English A Literature

for the IB Diploma

2nd Edition

JAN ADKINS • MICHELE LACKOVIC

Published by Pearson Education Limited, 80 Strand, London, WC2R 0RL

www.pearsonglobalschools.com

Text © Pearson Education Limited 2020
Development edited by Julia Sandford
Copy edited by Soo Hamilton
Proofread by Sarah Wright and Laurie Duboucheix-Saunders
Indexed by Georgie Bowden
Designed by © Pearson Education Limited 2020
Typeset by © SPi Global
Original illustrations © Pearson Education Limited 2020
Illustrated by © SPi Global
Cover design by © Pearson Education Limited 2020
Cover images: Front: © **Getty Images:** Eskay Lim / EyeEm
Inside front cover: **Shutterstock.com:** Dmitry Lobanov

The rights of Jan Adkins and Michele Lackovic to be identified as the
authors of this work have been asserted by them in accordance with the
Copyright, Designs and Patents Act 1988.

First published 2020

23 22 21 20
IMP 10 9 8 7 6 5 4 3 2 1

British Library Cataloguing in Publication Data
A catalogue record for this book is available from the British Library

ISBN 978 1 292 32052 6

Printed in Slovakia by Neografia

Acknowledgements
The authors and publisher would like to thank the following individuals
and organisations for their kind permission to reproduce copyright
material.

Photographs
(Key: b-bottom; c-centre; l-left; r-right; t-top)

123RF GB LIMITED: Moleks/123RF 208, Olegdudko/123RF 306, Ivelin
Radkov/123RF 307b; **ALAMY IMAGES:** Napa Valley Register/ZUMA
Press Inc/Alamy Stock Photo 109tr, Peter Horree/Alamy Stock Photo
137, Dinodia Photos/Alamy Stock Photo 156, Homer Sykes/Alamy Stock
Photo 167bl, Classic Image/Alamy Stock Photo 167br, Sjbooks/Alamy
Stock Photo 173, Sasa Kralj/JiwaFoto/ZUMA Press, Inc./Alamy Stock
Photo 180, Photo Researchers/Science History Images/Alamy Stock
Photo 185, Rehman Asad/Alamy Stock Photo 247, Caroline Penn/Alamy
Stock Photo 248t, Warner Bros/Everett Collection Inc/Alamy Stock
Photo 311t, Sergio Azenha/Alamy Stock Photo 274; **Color Factory,
NYC:** © Color Factory 2018 146; **Bob Dylan:** 115; **DC Comics, Inc:**
© 2018 DC Entertainment 41, 42, 44; **Errol Morris:** 153; **GETTY
IMAGES INCORPORATED:** Marén Wellmann/EyeEm/Getty Images 6,
LittleBee80/iStock/Getty Images 12tl, Bowie15/iStock/Getty Images 13tr,
Fcscafeine/iStock/Getty Images 13br, Daisy-Daisy/iStock/Getty Images
17, Thipjang/Moment/Getty Images 26, 26r, Jouni Pirhonen/EyeEm/
Getty Images 27rb, Bluejayphoto/iStock/Getty Images 28cl, Ulf
Andersen/Hulton Archive/Getty Images 63, Thomas Barwick/
DigitalVision/Getty Images 73, Matt Cardy/Getty Images News/Getty
Images 74, Mondadori Portfolio/Getty Images 76t, Ariel Skelley/
DigitalVision/Getty Images 76b, Ozgurdonmaz/E+/Getty Images 77c,
Robbie jack/Corbis Entertainment/Getty Images 79t, Europa Press
Entertainment/Europa Press/Getty Images 79c, Bruce Glikas/FilmMagic/
Getty Images 79b, Bernand/Gamma-Rapho/Getty Images 80,
AlenPopov/E+/Getty Images 109tl, Monzenmachi/E+/Getty Images
109bl, Andersen Ross Photography Inc/DigitalVision/Getty Images
109br, Marla Aufmuth/Getty Images Entertainment/Getty Images 111,
RB/Redferns/Getty Images 114, Gregg DeGuire/Getty Images
Entertainment/Getty Images 120, Dea/A. Dagli Orti/De Agostini/Getty
Images 136, Snapshot-photography/Ullstein bild/Getty Images 153,
Photo 12/Universal Images Group/Getty Images 154l, The LIFE Picture
Collection/Pix Inc./Getty Images 158, Pop_jop/DigitalVision Vectors/
Getty Images 160, Vipin Kumar/Hindustan Times/Getty Images 164,
Bettmann/Getty Images 167cl, S. Greg Panosian/iStock/Getty Images
171c, 171b, Bruce Gilbert/Newsday LLC/Getty Images 174, Livio
Anticoli/Gamma-Rapho/Getty Images 188, JoyImage/iStock/Getty
Images 198, BrianAJackson/iStock/Getty Images 204, Katleho Seisa/E+/
Getty Images 217, Alexander Vorotyntsev/iStock/Getty Images 222, Ali
Mufti Achmadi/EyeEm/Getty Images 223, Sovfoto/Universal Images
Group/Getty Images 248b, Damircudic/E+/Getty Images 252, Brijith
vijayan/iStock/Getty Images 260, Happy_vector/iStock/Getty Images
278, Zvukmedia/iStock/Getty Images 287, Radachynskyi/iStock/Getty
Images 288, Dave G Kelly/Moment/Getty Images 289, Devonyu/iStock/
Getty Images 308, Luis Alvarez/DigitalVision/Getty Images 23,106,
Matthew Micah Wright/The Image Bank/Getty Images 149, JLGutierrez/
E+/Getty Images 243; **HarperCollins Publishers, Inc:** From
Understanding Comics by Scott McCloud. Copyright (c) 1993, 1994 by
Scott McCloud. Used by permission of HarperCollins Publishers 40;
International Baccalaureate Organization: © International
Baccalaureate Organization 302; **Jan Adkins:** 33; **Penguin Random
House LLC:** Illustrations from PERSEPOLIS: THE STORY OF A
CHILDHOOD by Marjane Satrapi, translation copyright © 2003 by
L'Association, Paris, France. Used by permission of Pantheon Books, an
imprint of the Knopf Doubleday Publishing Group, a division of Penguin
Random House LLC. All rights reserved 2, 70, 262; **SHUTTERSTOCK:**
JessicaPichardo/Shutterstock 4, I am Corona/Shutterstock 12c, Conrado/
Shutterstock 12b, Konontsev Artem/Shutterstock 13c, Raditya/
Shutterstock 14, 88studio/Shutterstock 19, Rasstock/Shutterstock 25tl,

Tmcphotos/Shutterstock 25tr, Pigama/Shutterstock 25bl, Crazystocker/Shutterstock 25br, Nuchylee/Shutterstock 27t, Lakov Filimonov/Shutterstock 27c, Tupungato/Shutterstock 28bl, Andreiuc88/Shutterstock 34, Skolova/Shutterstock 36, Don Mammoser/Shutterstock 69, Alex Lentati/Evening Standard/Shutterstock 77tr, ID1974/Shutterstock 77bl, Pavel L Photo and Video/Shutterstock 77br, lev radin/Shutterstock 104, Roman Nerud/Shutterstock 154r, Alexskopje/Shutterstock 159tl, One photo/Shutterstock 159tr, EpicStockMedia/Shutterstock 159b, Stocksnapper/Shutterstock 167tr, Have a nice day Photo/Shutterstock 171t, MongPro/Shutterstock 203, NDT/Shutterstock 206, NEILRAS/Shutterstock 212, Kaisaya/Shutterstock 227t, Sdecoret/Shutterstock 227b, Calin Stan/Shutterstock 231, Mypokcik/Shutterstock 245,Dean Drobot/Shutterstock 249t, PopTika/Shutterstock 249b, Maxx-Studio/Shutterstock 253, Kayla Blundell/Shutterstock 277, Artur Szczybylo/Shutterstock 282, 305, Pathdoc/Shutterstock 307t, Krcil/Shutterstock 310, Magic pictures/Shutterstock 311b, Schusterbauer.com/Shutterstock 172, Yulia Grigoryeva/Shutterstock 197, Ryan DeBerardinis/Shutterstock 221, Debby Wong/Shutterstock 14b; Lapandr/Shutterstock 82; Lisima/Shutterstock 145b; **United Nations:** © United Nations 251; **WELLCOME COLLECTION:** Wellcome Collection 1; **Won McIntosh** 145, 147.

All other images © Pearson Education

Text

Sally Heckel: A Jury of her Peers, Making the Film. © Sally Heckel. Used with permission 84; **Women Make Movies:** A Jury Of Her Peers, A film by Sally Heckel, Review by Katharine T. Bartlett, Professor Duke University School of Law, © Women Make Movies. Used with permission 95; **Women Make Movies:** A JURY OF HER PEERS, A film by Sally Heckel, Review by Andrea Friedman, Hist. & Women's Studies, Washington University, © Women Make Movies. Used with permission 96; **Michael Meyer:** Michael Meyer, Ibsen: A Biography, © 1971, Michael Meyer 98; **TED Conferences LLC:** We Should all be Feminist by Chimamanda Ngozi Adichie, TEDxEuston, December 2012 © TED Conferences LLC. Used with permission 61, 104; **Oxford University Press:** Ellison, Ralph., Ralph Ellison's Invisible Man: A Casebook, © 2004, Oxford University Press. Used with permission 28; **Oxford University Press:** Machado de Assis, John Gledson.,Dom Casmurro: A Novel, © 1997, Oxford University Press 28; **Minerva:** Ninh, Bao, The Sorrow of War: A Novel, © 1998, Minerva. 29; **Chinua Achebe:** Chinua Achebe's, Things Fall Apart, © 1959, Chinua Achebe. Used with permission 29; **John C. Hurston and Joel Hurtson:** Zora Neale Hurston, Their Eyes Were Watching God, © 1969, John C. Hurston and Joel Hurtson. Used with permission 30; **Penguin Random House:** Gordimer, Nadine, July's People, © 1982, Penguin Books. 30-31; **Penguin Random House:** Lan Cao, Monkey Bridge, © 1997, Penguin Random House. Used with permission 31; **Rosetta Books:** E. M. Forster, Aspects of the Novel, © 2010, Rosetta Books. 32; **HarperCollins:** Marguerite Duras, The Lover, © 1992, HarperCollins. 35; **Penguin Random House Canada Limited:** Excerpt(s) from ATONEMENT by Ian McEwan, Copyright © 2001 Ian McEwan. Reprinted by permission of Vintage Canada/Alfred A. Knopf Canada, a division of Penguin Random House Canada Limited. All rights reserved. 37-38; **Penguin Random House UK Limited:** Excerpt(s) from ATONEMENT by Ian McEwan, Copyright © 2001 Ian McEwan. Reprinted by permission of Jonathan Cape, a division of Penguin Random House UK Limited. All rights reserved. 37-38; **Rogers, Coleridge & White Ltd.:** McEwan, Ian., Atonement, © 2001. Reproduced by permission of the author c/o Rogers, Coleridge & White Ltd., 20 Powis Mews, London W11 1JN 37-38; **W. W. Norton & Company:** Eisner, Will., Comics and Sequential Art: Principles and Practices from the Legendary Cartoonist, © 2008, W. W. Norton & Company 38-39; **Francisca Goldsmith:** A Brief History of Graphic Novels by Francisca Goldsmith, 24 April 2019, © Francisca Goldsmith. 39; **BBC:** Watchmen: The moment comic books grew up By Nicholas Barber, 9 August 2016, © BBC 43; **Houghton Mifflin Harcourt Publishing Company:** "A Good Man is Hard to Find" from A GOOD MAN IS HARD TO FIND AND OTHER STORIES by Flannery O'Connor. Copyright © 1955 by Flannery O'Connor and renewed 1983 by Regina O'Connor. Reprinted by permission of Houghton Mifflin Harcourt Publishing Company. All rights reserved. 46-52; **Faber & Faber:** O'Connor, Flannery., Mystery and Manners, © 2014, Faber & Faber 51; **Condé Nast:** Chimamanda Ngozi Adichie, "Cell One", The New Yorker, Jan 29, 2007. © 2007, Condé Nast. Used with Permission 53-62, 143; **Grove/Atlantic, Inc.:** Jorge Luis Borges, Ficciones, © 2015, Grove/Atlantic, Inc. Used with Permission 63-69; **Penguin Random House:** Brian Greene, The Hidden Reality: Parallel Universes and the Deep Laws of the Cosmos, © 2011, Penguin Random House 70; **New Directions:** Translated by Donald A. Yates. Labyrinths, © 1962, New Directions 69; **Barrie Jean Borich:** Barrie Jean Borich, What Is Creative Nonfiction?: An Introduction, © 2001, Barriejeanborich 151; **Hachette UK Limited:** Carlos Ruiz Zafón, The Angel's Game: The Cemetery of Forgotten, Translation by Lucia Graves, © 2009, Hachette UK Limited. 151; **Elsevier Ltd:** Sharpe, R. J., & Heyden, L. C. (2009). Honey bee colony collapse disorder is possibly caused by a dietary pyrethrum deficiency. Bioscience Hypotheses, 2(6), 439–440, © Elsevier Ltd 151; **Penguin Random House:** Hillenbrand, Laura., Unbroken: A World War II Story of Survival, Resilience, and Redemption, © 2014, Random House Trade Paperbacks. 151; **Condé Nast.:** Carr, Nicholas., Author Nicholas Carr: The Web Shatters Focus, Rewires Brains, © 2010, Condé Nast. 151; **Martin Luther King Jr:** Letter From Birmingham Jail Martin Luther King Jr, © Martin Luther King Jr. Used with Permission 151; **Aung San Suu Kyi:** "Freedom from Fear" 1990 Aung San Suu Kyi, as leader of Myanmar's National League for Democracy Party 152; **NPR:** Morris, Errol., There is such a thing as truth, 2 May 2005, © NPR. 153; **Publication Division of India:** Collected Works of Mahatma Gandhi, Letter to Adolf Hitler, Pg. 453-456, Vol. 79, 16 July, 1940-27 December, 1940 © Publication Division of India. Used with Permission 154-156; **Harcourt Brace Jovanovich:** Why I Write by George Orwell, © 1946, Harcourt Brace Jovanovich. Used with Permission 160; **Secker and Warburg:** A Hanging by George Orwell, August 1931, © Secker and Warburg. Used with Permission 161-163; **Guardian News & Media Limited:** Arundhati Roy, Literature provides shelter. That's why we need it, 13 May 2019, Guardian News & Media Limited. Used with Permission 165; **Guardian News & Media Limited:** Arundhati Roy: 'The point of the writer is to be unpopular' by Tim Lewis, 17 Jun 2018, Guardian News & Media Limited. 166; **Simon & Schuster, Inc.:** Walls, Jeanette., The Glass Castle: A Memoir, © 2009, Simon and Schuster. Used with Permission 169-170; **Taylor & Francis:** Carl Thompson, Travel Writing,

Contents

Introduction

From the authors

Welcome to our book!

With collectively 40 years of English A: literature teaching between us, we welcome you to the new English A: literature course (first exams 2021). We have attempted to combine our passion for literature with the particulars of the new course, its framework and its assessment, in a way that provides engaging activities, insightful discussions, and sample assessments.

Throughout this text we will challenge you to move from being a passive reader to an active one, and this is not a small task. We hope that you will use this text as you would a map, venturing out, taking those first steps into the particulars of the new course, but understanding as well that connections are key: connections between works (**intertextuality**) as well as connections to larger IB concerns like **international-mindedness**, **approaches to learning**, and **global issues**.

This journey to new places and unfamiliar cultures will ultimately lead you to new knowledge and insights into the world that we all share.

Enjoy the ride.

Jan and Michele

Detailed overview

- What is literature and why does it matter?
- What are the aims of the IB literature course?
- How does studying the IB literature aims and IB philosophy inspire us to understand, analyse, and participate in the world around us?
- How is the IB literature course organised? What are '**areas of exploration**' and '**course concepts**'?
- What are the required assessments for the IB literature course?
- What is the learner portfolio? Why is it required? How can it help with self-reflection and IB literature assessments?

Understanding literary forms (fiction, poetry, drama, and non-fiction)

- What is a literary form and what are the conventions (rules) for each literary form?
- How do the areas of exploration and course concepts help us to understand, analyse, evaluate, and appreciate a range of works across all literary forms?
- How might deepening our knowledge of each form help us interpret, analyse, and make distinctions between and among the forms? How is this helpful for assessment?

- How does each literary form chapter model **creative** and analytical activities for the learner portfolio?
- Why include TOK discussion points throughout each literary form chapter?
- Why is it important to link literary works to global issues? What are the implications for IB literature assessments, CAS, TOK and cross-curricular connections?
- How do the literature-based activities in each literary form chapter help us become more confident and competent in our literary studies as we prepare for assessments?

Assessments (Paper 1, Paper 2, individual oral, HL essay)

- What elements do the IB literature assessments have in common? What are the distinctions between the assessments and between HL and SL programmes?
- Which learner portfolio activities are best suited for specific assessments?
- How does the application of the assessment criteria change depending on the component being assessed?
- What is the benefit of reviewing student samples, practising for assessments, and participating in peer review activities?

Extended essay

- What are the requirements for an extended essay in the English language and literature subject area?
- What is the difference between the Category 1, Category 2, and Category 3 essay options?
- What is a literature review?
- What does methodology mean for English language and literature essays?
- What type of reflection is required for extended essays?
- What are the assessment criteria for the extended essay and what is the best way to interpret them for literature extended essays?

How to use this book

We recommend that you read the detailed overview chapter first and then work through the literary form chapters in any order. You can focus on each assessment chapter as needed, based on how your teacher has organised your course. Read the extended essay chapter if you plan to write your extended essay in the English language and literature subject area.

Bolded wording

As you read each chapter, you'll notice that some words are in **bold**. The IB English A: literature and IB philosophy words are bolded in black the first time they appear in each chapter. The bolding is simply there to draw your attention to course and IB terminology, as these conceptual ideas will give you a working vocabulary for reading, analysing, and evaluating.

The literary form chapters also contain words highlighted in **blue** that are either defined within the chapter or in the glossary at the back of the book. The blue words are linked to literary terminology and form conventions that you'll need to master as you analyse and evaluate literature throughout the course. Keep in mind that glossary words only appear in blue the first time they appear in the book.

Features

Throughout the book, you will see a number of coloured boxes and icons interspersed through each chapter. They may be in the margins or in the main text. Each of these boxes provides additional information as follows.

Learning objectives

You will find a box like this at the start of each chapter. These define the learning objectives for the chapter you are about to read, and they set out what content and aspects of learning are covered in the chapter.

Learning objectives

In this chapter you will…
- connect drama to approaches to learning, course concepts, and areas of exploration
- explore conventions and expectations of drama
- consider the advantages and limitations of staging
- understand the creation of momentum
- identify and interpret dramatic structures and their effects on the audience
- understand drama as performance literature
- communicate ideas through a variety of individual and collaborative activities
- analyse, evaluate, and appreciate a range of dramatic works through:
  - readers, writers, and texts
  - time and space
  - intertextuality
  - global issues.

Icons

The English A: literature course is organised into three different areas of exploration (AOE) – readers, writers, and texts; time and space; and intertextuality. You will find AOE icons throughout the text as a visual cue to the specific area of exploration.

Info boxes

Info boxes provide new information drawn from the main text that extends your knowledge and strengthens your interpretation skills.

TOK boxes

Theory of knowledge (TOK) boxes stimulate thought and consideration of any TOK issues as they arise in context. Often these boxes will just contain a question to stimulate your own thoughts and discussion. Sometimes they may direct you to write a reflection or response in your learner portfolio.

Info box

The 'fourth wall' is the imaginary wall through which the audience witnesses the action of a play.

TOK

What is the significance of inanimate objects such as books being able to produce a physical response? To what extent does this transformative theory apply to other objects? What is the effect?

Connections boxes

Connections boxes highlight aspects of the text that ask you to make connections. The connections can be implied or specific.

Connections

The more realistic the play, the more often the playwright intends to engage the audience emotionally. Less realistic drama, such as absurdist plays, often disregards the emotional sympathies of the audience in favour of their intellectual responses. Do not assume that every playwright wants their audiences to identify with characters or their situations.

Global issues boxes

Global issues boxes provide a broader and more **international-minded** insight into the topic you are studying or the skills you are developing. You will be studying global issues in many literary texts as preparation for assessments in English A: literature.

Global issue

To what degree is the conflict between individuals and society imposed by economic and social stereotyping? Is identity predetermined in violent conflict? Does the 'enemy' lose his humanity? Is this loss of common humanity essential to conflict?

Insights sections

Insights sections consolidate the material you have studied in the chapter. They are handy for reminding yourself of key themes and major points about the study of literature, and for providing guidance as you navigate the course.

Extra eBook activities and documents

The grey icon indicates where extra activities and documents are available for download from the eBook.

QR codes

Throughout the book you will find QR codes that link to external resources.

Detailed overview

Learning objectives

In this chapter you will…
- explore the question 'What is literature?'
- develop knowledge of the course through individual and collaborative activities
- engage with the aims of the IB literature course
- make connections between IB English A: literature and the IB philosophy course
- learn how the IB literature course is organised
- examine course areas of exploration:
  - readers, writers, and texts
  - time and space
  - intertextuality
- understand how the areas of exploration are linked to the course concepts
- learn about the required assessments for IB literature
- explore the purpose of the learner portfolio.

What is literature?

As we write this, the definition of literature is shifting and expanding to reflect the world around us. In simple terms, literature represents the **culture**, practices, and **communications** of people. From the Latin '*litaritura/litteratura*', literature translates to 'writing formed with letters'. Broadly speaking, civilisations from Egypt to China have celebrated literature in many forms, including texts that are spoken or sung. Ancient Greek poets such as Homer and Sophocles composed poems and plays such as *The Iliad* and *Oedipus Rex* that are still studied today. Such literature provides a window into different cultures and times. But literature is more than just a marker of civilisation: it can introduce us to fantastical worlds that are fuelled by pure imagination. Of course, not every book can be considered literature and the definition of what 'makes the cut' is often elusive. When British writer Aldous Huxley published his futuristic novel, *Brave New World*, in 1932, it was regarded by some critics as politicised propaganda. And yet today it is hailed as a timeless classic that helped define the **dystopian** genre.

Ancient texts were often spoken before they were rendered to written form.

The question remains: What is literature? While it is evident that instruction manuals or banal romances do not demonstrate literary merit, a quick internet search for a definition produces a wide range of results, revealing that there is no one accepted definition. 'For the times they are a-changin'', Bob Dylan proclaims through his music lyrics that earned him the Nobel Prize for Literature in 2016. As the definition of literature broadens, music and visual texts such as graphic novels are now classified as

The opening page of *Persepolis* ▶

literature. Marjane Satrapi's graphic memoir, *Persepolis*, a coming of age text that records Satrapi's life in Iran during and after the Islamic Revolution, is a prime example of this literary expansion. The work has been translated from French into many languages and is widely studied in literature programmes across the world.

So, who and what determines what is literature? Perhaps the more important question is 'Why should we read a specific work?' In the case of *Persepolis*, Satrapi's text gives a voice to a story that is often silent; her memoir style mixes history with personal experience, making her narrative believable and relatable. As she immerses us in emotive words and visuals, she allows us to experience her culture and community. This doesn't just give us a window into her world, it also gives us a better understanding of our own. Works that affect communities of readers in this way aren't placed in literary categories arbitrarily; they earn their place through readers and critics recognising their aesthetic value in local and global **contexts**.

Activity 1 Why does literature matter?

While there is no one set definition of literature, consider the observations below from literary-minded individuals across the globe who derive meaning from literature in specific ways. For these individuals, literature:

- 'allows us to be open, to listen, and to be curious' (Tracy K Smith)
- 'is dangerous: it awakens a rebellious attitude in us' (Mario Vargas Llosa)
- 'becomes the living memory of a nation' (Aleksandr Solzhenitsyn)
- 'is one of the most interesting and significant expressions of humanity' (PT Barnum)
- 'sucks you into another psyche. So the creation of empathy necessarily influences how you'll behave to other people' (Barbara Kingsolver)
- 'plays a huge role in examining difficult real-life issues' (Angie Thomas)
- 'helps us transcend ourselves' (Mohsin Hamid).

1) Which statement above most appeals to you? Why?
2) Create your own statement about literature and share it with your peers.
3) What do you notice about the statements that you and your peers have written? To what extent do they overlap or differ?
4) What does this activity reveal about the nature of literature?
5) Write your responses in your learner portfolio.

As a student of English A: literature, you'll engage with a range of literary texts, in a variety of forms (poetry, drama, fiction, and non-fiction), from different time periods and cultures. As you develop an understanding of the texts, you'll also be exposed to a variety of **perspectives**, cultural contexts, and local and **global issues**. Through literature you will read, write, speak, and perform. You'll learn to analyse and evaluate, communicate, and collaborate. But the aim isn't simply to pass your assessment; it's a way to make connections between literature and other subjects, and to foster empathy and understanding of diverse cultures and ideas.

Course aims for studies in language and literature

The aims of both the English A: literature course and the *Prescribed reading list* stress the **international-minded** nature of the IB programme, which encourages students to engage with a range of texts from different periods, styles, and cultures. Below is a list of aims which span all three Language A courses – Language A: literature; Language A: language and literature; and Language A: literature and performance.

Aims: studies in language and literature (including English A: literature)

	The aims of all subjects in studies in language and literature are to enable students to:
1	engage with a range of texts, in a variety of media and forms, from different periods, styles, and cultures
2	develop skills in listening, speaking, reading, writing, viewing, presenting, and performing
3	develop skills in interpretation, analysis, and evaluation
4	develop sensitivity to the formal and aesthetic qualities of texts and an appreciation of how they contribute to diverse responses and open up multiple meanings
5	develop an understanding of relationships between texts and a variety of perspectives, cultural contexts, and local and global issues, and develop an appreciation of how they contribute to diverse responses and open up multiple meanings
6	develop an understanding of the relationships between studies in language and literature and other disciplines
7	communicate and collaborate in a confident and creative way
8	foster a lifelong interest in and enjoyment of language and literature.

Activity 2 The aims of the English A: literature course

Given the elusive and evolving definition of literature, your task is to connect the opening paragraphs of this book with the aims of the English A: literature course listed on page 3 to help you select a handful of literary works that would be suitable for this course.

1) Carefully read the eight course aims in the table on page 3.
2) Working in small groups, discuss what types of literature would be appropriate for this course. Do some online research on literary works from around the globe. Your search can include a combination of works from any of the four literary forms: fiction, non-fiction, poetry, and drama.
3) Which texts show up on 'literary-minded' lists? Which works are other IB schools reading in their English A: literature programme?
4) Use chart paper or a computer program such as Padlet® to record at least five literary works that would be suitable for English A: literature.
5) Share your findings with a larger group and *justify* your choices.
6) Write a reflection in your learner portfolio regarding what this activity reveals about the **objective** or **subjective** nature of decisions that involve culture, content, and context.

Info box

Objective decisions are based on fact. Subjective decisions are based on assumptions and beliefs.

Connections

Even if the books you and your peers selected do not become part of your English A: literature course, keep your shared lists on hand. You may enjoy the texts on your own or find uses for them in other parts of the programme, such as Language B, Theatre, or the extended essay.

Mexico City's Biblioteca Vasconcelos or 'megalibrary'

Info box

Not all works studied in English A: literature have to be chosen from the *Prescribed reading list*. In the HL version of the course, teachers can select up to four free-choice texts. In the SL version of the course, teachers can select up to two free-choice texts. All free-choice texts must have literary merit.

The *Prescribed reading list*

Much like your collaborative group in the previous activity, the creators of this IB course sat down and developed a list of authors whose works were deemed worthy of literary exploration. The majority of the works you study in English A: literature will come from the IB's globally minded *Prescribed reading list*. While there are plenty of recognisable classic and popular authors on the list, such as William Shakespeare and Haruki Murakami, the broad nature of the *Prescribed reading list* encourages students and teachers to study multiple authors who write literary works from various cultures and time periods. The literary forms on the list are also varied. English A: literature includes the four standard forms of literature: drama, poetry, fiction, and non-fiction. But the *Prescribed reading list* expands the definition of a literary form: song lyrics are included as a type of poetry, and graphic novels and memoirs can fit into either fiction or non-fiction categories depending on their subject matter. In keeping with the course aims, the *Prescribed reading list* provides plenty of opportunity to engage with a range of literature that offers different perspectives in content, form, culture, place, and time period.

How does English A: literature connect to the IB framework?

Approaches to teaching and learning

While course content and its selection are certainly significant, the **approaches to teaching and learning** focus on deliberate strategies, skills, and perspectives that bring course content to life. How you learn is just as important as what you learn. With this axiom in mind, we've designed activities in this book that will help you meet the course aims, prepare for assessments, and make connections in literature, the IB core, and other disciplines. Approaches to teaching and learning make your learning more meaningful, so that you can reflect on how and what you learn matters, both inside and outside the classroom.

The IB Diploma Programme (DP) model shows the importance of the approaches to teaching and learning.

The six approaches to teaching develop teaching that is:	The five approaches to learning develop:
inquiry based	thinking skills
conceptually focused	social skills
developed in local and global contexts	communication skills
collaborative	self-management skills
differentiated for diverse learners	research skills
informed by assessment	

Throughout this book, you will have plenty of opportunities to deepen your knowledge and sharpen your **thinking** skills. You will closely read texts, **research** pertinent **contextual** information, explore **concepts**, and communicate your ideas both individually and **collaboratively** as you prepare for **assessments**.

The learner profile

The **IB learner profile** represents ten attributes valued by IB World Schools. Notice how closely the approaches to teaching and learning align with the learner profile.

As IB learners we strive to be:

- inquirers
- knowledgeable
- thinkers
- communicators
- principled
- open-minded
- caring
- risk-takers
- balanced
- reflective.

Activity 3 The literary learner profile

1) Using either one or several literary texts, identify characters who demonstrate one or more of the learner profile traits listed above. Linking a specific character to a learner profile trait will help you understand the character's values, motivations, and actions more fully. Now find quotes from your selected literary text about the character or characters that demonstrate a specific trait.
2) Once you have selected your learner profile quotes, visually represent your final product in a creative way. Feel free to use specialised software or coloured pens to create your piece.

International-mindedness

As we read, we can view literature as a mirror. When we hold up this mirror, it reflects characters who experience situations that are familiar to us. Since the culture and value

Literature can be viewed both as a window and a mirror.

systems of these characters may overlap with our own, reading about them gives us a sense of comfort. Peering into the mirror taps into our sense of **identity**; it helps us make sense of the world we know.

But as a student of English A: literature, you will read varied works from different time periods, cultures, and places. This emphasis on variety is deliberate. Literature can also be a window, providing a view of worlds that are unfamiliar to us. The windows aren't necessary closed. We can cast them open with our imagination, and experience cultures and customs quite different from our own. And once we have entered this new world, the window can again become a mirror 'transform[ing] human experience [as it] reflects it back to us, and in that reflection we can see our own lives and experiences as part of the larger human experience' (Rudine Sims Bishop, 1990). Indeed, visiting such worlds and considering different perspectives is an important part of participating in an international-minded curriculum.

Keep the mirror/window literature metaphor in mind as you read the statement below by African author, Chinua Achebe:

> I tell my students, it's not difficult to identify with somebody like yourself, somebody next door who looks like you. What's more difficult is to identify with someone you don't see, who's very far away, who's a different color, who eats a different kind of food. When you begin to do that then literature is really performing its wonders.

1) What do you think Achebe means by literature 'really performing its wonders'? What are these 'wonders'?
2) What does it mean to be internationally minded?

The IB core

All Diploma Programme (DP) students must complete the three core elements (TOK, CAS, and the extended essay) in order to be eligible for the IB Diploma.

Theory of knowledge

Theory of knowledge (TOK) is a course that connects to all DP subject courses and is related to a branch of philosophy called epistemology (the study of the nature of knowledge and its justified belief). As you examine the nature of knowledge, you will question how you know what you claim to know.

Literature links to TOK include inquiry-based questions such as:

- What is the purpose of literature?

- How does the knowledge we derive from literature differ from knowledge in other subject areas?

- To what extent can we determine how we make meaning from literary texts? How much are we influenced by authors' intentions? By our own background? By our knowledge of the work's culture and context? By our discussions with our peers? To what extent do these factors bias or build our knowledge?

- Given that literary texts can be interpreted from multiple perspectives, what does this reveal about the nature of knowledge? Is there a way to determine whether one interpretation is more effective than another?

- To what extent can we accurately interpret texts from cultures that are different from our own?

- How does knowledge of literary forms and their conventions (authorial choices) help us justify our interpretations of a text?

The English A: literature course is not a separate entity from TOK. The conceptual framework of the course encourages a TOK-type mindset as you study literary works.

Creativity, activity, service (CAS)

CAS allows you to transform your classroom learning into meaningful experiences that develop through local and global contexts. The seven learning outcomes in CAS are designed to give you an opportunity to explore multiple interests through both individual and collaborative experiences.

CAS learning outcomes

- Identify your own strengths and develop areas for growth.

- Demonstrate that challenges have been undertaken, developing new skills in the process.

- Demonstrate how to initiate and plan a CAS experience.

- Show commitment to and perseverance in CAS experiences.

- Demonstrate the skills and recognise the benefits of working collaboratively.

- Demonstrate engagement with issues of global significance.

- Recognise and consider the ethics of choices and actions.

CAS isn't about putting in hours; it's about making an investment in yourself and those around you so that life takes on meaning beyond the classroom walls. When you think of the three strands of CAS – creativity, activity, and service – you may not intuitively think of how your IB literature class connects to CAS.

Start by thinking about the literary works you are reading for the course. Is there a global issue that interests you? For example, if your class is reading Elie Wiesel's *Night* or Art Spiegelman's *Maus*, texts set in World War II, you can deepen your knowledge of the works by seeking out community events that focus on historical relevance, perhaps by attending a lecture on the Holocaust or visiting a war museum. You could also volunteer to work with local veterans, an act that would not only help you understand war through living historical accounts, but also enable you to make connections to individuals who have different experiences to you.

CAS is at the heart of the IB core, encouraging us to learn about the world around us in an active, tactile way. Becoming more familiar with the strands (creativity, activity, service) and the learning outcomes is the first step in your CAS journey.

Activity 5 Dramatic action with CAS literary learning outcomes

Every time you read a work for English A: literature, think about how CAS applies to characters in the texts. Even if the characters are in imagined situations, we can be aware of how CAS learning outcomes play out in these works. Such awareness of CAS will not only deepen your understanding of the characters' motivations, integrity, and contexts, but also perhaps give you ways to think about your own CAS experience.

1) Work in a group. Each person selects a character from a literary work that demonstrates a different CAS learning outcome: Which character can identify their own strengths and has developed areas for growth? Which character

has undertaken a new challenge and developed a new skill in the process? Which character initiates constructive plans? Demonstrates commitment and perseverance? Excels at collaboration? Engages with issues of global significance? Recognises and considers the ethics of choices and actions?

2) As a group, write a short drama scene that includes a conversation between these literary characters. Use your imaginations to create a situation where each character can demonstrate their CAS learning outcome. (Perhaps the characters are meeting each other for the first time at a dinner party or are trapped in a lift.) Perform it live or film it, and share your dramatic presentations with peers.

3) In your learner portfolio, explain how this activity helps you better understand your own CAS experiences. Perhaps it inspired you to take on a new experience or caused you to reflect on a CAS experience that is already underway.

The extended essay

The extended essay is a required component for all students achieving the IB Diploma. Over the course of the two-year programme, you will research and write a 4000-word essay under the guidance of a supervisor. The purpose of this independent assessment is for you to hone your research and writing skills in preparation for university level studies. As a first step, you will select a topic of interest that is linked to one of your six DP subject areas and be assigned to a supervisor who will guide you through the process. The entire process should take about 40 hours, but you will have reflection meetings with your supervisor along the way to help you construct your research question, discuss your working draft, and review your progress. Extended essays in the language and literature subject area fall into one of three categories. The first two categories are geared towards a literature essay; the third category focuses on studies in language. For more information about how to write an extended essay in the subject of language and literature, please see the extended essay chapter at the end of this book.

How is the IB English A: literature course organised?

The way any course is structured plays an important role in how and what is learned. A history course may be arranged chronologically according to **time and space** or thematically so that a concept such as civil rights can be studied across different places and time periods. Traditional literature courses were often structured geographically and chronologically so that the study of literature from one country covered many decades or even centuries.

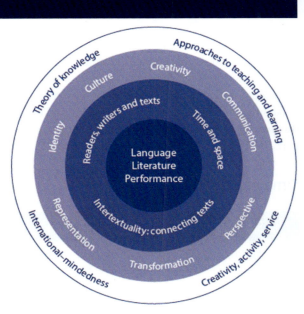

The diagram shows how the studies in language and literature courses are structured.

Another way to organise literature courses is by focusing on a specific author such as William Shakespeare, or type of literature such as drama, or through **thematic** groupings such as war poetry.

Unlike the examples above, which follow a prescribed format, English A: literature provides a fluid, conceptual path into the study of literature. The three courses at the centre are: language and literature; literature; and literature and performance. All three Language A courses work from the same course diagram. The English A: literature course includes some language and performance aspects, but its primary focus is literature. All the texts you study in this course will be works of literature, but it's important to remember that this course is concept driven. The framework in the diagram will not only provide important ways for you to understand, interpret, and analyse literature for success in assessment, but will also help you make connections that extend your learning into other courses and outside the classroom.

Areas of exploration

Three **areas of exploration – readers, writers, and texts**; **time and space**; and **intertextuality: connecting texts** – surround the inner circle of English A courses. Think of these areas of exploration as lenses which will help you find a way into a text. Your teacher will select a specific area of exploration from which to study each work, though some may overlap.

Readers, writers, and texts

> ### John M Ford, American science fiction and fantasy writer
> Every book is three books, after all; the one the writer intended, the one the reader expected, and the one that casts its shadow when the first two meet by moonlight.

In this area of exploration you will focus on the nature of literature and how and why we study it. As you read various works, pay close attention to the connection between readers, writers, and texts. While authors may make specific choices regarding textual features in terms of language, technique, and style, an important part of this equation is the effect those choices have on you, the reader. Your personal knowledge and experiences may enable you to find a unique way into the text. Of course, this type of knowledge does not define the entirety of your interpretation. Deepening your knowledge of textual features and how they create meaning will give you confidence and competence in your abilities to analyse and evaluate texts. Collaborative discussions with your peers can also extend your knowledge and reshape how you perceive a text.

Time and space

> ### *The Silent Language* by Edward T Hall
> One of the most effective ways to learn about oneself is by taking seriously the cultures of others. It forces you to pay attention to those details of life which differentiate them from you.

In this area of exploration you will consider how the culture and context of the literature you study affects how it is interpreted. No text is constructed in a vacuum. Understanding works in their time and space enriches our experience with the text. You'll need to occupy spaces that are very different from your own with an open mind. The authorial choices that shape character motivations are often influenced by the culture in which they were constructed. Also significant is how the reception of works changes over time and through space. Works that are banned in one region may be lauded in another. Dramatic works such as Shakespeare plays may be **transformed** depending on the time or place in which they are performed, or simply through a director's interpretation. How works are understood, received, and reinterpreted gives us a way to understand concepts such as culture, context, and identity.

Intertextuality: connecting texts

In this area of exploration you will consider how meaning is conveyed by examining texts in relation to one another: examining what this reveals about the texts themselves and the culture in which they were produced. The term *intertextuality* comes from the Latin phrase *intertexo* which translates to 'intermixing while weaving'. When Shakespeare makes Greek and Biblical allusions in his play, *Hamlet*, intertextuality is at work. Parodies are also a type of intertextuality as they transform one text into another, often with humorous results. In a broader sense, texts may influence or inspire other texts, or may be linked by a common theme.

Intertextuality does not have to be deliberate on the part of the author. As a student of English A: literature, you will make textual connections frequently. Texts can be grouped by form (drama, poetry, fiction, non-fiction), ideas or issues (corruption, justice, religious values, etc.), **course concepts** (community, culture, identity, etc.), or explicit allusions as mentioned in the *Hamlet* example above.

In terms of how this would work in practice, think about how examining gender inequalities in Sylvia Plath's poetry and Marjane Satrapi's graphic novel, *Persepolis*, provides some contrasting points of analysis. The texts represent different forms (genres) and cultures, and are written in different languages. Note that Satrapi's text includes a visual component. Consider how the forms and conventions (textual features associated with the forms) help you develop your analysis of gender inequality. Do you notice any overlapping commonalities between the two texts? What does this intertextual exploration reveal about the treatment of women in each text and culture? And about the human condition?

Course concepts

In addition to the three areas of exploration, the English A: literature course also includes seven course concepts to help you analyse texts through differing vantage points. The concepts are meant to be applied in multiple ways. The brief explanation of each below should give you an idea of how they are designed to develop your thinking skills. Later chapters in this book will show you how to apply them to your literary studies.

Connections

Since course concepts often focus on how knowledge is interpreted and constructed, the questions they raise naturally correspond with ideas discussed in TOK.

Identity

- Consider the identity of the writer. How might knowledge of the writer's culture and context (time and space) inform our understanding of a text?

- What about the identity of the characters? How are these identities established?

- What textual features help us understand how characters identify with each other and themselves?

- How does your own identity affect the way you make meaning from a text?

Culture

- How does a text relate to the context in which it is produced and received? What can it teach us about the values and beliefs of a particular community?

- How does the text you are reading relate to other texts from different time periods within the same culture (intertextuality)?

- How do cultural values and beliefs change over time? What is literature's role in this change?

- To what extent can we transcend our own biases when we read works from another culture?

- What is the benefit of learning about culture through a literary lens?

Creativity

- What role does imagination play in the construction of a literary work? How do such imaginative works of art give us insight into the human condition?

- How should we regard characters who produce art or who have active imaginations? To what extent are their creative thought processes an asset or a liability?

- Readers also use their imaginations as they respond to texts, constructing **images** and interpretations in their minds. How does each literary form engage your imagination differently?

- To what extent can our imagination deepen our knowledge and interpretation of a text?

How might knowledge of a writer's identity inform our understanding of a text?

What can a text tell us about the values and beliefs of a community?

Readers use their imaginations as they respond to texts.

Communication

- How is communication between readers and writers established through literary texts?

- How do authorial choices (textual features) affect this communication?

- According to Bijay Kumar Das, 'a translator is a reader, an interpreter and a creator all in one'. How do translators' choices affect the way a work is perceived?

- To what extent does the time and space in which a text is created, and the culture and context in which a reader resides, influence the process of communication?

- How can researching an author's culture, context, and literary style help you better understand what the author is trying to communicate?

- How can communicating about a literary work with your peers help you to build knowledge of the text?

- Given that language can be interpreted in various ways, to what extent can authentic communications between readers, writers, and texts be established?

▲ How do authorial choices affect communication?

Perspective

- How is the concept of perspective expressed in each literary form?

- What is the value of analysing a text from multiple perspectives or lenses?

- How important is the perspective of the writer?

- To what extent does our own background and experience influence our perspective of a text?

- How can we more authentically perceive a text from a culture and context that is different from our own?

- How might our perspective of a text change when reading it in relation to another text (intertextuality)?

- How does considering the perspectives of others encourage us to re-evaluate our own interpretations?

- How can a synthesis of multiple perspectives deepen our knowledge, analysis, and evaluation of a text?

▲ What is the value of analysing a text through a different lens?

Transformation

- How is literature transformative?

- How might a work transform in your mind when you research its culture and context (time and space)? When you discuss it within a community (communication)? When you analyse its textual features (readers, writers, and texts)? When you explore its connection to another work (intertextuality)?

- How is the act of borrowing aspects from one work to create another a transformative process?

▲ How is literature transformative?

- Consider how plays are transformed as they are performed for different audiences through time and space. How much of this **transformation** is attributed to the interpretation of the director? Or to the limitations of physical space? Or to the culture and context of the audience that views the play?

- To what extent do perceptions of works evolve over time, transforming how they are received and evaluated?

Representation

- What is the definition of literary **representation**?

- How does the representation (physical format) of a work affect how it is interpreted?

- How are such representations expressed across the literary forms?

- How does the representation of a drama or a poem as a written piece of text transform once it is performed?

- How do these different representations of the same text affect how it is interpreted?

How does the representation of a poem transform when it is performed?

Consider how the concept of representation applies to the standard definitions of fiction and non-fiction. Fictional works are often associated with imagined worlds while non-fiction texts reflect real-life events. How are these classifications of representation complicated by novels that are steeped in realistic depictions of history and non-fiction memoirs that take liberties with historical accuracy in favour of emotional dramatisations? It is important to note that the definition of representation in literature is as fluid as the lines between fact and fiction in literary forms. According to Italian poet Torquatto Tasso, 'Poetry is an imitation of human action, fashioned to teach us how to live', and novelist Henry James said, 'The only reason for the existence of a novel is that it does attempt to represent life'. Of course, not all novels represent life and not all poetry teaches us how to live, but as we need to remember, literary representations, like perspectives, are not fixed.

Connections

The areas of exploration and concepts overlap, but you won't study all of them simultaneously. If you glance back at the course diagram, picture the circular areas as wheels that are constantly in motion, so that you can experience and interpret a text differently depending on which area of exploration and/or concept becomes your focus. For example, comparing texts (intertextuality) from different cultures encourages you to consider different perspectives. Such experiences can be transformative, altering not just the way you perceive the literary work in front of you, but your own local context as well.

Activity 6 How and why we read literature

John Green, an American author and YouTube® content creator, hosts several educational series in the fields of literature, history, and science. The video entitled 'How and why we read' explains the significance of literature for what it can teach us about other cultures and ourselves, echoing the IB philosophy of international-mindedness.

The questions below are designed to help solidify your knowledge and understanding of the areas of exploration and course concepts in English A: literature. Use the QR code to watch the short video, 'How and why we read' and write your responses to the questions that follow in your learner portfolio.

1) In the beginning of the video, Green makes a connection between Homer's *The Odyssey* and Zora Neale Hurston's *Mules and Men*. What is this connection? Which area of exploration calls for a comparison of texts? What is the effect of connecting these texts?

2) Green argues that stories are about communication. How can Green's explanation of why we tell stories help us to better understand the course concepts of communication and culture?

3) Do you agree that reading is an act of empathy – that in reading literature we learn what it's like to be another person? Which learner profile traits connect to this idea? How does the course concept of creativity also apply?

4) What about authorial intent? To what extent should we consider the author's intentions when we read literature? Can we learn from literature without knowing an author's intent? If so, what does this imply about the connection between readers, writers, and texts?

5) When Green uses the terms hyperbole and metaphor to describe his own break-up, he says that his use of figurative language is not compelling or interesting so it does not draw empathy from his audience. What does this reveal about the relationship between language and emotion?

6) Green claims that learning about other cultures not only helps us to better understand others, but ourselves as well. To which course aim does his claim apply?

7) How does Green's video relate the study of literature to one of the following IB concepts: approaches to teaching and learning, the learner profile, the IB core, or international-mindedness?

▲
John Green

Course requirements

While the fluid construction of English A: Literature may seem a bit overwhelming at first, keep in mind that the specific course requirements listed below will give you a sense of structure as you work your way towards assessment.

The following checklist will help you sort out course requirements:

Course requirements for English A: literature (HL/SL)

HL	Requirement	SL	Requirement
Works	**Total: 13** • Minimum of 5 must be written in language studied, by authors on the PRL* • Minimum of 4 must be works in translation written by authors on PRL • 4 can be chosen freely from PRL or elsewhere	**Works**	**Total: 9** • Minimum of 4 must be written in language studied, by authors on the PRL • Minimum of 3 must be works in translation written by authors on PRL • 2 can be chosen freely from PRL or elsewhere
Areas of exploration	At least 3 works for each area of exploration: • Readers, writers, and texts • Time and space • Intertextuality	**Areas of exploration**	At least 2 works for each area of exploration: • Readers, writers, and texts • Time and space • Intertextuality
Concepts	7 concepts covered throughout syllabus: • identity • culture • creativity • communication • perspective • transformation • representation	**Concepts**	7 concepts covered throughout syllabus: • identity • culture • creativity • communication • perspective • transformation • representation
Literary forms	All 4: Drama, fiction, non-fiction, poetry	**Literary forms**	Choice of 3: Drama, fiction, non-fiction, poetry
Authors	None repeated anywhere in the syllabus or in any Language A or Language B syllabus	**Authors**	None repeated anywhere in the syllabus or in any Language A or Language B syllabus
Periods	3	**Periods**	3
Places	4 countries/regions; 2 continents	**Places**	3 countries/regions; 2 continents
Assessments	HL essay; Individual oral; Paper 1; Paper 2	**Assessments**	Individual oral; Paper 1; Paper 2

PRL – Prescribed reading list

Assessment in English A: literature

As you work your way through the English A: literature course, you will participate in formative (practice) assessments that will help you measure your achievement level. Some formative work may involve group or oral presentations, or may mirror the assessment that you are required to submit to the IB. Mastering any skill, whether you are in the classroom or on a sports team, takes time, effort, and practice. In terms of the required assessments for IB English A: literature, it is important to keep in mind that you are not competing with your peers. The focus is always on the assessment criteria, so it is essential to become familiar not just with course aims, but also with the specific assessment objectives and criteria.

Working towards any achievement requires practice, and English A: literature is no exception.

Assessment objectives

Activity 7 Comparing aims and objectives

Compare the assessment objectives below with the course aims discussed earlier in the chapter on page 3. What connections can you make between the course aims and the assessment objectives? What do these connections reveal about what and how you will learn in this course? Record your responses in your learner portfolio.

Assessment objectives for English A: literature (HL and SL)

Students in IB English A: literature will be able to:

Know, understand and interpret
• a range of texts, works, and/or performances, and their meanings and implications • contexts in which texts are written and/or received • elements of literary, stylistic, rhetorical, visual, and/or performance craft • features of particular text types and literary forms.
Analyse and evaluate
• ways in which the use of language creates meaning • uses and effects of literary, stylistic, rhetorical, visual, or theatrical techniques • relationships among different texts • ways in which texts may offer perspectives on human concerns.
Communicate
• ideas in a clear, logical and persuasive way • in a range of styles, **registers**, and for a variety of purposes and situations.

Required assessments

There are four required assessments at the HL level and three required assessments at the SL level. Each of these assessments are briefly outlined in the tables below and they will be fully explained in the assessment chapters.

Assessment snapshot: English A: literature HL

Type of assessment	Format of assessment	Marks	Time (hours)	Weighting of final grade
External				**80%**
Paper 1	**Guided literary analysis** Guided literary analysis of two unseen texts from two different literary forms.	40	2 hours 15 minutes	35%
Paper 2	**Comparative essay** Comparative essay based on two works studied.	30	1 hour 45 minutes	25%
HL essay	**Higher level essay** Literary essay on one work studied. 1200–1500 words in length.	20	Completed independently	20%
Internal				**20%**
Individual oral	**Individual oral** Individual oral based on two extracts that address the following prompt: Examine the ways in which the global issue of your choice is presented through the content and form of two of the works you have studied.	40	15 minutes	20%

Assessment snapshot: English A: literature SL

Type of assessment	Format of assessment	Marks	Time (hours)	Weighting of final grade
External				**70%**
Paper 1	**Guided literary analysis** Guided literary analysis of one unseen text.	20	1 hours 15 minutes	35%
Paper 2	**Comparative essay** Comparative essay based on two works studied.	30	1 hour 45 minutes	35%
Internal				**30%**
Individual oral	**Individual oral** Individual oral based on two extracts that address the following prompt: Examine the ways in which the global issue of your choice is presented through the content and form of two of the works you have studied.	40	15 minutes	30%

Assessment criteria

The assessments in English A: literature HL and SL courses share similar assessment criteria. The application of each criterion may shift according to the assessment task, but the shared criteria streamlines the assessments and makes the learning across all assessments more cohesive. Later chapters will discuss assessment criteria in more detail, but the snapshot below will give you a sense of the key elements that examiners focus on when they score your exams.

Assessment criteria for Paper 1, Paper 2, individual oral, HL essay	
Criterion A	Knowledge*, understanding, and interpretation
Criterion B	Analysis and evaluation
Criterion C	Focus and organisation
Criterion D	Language

*Paper 1 is the only assessment that does not focus on knowledge in Criterion A because the assessment task is based on an unseen text. See the assessment chapter for Paper 1 for more details on assessments.

The learner portfolio

The learner portfolio is a key element of the English A: literature course. Not only will it strengthen your self-management skills as you organise materials to be used for assessment, but it will also capture your literary journey through the course. It is an excellent tool for reflection.

What is the learner portfolio and why is it required?

The learner portfolio is a course requirement. While it won't necessarily contain every activity that you do, it will include many assignments and activities that you have compiled throughout the two-year programme. It won't be directly assessed or moderated by the IB, but your school is required to keep it on file for six months after you receive your IB results, and schools may be asked to submit learner portfolios to verify that students are following the guidelines of academic integrity. But the IB doesn't simply require the portfolio because it provides evidence of the work you've produced.

Your learner portfolio can be handwritten and/or electronic. It will capture your literary journey though the course.

The course is structured so that students have a great amount of freedom and autonomy in selecting texts for assessment. This means that you may choose to write your HL essay, prepare for your individual oral, or respond to a Paper 2 question using works that you studied throughout both years of the course. Keeping activities and assignments related to these works in one organised place will provide you with the materials necessary to prepare for upcoming assessments.

Is there a list of required portfolio products?

While there is not a list of required portfolio entries and works, your portfolio should reflect the fluid nature of the course. You may wish to organise it by work or text, but keep in mind that intertextual connections should be a constant over both years and your portfolio should reflect connections between areas of exploration, texts, ideas, global issues, and concepts. Consider also that the course encourages variety not just in the reading list, but in how you learn. Your portfolio should reflect your varied learning experiences and contain a mix of creative and intellectual works that cross all media. You may also want to use the portfolio as a place to park your thoughts on outside sources. If you watch a compelling TED Talk that helped you understand a global issue in a text, don't just include your reflection – also include the link to the talk so you can review it later.

The chapters ahead will provide plenty of practical ideas on what types of work can go into your portfolio. Portfolios are unique. Some entries may be reflective, others may be exploratory or research-based. Still others may include creative writing or filmed performances. Shared documents from group discussions and teacher feedback from mock IB exams or other formative assessments will also be valuable.

Is there a required format?

There is no required format for the learner portfolio. You may find it easier to keep an electronic portfolio or you may choose to organise hard copies in a binder. Some students will choose a hybrid of the two, electing to keep some work in digital form and some in print copy. Often there is no access to technology during a class period, so it isn't practical to retype a reflection or an assignment that is handwritten in class. In this case, it may be helpful to use an app such as Cam Scanner (CS)® that allows you to take pictures of your document in batches and save it as one PDF or JPG file. The file can then be uploaded to the rest of your digital entries. Teachers and students are free to select a portfolio format that works best for them.

It will be interesting to look back on your initial reflections as you continue your two-year journey. We often end up in places we did not expect. As a closing activity for the course, you may want to write a response to this earlier version of yourself, focusing on how your experiences in IB DP literature have influenced your personal and intellectual growth.

Activity 8 Learner portfolio reflection

For this activity you will create a reflective learner portfolio entry by answering the questions below. The activity is designed to help you think about yourself as a learner and a student of English A: literature.

1) Which subject do you enjoy the most in school? Why?
2) Which course do you enjoy the least? Why?
3) Review the list of learner profile traits on page 6. Explain how three of them apply to you.
4) Which trait do you feel least applies to you? Why?
5) What do you feel you do well in English class?
6) What gives you the most trouble or challenges you most in English?
7) What steps can you take to meet those challenges this year?
8) Which of the following approaches to learning skills do you feel is your strongest? Your weakest?
   - THINKING (reflection, metacognition, reasoning)
   - COMMUNICATION (speaking, listening, writing)

- SOCIAL (engaging with others, getting along with difficult people, being open-minded)
- SELF-MANAGEMENT (organisational skills, time management, resilience in the face of failure or difficulty, mindfulness, self-motivation)
- RESEARCH (finding, evaluating, analysing, and incorporating sources).

9) What steps can you take this year to strengthen your weakest approach to learning skills?
10) What space or place makes you feel happy, peaceful, or 'at home'? Why?
11) Where do you spend time? Draw a map (in whatever way works for you) of how you spend a day/week/ month, or otherwise describe the spaces, places, and people that make up your daily life.
12) Describe your ideal day.
13) What are you most excited and/or worried about this year in English? In IB in general?
14) Imagine yourself at age 30. Where are you and what are you doing?
15) How might what you do or don't do over the course of your DP studies affect or help or hurt that future you?

Insights into this overview chapter

1. The definition of literature is not static. A text's literary status reflects cultural values and the ever-evolving relationship between readers, writers, and texts.

2. The course aims for English A: literature and the *Prescribed reading list* stress the international-minded nature of the IB programme, which encourages students to engage with a range of texts from different time periods, styles, and cultures.

3. Aspects of the IB philosophy, such as approaches to learning, the learner profile, international-mindedness, and the IB core, complement the aims of English A: literature to support student learning.

4. The three areas of exploration – readers, writers, and texts, time and space, and intertextuality: connecting texts – work with the seven course concepts (identity, culture, creativity, communication, perspective, transformation, representation) to foster a student-centred multi-faceted approach to teaching and learning.

5. Structural aspects of English A: literature include requirements regarding works studied, areas of exploration, concepts, literary forms, authors, periods, places, and assessments.

6. Assessments for English A literature are directly connected to course aims and there is alignment in grading criteria across all required assessments.

7. There are three required assessments for English A: literature SL, which are: Paper 1: Guided literary analysis; Paper 2: Comparative essay; and the individual oral. The HL version of the course adds a fourth assessment (the HL essay) and requires students to write a second essay for the Paper 1 assessment.

8. The learner portfolio is a required component that is not formally assessed by the IB but is designed to keep your work organised for your assessments and enable you to reflect on your progress throughout the course.

Introduction to the 'approaches to learning' chapters

The English A: literature course includes the study of different types of literature. These types, commonly referred to as 'forms', include drama, fiction, poetry, and non-fiction. Each of these forms requires different **perspectives** from you as a reader, and it is important to know what these requirements are so that you can approach your reading with confidence. In the Detailed overview chapter, we discussed the **areas of exploration** and **concepts** that comprise the IB literature course. We also connected this literary framework to the broader IB concepts that govern all IB DP courses such as **approaches to teaching and learning**, **CAS**, **TOK**, the **learner profile**, and **international-mindedness**. This is a lot of theory. Studying each of the literary forms will help you apply theory to practice.

The following four chapters will focus on the approaches to learning in the conventions of drama, poetry, fiction, and literary non-fiction. Conventions, quite simply, are the established 'rules' that writers use. If we read with a sharp understanding of these conventions, then we can know what is expected of us as a reader and can judge whether the text before us is representative of a particular form. As an English A: literature student, you will be expected to **communicate** how literary writers use certain strategies to create their narratives. But you won't be expected to do this alone. There are opportunities in the next four chapters for both independent and **collaborative** activities that will show you how to build an effective learner portfolio. As you work through the chapters, you will learn what each form expects from you as a reader, what strategies you can expect to encounter as you read, and how these expectations will provide you with a basis for understanding, analysing, and interpreting a text.

Approaches to learning in fiction

1.1

Learning objectives

In this chapter you will…

- connect fiction to approaches to learning, course concepts, and areas of exploration
- explore conventions and expectations of fiction
- understand what it means to be an active, close reader
- actively explore the importance of point of view, voice, and tone
- engage with the variations of characterisation
- understand the function of plot, setting, time, and theme
- interpret and consider the value of visual literacy in texts such as graphic novels
- communicate ideas through a variety of individual and collaborative activities
- analyse, evaluate, and appreciate a range of fiction works/extracts through:
  - readers, writers, and texts
  - time and space
  - intertextuality
  - global issues.

Fiction writers create worlds through the endless possibilities that words provide. Visits to multiple cities or even universes are limited only by the author's imagination. Unlike other literary forms, a good fiction story is not dependent on a team of directors or actors, nor is it limited by compressed language. Truth is not required. But how fiction writers **communicate** their **creative** plots is essential in making their worlds believable.

As you delve into this chapter, you'll have the opportunity to develop your knowledge of this literary form through individual exercises and even hone your analytical and social skills as you collaborate with peers. After you become familiar with the literary conventions of fiction, you will analyse and evaluate various texts and examine **global issues** though **areas of exploration** and the **course concepts**. The journey ahead will not only strengthen your skills for assessment but also encourage a lifelong appreciation of the fiction form.

Conventions and expectations of fiction

When we read fiction, whether a short story or a novel, we most often read alone. The images associated with reading fiction – a comfy chair, a quiet space, the corner of a subway car – speak to the nature of the form itself. In most cases, with the exception of the graphic novel, the reader creates the images from words alone. It's a highly imaginative, creative process, one that enables the reader to **transform** the words on the page into a **representation** that is a combination of authorial choices and the prior knowledge that the reader associates with ideas in the text. This negotiation between **readers, writers, and texts** centres on the readers' ability to immerse themselves in the world of fiction, a world that originated in the mind of the writer but takes on a life of its own once a new reader begins to read the text.

Reading novels usually requires more than one sitting. Novels can be picked up and laid aside, sometimes for periods of weeks. As such, novelists structure their texts to accommodate this process. Sections, chapters, interstices (white space or gaps on a page) function as natural breaks for the reader, and novelists can use these breaks as part of their narrative strategy. Many graphic novels originated as separate issues or chapters to be read in instalments, and then were later combined to create one larger work. Spiegelman's *Maus* and Gibbons and Moore's *Watchmen* are two examples of this **transformation**. This type of reading is not new. Nineteenth-century writers Charles Dickens and Arthur Conan Doyle also published their works in instalments (much like modern-day TV episodes), building suspense in their readers, who would eagerly await the next publication.

According to Stephen King, 'A short story is like a quick kiss in the dark from a stranger '. Unlike novels, which take time to develop intricate plots and complex characters, short stories are compressed and intense; characters and plot lines are introduced quickly. Endings often leave the reader with more questions than answers, or tend to be punctuated with unexpected twists. It may be helpful to think of a short story like a one-act play or short film, as opposed to their more lengthy counterparts.

Fiction writers, whatever type of fiction they choose to write, share many of the same narrative strategies in creating their literary worlds. Features used by authors of this form to bring these worlds to life include:

- **point of view**
- **voice**
- **characterisation**
- **plot**
- **setting**
- **theme**
- **time**
- **structure.**

Reading can take place anywhere and everywhere.

Thinking vs feeling

When we experience a fiction text, we open ourselves to the effects of the text. Sometimes those effects trigger an emotional response, and other times the effect piques our intellectual curiosity, but a full and satisfying experience incorporates both thinking and feeling. In close reading you focus not only on the literal meaning of the words, but also on the subtlety of a writer's style – the use of descriptive language, the pace of sentences, the rhythm of **dialogue**, all influence a reader's emotional and intellectual responses. This is the heart of the readers, writers, and texts area of exploration. The more you practise close reading, the better close reader you become.

Click on the eBook activity to read now what the Nobel Prize-winning novelist, Toni Morrison, says about reading. Her essay, 'The Reader as Artist', defines the process of active reading. In this course you are expected to read, as Morrison says, by 'surrender[ing] to the narrator's world while remaining alert inside it'. By remaining 'alert', you can 'dig for the hidden, questioning and relishing the choices the author made', thereby constructing your own meaning from the text. Active reading is the guiding principle for the English A: literature course.

Connections
Aspire to be an active rather than a passive reader.

Considering point of view

Fiction writers decide on the manner and method of presenting their text. Their primary consideration is just how much information they want to reveal, or how much they want to conceal. Point of view is the **perspective** a writer determines for their reader – something like choosing a camera angle or lens. The choice is significant.

A chosen angle of vision, just as in point of view, limits what we see as well as what we know.

Imagine the difference in shooting a film from high atop a cliff a mile away from the action, as opposed to shooting the same scene from five metres away. Details in the close-up version would be sharp and clear, but the greater area where the scene plays out would be unseen. At the same time, the view from a cliff top would offer a perfect view of the panorama but details would be lost. In the same way, a fiction writer judiciously selects the angle of vision dependent upon the effects that they want to create for the reader. How close will the writer allow the reader to get to the story? How much will the reader 'know'? How much will the reader have to assume or surmise? Will there be information that the reader will never know? A writer's decision as to the point of view is perhaps the first, and most significant, choice to make.

Types of point of view

- First person
- third-person omniscient
- third-person limited omniscient
- objective.

First-person point of view is the perspective of one of the characters (either major or minor) in the text who narrates the story.

Example: *I knew from the moment that I saw her, that my life, as I knew it, would be changed forever.*

First-person point of view

Third-person omniscient point of view is the perspective of a narrator outside the action of the story, who knows what the characters think and feel and why they behave as they do. This narrator can potentially tell the reader everything about the characters and the situations of the text, but does not have to.

Example: *When they met, they exchanged pleasantries. Susan smiled and grabbed Gabriella's hands, as if she had met an old, dear friend, while Gabriella nodded and wrinkled her nose the way she always did when she was nervous. They both knew that their meeting may have been by chance but felt fated nonetheless.*

Third-person omniscient

Third-person limited point of view is similar to the perspective of the third-person omniscient narrator, but only with regard to a single character. This narrator can enter the mind and heart of that character, and virtually knows everything about this character, but cannot tell us what other characters are thinking and feeling.

Example: *When Susan saw her, standing there, looking that beautiful, she knew that she had to say something. Stop, get her attention, say something stupid. Anything. This meeting had to happen sometime and today was destined to be the day. She knew it.*

Third-person limited

The **objective** point of view is often called 'the fly on the wall' perspective. This narrator observes and describes but does not judge or offer insight into characters or situations within the text.

Example: *Both young women stopped suddenly, smiled, and stood apart. Susan spoke, but Gabriella said nothing. The sun was gleaming and hot. Susan put her hand to her forehead and smiled again, offering a gesture of friendship that was denied.*

Considering voice

Narrative voice is wholly dependent upon the authorial choice of narration. The voice can communicate rage or detachment or humour. The tone of the narrator's voice is a critical narrative feature. While a title may grab the attention of a reader, the voice in the opening paragraph can engage the reader so intensely that they don't want to stop reading.

Consider the following example:

The Invisible Man by Ralph Ellison (1952)

It goes a long way back, some twenty years. All my life I had been looking for something, and everywhere I turned someone tried to tell me what it was. I accepted their answers too, though they were often in contradiction and even self-contradictory. I was naive. I was looking for myself and asking everyone except myself questions which I, and only I, could answer. It took me a long time and much painful boomeranging of my expectations to achieve a realization everyone else appears to have been born with: That I am nobody by myself. But first I had to discover that I am an invisible man!

In first-person narration, like the example above, the voice of the narrator is the voice of the character. While engaging, this voice is subjective, has bias, and is not always believable.

To identify an unreliable narrator, the reader must be alert to clues that indicate that the narrator is unaware of the reality of a situation. In *Dom Cassmuro*, by Machado de Assis, the unreliable narrator's rants and ravings throughout the text provide evidence for his unreliability.

First-person narration

Dom Casmurro by Machado de Assis (1899)

I escaped from the dependent, I escaped from my mother by not going to her room, but I did not escape from myself. I ran to my room, and came in after myself. I talked to myself, I chased after myself, I threw myself on the bed and rolled around with myself, weeping and stifling sobs on the edge of the sheet.

Third-person narrators, because they have some degree of omniscience, either full or limited, are accepted as trustworthy because we believe that they offer honest insights into character, thought and feeling, and unbiased assessments of event and situation, when in fact, they may hold biases. The voice of the narrator appears direct and confident – we trust this perspective because the narrator appears familiar with

Third-person narration

the characters, the setting, or the events. It is important, however, to examine the narrator's voice for clues to bias. Information can be revealed sympathetically or disdainfully, and the reader's judgement of character and situation is always directed by narrative voice.

As you can see in the following example, the voice of the third-person narrator describes a character in such detail that we accept the description at face value.

The Sorrow of War by Bao Ninh (1991)

She stood, feet slightly apart, looking directly at him. Not nineteen, but sure of herself. A little paler, a little less healthy than he had first thought. And on closer scrutiny her bright clothes, attractive from a distance, had seen better days.

In the example below, the narrative voice makes a judgement of the character based on what appears to be close observation over a period of time. This voice is self-assured and is, therefore, believable.

Things Fall Apart by Chinua Achebe (1958)

When he walked, his heels hardly touched the ground and he seemed to walk on springs, as if he was going to pounce on somebody. And he did pounce on people quite often. He had a slight stammer and whenever he was angry and could not get words out quickly enough, he would use his fists. He had no patience with unsuccessful men. He had had no patience with his father.

The voice of an objective narrator is often mechanical and disembodied, and lends itself to texts where information is revealed matter-of-factly without opinion or bias. This voice simply reports what it sees.

A Rose for Emily by William Faulkner (1930)

When Miss Emily Grierson died, our whole town went to her funeral: the men through a sort of respectful affection for a fallen monument, the women mostly out of curiosity to see the inside of her house, which no one save an old manservant—a combined gardener and cook—had seen in at least ten years.

Connections

The author's choice of point of view is purposeful and strategic. A narrator's distance from the action determines the reader's response to that action.

Considering tone

Every work of fiction has an associated tone that conveys the attitude of the narrator. It can express the full range of emotions, from passion and anger to boredom and indifference. This attitude is revealed through the action and situation of the text as well as the reactions of characters. Just as tone of voice can soften the effect of a reprimand, the tone in a work of fiction can modify or direct a reader's response to a character, action, or situation. In Activity 1 you will consider tone, point of view, and voice as you read, analyse, evaluate, and transform the passages below.

Activity 1 Point of view, voice, and tone

Each of the following passages, taken from several novels, demonstrates a wide range of points of view and voice. Determine the type of narrative point of view (perspective) for each passage. Then, determine all that you can about the narrator including age, gender, and tone of voice.

NOTE: There are additional passages in the eBook if you would like to expand this activity or come back to it for more practice.

Part 1: Read, analyse, and evaluate the following questions:

- Can you sense if the tone of voice of the narrator is sympathetic, detached, or indifferent?
- What specific words or phrases indicate the narrator's attitude towards the subject matter?
- Does the voice reveal anything about their **culture** or **identity**?
- Do you seem to connect with one character or situation more than another? Explain why you think this is.
- Write your responses in your **learner portfolio**.

1) *Her marriage to Leonce Pontellier was purely an accident, in this respect resembling many other marriages which masquerade as the decrees of Fate. It was in the midst of her secret great passion that she met him. He fell in love, as men are in the habit of doing, and pressed his suit with an earnestness and an ardor which left nothing to be desired. He pleased her; his absolute devotion flattered her. She fancied there was a sympathy of thought and taste between them, in which fancy she was mistaken.*

    – Kate Chopin, The Awakening (1899)

2) *The people all saw her come because it was sundown. The sun was gone, but he had left his footprints in the sky. It was the time for sitting on porches beside the road. It was the time to hear things and talk. These sitters had been tongueless, earless, eyeless conveniences all day long. Mules and other brutes had occupied their skins. But now, the sun and the bossman were gone, so the skins felt powerful and human. They became lords of sounds and lesser things. They passed notions through their mouths. They sat in judgment.*

    – Zora Neale Hurston, Their Eyes Were Watching God (1937)

3) *People in delirium rise and sink, rise and sink, in and out of lucidity. The swaying, shuddering, thudding, flinging stops, and the furniture of life falls into place. The*

vehicle was the fever. Chattering metal and raving dance of loose bolts in the smell of the children's car-sick. She rose from it gradually for longer and longer intervals. At first what fell into place was what had vanished, the past.

– Nadine Gordimer, *July's People* (1981)

4) *I knew I was not in Saigon. I was not a hospital volunteer. It was not 1968 but 1978. Yet I also knew, as I passed a wall of smoked-glass windows, that I would see the quick movements of green camouflage fatigues, and I knew. I knew the medic insignia on his uniform and I knew, I knew, what I would see next. His face, not the face before the explosion, but the face after, motionless in the liquefied red that poured from a tangle of delicate veins. 'Oh God, oh God, oh my God!' people cried. The doctor, the medic, and the operating-room crew killed in a cramped, battered room reinforced by rows of military-green sandbags. The calm of Saigon had always been unreliable, narcotically unreal. Who could have known before the man was cut up that an unexploded grenade, fired from a launcher—not a dead bullet—had lodged in the hollowness of his stomach?*

– Lan Cao, *Monkey Bridge* (1997)

Part 2: Transformation: from flat text to tableau

- A tableau is dramatic teaching strategy where you freeze in poses to represent a specific scene. The purpose is to transform close reading skills into a visual representation that conveys voice, tone, and perspective.
- For this part of the activity, you will work in a group to create a tableau for one of the passages you analysed in Part 1.
- Once you have been assigned to your group, discuss the questions from Part 1 associated with your passage and plan how you will express your assigned scene through a freeze frame. Even if there is little action in your scene, remember you are trying to capture voice, perspective, and tone.
- Put energy into your body and expression. Consider posing at different levels (close to floor, mid-level, higher up); interact with each other to increase the dramatic effect.
- Once you have selected your freeze frame, practise as if someone is taking a picture. Have one person narrate the text and then afterward count 1, 2, 3 'freeze' to set your tableau.
- Present your tableaus for each other in groups.
- Write a reflection in your learner portfolio about how this transformative activity helps you better understand tone, perspective, and voice. How can borrowing strategies from drama improve literary analysis and interpretation skills?

Considering characterisation

There are two methods of characterisation in fiction – direct and indirect.

Direct characterisation relies on the narrator's descriptions and judgements about a specific character. If a narrator describes a character as tall and thin with a slight limp, we classify that as direct characterisation. If the narrator tells us that a character dislikes small children and avoids them at every opportunity, once again, we have direct characterisation. But, if we witness a character struggling up a narrow staircase, or holding his hands over his ears and moving nervously aside when small children run past him screaming with delight, we experience indirect characterisation. If another character describes a character as 'skinny as a bean pole and not a friend to children', we classify this observation as indirect characterisation as well. Think of direct characterisation in terms of *telling* and indirect characterisation in terms of *showing*. Such representations reveal the author's style of communication with the reader and provide us with a window into character identities.

Characters may also either be dynamic or static in terms of their presentation within fiction. Dynamic characters change within the text. Experiences affect these characters and they may act or think differently because of these experiences. Static characters, on the other hand, do not change, although the reader's perception of such a character can change over time.

Connections

A narrator's bias regarding a character must be evaluated in terms of textual evidence to support the truth or falsity of that bias.

Click on the link to the online exercise in the eBook.

Considering plot

If a friend asked you to tell them what a film was about, you would probably give them a quick summary of the main events of the film. Those main events, linked together through time, create a unified whole. Aristotle, in his *Poetics*, wrote about plot in this way. He said that plot is the 'imitation of an action' and 'the arrangement of the incidents'. This arrangement would have to be unified: it would have a beginning, middle, and an end, and each part could be recognised within a chain of causality better known as cause and effect. Stories have beginnings, and middles, and ends, so is a story the same thing as a plot?

EM Forster distinguishes between a story and a plot. He says that a story is 'a narrative of events arranged in their time sequence'. Plot, he continues, 'is also a narrative of events, but the emphasis falls on causality'. He gives this example: '"The king died, and then the queen died" is a story; "The king died, and then the queen died of grief" is a plot. Causality takes precedence over time sequence in plot. Time sequence is still there, but it is secondary to cause and effect.'

Novels are developed in such a way that they may have more than one plot. These **subplots** have a number of functions. They can deepen suspense, serve as ironic **contrast** to the main plot, or function as a means to develop character. The intricacy of plot within a text is one of the many narrative strategies that fiction writers have at their disposal; they can create simple, unified plot lines, or they can interweave plot and subplot, creating a tangle of action.

Activity 2 Sequencing plot events

1) Read through the plot events below and arrange them in order. If you are not familiar with the plot of *Cinderella*, research a brief summary before beginning the activity.
   - Cinderella dances with the Prince and the couple falls in love.
   - The glass slipper fits Cinderella's foot and she marries the Prince.
   - The Fairy Godmother visits Cinderella and provides her with what she needs for the ball.
   - An invitation to the Royal Ball is delivered to the home.
   - The clock strikes midnight and Cinderella leaves her glass slipper behind.
   - The Prince and Cinderella live happily ever after.
   - The Prince goes from home to home having maidens try on the glass slipper.
   - Cinderella's father dies and she is made to do housework by her stepmother and stepsisters.

   Obviously, you had to do some rearranging, but even if the events were in sequential order, you may feel that some key details were left out. When you retell a story, what you choose to include or leave out depends largely on your personal experience with the text.

2) Next, you and a partner will *individually* create plot events for a text you have both read, using strips of paper, note cards, or a program like Padlet®, if available. Once you have both completed this task, trade with each other and put the events in order.

   What do you notice about your plot lines? Where do they overlap? Where are the discrepancies? What do you think accounts for the differences? Consider what this exercise reveals about the nature of storytelling and write your response in your learner portfolio.

Students recording events for Ian McEwan's novel, *Atonement*

Considering setting and time

Settings, like plots, can be complex or simple. The setting of a novel, for example, can be limited to a single place, or more than one place, dependent upon the aims of the writer. What is perhaps most important, however, is not the number of settings, but what we might call the 'rendering' of setting within a text. The IB English A: literature course embeds this terminology into the course by including the **time and space** area of exploration. Setting or 'space' includes the geographical, historical, and social background in which the action takes place. In some fiction, setting can take on the significance of character or theme. For example, a wall could take on thematic significance if a character witnesses a crime through a crevice in that wall. Every

To devise a setting is to create a fictional world that readers can envision.

time that character sees that wall, the memory of what he saw or heard is relived; or, perhaps with the passing of time, the wall crumbles like the memory itself.

Fiction writers create and manipulate setting because it comprises the fictional world where their characters reside. All action takes place within a setting, but the setting can change with the passage of time.

Time, then, or rather the passing of time within a work of fiction, is relative to other conventions of fiction. What this means is that many aspects of fiction – the characters, the plot, the setting, the revelation of themes, even the structure of a text – relate to the passing of time. Some writers unfold their text as a strict chronology while others break the sequence of time from past to present and to future. One tool writers use to do this is **flashback**, where the present tense of the action of a text is suspended to reveal some moment in the past. The significance of such a moment may or may not be apparent when it occurs. As a close reader, your ability to recognise the flashback is key, but even more important is your ability to consider the effect of the flashback. Does that effect inform your understanding of some aspect of the text? For example, is your understanding of a character enhanced through the flashback? Would a series of flashbacks work as a progressive understanding of character in the present time of the text?

Time and space: literature as a path to the past

The time and space area of exploration aligns with the concepts of culture and identity, which often connect to personal histories. Marguerite Duras' French novel, *The Lover*, is a **reflective** text that explores the implications of choices made during times of duress. Because the novel is based on the author's own experiences as an impoverished young woman in Indochina during pre- and post-World War II, fact and fiction are blurred as the narrator reaches back in time to recollect her story.

The combination of poverty and her outsider status as a colonist living in French-occupied Indochina creates a sense of isolation for the narrator. Seeking human connection and a way to support her family, she chose to become a prostitute at the age of 15. Shame, sorrow, and regret follow this decision through many decades. The passage below takes place just moments before the unnamed narrator, who is now an elderly woman, describes her memories of meeting the man who will become her lover and source of shame. As you read the passage, consider time and space in terms not only of geography, but also in terms of the considerable number of years that span between the event and the reflection.

The Lover by Marguerite Duras (1984)

I think it was during this journey [on a ferry to Saigon] that the image became detached, removed from the rest. It might have existed, a photograph might have been taken, just like any other, somewhere else, in other circumstances. But it wasn't. The subject was too slight. Who would have thought of such a thing? The photograph could only have been taken if someone could have known in advance how important it was to be in my life, that event, that crossing of the river. But while it was happening, no one even knew of its existence. Except God. And that's why—it couldn't have been otherwise—the image doesn't exist. It was omitted. Forgotten. It never was detached or removed from the rest. And it's to this, this failure to be created, that the image owes its virtue: the virtue of representing, of being the creator of, an absolute.

Here the narrator speaks of an image, a memory, a moment where a choice she made had a significant impact on the course of her life. We all make choices, but rarely do we know which choices will be our 'defining moments', moments that forge our destiny, our development, our identity. In **TOK** fashion, the narrator questions if such a moment can even exist if no one records it. There is no record, no photograph of her on the ferry that day, yet every cell in her being 'knows' that this moment when she makes a choice after stepping off the ferry will cause 'regrets for everything [she does], everything [she's] gained, everything [she's] lost, good and bad…'.

Activity 3 Analysing a snapshot moment

1) **Inquiry:** Choose a 'snapshot' of a memory from at least 5–10 years ago. It's okay if you don't remember all the details. It does not have to be a 'defining moment'. It can simply be something that you remember from your childhood. It should be something that someone you know (mother, father, sibling, grandparent) also remembers.
2) **Thinking:** Write a short recollection of this event.
3) **Communication:** Discuss your event with the person who also remembers it and take notes from your discussion.
4) **Analysis:** What do you notice about the recollections? Which details match yours? Which ones are different? How does the passage of time affect the interpretation of events?
5) **Reflection:** Consider the purpose of reflecting on past experiences. What is gained in terms of knowledge? Identity? Perspective?
6) Write your responses to these questions in your learner portfolio.

Considering theme

Theme is best understood as a lesson about human nature that emerges from the action and interaction within a text. A work of fiction is not limited by the number of themes that can unfold as you read a text. Essentially, there are two types of themes: those that are explicitly stated, and those that are subtly implied.

The messages, or themes, in children's literature are always clearly stated.

Explicit themes are stated outright by a narrator or a character. In children's literature, explicit themes abound because writers want the message to be absolutely clear, spelled out directly for the child to consider. In more sophisticated reading, the themes are seldom explicit.

Implicit themes are inferred by the reader over time. These messages about human nature are subtle, rather than **didactic**, and are discovered through examining character action and interaction. At best, the convention of theme emerges as the text unfolds.

Implicit themes are not directly stated, as explicit themes are, but are instead implied over the course of reading the text. These messages that emerge about some aspect of human nature are inferred by the reader, and are, therefore, constructed by a reader's ability to grasp some understanding of character action and interaction. The writer doesn't 'spell out' these themes; readers construct them.

Considering structure

The structure of a novel or short story is a narrative strategy that can greatly affect the reader's understanding of a text. Alice Walker's structuring of her short story, *Roselily* is a case in point. Walker enables the reader to be inside the mind of the character as her wedding vows are being spoken, allowing for great understanding of the character, her situation, her fears, and her hopes. **Irony** is also heightened through the connection of Roselily's thoughts to a particular segment of the vow. The structure of the story creates very specific effects on the reader.

So, if a writer chooses to switch point of view every other chapter, or to use the present time of the novel for the odd-numbered chapters and flashbacks for the even-numbered chapters, they would do so to create very specific effects for the reader. Always consider the structure of a novel – the number of chapters and the use of groupings of chapters within sections of the text may seem arbitrary considerations, but they are not. They are purposeful manipulations of the convention with intended results.

Activity 4 A readers, writers, and texts approach to the opening of Ian McEwan's *Atonement*

Note that when you begin to read a novel, you formulate first impressions that will likely shift or transform after you have read the entire work. For this activity, don't worry about where the story is going. Just steep yourself in the opening paragraphs of the text and allow your close reading to connect with language, characters, and content. You will navigate between *academic* and *personal* responses as you try to make sense of the world Ian McEwan constructs.

Directions: Read the opening paragraphs of Ian McEwan's *Atonement* (below the questions) and write down your responses to the questions in your learner portfolio.

1) **Diction:** Consider the two opening words of the novel: 'The play'. How long did it take the writer to complete the task of writing the play? What is the significance of the word 'tempest' in describing how the play was written? What might this reveal about the writer?

2) **Form/Genre:** The second paragraph explains the plot of Briony's play. The play itself falls into the genre of melodrama. Look up the meaning of melodrama and copy the definition in your response (don't forget your citation). How does Briony's melodrama end? You may be interested to know that Briony is only 13 years old. What might the melodrama genre and the ending suggest about her character?

3) **Characterisation:** Consider the sentence 'Briony studied her mother's face for every trace of shifting emotion, and Emily Tallis obliged with looks of alarm, snickers of glee and, at the end, grateful smiles and wise, affirming nods.' What does this interaction reveal about the relationship between the two? What do they value?

4) **Foreshadowing:** Why is it significant that the narrator says, 'Briony was hardly to know it then, but this was the project's highest point of fulfilment'? What impact does such foreshadowing have on the reader?

5) **TOK connections:** What does the last paragraph of the passage reveal about Briony's <u>imagination</u>? How does she feel about her older brother, Leon? How might her desire to be a bridesmaid in his (imagined) upcoming wedding be linked to Briony's choice of genre for her play?

6) **Point of view:** What is the significance of point of view here? How might the effect of the story be different if we learned about Briony through a first person rather than a third person perspective?

7) **Personal connection:** Speaking of point of view, consider your own context here. Briony clearly has a passion for writing. Think about one of your passions – art, cooking, sports, music, photography… really anything. How important is it for you to share your passion with others? If it is important, why is this important to you? How does 'sharing' this personal knowledge work? If sharing is not instrumental to your passion, why is this so? What do you think your passion reveals about you? Your values? Your personality?

8) **One-sentence summary:** Based on your reading of the opening paragraphs of *Atonement*, write a one-sentence summary about Briony. What is she like? What does she value? What do you notice between the lines?

9) **Transformation, representation, and perspective:** If you were to film the opening passage from *Atonement*:
   - what choices would you make in terms of set design, character placement and movement, camera angles, sound?
   - How would you communicate Briony's attitude and personality? The content of her play? Her mother's response?
   - Compare your representation of the scene with that of your peers. What did you notice about the choices you made? What overlapped? What differed? What does this transformative activity reveal about the connection between close reading and interpretation?

10) **Intertextual connections:** In 2007, *Atonement* was produced as a major motion picture directed by Joe Wright. In addition to numerous prestigious nominations, it won the Golden Globe Award for Best Motion Picture in 2008.

- Watch the opening scene of the film. To what extent did the director accurately convey the opening passage of McEwan's novel? What was lost in the transformation to this different medium? Was anything gained? Explain the strengths and limitations of each version of the text (film vs print).

Atonement by Ian McEwan (2001)

Chapter One

The play – for which Briony had designed the posters, programmes and tickets, constructed the sales booth out of a folding screen tipped on its side, and lined the collection box in red crepe paper – was written by her in a two-day tempest of composition, causing her to miss a breakfast and a lunch. When the preparations were complete, she had nothing to do but contemplate her finished draft and wait for the appearance of her cousins from the distant north. There would be time for only one day of rehearsal before her brother arrived. At some moments chilling, at others desperately sad, the play told a tale of the heart whose message, conveyed in a rhyming prologue, was that love which did not build a foundation on good sense was doomed. The reckless passion of the heroine, Arabella, for a wicked foreign count is punished by ill fortune when she contracts cholera during an impetuous dash towards a seaside town with her intended. Deserted by him and nearly everybody else, bed-bound in a garret, she discovers in herself a sense of humour. Fortune presents her a second chance in the form of an impoverished doctor – in fact, a prince in disguise who has elected to work among the needy. Healed by him, Arabella chooses judiciously this time, and is rewarded by reconciliation with her family and a wedding with the medical prince on 'a windy sunlit day in spring.'

Mrs Tallis read the seven pages of *The Trials of Arabella* in her bedroom, at her dressing table. With the author's arm around her shoulder the whole while, Briony studied her mother's face for every trace of shifting emotion, and Emily Tallis obliged with looks of alarm, snickers of glee and, at the end, grateful smiles and wise, affirming nods. She took her daughter in her arms, onto her lap – ah, that hot smooth little body she remembered from its infancy, and still not gone from her, not quite yet – and said that the play was 'stupendous,' and agreed instantly, murmuring into the tight whorl of the girl's ear, that this word could be quoted on the poster which was to be on an easel in the entrance hall by the ticket booth.

Briony was hardly to know it then, but this was the project's highest point of fulfilment. Nothing came near it for satisfaction, all else was dreams and frustration. There were moments in the summer dusk after her light was out, burrowing in the delicious gloom of her canopy bed, when she made her heart thud with luminous, yearning fantasies, little playlets in themselves, every one of which featured Leon. In one, his big, good-natured face buckled in grief as Arabella sank in loneliness and despair. In another, there he was, cocktail in hand at some fashionable city watering hole, overheard boasting to a group of friends: Yes, my younger sister, Briony Tallis the writer, you must surely have heard of her. In a third, he punched the air in exultation as the final curtain fell, although there was no curtain, there was no possibility of a curtain. Her play was not for her cousins, it was for her brother, to celebrate his return, provoke his admiration and guide him away from his careless succession of girlfriends, towards the right form of wife, the one who would persuade him to return to the countryside, the one who would sweetly request Briony's services as a bridesmaid.

Expanding our view of texts – the graphic novel and fiction

Although the term graphic novel is not new, the acceptance of it as a literary form has gained traction in the past decade. An earlier term for the graphic novel is sequential art: 'the arrangement of pictures or images and words to narrate a story or dramatise an idea' (Will Eisner, 1985, *Comics & Sequential Art*). From the Bayeux Tapestry to Egyptian hieroglyphics, stories have been told visually since the early beginnings of human communication. As the definition of text and literacy broadens in the twenty-first century, the distinction between highbrow and lowbrow literature narrows.

Today, graphic novels are considered works of literature in their own right. As a student of English A: literature, you may encounter a passage from a graphic novel in the Paper 1 exam or you may choose to focus on a graphic novel for any other assessment including Paper 2, the HL essay, or the individual oral. In the bigger picture, studying graphic texts not only helps us understand culture and context through time and space, but also our own place in it.

Like fiction, graphic novels can be analysed using classic terms such as plot, setting, characterisation, and point of view, but **visual literacy**, which focuses on creating meaning from images, requires knowledge of additional terminology. In his primer, *Understanding Comics*, Scott McCloud explains how to interpret graphic works through the form itself. On the next page we've annotated his pages to help you review the vocabulary, but as you read his panels, take note of how you are processing the words and images.

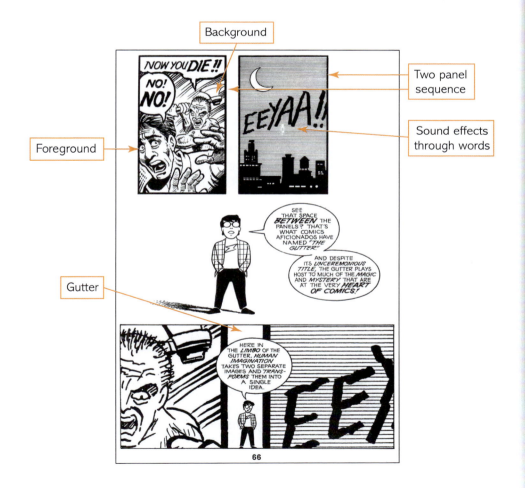

How to interpret graphic works ▶

Visual vocabulary for graphic texts

Panel: Single frames placed in a sequence.

Gutter: The area between the panels.

Speech balloon: Area that serves as dialogue in the text.

Thought balloon: Like a speech balloon but the blank circles before the balloon indicate thought rather than dialogue.

Bleed: When an image extends beyond the frame/page.

Sound effects: Sound can be conveyed through specific font lettering or through visual images such as lines.

Figure: Often a character (not necessarily human). Aspects of figures, such as hands, faces, etc. can convey tone through body language.

Closure: The 'grammar' aspect of visual literacy where the viewer makes sense of a sequence by filling in the gaps between the gutters.

Foreground: The part of the panel that is closest to the viewer.

Midground: The centre of the panel; our eyes tend to gravitate towards the centre, so the author can make use of this space for emphasis or place characters off-centre for a slightly different effect.

Background: The backdrop of the panel that may contain subtext, foreshadowing and/or other not so obvious (but key) information.

Layout: The arrangement of panels on the page. Are they uniform? Are there breaks in the uniformity? If so, where?

Style: Varies by writer and time period. Realistic? Cartoonish? Abstract? How is colour used? To what effect? Does point of view shift?

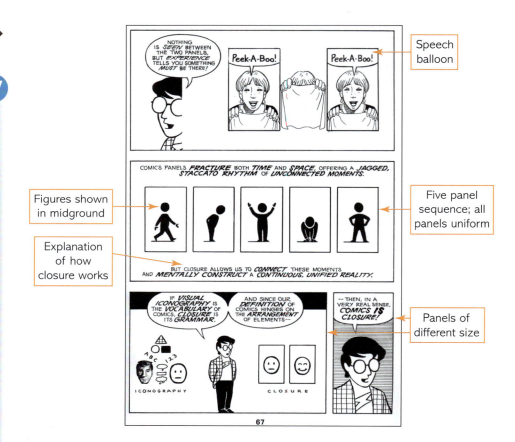

Speech balloon

Figures shown in midground

Five panel sequence; all panels uniform

Explanation of how closure works

Panels of different size

Note how McCloud defines the words 'gutter' (the space between the panels) and 'closure' (our ability to connect frames and mentally construct a unified reality) in a visual way that replicates the process of analysing this newer literary form. The viewer must *imagine*, must *create* the action that exists between the panels. Graphic novels use a combination of visual and written cues to make this happen, but types of closure exist in other literary forms as well.

Connections

When you make meaning from compressed lines in poetry, when you recognise what happens offstage between scenes in drama, and when you read between the lines in fiction and non-fiction, you are practising a form of closure.

While similarities exist across all forms of literature, interpreting graphic texts involves a multilayered type of thinking. As Francisca Goldsmith, author of *The Readers Advisory Guide to Graphic Novels,* points out, 'Reading graphic novels requires transliteracy skills as the pictures and words presented are bound together to form a higher level of conceptual communication than either text or image can deliver on its own.'

In the next two activities you will have the opportunity to put these transliterary skills to work as you review student-created storyboards and reflections (Activity 5) and create your own storyboard and reflection (Activity 6).

In Arthur Conan Doyle's short story, 'The Adventure of the Speckled Band', Sherlock Holmes saves a young woman's life by forcing her would-be assailant to come face to face with his own murder weapon. In this activity you will read an excerpt from the end of the story and compare two student-created graphic panels (storyboards) and reflections based on the excerpt.

Excerpt from 'The Adventure of the Speckled Band' by Arthur Conan Doyle (1892)

'What can it mean?' I gasped.

'It means that it is all over,' Holmes answered. 'And perhaps, after all, it is for the best. Take your pistol, and we will enter Dr. Roylott's room.'

With a grave face he lit the lamp and led the way down the corridor. Twice he struck at the chamber door without any reply from within. Then he turned the handle and entered, I at Analhi's heels, with the cocked pistol in my hand.

It was a singular sight which met our eyes. On the table stood a dark-lantern with the shutter half open, throwing a brilliant beam of light upon the iron safe, the door of which was ajar. Beside this table, on the wooden chair, sat Dr. Grimesby Roylott clad in a long grey dressing-gown, his bare ankles protruding beneath, and his feet thrust into red heelless Turkish slippers. Across his lap lay the short stock with the long lash which we had noticed during the day. His chin was cocked upward and his eyes were fixed in a dreadful, rigid stare at the corner of the ceiling. Round his brow he had a peculiar yellow band, with brownish speckles, which seemed to be bound tightly round his head. As we entered he made neither sound nor motion.

'The band! the speckled band!' whispered Holmes.

I took a step forward. In an instant his strange headgear began to move, and there reared itself from among his hair the squat diamond-shaped head and puffed neck of a loathsome serpent.

'It is a swamp adder!' cried Holmes, 'the deadliest snake in India. He has died within ten seconds of being bitten. Violence does, in truth, recoil upon the violent, and the schemer falls into the pit which he digs for another. Let us thrust this creature back into its den, and we can then remove Miss Stoner to some place of shelter and let the county police know what has happened.'

Now that you have read the print text, review the two student graphic panels and reflections below and respond to the questions on page 42. To view the panels in more detail along with other student samples, click on the link in the eBook.

Student A storyboard and reflection

My storyboard is a scene from 'The Adventure of the Speckled Band', where Holmes and Watson go to confront Dr Roylott for murdering Julia, only to discover that he had been killed in the very way he had killed her and planned to kill Helen. In the original stories, Holmes is described as being tall and having sharp features, which I applied to my storyboard. This storyboard has many dark backgrounds and silhouettes, with very little visible minus what Holmes' lamp illuminates, to create a sense of darkness and mystery from the original story. In mysteries and detective fiction, the readers are, for the most part, in the dark for what the solution could be, with all what we can see being what the narrator lights up for us. Each panel gets a little brighter as it goes on as the answer to the mystery is revealed. The last panel then becomes dark again with a black background to convey Holmes' fear of the creature.

Student B storyboard and reflection

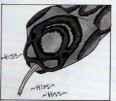

For my storyboard, I decided to do the scene from 'The Adventures of the Speckled Band' where Sherlock and Watson venture into Dr Roylott's room to see him dead with the snake wrapped around him, bringing the case to a close. There were many parts of this story I wanted to capture, but I felt like this was the most crucial moment, where everything comes together. For character revealing, this board shows how philosophical Sherlock can be at moments, when he goes on about how violence will always turn back onto the one causing it, as it did with Dr Roylott. Thematically it reveals the dangers of violence and greed, as Dr Roylott was killing for settlement money. The tone of this story is very dim, with the only 'light' being the one Sherlock holds. For the medium, I decided to use a completely black/white scheme in order to capture a noir effect, similar to what old detective stories and even tv shows used to be like. It adds a sense of grit and mystery to both the story and the storyboard. Being able to use shadows and shading adds a deeper perspective when looking at the storyboard, as there is little color and detail, but Sherlock is still able to pull out so much information in such a plain medium, which truly shows his mastery in deduction.

1) What do the graphic panels and the student reflections reveal about their interpretations of the text?
2) How might creating panels help you develop skills in literary analysis? What literary skills are involved in creating graphic panels based on works of fiction?
3) If you had to design panels for this scene, what artistic choices would you make?
4) Share your responses with a small group and record them in your learner portfolio.

Activity 6 Creating a graphic storyboard

Now that you have reviewed student samples, you will have the opportunity to create your own storyboard and reflection.

1) Choose a work of fiction from your IB syllabus and focus on a scene or situation from the text.
2) Think about the following as you create your storyboard:
   - Consider how the visual images will mix with the written text.
   - Will you use colour? If so, to what effect?
   - Your medium is visual, but this is a literary task. What tone are you creating? How do the words and visuals help establish the tone?
   - How will your readers draw inferences from one panel to the next? What is assumed between the panels? (See Scott McCloud's comments from his 'Understanding comics' panels on pages 39–40 for more details on this idea.)
   - What is the focal point of each frame? How have you drawn your reader's attention to this point? How is point of view established?
   - How will you design your layout? Will it be uniform? Will some panels be different sizes?
   - What style will define your storyboard? Realistic, cartoonish? Abstract? To what extent do your stylistic choices authentically convey the original text or perhaps redefine the text and create something new?
3) Create your graphic storyboard based on any specific scene from one of the works of fiction that you have studied in your two-year course.
4) Write a reflection that justifies your literary and artistic choices. Explain your decision-making process as you constructed your board. What 'story' does your board tell? What does your board reveal about characters? Themes? Tone? How does this visual medium help you convey meaning in a way that words alone cannot?
5) Once you have completed your storyboard, share and comment on the storyboards of your peers either electronically or in small groups.

The graphic novel, *Watchmen*, redefines the role and perception of superheroes.

Info box

For a full discussion of the history and impact of the graphic novel *Watchmen*, search for the YouTube video titled *'Watchmen – The Phenomenon: The Comic that Changed Comics'*.

The rise of the graphic novel

When Gibbons and Moore began publishing *Watchmen* in issue form over the course of 1986–87, they did not anticipate how their work would affect the literary world. 'Before DC Comics' *Watchmen* in 1986, liking comic books was a guilty secret – but Alan Moore's graphic novel changed all that and paved the way for a current cultural obsession,' writes Nicholas Barber in a BBC article. And this cultural obsession marked a shift in how communities defined works of literary merit.

Perhaps most notably, in 2005, *TIME Magazine* named *Watchmen* as one of the 100 best English-language novels from 1923 to the present, the first comic to ever make the list. What followed were numerous accolades including: Kirby Awards for Best Finite Series, Best New Series, Best Writer, and Best Writer/Artist; Eisner Awards for Best Finite Series, Best Graphic Album, Best Writer, and Best Writer/Artist; and a Hugo Award for Other Forms. In 2009, Warner Bros Studios transformed *Watchmen* into an American superhero film directed by Zach Snyder.

Summary and background

Watchmen begins with a murder investigation and it can certainly be read on one level as a crime thriller that includes superhero elements. But as the plot unfolds and the multifaceted characters come to life, it's clear that Gibbons and Moore transcend the traditional superhero comic formula. Set in a re-imagined 1985 where Richard Nixon is president and the United States won the Vietnam War, *Watchmen* channels the angst of the Cold War 1980s as Gibbons and Moore position the Soviet Union and the United States as adversaries headed toward nuclear war. The superheroes in *Watchmen* aren't caped heroes. They are presented as enigmatic, flawed people who are faced with impossible ethical dilemmas. Significantly, Gibbons and Moore invert that conventional superhero archetype so that lines between right and wrong, good and evil, triumph and destruction are never quite clear. And perhaps most notably for IB English A: literature students studying global issues, *Watchmen* reveals the dangers that come when technological growth eclipses social responsibilities, when conflicting political ideologies lead to violence on a local and global scale, and when the common-sense theories behind utilitarianism translate into the deaths of millions. There are no easy decisions when the stakes are so high – even for superheroes. But Gibbons and Moore render these complexities through intricate plot lines, deep characters, fractured linearity, and detailed visuals, thus creating a thought-provoking literary experience.

Connections: A few words on context

Sometimes, just jumping into a new text without any idea about its content or background activates our **creativity** and allows us to interpret it uniquely without any preconceived notions to temper our experience. *Watchmen* can be experienced this way, but knowing some facts about the Cold War during the 1980s and the fear of nuclear arms stand-offs with the USSR helps readers to understand characters' motivations. Individuals may act in a paranoid fashion because they are in a constant state of distrust, wary of other cultures and even of their own government. No one feels safe. The dark, complex characters in *Watchmen* arise from this ominous world, not from an art studio vacuum.

What's in a name?

Allusions and intertextual references abound in *Watchman* and knowing these references can certainly enrich your reading experience. Some names are direct allusions while others just hint at a connection. The character Ozymandias bears the same name as the title of a Percy Bysshe Shelley poem from the English Romantic era and also has connections to another comic character named Thunderbolt. Dr Manhattan, who is literally a nuclear character, has a similar name to the Manhattan Project but comic fans may recognise him as Captain Atom. Rorschach wears an ink-blotted mask, but he too resembles another comic character, Question. What you make of these connections and how they help you understand the text corresponds to your prior knowledge. Understanding time and space allows us to build our own representation of the text, transforming it with not just our creativity, but also with the background information we bring to the table.

Global issue

As mentioned earlier, the storyline in *Watchmen* lends itself to a discussion of global issues, particularly those related to science, technology, and the environment.

In pairs or a small group discuss the following global issue with reference to *Watchmen* **or** any other text you have studied. What are the implications when technological growth eclipses moral responsibility to the environment and its inhabitants? Record your responses in your learner portfolio.

Activity 7 Movie trailers

Movie trailers have become a popular way to encourage viewers to see a film. Search for *Watchmen – Official Graphic Novel Trailer* (YouTube) which provides a 30-second trailer for the novel, not the film.

1) How does this trailer encourage people to read *Watchmen*? What verbal, visual, and auditory effects are used? To what effect?
2) Create your own trailer for any work on your IB syllabus. Upload your trailer to your school platform or to the internet.
3) Watch your peers' trailers and discuss how creating a trailer sharpens your literary interpretive skills.

Areas of exploration: analyse, evaluate, appreciate

1) *A Good Man is Hard to Find* by Flannery O'Connor

2) *Cell One* by Chimamanda Ngozi Adichie

3) *The Garden of Forking Paths* by Jorge Luis Borges

1) Readers, writers, and texts: an approach to Flannery O'Connor's *A Good Man is Hard to Find* (1953)

Approaching any piece of fiction, whether a novel, a short story, or a graphic novel through the lens of readers, writers, and texts requires you to read slowly and closely, observing, as Toni Morrison says, both what is there and what is not. Close reading requires sharply focused observation of how the writer has used the conventions of the form of fiction to create specific effects in the reading. The meaning of the text and its interpretation lies at the intersection of observation and insight to those observations. Flannery O'Connor's short story begins as a comedic tale of a family of six driving to Florida for a family vacation. O'Connor herself says: 'I'll tell you that this is the story of a family of six which, on its way driving to Florida, gets wiped out by an escaped convict who calls himself the Misfit. The family is made up of the Grandmother and her son, Bailey, and his children, John Wesley and June Star and the baby, and there is also the cat and the children's mother. The cat is named Pitty Sing, and the Grandmother is taking him with them, hidden in a basket.'

It is in the first half of the story where we see these characters for what they are – two selfish, outspoken and rude children; a self-centred, superficial grandmother, dressed so that 'in case of an accident, anyone seeing her dead on the highway would know at once she was a lady'; and two parents who are either too tired, or too self-absorbed, to exercise any control over their children or their situation. The mother does not speak in the first half of the story – she holds the baby in the front seat and does not seem to hear or acknowledge any conversation between her children and their grandmother. Bailey, her husband, who does not have 'a naturally sunny disposition' like his mother and gets 'nervous' on trips, is equally absent from the conversation in the back seat.

According to Robert H Brinkmeyer Jr, an O'Connor scholar, 'The tone and direction of the story takes a sudden and drastic turn after the family's car overturns and the Misfit and his two henchmen drive up. What began as a satire of the family vacation now becomes a tale of terror as the family is led away and shot until only the grandmother and the Misfit remain alone together.'

For more information about how O'Connor views this dramatic shift in her own story, click on the activity in the eBook.

There are references, however, in the first part of the story, to the drastic turn that awaits them in the second half of the story:

- The grandmother reads about the Misfit's escape from the Federal Pen. and learns he is headed to Florida. She says, 'I wouldn't take my children in any direction with a criminal aloose in it. I couldn't answer my conscience if I did.'

- They passed a large cotton field with five or six graves fenced in the middle of it, like a small island.

- At lunch at Red Sammy Butts' restaurant, The Tower, his wife remarked, 'It isn't a soul in this green world of God's that you can trust.'

- 'A good man is hard to find,' Red Sammy said. 'Everything is getting terrible.'

- Outside of Toombsboro she woke up and recalled an old plantation that she had visited in this neighborhood once when she was a young lady… She recalled exactly which road to turn off to get to it… The road looked as if no one had travelled on it in months.

Reading closely, you may have observed one or more of these elements of foreshadowing. Close readers are always aware that clues may be provided by the writer, either directly or indirectly, to anticipate future action in the story. Practise this close reading skill as you read the second half of O'Connor's story. In particular, examine verbal expressions as well as physical actions that are **symbolic** or representative of some larger context or understanding.

Here is the second half of O'Connor's story: the bolded, underlined, and italicised portions will help you with the specific activities that follow the extract.

A Good Man is Hard to Find by Flannery O'Connor

The road was about ten feet above and they could see only the tops of the trees on the other side of it. Behind the ditch they were sitting in there were more woods, tall and dark and deep. In a few minutes they saw a car some distance away on top of a hill, coming slowly as if the occupants were watching them. **The grandmother stood up and waved both arms dramatically to attract their attention.** The car continued to come on slowly, disappeared around a bend and appeared again, moving even slower, on top of the hill they had gone over. It was <u>a big black battered hearse-like automobile</u>. There were three men in it.

It came to a stop just over them and for some minutes, the driver looked down with a steady expressionless gaze to where they were sitting, and didn't speak. Then he turned his head and muttered something to the other two and they got out. One was a fat boy in black trousers and a red sweat shirt with a silver stallion embossed on the front of it. He moved around on the right side of them and <u>stood staring, his mouth partly open in a kind of loose grin</u>. The other had on khaki pants and a blue striped coat and <u>a gray hat pulled down very low, hiding most of his face.</u> He came around slowly on the left side. <u>Neither spoke.</u>

The driver got out of the car and stood by the side of it, <u>looking down at them</u>. He was an older man than the other two. His hair was just beginning to gray and <u>he wore silver-rimmed spectacles that gave him a scholarly look</u>. He had a long creased face and didn't have on any shirt or undershirt. He had on blue jeans that were too tight for him and was holding a black hat and a gun. The two boys also had guns.

'We've had an ACCIDENT!' the children screamed.

The grandmother had the peculiar feeling that the bespectacled man was someone she knew. His face was as familiar to her as if she had known him all her life but she could not recall who he was. He moved away from the car and began to come down the embankment, placing his feet carefully so that he wouldn't slip. He had on tan and white shoes and no socks, and his ankles were red and thin. 'Good afternoon,' he said. 'I see you all had you a little spill.'

'We turned over twice!' said the grandmother.

'Once,' he corrected. *'We seen it happen. Try their car and see will it run, Hiram,'* he said quietly to the boy with the gray hat.

'What you got that gun for?' John Wesley asked. 'Whatcha gonna do with that gun?'

'Lady,' the man said to the children's mother, 'would you mind calling them children to sit down by you? Children make me nervous. *I want all you all to sit down right together there where you're at.'*

'What are you telling US what to do for?' June Star asked.

<u>Behind them the line of woods gaped like a dark open mouth</u>. 'Come here,' said their mother.

'Look here now,' Bailey began suddenly, 'we're in a predicament! We're in…'

The grandmother shrieked. She scrambled to her feet and stood staring. 'You're The Misfit!' she said. 'I recognized you at once!'

'Yes'm,' the man said, smiling slightly as if he were pleased in spite of himself to be known, *'but it would have been better for all of you, lady, if you hadn't of reckernized me.'*

Bailey turned his head sharply and said something to his mother that shocked even the children. The old lady began to cry and The Misfit reddened.

'Lady,' he said, 'don't you get upset. Sometimes a man says things he don't mean. *I don't reckon he meant to talk to you thataway.'*

'You wouldn't shoot a lady, would you?' the grandmother said and removed a clean handkerchief from her cuff and began to slap at her eyes with it.

The Misfit pointed the toe of his shoe into the ground and made a little hole and then covered it up again. 'I would hate to have to,' he said.

'Listen,' the grandmother almost screamed, 'I know you're a good man. You don't look a bit like you have common blood. I know you must come from nice people!'

'Yes mam,' he said, 'finest people in the world.' When he smiled he showed a row of strong white teeth. 'God never made a finer woman than my mother and my daddy's heart was pure gold,' he said. The boy with the red sweat shirt had come around behind them and was standing with his gun at his hip. The Misfit squatted down on the ground. 'Watch them children, Bobby Lee,' he said. 'You know they make me nervous.' He looked at the six of them huddled together in front of him and he seemed to be embarrassed as if he couldn't think of anything to say. 'Ain't a cloud in the sky,' he remarked, looking up at it. 'Don't see no sun but don't see no cloud neither.'

'Yes, it's a beautiful day,' said the grandmother. 'Listen,' she said, 'you shouldn't call yourself The Misfit because I know you're a good man at heart. I can just look at you and tell. '

'Hush!' Bailey yelled. 'Hush! Everybody shut up and let me handle this!' He was squatting in the position of a runner about to sprint forward but he didn't move.

'I prechate that, lady,' The Misfit said and drew a little circle in the ground with the butt of his gun.

'It'll take a half a hour to fix this here car,' Hiram called, looking over the raised hood of it.

'Well, first you and Bobby Lee get him and that little boy to step over yonder with you,' The Misfit said, pointing to Bailey and John Wesley. 'The boys want to ast you something,' he said to Bailey. 'Would you mind stepping back in them woods there with them?'

'Listen,' Bailey began, 'we're in a terrible predicament! Nobody realizes what this is,' and his voice cracked. His eyes were as blue and intense as the parrots in his shirt and he remained perfectly still.

The grandmother reached up to adjust her hat brim as if she were going to the woods with him but it came off in her hand. She stood staring at it and after a second she let it fall on the ground. Hiram pulled Bailey up by the arm as if he were assisting an old man. John Wesley caught hold of his father's hand and Bobby Lee followed. They went off toward the woods and just as they reached the dark edge, Bailey turned and supporting himself against a gray naked pine trunk, he shouted, 'I'll be back in a minute, Mamma, wait on me!'

'Come back this instant!' his mother shrilled but they all disappeared into the woods.

'Bailey Boy!' the grandmother called in a tragic voice but she found she was looking at The Misfit squatting on the ground in front of her. **'I just know you're a good man,' she said desperately. 'You're not a bit common!'**

'Nome, I ain't a good man,' The Misfit said after a second as if he had considered her statement carefully, 'but I ain't the worst in the world neither. My daddy said I was a different breed of dog from my brothers and sisters. "You know," Daddy said, "it's some that can live their whole life out without asking about it and it's others has to know why it is, and this boy is one of the latters. He's going to be into everything!"' He put on his black hat and looked up suddenly and then away deep into the woods as if he were embarrassed again. 'I'm sorry I don't have on a shirt before you ladies,' he said, hunching his shoulders slightly. 'We buried our clothes that we had on when we escaped and we're just making do until we can get better. We borrowed these from some folks we met,' he explained.

'That's perfectly all right,' the grandmother said. 'Maybe Bailey has an extra shirt in his suitcase.'

'I'll look and see terrectly,' The Misfit said.

'Where are they taking him?' the children's mother screamed.

'Daddy was a card himself,' The Misfit said. 'You couldn't put anything over on him. He never got in trouble with the Authorities though. Just had the knack of handling them.'

'You could be honest too if you'd only try,' said the grandmother. 'Think how wonderful it would be to settle down and live a comfortable life and not have to think about somebody chasing you all the time.'

The Misfit kept scratching in the ground with the butt of his gun as if he were thinking about it. '*Yes'm, somebody is always after you,*' he murmured.

The grandmother noticed how thin his shoulder blades were just behind his hat because she was standing up looking down on him. 'Do you ever pray?' she asked.

He shook his head. All she saw was the black hat wiggle between his shoulder blades. 'Nome,' he said.

There was a pistol shot from the woods, followed closely by another. Then silence. The old lady's head jerked around. She could hear the wind move through the tree tops like a long satisfied insuck of breath. 'Bailey Boy!' she called.

'I was a gospel singer for a while,' The Misfit said. '*I been most everything. Been in the arm service, both land and sea, at home and abroad, been twict married, been an undertaker, been with the railroads, plowed Mother Earth, been in a tornado, seen a man burnt alive oncet,*' and he looked up at the children's mother and the little girl who were sitting close together, their faces white and their eyes glassy; '*I even seen a woman flogged,*' he said.

'Pray, pray,' the grandmother began, 'pray, pray...'

'I never was a bad boy that I remember of,' The Misfit said in an almost dreamy voice, '*but somewhere along the line I done something wrong and got sent to the penitentiary. I was buried alive,*' and he looked up and held her attention to him by a steady stare.

'That's when you should have started to pray,' she said 'What did you do to get sent to the penitentiary that first time?'

'*Turn to the right, it was a wall,*' The Misfit said, looking up again at the cloudless sky. '*Turn to the left, it was a wall. Look up it was a ceiling, look down it was a floor. I forget what I done, lady. I set there and set there, trying to remember what it was I done and I ain't recalled it to this day. Oncet in a while, I would think it was coming to me, but it never come.*'

'Maybe they put you in by mistake,' the old lady said vaguely.

'Nome,' he said. 'It wasn't no mistake. They had the papers on me.'

'You must have stolen something,' she said.

The Misfit sneered slightly. 'Nobody had nothing I wanted,' he said. '*It was a head-doctor at the penitentiary said what I had done was kill my daddy but I known that for a lie.* My daddy died in nineteen ought nineteen of the epidemic flu and I never had a thing to do with it. He was buried in the Mount Hopewell Baptist churchyard and you can go there and see for yourself.'

'If you would pray,' the old lady said, 'Jesus would help you.'

'That's right,' The Misfit said.

'Well then, why don't you pray?' she asked trembling with delight suddenly.

'*I don't want no hep,*' he said. 'I'm doing all right by myself.'

Bobby Lee and Hiram came ambling back from the woods. Bobby Lee was dragging a yellow shirt with bright blue parrots in it.

'*Thow me that shirt, Bobby Lee,*' The Misfit said. The shirt came flying at him and landed on his shoulder and he put it on. The grandmother couldn't name what the shirt reminded her of. 'No, lady,' The Misfit said while he was buttoning it up, '<u>I found out the crime don't matter. You can do one thing or you can do another, kill a man or take a tire off his car, because sooner or later you're going to forget what it was you done and just be punished for it.</u>'

The children's mother had begun to make heaving noises as if she couldn't get her breath. 'Lady,' he asked, 'would you and that little girl like to step off yonder with Bobby Lee and Hiram and join your husband?'

'Yes, thank you,' the mother said faintly. Her left arm dangled helplessly and she was holding the baby, who had gone to sleep, in the other. '*Hep that lady up, Hiram,*' The Misfit said as she struggled to climb out of the ditch, 'and Bobby Lee, you hold onto that little girl's hand.'

'I don't want to hold hands with him,' June Star said. 'He reminds me of a pig.'

The fat boy blushed and laughed and caught her by the arm and pulled her off into the woods after Hiram and her mother.

<u>Alone with The Misfit, the grandmother found that she had lost her voice. There was not a cloud in the sky nor any sun. There was nothing around her but woods.</u> She wanted to tell him that he must pray. She opened and closed her mouth several times before anything came out. Finally she found herself saying, 'Jesus. Jesus,' meaning, Jesus will help you, but the way she was saying it, <u>it sounded as if she might be cursing</u>.

'Yes'm,' The Misfit said as if he agreed. '*Jesus thown everything off balance. It was the same case with Him as with me except He hadn't committed any crime and they could prove I had committed one because they had the papers on me. Of course,*' he said, '*they never shown me my papers. That's why I sign myself now. I said long ago, you get you a signature and sign everything you do and keep a copy of it. Then you'll know what you done and you can hold up the crime to the punishment and see do they match and in the end you'll have something to prove you ain't been treated right. I call myself The Misfit,*' he said, '*because I can't make what all I done wrong fit what all I gone through in punishment.*'

There was a piercing scream from the woods, followed closely by a pistol report. '*Does it seem right to you, lady, that one is punished a heap and another ain't punished at all?*'

'Jesus!' the old lady cried. **'You've got good blood! I know you wouldn't shoot a lady! I know you come from nice people! Pray! Jesus, you ought not to shoot a lady. I'll give you all the money I've got!'**

'Lady,' The Misfit said, looking beyond her far into the woods, '*there never was a body that give the undertaker a tip.*'

There were two more pistol reports and the grandmother raised her head like a parched old turkey hen crying for water and called, 'Bailey Boy, Bailey Boy!' as if her heart would break.

'*Jesus was the only One that ever raised the dead,*' The Misfit continued, '*and He shouldn't have done it. He thown everything off balance. If He did what He said, then it's nothing for you to do but thow away everything and follow Him, and if He didn't, then it's nothing for you to do but enjoy the few minutes you got left the best way you can – by killing somebody or burning down his house or doing some other meanness to him. No pleasure but meanness,*' he said and <u>his voice had become almost a snarl.</u>

'Maybe He didn't raise the dead,' the old lady mumbled, not knowing what she was saying and feeling so dizzy that she sank down in the ditch with her legs twisted under her.

'*I wasn't there so I can't say He didn't,*' The Misfit said. '*I wisht I had of been there,*' he said, hitting the ground with his fist. '*It ain't right I wasn't there because if I had of been there I would of known. Listen lady,*' he said in a high voice, '*if I had of been there I would of known and I wouldn't be like I am now.*' **His voice seemed about to crack and the grandmother's head cleared for an instant. She saw the man's face twisted close to her own as if he were going to cry and she murmured, 'Why you're one of my babies. You're one of my** own children!' **She reached out and touched him on the shoulder.** The Misfit sprang back as if a snake had bitten him and shot her three times through the chest. Then he put his gun down on the ground and took off his glasses and began to clean them.

Hiram and Bobby Lee returned from the woods and stood over the ditch, looking down at the grandmother who half sat and half lay in a puddle of blood with her legs crossed under her like a child's and her face smiling up at the cloudless sky.

Without his glasses, The Misfit's eyes were red-rimmed and pale and defenseless-looking. *'Take her off and thow her where you thown the others,'* he said, picking up the cat that was rubbing itself against his leg.

'She was a talker, wasn't she?' Bobby Lee said, sliding down the ditch with a yodel.

'She would of been a good woman,' The Misfit said, *'if it had been somebody there to shoot her every minute of her life.'*

'Some fun!' Bobby Lee said.

'Shut up, Bobby Lee' The Misfit said. *'It's no real pleasure in life.'*

Activity 8

What do the **bold** portions of the story indicate about the grandmother's character? Are there any other lines or phrases that you believe should also be made bold as indicators/clues of direct and/or indirect characterisation?

Activity 9

Consider the following critical statements made by O'Connor as they relate to the *italicised* portions of the story:

'If my characters speak Southern, it's because I do… Our history, customs, vices, and virtues are inherent in our idiom.'

'An idiom characterizes a society, and when you ignore the idiom, you are very likely ignoring the whole social fabric that could make a meaningful character… The sound of our talk is too definite to be discarded with impunity… In most good stories it is the character's personality that creates the action of the story.'

Choose five idiomatic expressions that are *italicised* that you believe most effectively address one of the above critical statements and explain why.

Activity 10

Choose 15 of the underlined portions of the story – five that relate to the grandmother, five that relate to The Misfit, and five that relate to establishing a specific tone in the story. Specify which of your selections are verbal expressions and which are physical actions. Then, in a group of no more than three, share your selections and come to a consensus as to which five are the most effective in establishing a specific tone. Each group will present the larger context and/or understanding of character that these symbolic actions and expressions address.

Activity 11

Select one of the following observations made by O'Connor regarding *A Good Man is Hard to Find* and prepare notes and quotes in your learner portfolio. Do not write in complete sentences – use bullet points only. Select a minimum of five direct quotations that you can cite from the text of the story to support the statement you have chosen. You may be asked to write an essay response only using your notes and quotes, so be sure to choose your textual support wisely.

A. 'There is change in tension from the first part of the story to the second where the Misfit enters, but this is not lessening of reality. This story is, of course, not meant to be realistic in the sense that it portrays the everyday doings of people in Georgia. It is stylised and its conventions are comic even though its meaning is serious… **The story is a duel of sorts between the grandmother and her superficial beliefs and the Misfit's more profoundly felt [sense of a] world off balance for him.**'

B. ' I often ask myself what makes a story work, and what makes it hold up as a story, and I have decided that **it is probably some action, some gesture of a character that is unlike any other in the story, one which indicates where the real heart of the story lies**. This would have to be an action or a gesture which was both totally right and totally unexpected…'

C. '… in my own stories I have found that **violence is strangely capable of returning my characters to reality and preparing them to accept their moment of grace.** Their heads are so hard that almost nothing else will work…. With the serious writer, violence is never an end in itself. **It is the extreme situation that best reveals what we are essentially,** and I believe these are times when writers are more interested in what we are essentially than in the tenor of our daily lives.'

2) Time and space: an approach to Chimamanda Ngozi Adichie's short story, *Cell One*

Contemporary Nigerian writer, Chimamanda Ngozi Adichie, writes, 'In some ways I think fiction is one's way of making sense of things that don't make sense. It informs my fiction; that whole idea of "what are you?" and "what's your identity?" Again, I don't set out writing fiction to make a point – about how the world is full of inequality, even though it is. I hope it's more thoughtful and a bit more complicated. Things always are complicated, there's just never anything that is easy.'

In Adichie's short story, *Cell One*, we encounter a Nigerian family in the late 1990s through the eyes of the younger sister. What we learn about this family, their university community, and their community at large, is filtered through her perspective. As an adolescent narrator, she becomes a kind of cultural witness for the reader through her observations of her suddenly complicated world.

Cell One by Chimamanda Ngozi Adichie (2009)

The first time our house was robbed, it was our neighbor Osita who climbed in through the dining room window and stole our TV, our VCR, and the *Purple Rain* and *Thriller* videotapes my father had brought back from America. The second time our house was robbed, it was my brother Nnamabia who faked a break-in and stole my mother's jewelry. It happened on a Sunday. My parents had traveled to our hometown, Mbaise, to visit our grandparents, so Nnamabia and I went to church alone. He drove my mother's green Peugeot 504. We sat together in church as we usually did, but we did not nudge each other and stifle giggles about somebody's ugly hat or threadbare caftan, because Nnamabia left without a word after about ten minutes. He came back just before the priest said, "The Mass is ended. Go in peace." I was a little piqued. I imagined he had gone off to smoke and to see some girl, since he had the car to himself for once, but he could at least have told me where he was going. We drove home in silence and, when he parked in our long driveway, I stopped to pluck some ixora flowers while Nnamabia unlocked the front door. I went inside to find him standing still in the middle of the parlor.

"We've been robbed!" he said in English.

It took me a moment to understand, to take in the scattered room. Even then, I felt that there was a theatrical quality to the way the drawers were flung open, as if it had been done by somebody who wanted to make an impression on the discoverers. Or perhaps it was simply that I knew my brother so well. Later, when my parents came home and neighbors began to troop in to say *ndo*, and to snap their fingers and heave their shoulders up and down, I sat alone in my room upstairs and realized what the queasiness in my gut was: Nnamabia had done it, I knew. My father knew, too. He pointed out that the window louvers had been slipped out from the inside, rather than outside (Nnamabia was really much smarter than that; perhaps he had been in a hurry to get back to church before Mass ended), and that the robber knew exactly where my mother's jewelry was—the left corner of her metal trunk. Nnamabia stared at my father with dramatic, wounded eyes and said, "I know I have caused you both terrible pain in the past, but I would never violate your trust like this." He spoke English, using unnecessary words like "terrible pain" and "violate," as he always did when he was defending himself. Then he walked out through the back door and did not come home that night. Or the next night. Or the night after. He came home two weeks later, gaunt, smelling of beer, crying, saying he was sorry and he had pawned the jewelry to the Hausa traders in Enugu and all the money was gone.

"How much did they give you for my gold?" my mother asked him. And when he told her, she placed both hands on her head and cried, "Oh! Oh! *Chi m egbuo m!* My God has killed me!" It was as if she felt that the least he could have done was get a good price. I wanted to slap her. My father asked Nnamabia to write a report: how he had sold the jewelry, what he had spent the money on, with whom he had spent it. I didn't think Nnamabia would tell the truth, and I don't think my father thought he would, either, but he liked reports, my professor father, he liked things written down and nicely documented. Besides, Nnamabia was seventeen, with a carefully tended beard. He was in that space between secondary school and university and was too old for caning. What else could my father have done? After Nnamabia wrote the report, my father filed it in the steel drawer in his study where he kept our school papers.

"That he could hurt his mother like this" was the last thing my father said, in a mutter.

But Nnamabia really hadn't set out to hurt her. He did it because my mother's jewelry was the only thing of any value in the house: a lifetime's collection of solid gold pieces. He did it, too, because other sons of professors were doing it. This was the season of thefts on our serene Nsukka campus. Boys who had grown up watching *Sesame Street*, reading Enid Blyton, eating cornflakes for breakfast, attending the university staff primary school in smartly polished brown sandals, were now cutting through the mosquito netting of their neighbors' windows, sliding out glass louvers, and climbing in to steal TVs and VCRs. We knew the thieves. Nsukka campus was such a small place—the houses sitting side by side on tree-lined streets, separated only by low hedges—that we could not but know who was stealing. Still, when their professor parents saw one another at the staff club or at church or at a faculty meeting, they continued to moan about riffraff from town coming onto their sacred campus to steal.

The thieving boys were the popular ones. They drove their parents' cars in the evening, their seats pushed back and their arms stretched out to reach the steering wheel. Osita, the neighbor who had stolen our TV only weeks before the Nnamabia incident, was lithe and handsome in a brooding sort of way and walked with the grace of a cat. His shirts were always sharply ironed; I used to look across the hedge and see him and close my eyes and imagine that he was walking toward me, coming to claim me as his. He never noticed me. When he stole from us, my parents did not go over to Professor Ebube's house to ask him to ask his son to bring back our things. They said publicly that it was riffraff from town. But they knew it was Osita. Osita was two years older than Nnamabia; most of the thieving boys were a little older than Nnamabia, and perhaps that was why Nnamabia did not steal from another person's house. Perhaps he did not feel old enough, qualified enough, for anything bigger than my mother's jewelry.

Nnamabia looked just like my mother, with that honey-fair complexion, large eyes, and a generous mouth that curved perfectly. When my mother took us to the market, traders would call out, "Hey! Madam, why did you waste your fair skin on a boy and leave the girl so dark? What is a boy doing with all this beauty?" And my mother would chuckle, as though she took a mischievous and joyful responsibility for Nnamabia's good looks. When, at eleven, Nnamabia broke the window of his classroom with a stone, my mother gave him the money to replace it and did not tell my father. When he lost some library books in class two, she told his form-mistress that our houseboy had stolen them. When, in class three, he left early every day to attend catechism and it turned out he never once went and so could not receive Holy Communion, she told the other parents that he had malaria on the examination day. When he took the key of my father's car and pressed it into a piece of soap that my father found before Nnamabia could take it to a locksmith, she made vague sounds about how he was just experimenting and it didn't mean a thing. When he stole the exam questions from the study and sold them to my father's students, she shouted at him but then told my father that Nnamabia was sixteen, after all, and really should be given more pocket money.

I don't know whether Nnamabia felt remorse for stealing her jewelry. I could not always tell from my brother's gracious, smiling face what it was he really felt. And we did not talk about it. Even though my mother's sisters sent her their gold earrings, even though she bought an earring-and-pendant set from Mrs. Mozie, the glamorous woman who imported gold from Italy, and began to drive to Mrs. Mozie's house once a month to pay for it in installments, we never talked, after that day, about Nnamabia's stealing her jewelry. It was as if pretending that Nnamabia had not done the things he had done would give him the opportunity to start afresh. The robbery might never have been mentioned again if Nnamabia had not been arrested three years later, in his third year in the university, and locked up at the police station.

It was the season of cults on our serene Nsukka campus. It was the time when signboards all over the university read, in bold letters, SAY NO TO CULTS. The Black Axe, the Buccaneers, and the Pirates were the best known. They may once have been benign fraternities, but they had evolved and were now called "cults"; eighteen-year-olds who had mastered the swagger of American rap videos were undergoing secret and strange initiations that sometimes left one or two of them dead on Odim Hill. Guns and tortured loyalties and axes had become common. Cult wars had become common: a boy would leer at a girl who turned out to be the girlfriend of the Capone of the Black Axe, and that boy, as he walked to a kiosk to buy a cigarette later, would be stabbed in the thigh, and he would turn out to be a member of the Buccaneers, and so his fellow Buccaneers would go to a beer parlor and shoot the nearest Black Axe boy in the shoulder, and then the next day a Buccaneer member would be shot dead in the refectory, his body falling against aluminum bowls of soup, and that evening a Black Axe boy would be hacked to death in his room in a lecturer's Boys' Quarters, his CD player splattered with blood. It was senseless. It was so abnormal that it quickly became normal. Girls stayed inside their hostel rooms after lectures and lecturers quivered and when a fly buzzed too loudly, people were afraid. So the police were called in. They sped across campus in their rickety blue Peugeot 505, rusty guns poking out of the car windows, and glowered at the students. Nnamabia came home from his lectures laughing. He thought the police would have to do better; everyone knew the cult boys had more modern guns.

My parents watched Nnamabia's laughing face with silent concern and I knew that they, too, were wondering whether he was in a cult. Sometimes I thought he was. Cult boys were popular and Nnamabia was very popular. Boys yelled out his nickname—"The Funk!"—and shook his hand whenever he passed by, and girls, especially the popular Big Chicks, hugged him for too long when they said hello. He went to all the parties, the tame ones on campus and the wilder ones in town, and he was the kind of ladies' man who was also a guy's guy, the kind who smoked a pack of Rothmans a day and was reputed to be able to finish a carton of Star beer in a sitting. Other times I thought he was not in a cult, because he *was* so popular and it seemed more his style that he would befriend all the different cult boys and be the enemy of none. And I was not entirely sure, either, that my brother had whatever it took—guts or insecurity—to join a cult. The only time I asked him if he was in a cult, he looked at me with surprise, his eyelashes long and thick, as if I should have known better than to ask, before he said, "Of course not." I believed him. My father believed him, too. But our believing him made little difference, because he had already been arrested and accused of belonging to a cult. He told me this—"Of course not"—on our first visit to the police station where he was locked up.

This is how it happened. On a humid Monday, four cult members waited at the campus gate and waylaid a professor driving a red Mercedes. They pressed a gun to her head, shoved her out of the car, and drove it to the Faculty of Engineering, where they shot three boys walking out of their lecture halls. It was noon. I was in a class nearby, and when we heard the sharp bangs, our lecturer was the first to run out of the room. There was loud screaming and suddenly the staircases were packed with scrambling students unsure in which direction to run. Outside, three bodies lay on the lawn. The red Mercedes had screeched away. Many students packed hasty bags and *okada* drivers charged twice the usual fare to take them to the motor park. The vice chancellor announced that all evening classes were canceled and everyone had to be indoors after 9 p.m. This did not make much sense to me, since the shooting happened in sparkling daylight, and perhaps it did not make sense to Nnamabia, either, because on the first day of the curfew, he was not home at 9 p.m. and did not come home that night. I assumed he had stayed at a friend's; he did not always come home anyway. The next morning, a security man came to tell my parents that Nnamabia had been arrested with some cult boys at a bar and had been taken away in a police van. My mother screamed, "*Ekwuzikwana!* Don't say that!" My father calmly thanked the security man. He drove us to the police station in town. There, a constable chewing on a dirty pen cover said, "You mean those cult boys arrested yesterday night? They have been taken to Enugu. Very serious case! We must stop this cult trouble once and for all!"

We got back into the car and a new fear gripped us all. Nsukka—our slow, insular campus and the slower, more insular town—was manageable; my father would know the police superintendent. But Enugu was anonymous, the state capital with the Mechanized Division of the Nigerian Army and the police headquarters and the traffic wardens at busy intersections. It was where the police could do what they were famed for when under pressure to produce results: kill people.

The Enugu police station was in a walled-around, sprawling compound full of buildings; dusty, damaged cars were piled by the gate, near the sign that said OFFICE OF THE COMMISSIONER OF POLICE. My father drove toward the rectangular bungalow at the other end of the compound. My mother bribed the two policemen at the desk with money and with *jollof* rice and meat, all tied up in a black waterproof bag, and they allowed Nnamabia to come out of his cell and sit on a bench with us under an umbrella tree. Nobody asked why he stayed out that night when he knew that a curfew had been imposed. Nobody said that the policemen were irrational to walk into a bar and arrest all the boys drinking there, as well as the barman. Instead we listened to Nnamabia talk. He sat straddling the wooden bench, a food flask of rice and chicken in front of him, his eyes brightly expectant: an entertainer about to perform.

"If we ran Nigeria like this cell," he said, "we would have no problems in this country. Things are so organized. Our cell has a chief called General Abacha and he has a second in command. Once you come in, you have to give them some money. If you don't, you're in trouble."

"And did you have any money?" my mother asked.

Nnamabia smiled, his face even more beautiful with a new pimple-like insect bite on his forehead, and said in Igbo that he had slipped his money into his anus shortly after the arrest at the bar. He knew the policemen would take it if he didn't hide it arid he knew he would need it to buy his peace in the cell. He bit into a fried drumstick and switched to English. "General Abacha was impressed with how I hid my money. I've made myself amenable to him. I praise him all the time. When the men asked all of us newcomers to hold our ears and frog-jump to their singing, he let me go after ten minutes. The others had to do it for almost thirty minutes."

My mother hugged herself, as though she felt cold. My father said nothing, watching Nnamabia carefully. And I imagined him, my *amenable* brother, rolling one-hundred-naira notes into thin cigarette shapes and then slipping a hand into the back of his trousers to slide them painfully into himself.

Later, as we drove back to Nsukka, my father said, "This is what I should have done when he broke into the house. I should have had him locked up in a cell."

My mother stared silently out of the window.

"Why?" I asked.

"Because this has shaken him for once. Couldn't you see?" my father asked with a small smile. I couldn't see it. Not that day. Nnamabia seemed fine to me, slipping his money into his anus and all.

. . .

Nnamabia's first shock was seeing the Buccaneer sobbing. The boy was tall and tough, rumored to have carried out one of the killings, to be in line for Capone next semester, and yet there he was in the cell cowering and sobbing after the chief had given him a knock behind the head. Nnamabia told me this on our visit the following day, in a voice lined with both disgust and disappointment; it was as if he had suddenly been made to see that the Incredible Hulk was really just green paint. His second shock, a few days later, was Cell One, the cell beyond his. Two policemen had carried out a swollen dead man from Cell One and stopped by Nnamabia's cell to make sure the corpse was seen by all.

Even the chief of his cell seemed afraid of Cell One. When Nnamabia and his cell mates, those who could afford to buy bathing water in the plastic buckets that had once held paint, were let out to bathe in the open yard, the policemen watched them and often shouted, "Stop that or you are going to Cell One now!" Nnamabia had nightmares about Cell One. He could not imagine a place worse than his cell, which was so crowded he often stood pressed against the cracked wall. Tiny *kwalikwata* lived inside the cracks and their bites were vicious, and when he yelped his cell mates called him Milk and Banana Boy, University Boy, Yeye Fine Boy.

They were too tiny to bite so painfully, those bugs. The biting was worse during the night, when they all had to sleep on their sides, head to foot, except the chief with his whole back lavishly on the floor. It was the chief who shared the plates of *garri* and watery soup that were pushed into the cell everyday. Each person got two mouthfuls. Nnamabia told us this during the first week. As he spoke I wondered if the bugs in the wall had bitten his face, too, or if the bumps spreading all over his forehead had come from an infection. Some of them were tipped with pus the color of cream. He scratched at them as he said, "I had to shit in a waterproof bag today, standing up. The toilet was too full. They flush it only on Saturdays."

His tone was histrionic. I wanted to ask him to shut up, because he was enjoying his new role as the sufferer of indignities, and because he did not understand how lucky he was that the policemen allowed him to come out and eat our food, how stupid he'd been to stay out drinking that night, how uncertain his chances were of being released.

We visited him every day of the first week. We went in my father's old Volvo because my mother's older Peugeot 504 was considered unsafe for trips outside Nsukka. When we passed the police checkpoints on the road, I noticed that my parents were different—subtly so, but different. My father no longer delivered a monologue, as soon as we were waved on, on how-illiterate and corrupt the police were. He did not bring up the day they had delayed us for an hour because he refused to bribe them, or the way they had stopped a bus in which my beautiful cousin Ogechi was traveling and singled her out and called her a whore because she had two cell phones and asked her for so much money that she knelt on the ground in the rain begging them to let her go since her bus had already been allowed to go. My mother did not mumble, They are symptoms of a larger malaise. Instead my parents remained silent. It was as if refusing to criticize the police as usual would somehow make Nnamabia's freedom imminent. "Delicate" was the word the superintendent at Nsukka had used. Getting Nnamabia out anytime soon would be delicate, especially with the police commissioner in Enugu giving gloating, preening interviews on television about the arrested cultists. The cult problem was serious. Big Men in Abuja were following events. Everybody wanted to appear to be doing something.

The second week, I told my parents we were not going to visit Nnamabia. We did not know how long we would have to keep doing this and petrol was too expensive to drive three hours every day and it would not hurt Nnamabia to fend for himself for a day.

My father looked at me, surprised, and asked, "What do you mean?" My mother eyed me up and down and headed for the door and said nobody was begging me to come; I could sit there and do nothing while my innocent brother suffered. She was walking toward the car and I ran after her, and when I got outside I was not sure what to do, so I picked up a stone near the ixora bush and hurled it at the windshield of the Volvo. The windshield cracked. I heard the brittle sound and saw the tiny lines spreading like rays on the glass before I turned and dashed upstairs and locked myself in my room to protect myself from my mother's fury. I heard her shouting. I heard my father's voice. Finally there was silence, and I did not hear the car start. Nobody went to see Nnamabia that day. It surprised me, this little victory.

We visited him the next day. We said nothing about the windshield, although the cracks had spread out like ripples on a frozen stream. The policeman at the desk, the pleasant dark-skinned one, asked why we had not come the day before; he had missed my mother's *jollof* rice. I expected Nnamabia to ask, too, even to be upset, but he looked oddly sober, an expression I had not seen before. He did not eat all of his rice. He kept looking away, toward the cluster of half-burned cars at the end of the compound, the remnants of accidents.

"What is wrong?" my mother asked, and Nnamabia began to speak almost immediately, as if he had been waiting to be asked. His Igbo was even-toned, his voice neither rising nor falling. An old man had been pushed into his cell the day before, a man perhaps in his mid-seventies, white-haired, skin finely wrinkled, with the old-fashioned refinement of an incorruptible retired civil servant. His son was wanted for armed robbery, and when the police could not find the son, they decided to lock him up instead.

"The man did nothing," Nnamabia said.

"But you did nothing, too," my mother said.

Nnamabia shook his head as if she did not understand. In the following days, he was more subdued. He spoke less, and mostly about the old man: how he had no money and could not buy bathing water, how the other men made fun of him or accused him of hiding his son, how the chief ignored him, how he looked frightened and so terribly small.

"Does he know where his son is?" my mother asked.

"He has not seen his son in four months," Nnamabia said.

My father said something about how it was irrelevant whether or not the man knew where his son was.

"Of course," my mother said. "It is wrong, but this is what the police do all the time. If they do not find the person they are looking for, they will lock up his father or his mother or his relative."

My father brushed at something on his knee—an impatient gesture. He did not understand why my mother was stating the obvious.

"The man is ill," Nnamabia said. "His hands shake and shake, even when he's asleep."

My parents were silent. Nnamabia closed the food flask of rice and turned to my father. "I want to give him some of this, but if I bring it into the cell General Abacha will take it."

My father went over and asked the policeman at the desk if we could be allowed to see the old man in Nnamabia's cell for a few minutes. The policeman was the light-skinned, acerbic one who never said thank you when my mother handed over the rice and money bribe. Now he sneered in my father's face and said he could well lose his job for letting Nnamabia out and yet we were asking for another person to be allowed out? Did we think this was a boarding school visiting day? Didn't we know that this was a high-security holding place for criminal elements of society? My father came back and sat down with a sigh and Nnamabia silently scratched at his bumpy face.

The next day, Nnamabia barely touched his rice. He said that the policemen had splashed detergent water on the floor and walls of the cell in the name of cleaning as they usually did and that the old man, who could not afford water, who had not bathed in a week, had hurried into the cell and yanked his shirt off and rubbed his frail back against the detergent-wet floor. The policemen started to laugh when they saw him do this and they asked him to take all his clothes off and parade in the corridor outside the cell, and as he did they laughed louder and asked whether his son the thief knew that papa's penis was so shriveled. Nnamabia was staring at his yellow-orange rice as he spoke, and when he looked up I saw my brothers eyes fill with tears—my worldly brother—and I felt a tenderness for him that I could not have explained had I been asked to.

. . .

Two days later, there was another cult attack on campus: a boy hacked another boy with an axe right in front of the music department building.

"This is good," my mother said as she and my father got ready to go and see the Nsukka police superintendent again. "They cannot say now that they have arrested all the cult boys." We did not go to Enugu that day, because my parents spent so long at the superintendents, but they came back with good news. Nnamabia and the barman were to be released immediately. One of the cult boys had become an informer, and he insisted that Nnamabia was not a member. We left earlier than usual in the morning, without *jollof* rice, the sun already so hot that all the car windows were down. My mother was jumpy on the drive. She was used to saying "*Nekwa ya!* Watch out!" to my father as if he could not see the cars making dangerous turns in the other lane, but this time she did it so often that just before we got to Ninth Mile, where hawkers crowded around the car with their trays of *okpa* and boiled eggs and cashew nuts, my father stopped the car and snapped, "Just who is driving this car, Uzoamaka?"

Inside the sprawling station compound, two policemen were flogging somebody who was lying on the ground under the umbrella tree. At first I thought, with a lurch in my chest, that it was Nnamabia, but it was not. I knew the boy who lay on the ground, writhing and shouting with each lash of a policeman's *koboko*. He was called Aboy, and he had the grave, ugly face of a hound and drove a Lexus on campus and was said to be a Buccaneer. I tried not to look at him as we walked into the station. The policeman on duty, the one with tribal marks on his cheeks who always said "God bless you" when he took his bribe, looked away when he saw us. Prickly hives spread over my skin. I knew then that something was wrong. My parents gave him the note from the superintendent. The policeman did not look at it. He knew about the release order, he told my father, the bar man had already been released but there was a complication with the boy. My mother began to shout. "The boy? What do you mean? Where is my son?"

The policeman got up. "I will call my senior to explain to you."

My mother rushed at him and pulled at his shirt. "Where is my son? Where is my son?" My father pried her away and the policeman brushed at his shirt, as if she had left some dirt there, before he turned to walk away.

"Where is our son?" my father asked in a voice so quiet, so steely, that the policeman stopped.

"They took him away, sir," he said.

"They took him away?" my mother broke in. She was still shouting. "What are you saying? Have you killed my son? Have you killed my son?"

"Where is he?" my father asked again in the same quiet voice. "Where is our son?"

"My senior said I should call him when you come," the policeman said, and this time he turned and hurried through a door.

It was after he left that I felt chilled by fear, that I wanted to run after him and like my mother pull at his shirt until he produced Nnamabia. The senior policeman came out and I searched his completely blank face for an expression.

"Good day, sir," he said to my father.

"Where is our son?" my father asked. My mother was breathing noisily. Later I would realize that at that moment each of us suspected privately that Nnamabia had been killed by trigger-happy policemen and that this man's job was to find the best lie to tell us about how he had died.

"No problem, sir. It is just that we transferred him. I will take you there right away." There was something nervous about the policeman; his face remained blank but he did not meet my father's eyes.

"Transferred him?"

"We got the release order this morning, but he had already been transferred. We don't have petrol, so I was waiting for you to come so that we go together to where he is."

"Where is he?"

"Another site. I will take you there."

"Why was he transferred?"

"I was not here, sir. They said he misbehaved yesterday and they took him to Cell One and then there was a transfer of all the people in Cell One to another site."

"He misbehaved? What do you mean?"

"I was not here, sir."

My mother spoke then in a broken voice. "Take me to my son! Take me to my son right now!"

I sat in the back with the policeman. He smelled of the kind of old camphor that seemed to last forever in my mother's trunk. We did not speak except for his giving my father directions until we arrived about fifteen minutes later, my father driving inordinately fast, as fast as my heart was beating. The small compound looked neglected, with patches of overgrown grass, with old bottles and plastic bags and paper strewn everywhere. The policeman hardly waited for my father to stop the car before he opened the door and hurried out, and again I felt chilled by fear. We were in this part of town with untarred roads and there had been no sign that said Police Station and there was a stillness in the air, a strange deserted feeling. But the policeman came out with Nnamabia. There he was, my handsome brother, walking toward us, unchanged, it seemed, until he came close enough for my mother to hug him and I saw him wince and back away; his left arm was covered in soft-looking welts. Dried blood was caked around his nose.

"Nna-Boy, why did they beat you like this?" my mother asked him. She turned to the policeman. "Why did you people do this to my son?"

The man shrugged, a new insolence to his demeanor; it was as if he had been uncertain about Nnamabia's well-being but now could let himself talk. "You cannot raise your children well, all of you people who feel important because you work in the university. When your children misbehave, you think they should not be punished. You are lucky, madam, very lucky that they released him."

My father said, "Let's go."

He opened the door and Nnamabia climbed in and we drove home. My father did not stop at any of the police checkpoints on the road; once, a policeman gestured threateningly with his gun as we sped past. The only thing my mother said on the silent drive was, Did Nnamabia want us to stop at Ninth Mile and buy some *okpa*? Nnamabia said no. We had arrived in Nsukka when he finally spoke.

"Yesterday the policemen asked the old man if he wanted a free bucket of water. He said yes. So they told him to take his clothes off and parade the corridor. My cell mates were laughing. But some of them said it was wrong to treat an old man like that." Nnamabia paused, his eyes distant. "I shouted at the policeman. I said the old man was innocent and ill and if they kept him here they would never find his son because he did not even know where his son was. They said I should shut up immediately or they would take me to Cell One. I didn't care. I didn't shut up. So they pulled me out and beat me and took me to Cell One."

Nnamabia stopped there and we asked him nothing else. Instead I imagined him raising his voice, calling the policeman a stupid idiot, a spineless coward, a sadist, a bastard, and I imagined the shock of the policemen, the shock of the chief staring openmouthed, the other cell mates stunned at the audacity of the handsome boy from the university. And I imagined the old man himself looking on with surprised pride and quietly refusing to undress. Nnamabia did not say what had happened to him in Cell One, or what happened in the new site, which seemed to me like where they kept people who would later disappear. It would have been so easy for him, my charming brother, to make a sleek drama of his story, but he did not.

After your reading of the story, consider how much or how little you know about the Igbo culture of modern day Nigeria. If you know very little, think about how much more insight you might draw from Adichie's story if you were aware of the political and social context in which this story is set – late 1990s south-eastern Nigeria.

Activity 12

1) Research the political and social unrest in south-west Nigeria at this time (late 1990s) and determine when and where this unrest began.

2) Research the university 'cults' that are at the root of Nnamabia's troubles with the police. Why might his parents be reluctant to admit that their son was a member of such a group? Did the Black Aces, Buccaneers, and Pirates exist as confraternities/campus cults? Speculate as to why such organisations came into existence?

3) Determine the role of gender and class in this unrest.

Use your learner portfolio to record your findings.

Activity 13

Read the following statement, made by Adichie from a TED talk, 'We Should all be Feminists', and respond to the questions that follow (either individually or in pairs) in your learner portfolio.

'We Should all be Feminists', TED talk by Chimamanda Ngozi Adichie

And I would like today to ask that we begin to dream about and plan for a different world, a fairer world, a world of happier men and happier women who are truer to themselves. And this is how to start: we must raise our daughters differently. We must also raise our sons differently. We do a great disservice to boys on how we raise them; we stifle the humanity of boys. We define masculinity in a very narrow way, masculinity becomes this hard, small cage and we put boys inside the cage. We teach boys to be afraid of fear. We teach boys to be afraid of weakness, of vulnerability. We teach them to mask their true selves, because they have to be, in Nigerian speak, 'hard man!'

1) How does the title of the story underscore Adichie's reference to the 'cage we put boys inside?'

2) What relationship is there between 'masking' a true self and the function of silence within the story? Note when there is an absence of dialogue. Note as well when 'silence' is referenced. Does the narrator's awareness of 'speaking' and 'silence' indicate an understanding of power within the family? Track the narrator's references to silence and offer some conclusion as to what we learn about characters from their chosen silences.

3) What cultural norms regarding gender and class are revealed through the young female narrator? What do we learn about her place within the family? Her brother's place? Her father's? Her mother's?

4) Observe the structure of the story. The narrator seems to set up a five-part structure to the story:
   'The first time our home was robbed…'
   'By then, it was the season of cults on the Nsukka campus…'
   'This is how it happened.'
   'We visited him every day for the first week…'
   'There was another attack on campus…'
   In each of these sections, determine what we learn about the narrator, her parents, her brother, and her culture. Do they evolve as characters or remain the same? Do the cultural issues develop as well?

5) Nnamabia's character makes the most dramatic change of any of the characters, though it can be said that his sister makes an equally dramatic change. What evidence can you provide to argue that one character changes more than the other? What is the significance of these changes?

Activity 14

The idea for *Cell One*, according to Adichie, came from a story she'd heard about an old man who was arrested, humiliated, and abused by the Nigerian police. Originally, the police went to the old man's home to arrest his son, but when they couldn't find the son, they arrested the father. This absurd practice was common in Nigeria and it haunted Adichie. Even if the father was old and sick, they would arrest and brutalise him. Another phenomenon that influenced her story was the existence of cults. These cults were made up of young, privileged men from upper-class families who had good educations but were drawn to these lawless groups of violent young men. Adichie could not understand why these young men made the choices they made. In writing *Cell One* Adichie could juxtapose these two incongruities that she saw in her culture and try and reconcile them. The result was a young man who challenged police procedure and suffered the price, only to find his redemption.

Think about redemption in terms of Nnamabia's account of what he did to be taken to Cell One. When his sister, our narrator, says, 'It would have been so easy for him, my charming brother, to make a sleek drama of his story, but he did not', what are we to believe? Has he, like Flannery O'Connor's characters, found his moment of grace? Has he found his humanity? What evidence could you use to argue that Nnamabia is a changed man?

Activity 15

Near the end of the story, Nnamabia's mother sees that he has been beaten, and so she turns to a policeman and questions, 'Why did you people do this to my son? Why?' The policeman shrugs, insolently, and replies, 'You cannot raise your children properly – all of you who feel important because you work at the university – and when your children misbehave you think they should not be punished. You are lucky they released him.'

1) What does this verbal exchange reveal about cultural attitudes regarding class?
2) What understanding, or lack of understanding, does this exchange reveal?

Global issue

To what degree is the conflict between individuals and society imposed by economic and social stereotyping? Is identity predetermined in violent conflict? Does the 'enemy' lose his humanity? Is this loss of common humanity essential to conflict?

3) Areas of exploration in *The Garden of Forking Paths* with focus on intertextual activities

In this section you will delve into intertextuality – an area of exploration that encourages you to consider how texts work in relation to each other. Luis Borges' short story, *The Garden of Forking Paths*, from his *Ficciones* collection, is the primary focus of our study. While his birth place and roots are in Buenos Aires, Borges moved to Geneva with his family in 1914 on the eve of World War I and travelled extensively through Europe and eventually back to South America. As a man who wrote in many different literary forms (fiction, non-fiction, poetry) and who spoke several languages, Borges encapsulates the spirit of **international-mindedness**, skilfully weaving different parts of the world into his cohesive tales.

The Garden of Forking Paths is a prime example of this cohesiveness. On one level, the story is a multilayered detective narrative set in World War I Europe that involves the stealthy world of spies from different culture**s** and their respective missions. But beyond the primary plot, Borges unravels a mystery that transcends war and politics and makes us question the nature of our existence. Because the work is so complex we have annotated it below, ultimately showing how all three areas of exploration naturally overlap. As you read the story, feel free to write notes in your learner portfolio in response to the questions.

Luis Borges

The Garden of Forking Paths by Luis Borges (1941)

To Victoria Ocampo

In his *A History of the World War* (page 216), Captain Liddell Hart reports that a planned offensive by thirteen British divisions, supported by fourteen hundred artillery pieces, against the German line at Serre-Montauban, scheduled for July 24, 1916, had to be postponed until the morning of the 29th. He comments that torrential rain caused this delay-which lacked any special significance. The following deposition, dictated by, read over, and then signed by Dr Yu Tsun, former teacher of English at the Tsingtao Hochschule, casts unsuspected light upon this event. The first two pages are missing.

* * *

… and I hung up the phone. Immediately I recollected the voice that had spoken in German. It was that of Captain Richard Madden. Madden, in Viktor Runeberg's office, meant the end of all our work and – though this seemed a secondary matter, or should have seemed so to me – of our lives also. His being there meant that Runeberg had been arrested or murdered.[1]

Before the sun set on this same day, I ran the same risk. Madden was implacable. Rather, to be more accurate, he was obliged to be implacable. An Irishman in the service of England, a man suspected of equivocal feelings if not of actual treachery, how could he fail to welcome and seize upon this extraordinary piece of luck: the discovery, capture and perhaps the deaths of two agents of Imperial Germany?

> What does the opening paragraph tell you about the setting? Describe the point of view and tone. What type of text is *A History of the World War*?

> How does the tone and point of view shift in the second paragraph? Who is telling this next part of the story? What is the effect of moving to a first-person point of view?

> What is the historical background regarding English and Irish relations in the early 20th century? Why might Madden be suspected of treachery?

---

[1] A malicious and outlandish statement. In point of fact, Captain Richard Madden had been attacked by the Prussian spy Hans Rabener, alias Viktor Runeberg, who drew an automatic pistol when Madden appeared with orders for the spy's arrest. Madden, in self-defense, had inflicted wounds of which the spy later died.

I went up to my bedroom. Absurd though the gesture was, I closed and locked the door. I threw myself down on my narrow iron bed, and waited on my back. The never changing rooftops filled the window, and the hazy six o'clock sun hung in the sky. It seemed incredible that this day, a day without warnings or omens, might be that of my implacable death. In despite of my dead father, in despite of having been a child in one of the symmetrical gardens of Hai Feng, was I to die now?

What do you think the narrator means when he says that 'things happen only in the present'?

Then I reflected that all things happen, happen to one, precisely now. Century follows century, and things happen only in the present. There are countless men in the air, on land and at sea, and all that really happens happens to me... The almost unbearable memory of Madden's long horseface put an end to these wandering thoughts.

What is the narrator's military mission? What information does he possess that is valuable to the Germans? If the narrator regards the German 'Chief' as a 'sick and hateful man', why is he so willing to spy for him?

In the midst of my hatred and terror (now that it no longer matters to me to speak of terror, now that I have outwitted Richard Madden, now that my neck hankers for the hangman's noose), I knew that the fast-moving and doubtless happy soldier did not suspect that I possessed the Secret – the name of the exact site of the new British artillery park on the Ancre. A bird streaked across the misty sky and, absently, I turned it into an airplane and then that airplane into many in the skies of France, shattering the artillery park under a rain of bombs. If only my mouth, before it should be silenced by a bullet, could shout this name in such a way that it could be heard in Germany... My voice, my human voice, was weak. How could it reach the ear of the Chief? The ear of that sick and hateful man who knew nothing of Runeberg or of me except that we were in Staffordshire. A man who, sitting in his arid Berlin office, leafed infinitely through newspapers, looking in vain for news from us. I said aloud, 'I must flee.'

After you finish the story, come back to the last line of this paragraph. Most readers miss the subtle foreshadowing the first time around.

I sat up on the bed, in senseless and perfect silence, as if Madden was already peering at me. Something – perhaps merely a desire to prove my total penury to myself – made me empty out my pockets. I found just what I knew I was going to find. The American watch, the nickel-plated chain and the square coin, the key ring with the useless but compromising keys to Runeberg's office, the notebook, a letter which I decided to destroy at once (and which I did not destroy), a five shilling piece, two single shillings and some pennies, a red and blue pencil, a handkerchief – and a revolver with a single bullet. Absurdly I held it and weighed it in my hand, to give myself courage. Vaguely I thought that a pistol shot can be heard for a great distance.

In ten minutes I had developed my plan. The telephone directory gave me the name of the one person capable of passing on the information. He lived in a suburb of Fenton, less than half an hour away by train.

Who is John Wolfgang von Goethe? What does this allusion reveal about the author's regard for the Englishman he describes?

I am a timorous man. I can say it now, now that I have brought my incredibly risky plan to an end. It was not easy to bring about, and I know that its execution was terrible. I did not do it for Germany – no! Such a barbarous country is of no importance to me, particularly since it had degraded me by making me become a spy. Furthermore, I knew an Englishman – a modest man – who, for me, is as great as Goethe. I did not speak with him for more than an hour, but during that time, he was Goethe.

There is a global issue within these paragraphs. What does the narrator reveal about the connection between culture, power, and pride?

I carried out my plan because I felt the Chief had some fear of those of my race, of those uncountable forebears whose culmination lies in me. I wished to prove to him that a yellow man could save his armies. Besides, I had to escape the Captain. His hands and voice could, at any moment, knock and beckon at my door.

Silently, I dressed, took leave of myself in the mirror, went down the stairs, sneaked a look at the quiet street, and went out. The station was not far from my house, but I thought it more prudent to take a cab. I told myself that I thus ran less chance of being recognized. The truth is that, in the deserted street, I felt infinitely visible and vulnerable. I recall that I told the driver to stop short of the main entrance. I got out with a painful and deliberate slowness.

Intertextual connection: Look up the reference to Tacitus' *Annals*. What is the significance?

I was going to the village of Ashgrove, but took a ticket for a station further on. The train would leave in a few minutes, at eight-fifty. I hurried, for the next would not go until half past nine. There was almost no one on the platform. I walked through the carriages. I remember some farmers, a woman dressed in mourning, a youth deep in Tacitus' *Annals* and a wounded, happy soldier.

At last the train pulled out. A man I recognized ran furiously, but vainly, the length of the platform. It was Captain Richard Madden. Shattered, trembling, I huddled in the distant corner of the seat, as far as possible from the fearful window. From utter terror I passed into a state of almost abject happiness. I told myself that the duel had already started and that I had won the first encounter by besting my adversary in his first attack – even if it was only for forty minutes – by an accident of fate. I argued that so small a victory prefigured a total victory. I argued that it was not so trivial, that were it not for the precious accident of the train schedule, I would be in prison or dead. I argued, with no less sophism, that my timorous happiness was proof that I was man enough to bring this adventure to a successful conclusion. From my weakness I drew strength that never left me.

How do the juxtapositions in this paragraph: utter terror/abject happiness; accident/fate; weakness/strength reveal the narrator's state of mind?

I foresee that man will resign himself each day to new abominations, that soon only soldiers and bandits will be left. To them I offer this advice: Whosoever would undertake some atrocious enterprise should act as if it were already accomplished, should impose upon himself a future as irrevocable as the past.

Thus I proceeded, while with the eyes of a man already dead, I contemplated the fluctuations of the day which would probably be my last, and watched the diffuse coming of night.

The train crept along gently, amid ash trees. It slowed down and stopped, almost in the middle of a field. No one called the name of a station. 'Ashgrove?' I asked some children on the platform. 'Ashgrove,' they replied. I got out.

A lamp lit the platform, but the children's faces remained in a shadow. One of them asked me: 'Are you going to Dr Stephen Albert's house?' Without waiting for my answer, another said: 'The house is a good distance away but you won't get lost if you take the road to the left and bear to the left at every crossroad.' I threw them a coin (my last), went down some stone steps and started along a deserted road. At a slight incline, the road ran downhill. It was a plain dirt way, and overhead the branches of trees intermingled, while a round moon hung low in the sky as if to keep me company.

TOK

How could the children 'know' where the narrator is going? Why do you think the narrator is not surprised that they know?

For a moment I thought that Richard Madden might in some way have divined my desperate intent. At once I realized that this would be impossible. The advice about turning always to the left reminded me that such was the common formula for finding the central courtyard of certain labyrinths. I know something about labyrinths. Not for nothing am I the great grandson of Ts'ui Pen. He was Governor of Yunnan and gave up temporal power to write a novel with more characters than there are in the Hung Lou Meng, and to create a maze in which all men would lose themselves. He spent thirteen years on these oddly assorted tasks before he was assassinated by a stranger. His novel had no sense to it and nobody ever found his labyrinth.

This digression can be confusing. What makes the narrator think of his great grandfather's affinity for complex novel writing and mazes?

Under the trees of England I meditated on this lost and perhaps mythical labyrinth. I imagined it untouched and perfect on the secret summit of some mountain; I imagined it drowned under rice paddies or beneath the sea; I imagined it infinite, made not only of eight-sided pavilions and of twisting paths but also of rivers, provinces and kingdoms… I thought of a maze of mazes, of a sinuous, ever growing maze which would take in both past and future and would somehow involve the stars.

Lost in these imaginary illusions I forgot my destiny – that of the hunted. For an undetermined period of time I felt myself cut off from the world, an abstract spectator. The hazy and murmuring countryside, the moon, the decline of the evening, stirred within me. Going down the gently sloping road I could not feel fatigue. The evening was at once intimate and infinite.

The road kept descending and branching off, through meadows misty in the twilight. A high-pitched and almost syllabic music kept coming and going, moving with the breeze, blurred by the leaves and by distance.

I thought that a man might be an enemy of other men, of the differing moments of other men, but never an enemy of a country: not of fireflies, words, gardens, streams, or the West wind.

What distinction does the narrator make between men of a country and the actual physical setting of a country? Why does he have trouble understanding how a man could be an enemy of a place?

Meditating thus I arrived at a high, rusty iron gate. Through the railings I could see an avenue bordered with poplar trees and also a kind of summer house or pavilion. Two things dawned on me at once, the first trivial and the second almost incredible: the music came from the pavilion and that music was Chinese. That was why I had accepted it fully, without paying it any attention. I do not remember whether there was a bell, a push-button, or whether I attracted attention by clapping my hands. The stuttering sparks of the music kept on.

But from the end of the avenue, from the main house, a lantern approached; a lantern which alternately, from moment to moment, was crisscrossed or put out by the trunks of the trees; a paper lantern shaped like a drum and colored like the moon. A tall man carried it. I could not see his face for the light blinded me.

He opened the gate and spoke slowly in my language.

'I see that the worthy Hsi P'eng has troubled himself to see to relieving my solitude. No doubt you want to see the garden?'

Recognizing the name of one of our consuls, I replied, somewhat taken aback.

'The garden?'

'The garden of forking paths.'

Something stirred in my memory and I said, with incomprehensible assurance:

'The garden of my ancestor, Ts'ui Pen.'

'Your ancestor? Your illustrious ancestor? Come in.'

The damp path zigzagged like those of my childhood. When we reached the house, we went into a library filled with books from both East and West. I recognized some large volumes bound in yellow silk – manuscripts of the Lost Encyclopedia which was edited by the Third Emperor of the Luminous Dynasty. They had never been printed. A phonograph record was spinning near a bronze phoenix. I remember also a rose-glazed jar and yet another, older by many centuries, of that blue color which our potters copied from the Persians…

Stephen Albert was watching me with a smile on his face. He was, as I have said, remarkably tall. His face was deeply lined and he had gray eyes and a gray beard. There was about him something of the priest, and something of the sailor. Later, he told me he had been a missionary in Tientsin before he 'had aspired to become a Sinologist.'

We sat down, I upon a large, low divan, he with his back to the window and to a large circular clock. I calculated that my pursuer, Richard Madden, could not arrive in less than an hour. My irrevocable decision could wait.

'A strange destiny,' said Stephen Albert, 'that of Ts'ui Pen-Governor of his native province, learned in astronomy, in astrology and tireless in the interpretation of the canonical books, a chess player, a famous poet and a calligrapher. Yet he abandoned all to make a book and a labyrinth. He gave up all the pleasures of oppression, justice, of a well-stocked bed, of banquets, and even of erudition, and shut himself up in the Pavilion of the Limpid Sun for thirteen years. At his death, his heirs found only a mess of manuscripts. The family, as you doubtless know, wished to consign them to the fire, but the executor of the estate a Taoist or a Buddhist monk – insisted on their publication.'

'Those of the blood of Ts'ui Pen,' I replied, 'still curse the memory of that monk. Such a publication was madness. The book is a shapeless mass of contradictory rough drafts. I examined it once upon a time: the hero dies in the third chapter, while in the fourth he is alive. As for that other enterprise of Ts'ui Pen… his Labyrinth…'

'Here is the Labyrinth,' Albert said, pointing to a tall, laquered writing cabinet.

'An ivory labyrinth?' I exclaimed. 'A tiny labyrinth indeed… !'

'A symbolic labyrinth,' he corrected me. 'An invisible labyrinth of time. I, a barbarous Englishman, have been given the key to this transparent mystery. After more than a hundred years most of the details are irrecoverable, lost beyond all recall, but it isn't hard to image

---

If the title of the story still doesn't make sense, don't worry. Borges is building momentum for its significance. What image does a 'forking path' put in your mind?

What does a sinologist do? Hint, if you are familiar with Dan Brown's novel, *The Da Vinci Code*, you already know the answer to this question.

What did the narrator think of his ancestor's book when he read it long ago?

what must have happened. At one time, Ts'ui must have said: "I am going into seclusion to write a book," and at another, "I am retiring to construct a maze." Everyone assumed these were separate activities. No one realized that the book and the labyrinth were one and the same. The Pavilion of the Limpid Sun was set in the middle of an intricate garden. This may have suggested the idea of a physical maze.

'Ts'ui Pen died. In all the vast lands which once belonged to your family, no one could find the labyrinth. The novel's confusion suggested that it was the labyrinth.

Two circumstances showed me the direct solution to the problem. First, the curious legend that Ts'ui Pen had proposed to create an infinite maze, second, a fragment of a letter which I discovered.'

Albert rose. For a few moments he turned his back to me. He opened the top drawer in the high black and gilded writing cabinet. He returned holding in his hand a piece of paper which had once been crimson but which had faded with the passage of time: it was rose colored, tenuous, quadrangular. Ts'ui Pen's calligraphy was justly famous. Eagerly, but without understanding, I read the words which a man of my own blood had written with a small brush: 'I leave to various future times, but not to all, my garden of forking paths.'

I handed back the sheet of paper in silence. Albert went on:

'Before I discovered this letter, I kept asking myself how a book could be infinite. I could not imagine any other than a cyclic volume, circular. A volume whose last page would be the same as the first and so have the possibility of continuing indefinitely. I recalled, too, the night in the middle of The Thousand and One Nights when Queen Scheherezade, through a magical mistake on the part of her copyist, started to tell the story of The Thousand and One Nights, with the risk of again arriving at the night upon which she will relate it, and thus on to infinity. I also imagined a Platonic hereditary work, passed on from father to son, to which each individual would add a new chapter or correct, with pious care, the work of his elders.

'These conjectures gave me amusement, but none seemed to have the remotest application to the contradictory chapters of Ts'ui Pen. At this point, I was sent from Oxford the manuscript you have just seen.

'Naturally, my attention was caught by the sentence, "I leave to various future times, but not to all, my garden of forking paths". I had no sooner read this, than I understood. The Garden of Forking Paths was the chaotic novel itself. The phrase "to various future times, but not to all" suggested the image of bifurcating in time, not in space. Rereading the whole work confirmed this theory. In all fiction, when a man is faced with alternatives he chooses one at the expense of the others. In the almost unfathomable Ts'ui Pen, he chooses – simultaneously – all of them. He thus creates various futures, various times which start others that will in their turn branch out and bifurcate in other times. This is the cause of the contradictions in the novel.

'Fang, let us say, has a secret. A stranger knocks at his door. Fang makes up his mind to kill him. Naturally there are various possible outcomes. Fang can kill the intruder, the intruder can kill Fang, both can be saved, both can die and so on and so on. In Ts'ui Pen's work, all the possible solutions occur, each one being the point of departure for other bifurcations. Sometimes the pathways of this labyrinth converge. For example, you come to this house; but in other possible pasts you are my enemy; in others my friend.

'If you will put up with my atrocious pronunciation, I would like to read you a few pages of your ancestor's work.'

His countenance, in the bright circle of lamplight, was certainly that of an ancient, but it shone with something unyielding, even immortal.

With slow precision, he read two versions of the same epic chapter. In the first, an army marches into battle over a desolate mountain pass. The bleak and somber aspect of the rocky landscape made the soldiers feel that life itself was of little value, and so they won the battle easily. In the second, the same army passes through a palace where a banquet is in progress. The splendor of the feast remained a memory throughout the glorious battle, and so victory followed.

Why might it be significant that the book Ts'ui wrote and the labyrinth he constructed are one and the same?

We've been presented with several examples of intertextuality here. Ts'ui Pen's book is referenced within Borges' short story and The Thousand and One Nights is referenced in relation to Ts'ui Pen's work. What is the effect of layering texts within texts?

Borges is at his most complex here. Ts'ui Pen's novel suggests that it is possible to make more than one choice that leads to multiple timelines that all exist simultaneously. Can you think of any other texts (films or television programs count as well) that suggest the idea of parallel universes?

Dr Albert poses a hypothetical situation as an example. How do you think the narrator regards his host in this situation – as a friend or an enemy?

How does the narrator's physical connection to Ts'ui Pen affect how he regards his ancestor's work? What does this reveal about ancestry (cultural connections)?

With proper veneration I listened to these old tales, although perhaps with less admiration for them in themselves than for the fact that they had been thought out by one of my own blood, and that a man of a distant empire had given them back to me, in the last stage of a desperate adventure, on a Western island. I remember the final words, repeated at the end of each version like a secret command: 'Thus the heroes fought, with tranquil heart and bloody sword. They were resigned to killing and to dying.'

At that moment I felt within me and around me something invisible and intangible pullulating. It was not the pullulation of two divergent, parallel, and finally converging armies, but an agitation more inaccessible, more intimate, prefigured by them in some way. Stephen Albert continued:

'I do not think that your illustrious ancestor toyed idly with variations. I do not find it believable that he would waste thirteen years laboring over a never ending experiment in rhetoric. In your country the novel is an inferior genre; in Ts'ui Pen's period, it was a despised one. Ts'ui Pen was a fine novelist but he was also a man of letters who, doubtless, considered himself more than a mere novelist. The testimony of his contemporaries attests to this, and certainly the known facts of his life confirm his leanings toward the metaphysical and the mystical. Philosophical conjectures take up the greater part of his novel. I know that of all problems, none disquieted him more, and none concerned him more than the profound one of time. Now then, this is the only problem that does not figure in the pages of The Garden. He does not even use the word which means time. How can these voluntary omissions be explained?'

I proposed various solutions, all of them inadequate. We discussed them. Finally Stephen Albert said: 'In a guessing game to which the answer is chess, which word is the only one prohibited?' I thought for a moment and then replied:

'The word is chess.'

Why is it significant that Ts'ui Pen's novel never specifically mentions the word 'time'?

'Precisely,' said Albert. 'The Garden of Forking Paths is an enormous guessing game, or parable, in which the subject is time. The rules of the game forbid the use of the word itself. To eliminate a word completely, to refer to it by means of inept phrases and obvious paraphrases, is perhaps the best way of drawing attention to it. This, then, is the tortuous method of approach preferred by the oblique Ts'ui Pen in every meandering of his interminable novel. I have gone over hundreds of manuscripts, I have corrected errors introduced by careless copyists, I have worked out the plan from this chaos, I have restored, or believe I have restored, the original. I have translated the whole work. I can state categorically that not once has the word time been used in the whole book.

After you finish the story, reread this paragraph. How might Ts'ui Pen's definition of time affect the narrator's actions at the end of the story? Do you think the narrator acts by choice, by chance, or by destiny? Why or why not?

'The explanation is obvious. The Garden of Forking Paths is a picture, incomplete yet not false, of the universe such as Ts'ui Pen conceived it to be. Differing from Newton and Schopenhauer, your ancestor did not think of time as absolute and uniform. He believed in an infinite series of times, in a dizzily growing, ever spreading network of diverging, converging and parallel times. This web of time – the strands of which approach one another, bifurcate, intersect or ignore each other through the centuries – embraces every possibility. We do not exist in most of them. In some you exist and not I, while in others I do, and you do not, and in yet others both of us exist. In this one, in which chance has favored me, you have come to my gate. In another, you, crossing the garden, have found me dead. In yet another, I say these very same words, but am an error, a phantom.'

'In all of them,' I enunciated, with a tremor in my voice. 'I deeply appreciate and am grateful to you for the restoration of Ts'ui Pen's garden.'

'Not in all,' he murmured with a smile. 'Time is forever dividing itself toward innumerable futures and in one of them I am your enemy.'

What does Borges mean by the word 'pullulation'?

Once again I sensed the pullulation of which I have already spoken. It seemed to me that the dew-damp garden surrounding the house was infinitely saturated with invisible people. All were Albert and myself, secretive, busy and multiform in other dimensions of time. I lifted my eyes and the short nightmare disappeared. In the black and yellow garden there was only a single man, but this man was as strong as a statue and this man was walking up the path and he was Captain Richard Madden.

'The future exists now,' I replied. 'But I am your friend. Can I take another look at the letter?'

Albert rose from his seat. He stood up tall as he opened the top drawer of the high writing cabinet. For a moment his back was again turned to me. I had the revolver ready. I fired with the utmost care: Albert fell without a murmur, at once. I swear that his death was instantaneous, as if he had been struck by lightning.

What remains is unreal and unimportant. Madden broke in and arrested me. I have been condemned to hang. Abominably, I have yet triumphed! The secret name of the city to be attacked got through to Berlin. Yesterday it was bombed. I read the news in the same English newspapers which were trying to solve the riddle of the murder of the learned Sinologist Stephen Albert by the unknown Yu Tsun. The Chief, however, had already solved this mystery. He knew that my problem was to shout, and that I had no other course open to me than to kill someone of that name. He does not know, for no one can, of my infinite penitence and sickness of the heart.

Translated by Helen Temple and Ruthven Todd

In his prologue to *Ficciones*, Luis Borges contends that *'The Garden of Forking Paths* is a detective story; its readers will assist at the execution, and all the preliminaries, of a crime, a crime whose purpose will not be unknown to them, but which they will not understand – it seems to me – until the last paragraph.' What do you understand about the narrator and the choices he makes, now that you've read the story?

Activity 16

Discuss the following questions and write down responses in your learner portfolio.

1) Given the rapport that the narrator developed with Dr Albert, why does he shoot him?
2) How does the narrator feel about his own actions?
3) What does the last line of the text reveal about the complexity of his character, of war, of cultural differences?
4) Do you think the narrator's knowledge of his ancestor's maze-like book has any effect on the outcome of the story? Why or why not?

The Borges Labyrinth, a greenery maze. The maze garden is located on Venice's island of San Giorgio Maggiore. It opened in 2011 and was dedicated to Borges on the 25th anniversary of his death.

Global issue

Work with a partner and discuss the global issue below. Record responses in your learner portfolio.

Why is it significant that so many cultures and nationalities are cobbled together in this story? What do such juxtapositions suggest about the connections between Nationalism, war, and culture?

TOK What is the significance of inanimate objects such as books being able to produce a physical response? To what extent does this transformative theory apply to other objects? What is the effect?

Activity 17 Intertextual links to natural science and mathematics

Scientist Brian Greene readily admits that the idea of parallel universes has applications in other fields, and even mentions Borges' story by name in his book, *The Hidden Reality: Parallel Universes and the Deep Laws of the Cosmos*:

'[An] early version of parallel universes resonated with themes of separate lands or alternative histories that were being explored in literature, television, and film, creative forays that continue today. (My favorites since childhood include The Wizard of Oz, It's a Wonderful Life..., the Borges story 'The Garden of Forking Paths') Collectively, these and many other works of popular culture have helped integrate the concept of parallel realities into the zeitgeist and are responsible for fueling much public fascination with the topic.'

1) In a small group, come up with a list of literary or other texts (films, TV series) in popular culture that explore time and space in parallel terms. What draws audiences to such narratives?
2) What is the significance of discussing the physics of time and space in a literary context? What might such intertextual connections yield beyond 'fuelling much public fascination with the topic'?

Connections

In 2015, the manuscript for *The Garden of the Forking Paths* was auctioned in New York for an estimated $200,000–300,000. Beyond its merits as a quality detective fiction story, it is perhaps best known as the first example of hypertext, a key component of the World Wide Web that links one text to another in a seemingly endless maze.

Intertextual research activity:
Using the QR code and the Internet, research Borges' connection to hypertext.

1) What types of articles did you find? Which subject areas are represented?
2) To what extent did this experience alter your understanding of Borges and/or *The Garden of Forking Paths*?
3) Why is it significant that Borges, a man of literature, is often cited as the original source for the idea of hypertext?

A manuscript page from Borges' 1941 story, *The Garden of the Forking Paths.*

Activity 18 Lost and found in translation

For this activity you will read two different English translations of the last paragraph of *The Garden of Forking Paths* and then use a chart to compare your findings. Translation is an exercise in interpretation. While the translator's job is to accurately convey the meaning of the original text, meanings of words are often not exact, so different translations of the same text will include variations. As you complete the activity below, consider the following:

1) To what extent can different translations of the same text affect meaning?

2) How can we trust a translation when we are not familiar with the original language of the text?
3) Can translations ever convey reliable knowledge?

Ending A: Translated by Helen Temple and Ruthven Todd

What remains is unreal and unimportant. Madden broke in and arrested me. I have been condemned to hang. Abominably, I have yet triumphed! The secret name of the city to be attacked got through to Berlin. Yesterday it was bombed. I read the news in the same English newspapers which were trying to solve the riddle of the murder of the learned Sinologist Stephen Albert by the unknown Yu Tsun. The Chief, however, had already solved this mystery. He knew that my problem was to shout, with my feeble voice, above the tumult of war, the name of the city called Albert, and that I had no other course open to me than to kill someone of that name. He does not know, for no one can, of my infinite penitence and sickness of the heart.

Ending B: Translated by Donald A Yates

The rest is unreal, insignificant. Madden broke in, arrested me. I have been condemned to the gallows. I have won out abominably; I have communicated to Berlin the secret name of the city they must attack. They bombed it yesterday; I read it in the same papers that offered to England the mystery of the learned Sinologist Stephen Albert who was murdered by a stranger, one Yu Tsun. The Chief had deciphered this mystery. He knew my problem was to indicate (through the uproar of the war) the city called Albert, and that I had found no other means to do so than to kill a man of that name. He does not know (no one can know) my innumerable contrition and weariness.

Read each text once through. Then read each again and highlight specific sentences. Find three corresponding sentences (or parts of sentences) and consider the differences in the effects of the writer's choices in each. Then, in the table, make observations about the effects. We have provided an example in the first row.

Sentence from Ending A	Sentence from Ending B	Effects of writer's choices (include notes on diction, punctuation, **syntax**, tone, style)
EXAMPLE: *What remains is unreal and unimportant.*	*The rest is unreal, insignificant.*	The word 'rest' in B is less formal than 'remains'. The comma in B makes the sentence feel more like a fragmented thought than a carefully designed sentence.
1		
2		
3		

Insights into fiction

All three areas of exploration and the seven course concepts work in tandem with the conventions of fiction that we have studied throughout this chapter. As you read the insights below, take note of how specific fiction conventions connect to areas of exploration and concepts so that you have a better understanding of not just how fiction works, but why reading it matters.

1. Determining point of view, the perspective through which a story is told, is critical. Once a reader is aware of perspective, they understand the limitations that the point of view may intrinsically provide. Why does narrative perspective matter and to what degree is the narrator sharing or perhaps purposely manipulating the events in the story?

2. Voice is an essential element of point of view. While point of view is the angle of vision – the perspective from which a story is told – the voice of the narrator informs that perspective. How does this voice communicate?

3. When you examine the structure of a work of fiction, you are examining it as a world that has been constructed for you (representation). The structure of the plot relates to the presentation of time within the work as well as the presentation of place (or space). Is the ordering of events chronological (linear) or does the story begin and end in the same place (circular)? Are chapters within a novel arranged purposefully to accommodate plot? Or, are chapters arranged seemingly at random? What is the effect of such structure on the story's meaning?

4. Consider how characters are developed and portrayed. Undoubtedly, you will encounter stereotypical characters: flat or round characters and stock characters such as evil villains or innocent maidens. But in much fiction you'll be drawn to more complex characters whose good or evil nature depends on how a situation is viewed. A hero can be seen as a villain, particularly if they perform acts that are against the law. Dynamic characters change; static ones do not. Whether change or stasis is positive or negative is not fixed. It often depends on perspective. Culture and context build characters, helping us understand their motives and identities and perhaps allowing us to reflect upon our own.

5. A writer's style is determined by their use of language and syntax (sentence structure). This creative footprint gives the writer a type of identity. Like poets, fiction writers communicate through figurative language. Syntactic patterns, the use of complex sentences, or even the use of fragments are also important to note. Is there a rhythm created by the pattern of sentences? Does the rhythm speed up or slow down as a way to underscore, or emphasise, the fictional situation? Looking closely, the language and devices that make up a work of fiction will allow you to understand how its representation (of plot, character, and theme) is constructed and communicated.

6. The conventions of fiction such as point of view, characterisation, voice, setting, and plot bring us into worlds that are like and unlike our own. As you explore different cultures you will be exposed to different perspectives that will enable you to understand, analyse, and interpret varied texts.

7. Themes are part of this deep inquiry. You may be intrigued by a plot event in the text that prompts you to explore a global issue. Or perhaps a character will help you better understand the concept of identity. Or a particular time and space will encourage you to analyse the effects of setting on culture. All of these concepts provide you with lenses through which to engage with the text and construct themes that go beyond forced observations. Read closely. Consider context. Make text to text connections. And don't forget your conceptual lenses. They'll serve you well for your upcoming assessments and beyond.

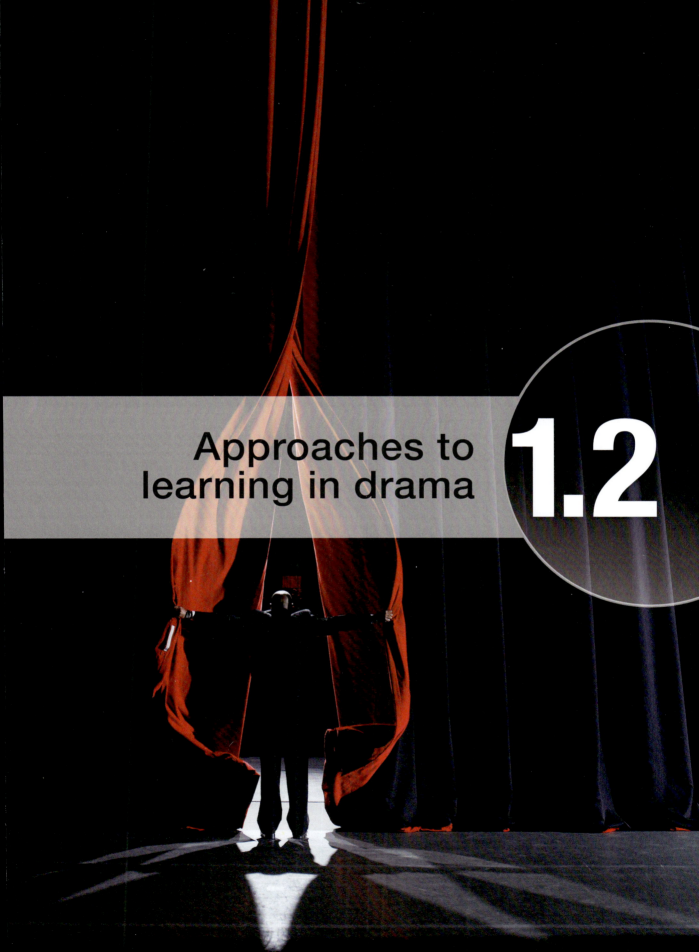

Approaches to learning in drama

1.2

Learning objectives

In this chapter you will…
- connect drama to approaches to learning, course concepts, and areas of exploration
- explore conventions and expectations of drama
- consider the advantages and limitations of staging
- understand the creation of momentum
- identify and interpret dramatic structures and their effects on the audience
- understand drama as performance literature
- communicate ideas through a variety of individual and collaborative activities
- analyse, evaluate, and appreciate a range of dramatic works through:
  - readers, writers, and texts
  - time and space
  - intertextuality
  - global issues.

Every play has one common aspect: it is written to be performed. What this means for you as a reader is that you must call upon your imagination to see the characters and to hear the same words, sounds, actions, and movements that you would experience as a member of an audience viewing a play. Imagination plays a role in many disciplines, but in drama it activates a reader's **creativity**, **transforming** flat text on a page into an animated form ready for life on the stage. As readers turn themselves into viewers, they negotiate a new role with writers and text, a role that makes the study of drama quite different from other literary forms.

The collaborative nature of drama also means that **representations** of a single text are always changing. Staging, directing, and even the context in which a play is performed affect how it is interpreted. We've devoted the first part of this chapter to the study of the conventions of drama so that you can ground your interpretations in foundational knowledge of the form. Once you've mastered the conventions, you'll read, analyse, and evaluate works of drama through the three **areas of exploration**, **course concepts** and **global issues**. This part of the chapter will allow you engage with texts through both collaborative and individual activities. The end goal is to build solid entries for your learner portfolio, skills for your upcoming assessments, and an appreciation for this performance-inspired literary form.

Theatrical performances are among the most immediate forms of literary presentation.

While drama and prose fiction share the common elements of plot, characters, and themes, the ways in which playwrights **communicate** these elements is quite distinct. The stage, and the position of the audience in relation to that stage, impose limitations which the prose fiction writer does not have. For example, the physical space limits the types of action a playwright can display. While in prose fiction readers can imagine descriptions of horses stampeding, elephants parading, or characters water-skiing, such action is generally more difficult to achieve on stage. Prose fiction writers also have a variety of **perspectives** or angles of vision to use in their works. The playwright essentially has one point of view, and that is the dramatic perspective of the audience members, sometimes referred to as the 'fourth wall'. This localised perspective creates a different way of considering **time and space**. Certainly, **cultural** and historical contexts shape meaning, but the physical world of the stage does this as well. If a playwright wants to reveal motivation for an action, that motivation must be revealed directly to the audience. We have to listen and watch the characters to discover their interior thoughts. Dialogue, then, becomes the primary vehicle for the playwright. Character movement or lack of movement, action and interaction, gestures, props, lighting and sound – the configuration of the stage itself – all contribute to the experience of the audience. But the playwright's words, and how they are spoken by the actors, often produce the greatest effects on the audience.

Even if you are unable to watch a play physically, learning the conventions and expectations of drama will enable you to 'see' the play in your mind's eye as you read it. This ability to imagine the play from an audience member's perspective is transformative. The type of creativity activated here is critical for the reader's immersion into the world that the playwright has created to be witnessed on a stage.

The 'fourth wall'

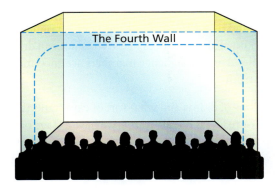

The Fourth Wall

Conventions and expectations of drama

Drama as an 'artifice', a creative construct, employs a number of strategies that bring to life the imaginary world of the play. Playwrights may want their audiences to embrace the world on stage wholly or in part. Realistic drama invites audiences to view the world on stage as a familiar one. The characters, words, actions, and stage sets, regardless of **culture** or time frame, are typically intended to be approachable rather than alienating. The characters' emotions are intended to provoke a sympathetic response. The outcome of this response is often seen as minimising the emotional distance between audience and performance.

In plays, the audience experiences more emotion and participates actively from behind the fourth wall. This 'active' participation means that the audience willingly 'suspends

Bertolt Brecht was particularly known for the 'alienation effect' in his plays. ▼

disbelief' and accepts the world on stage before them as realistic and, therefore, that it can offer them emotional intensity and relief. The writer, and by extension the director and actors, work to create a specific type of representation of reality that offers an immersion in a world that does not exist beyond the stage, but is unquestionably believable in the moment.

Other playwrights may want their audiences to be fully aware of the artifice of their presentation, and may consciously work at dissolving the fourth wall so that audiences are reminded throughout the performance that the presentation before them is just that – a presentation that challenges the audience's subjectivity. This dramatic experience keeps audiences at a purposeful distance from the emotional impact of the work. A detached, somewhat objective, audience perspective is the goal, similar to Bertolt Brecht's 'alienation effect'. This alienation effect seeks to keep audience members aware that what they are witnessing on stage is purely artificial; in this way, it is intended that audiences will remain alienated, or emotionally distant, from the world they witness on stage. The **intertextual** process of analysing such disparate representations, one that draws in audiences, another that keeps them at a distance, reveals how the form of a play can steer viewer perspectives and affect how meaning is negotiated between **readers, writers, and texts**.

The audience's emotional investment in a play can be manipulated by the playwright, and those involved in the play's performance, to great effect. **Dramatic irony**, for example, where the audience recognises the truth or falsity of words or actions when characters do not, can heighten the emotional investment of the audience. In Act 3 of *Hamlet*, young Hamlet has the perfect opportunity to avenge his father's death by killing King Claudius in the chapel, but decides not to kill a man in prayer who will likely be forgiven by God for repenting. The audience is fully aware that Claudius' prayers are not sincere and that Hamlet is missing a perfect opportunity for revenge. The tension that such knowledge produces in the audience can drive the play forward, creating a kind of **momentum**, as audience members are encouraged to anticipate an eventual revelation of truth.

What are the conventions of drama and what sort of expectations do we bring to plays as audience members or readers? For all drama, we have a stage on which actors play

A proscenium stage ▶

out the words and actions described by the playwright. Stages come in various shapes and sizes with equally varied configurations of audience seating. The stage is the setting of the play's action, and the world of character interaction. To stage a play means to bring the play to life, to have its characters move through a particular type of time and (physical) space. Staging, then, refers to all of the decisions involved in a play's production including the positioning of actors, their movements on stage, and the construction of the set (including the placement and physical attributes of props), as well as lighting, costume, and sound devices. A filmed version of a play offers a different type of staging and additional possibilities for settings in multiple contexts.

Your task, as a reader of a play, is to pay attention to every detail of the stage. As you participate in this creative, transformative process, you may construct the stage in your imagination, noting positions, shapes, colours, and sizes of every detail provided in the stage directions. Note where doors and windows are located because these staging devices differentiate the interior world of the play (on stage) from its exterior world (off stage). Even in plays where the stage directions are few, clues in dialogue that mention time of day or weather patterns affect how you imagine a scene.

Characterisation

Actors assume the roles of characters. And, just as in prose fiction, a play can have major and minor characters, **foil** characters, a **protagonist**, an **antagonist**, and, in the case of memory plays, a narrator.

You will need to examine characters carefully and pay particular attention to stage directions regarding the way that a character is described initially. Note any physical and costume descriptions that appear in the stage directions so that you can imagine a character visually. Also note any stage direction that describes the way a character speaks. Often, the manner in which a line is delivered can be just as important, or more so, than the words themselves. In watching a play, we have the added benefit of the actor's voice, which can suggest subtle meanings beyond the words themselves. When reading, however, voice moderation, accenting, and pacing of the playwright's words can only be inferred through written stage directions.

Actions on stage, whether overt or subtle, together with the words spoken by characters, advance the plot of the play. Momentum, which is what drives the play forward, is often associated with increasing tension. As you read, you must be sensitive to those actions or situations that create reaction in one or more of the characters. These reactions allow you to follow character development. By reading closely you can identify what subject matter, action, or interaction triggers, for example, reactions such as an explosively tense moment or a moment of absolute silence. Both reactions are important to recognise because in either situation momentum builds. In a sense, the reader and the text are caught in a tactile interplay.

By creating the forward motion, the momentum, of a play, the playwright allows the audience or reader to invest emotionally in the characters and their situations on stage. Tension, whether overt or subtly presented, extends to the audience/reader. Ideally, the audience/reader embraces this tension, driving forward their engagement with the plot. Quite simply, momentum begins the moment that the audience/reader wants to know what is going to happen next.

▲ Dramatic action can be the fulfilment of rising tension, or can create new tensions in itself.

▲ A theatre in the round

◄ Facial expressions can be at least as important as the words themselves.

◄ Silence on stage often prompts silence from the audience, as they are waiting for something important to happen or be said.

Dramatic structure

In 1863, German dramatist and novelist Gustav Freytag created his 'Pyramid' to explain the predictable order for the unfolding of a play. The five-part structure was basically as follows:

- **exposition**

- **rising action**

- **climax/crisis** (a turning point)

- **falling action/reversal**

- **dénouement**.

Freytag's Pyramid ▶

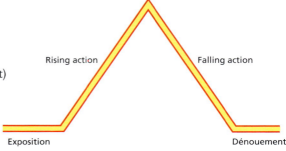

Of course, not all dramas follow this model. Rather than beginning with the prescribed exposition or background, many playwrights choose to engage their audience from the outset, seemingly dropping their audiences into the action of the play. This immediate engagement in the middle of action – '**in medias res**' – is often provocative. Audiences and readers alike have little time to ease into the action of the play. The effects are sometimes startling, or confusing, but the expectation is that spectators are actively engaged from the onset. Some playwrights seem to 'play off' the audience's reaction by allowing characters to 'break the fourth wall' and speak directly to the audience members. Note how the form changes over time and through space. Place, period, and culture inform the choices playwrights make in shaping their plays, and such choices affect how the final work is produced and received.

The well-made play

One modification of Freytag's traditional five-part structure is the structure that 19th-century Norwegian playwright Henrik Ibsen used to great effect – the well-made play. In this format, the plot involves a character withholding a secret. Through a series of events and actions, tension and suspense build steadily to the moment of climax when the secret is revealed and the character's fear of ultimate loss is translated into gain. Death and destruction give way to freedom and understanding – a new life, so to speak, emerges for the character.

A well-made play incorporates many of the following elements:

- a protagonist's secret

- mistaken identity

- misplaced documents

- well-timed entrances and exits

- a battle of wits

- a climactic scene revealing the secret

- logical dénouement.

We will examine these elements in detail later in this chapter in our areas of exploration section. In this section you will have the opportunity to apply the concepts of dramatic convention and the subsequent expectations for you as a reader of drama. You will also expand your understanding of the three areas of exploration, or lenses of analysis, that you will encounter in this course, along with the seven conceptual understandings that provide a sense of continuity as you move from one text to another, from one form to another. These seven concepts establish a framework for comparative observations of texts within a form (two plays) or texts in differing forms (a play and a poem).

◀ Ibsen's *A Doll's House*

◀ *Medea*

◀ *Waiting for Godot*

Other dramatic classifications

In addition to the traditional five-part play and the well-made play, there are a number of other types of plays that you may study in one or more parts of the programme including theatre of the absurd, classical or Elizabethan comedy and tragedy, and **tragicomedy**.

Theatre of the absurd, a term coined by dramatist and critic Martin Esslin, refers to a non-realistic form of drama. Characters, staging, and action all run counter to our expectations of realistic drama. The world of the absurd is peopled with confusion, despair, illogicality, and incongruity. Action is frequently repetitive or seemingly irrational. Characters are often confused, and metaphysical themes tend to reinforce that the world is incomprehensible. Ionesco's *The Bald Soprano* and Beckett's *Waiting for Godot* are well-known plays of this form. Texts of this type connect to the concept of representation as they challenge our perception of reality.

The Bald Soprano ▶

Connections

The more realistic the play, the more often the playwright intends to engage the audience emotionally. Less realistic drama, such as absurdist plays, often disregards the emotional sympathies of the audience in favour of their intellectual responses. Do not assume that every playwright wants their audiences to identify with characters or their situations.

Considering theme in drama

Themes in drama, like those in prose fiction, are ideas that express some aspect of human nature. Theme expresses lessons common to the human condition, so the time and place of the play is inconsequential to the lessons about what it means to be human. While thematic ideas can be expressed in single words or short phrases, theme is expressed in sentence form. For example, the word 'fear' is a thematic idea while the phrase 'Anger and rage are often manifestations of fear' would be a statement of theme.

Themes often transcend time and space but they do not exist in a vacuum. The readers' experiences – their culture and their perspectives – give rise to how themes are transformed and interpreted for each text.

Activity 1

See what themes you can construct from the following thematic ideas.
- jealousy
- forgiveness
- love
- freedom
- competition
- revenge

Considering time in drama

In earlier chapters we discussed how time and space provide a sense of culture and context, a backdrop that helps us interpret aspects of a text such as character actions and motivations. Time here is historical in nature.

But how does a playwright account for the passage of time on stage? Time can take on a meaning of its own. Although the play unfolds in real time in front of the audience, the time it covers within the story is often much longer.

In some instances, a playwright can use a variety of devices to indicate the passing of time. We know that closing the curtain or blacking out the stage implicitly signals that there may be a significant change when the curtain opens or the lights on stage come up. The scene could be changed to a different location, the set could be modified to indicate some significant action has taken place, or the time frame could have changed – moving forward or backward in time. These mechanical devices work the way that a chapter break or a noticeable white space (an interstices) works in prose fiction. They enable audiences to anticipate, and be open to, change. Other stage actions can also be effective in showing the passing of time – winding a clock, lighting a lamp, or using visuals such as a sunset visible to the audience through a stage window can convey time passing. Sounds, like the ringing of an alarm clock or a rooster crowing, can also signal a change in time, as can characters donning nightclothes or simply saying, 'Goodnight, we'll speak more of this in the morning'.

As a reader, you can expect that time will progress within the literal time span of the performance. Apart from the passage of time that an audience member observes as it occurs on stage, time can also function in relation to other conventions of drama. For example, the pacing of a scene can influence the momentum of the play itself, as well as how we respond to characters and their interactions. In Ibsen's *A Doll's House*, for example, time functions as an antagonist. Time is Nora's enemy. Ibsen chooses to slow the pace of some scenes and heighten the pace of others. When observing a play, the pace of dialogue is obvious. When reading a play, however, this determination is a bit more difficult. The reader will need to observe the dialogue between two characters. Short lines, spoken in rapid fire, will create a quicker pace, a staccato effect much like bantering. Slowing the pace of dialogue is created through starts and stops, pauses, and repetitions. Stage directions also work to slow the pace of dialogue. Actor movement, entering or exiting the stage, moving from one side of the stage to the other, or standing motionless without saying a word, slows the momentum of a scene.

Activity 2

Imagine that you are a director. How would you reveal the passage of time to an audience in a theatre in the following situations?

1) A shift from night to day.
2) A character dies in one scene and several months have passed in the next scene.
3) A character has been on a long trip and has now arrived in a different location.
4) A character must hurry because he/she is running out of time.
5) A young child is now much older, perhaps a young adult.

Live dramatic performances draw on energy from both the actors on the stage and the audience, creating a direct connection between performers and viewers.

Areas of exploration: analyse, evaluate, appreciate

Now that you have a working knowledge of dramatic conventions, we will take a closer look at how these conventions work in tandem with course concepts and areas of exploration. You will study three specific dramatic works in this section, each focusing on a different area of exploration. As you work through the activities, consider how the areas of exploration, along with accompanying concepts, help deepen your understanding of dramatic conventions and open up the texts in different ways.

1) *Trifles* by Susan Glaspell

2) *A Doll's House* by Henrik Ibsen

3) *The Father* by August Strindberg

1) Readers, writers, and texts: an approach to Susan Glaspell's *Trifles* (1916)

At the heart of this area of exploration, as with any of the four forms, is close reading, a type of **research/inquiry** that requires paying attention to every word, every detail that is provided by a writer, as well as observing what is not stated but implied. The choices that writers make contribute to the meaning of their texts regardless of form. But the role of the reader is also crucial to generating meaning.

The subject matter of a play, and the playwright's attitude towards it, along with dramatic strategies that a playwright chooses, produce effects in the audience and the reader alike. Our thoughts and feelings hinge on the words and actions of characters, the way those words are stated (tone), and our individual experiences as readers or observers. Recognising the aesthetic nature of literature means that, as readers, we admit a degree of subjectivity, based on our individual experiences. This admission works in tandem with the objective mindset of analysis. Meaning is negotiated and constructed within the interaction of these two distinct responses – personal experience and analytical perspective. The more you know about drama and its conventions and the strategies available to the playwright, coupled with your own experience as a reader, the more opportunity you have to negotiate meaning.

Readers of drama must also be aware of their own processes as readers, their own emotional reactions and intellectual awareness. For example, when is your disbelief suspended – when do you embrace the play as its own reality? When are you moved to laugh, to cry, to feel anger or pity? Are you aware of your own tension, or anticipation, as the play moves forward? Are there moments in the action of the play when it is difficult to maintain focus? Why? Does the play engage you from the opening scene, or does your engagement grow in accordance with the momentum the playwright produces? Do you like one character more than another? And, if so, do you know why?

In Susan Glaspell's one-act play, *Trifles*, close reading begins with her initial observations noted as 'Scene'. While a list of characters and/or a description of the staging may seem matter of fact and insignificant to the dialogue, they are not. Skimming over these initial descriptions, which unfortunately many students tend to do, will deny you an opportunity for significant insights into the characters, the staging, and, ultimately, the meaning.

TOK What is the difference between reading a play (and imagining the actions on stage) and viewing a play (and actually watching scenes unfold)?

As you read through *Trifles* in its entirety, you will see that we have divided it into six activity sections. Each of these sections will ask you questions that rely on your ability to close read. Jot down your responses in your learner portfolio and be prepared to share your findings with others.

Note: Observe bold elements in the play as close reading details that are significant to the development of character, theme(s), verbal or dramatic irony, and/or dramatic strategies (entries/exits, props, lighting, sound, gesture, silence, movement/**blocking**, the passage of time).

Trifles by Susan Glaspell

Characters

George Henderson, County Attorney

Lewis Hale, a neighboring farmer

Henry Peters, Sheriff

Mrs. Peters

Mrs. Hale

Scene: The kitchen in the now abandoned farmhouse of John Wright, a gloomy kitchen, and left without having been put in order—unwashed pans under the sink, a loaf of bread outside the breadbox, a dish towel on the table—other signs of incompleted work.

As the rear outer door opens, and the Sheriff comes in, followed by the County Attorney and Hale. The Sheriff and Hale are men in middle life, the County Attorney is a young man; all are much bundled up and go at once to the stove. They are followed by the two women— the Sheriff's wife first; she is a slight, wiry woman, a thin nervous face. Mrs. Hale is larger and would ordinarily be called more comfortable looking, but she is disturbed now and looks fearfully about as she enters. The women have come in slowly and stand close together near the door.

Activity 3 Focus on preliminary staging information

In the opening sentence, Glaspell's choice of language triggers a tone: words like 'abandoned', 'gloomy', and 'unwashed', coupled with incompleted actions, establish that tone. How would you characterise this tone? What might Glaspell be suggesting with the use of the word 'now'?

1) In the remaining five sentences of the scene, what does Glaspell manage to establish about the characters, either directly (stated) or indirectly (implied)?
2) Note the positioning of the two women and three men on the stage. Can we infer anything about them from their places on stage? What do you think the playwright is trying to communicate through these detailed descriptions?

TOK

To what extent are both research and imagination necessary in designing an accurate representation of a play?

Connections

When filmmaker Sally Heckel remade the short-story version of Glaspell's play into a 30-minute Oscar-nominated film in 1980, she had this to say about the kitchen described in the text: 'I considered the kitchen to be another character in the film, more than just a background. Its atmosphere and the objects in it had to create a mood and reveal their own story. Very little has been recorded about the way poor rural people lived at that time, and even less about their kitchens. I was able to find a few illustrations, but photographs were virtually non-existent. Much of the information came from people's reminiscences, and from letters in women's magazines from that era.'

Activity 4 Considering tone

Now that you've thought about how Glaspell's opening language builds a scene in your imagination, take a few minutes and view the openings of two different film versions of Glaspell's text. Sally Heckel (mentioned above) and Alfred Hitchcock both made short films in 1980 and 1961 respectively, based on Glaspell's short-story version of her one-act play.

Watch the opening of each film before the dialogue begins and consider the tools that the filmmakers use to establish tone and transform the texts into a visual reality.

1) What is the first image you see in each version? How does the image help establish the tone?
2) What do you notice about sound and lighting? How do these elements work with the visuals to establish tone?
3) How is the weather **communicated**? What is the effect?
4) What is the effect of moving from outdoors to indoors? This shift is not in the print version of the text and has been added by both directors. Why do you think they made this choice?
5) If you were to direct the opening of this scene, what might you do differently?

Trifles by Susan Glaspell continued, opening dialogue

COUNTY ATTORNEY: [*Rubbing his hands.*] This feels good. Come up to the fire, ladies.

MRS. PETERS: [*After taking a step forward.*] I'm not—cold.

SHERIFF: [*Unbuttoning his overcoat and stepping away from the stove as if to mark the beginning of official business.*] Now, Mr. Hale, before we move things about, you explain to Mr. Henderson just what you saw when you came here yesterday morning.

COUNTY ATTORNEY: By the way, has anything been moved? **Are things just as you left them yesterday?**

SHERIFF: [*Looking about.*] It's just the same. When it dropped below zero last night I thought I'd better send Frank out this morning to make a fire for us—no use getting pneumonia with a big case on, but I told him not to touch anything except the stove—and you know Frank.

COUNTY ATTORNEY: Somebody should have been left here yesterday.

SHERIFF: Oh—yesterday. When I had to send Frank to Morris Center for that man who went crazy—I want you to know I had my hands full yesterday. I knew you could get back from Omaha by today and as long as **I went over everything here myself—**

COUNTY ATTORNEY: Well, Mr. Hale, tell just what happened when you came here yesterday morning.

HALE: Harry and I had started to town with a load of potatoes. We came along the road from my place and as I got here I said, 'I'm going to see if I can't get John Wright to go in with me on a party telephone'. I spoke to Wright about it once before and he put me off, saying folks talked too much anyway, and all he asked was peace and quiet—I guess you know about how much he talked himself; but I thought maybe if I went to the house and talked about it before his wife, though I said to Harry that **I didn't know as what his wife wanted made much difference to John—**

COUNTY ATTORNEY**: Let's talk about that later, Mr. Hale.** I do want to talk about that, but tell now just what happened when you got to the house.

HALE: I didn't hear or see anything; I knocked at the door, and still it was all quiet inside. I knew they must be up, it was past eight o'clock. So I knocked again, and I thought I heard somebody say, 'Come in'. I wasn't sure, I'm not sure yet, but I opened the door—this door [*indicating **the door by which the two women are still standing**.*] and there in that rocker—[*pointing to it*] sat Mrs. Wright.

[*They all look at the rocker.*]

COUNTY ATTORNEY: What—was she doing?

HALE: She was **rockin' back and forth.** She had her apron in her hand and was kind of— **pleating it.**

COUNTY ATTORNEY: And how did she—look?

HALE: Well, she looked queer.

COUNTY ATTORNEY: How do you mean—queer?

HALE: Well, as if she didn't know what she was going to do next. And **kind of done up.**

COUNTY ATTORNEY: How did she seem to feel about your coming?

HALE: Why, I don't think she minded—one way or other. She didn't pay much attention. I said, 'How do, Mrs. Wright it's cold, ain't it?' And she said, 'Is it?'—and **went on kind of pleating at her apron.** Well, I was surprised; she didn't ask me to come up to the stove, or to set down, but just sat there, not even looking at me, so I said, 'I want to see John'. And then she—laughed. I guess you would call it a laugh. I thought of Harry and the team outside, so I said a little sharp: 'Can't I see John?' 'No', she says, kind o' dull like. 'Ain't he home?' says I. 'Yes', says she, 'he's home'. 'Then why can't I see him?' I asked her, out of patience. "Cause he's dead', says she. 'Dead?' says I. She just nodded her head, not getting a bit excited, but **rockin' back and forth.** 'Why—where is he?' says I, not knowing what to say. She just pointed upstairs—like that [*himself pointing to the room above*]. I got up, with the idea of going up there. I walked from there to here—then I says, 'Why, what did he die of?' 'He died of a rope round his neck', says she, and **just went on pleatin' at her apron.** Well, I went out and called Harry. I thought I might—need help. We went upstairs and there he was lyin'—

COUNTY ATTORNEY: I think I'd rather have you go into that upstairs, where you can point it all out. Just go on now with the rest of the story.

HALE: Well, my first thought was to get that rope off. It looked… [*Stops, his face twitches.*]… but Harry, he went up to him, and he said, 'No, he's dead all right, and we'd better not touch anything'. So we went back down stairs. She was still sitting that same way. 'Has anybody been notified?' I asked. 'No', says she unconcerned. 'Who did this, Mrs. Wright?' said Harry. He said it business-like—and **she stopped pleatin'** of her apron. 'I don't know', she says. 'You don't know?' says Harry. 'No', says she. 'Weren't you sleepin' in the bed with him?' says Harry. 'Yes', says she**, 'but I was on the inside'.** 'Somebody slipped a rope round his neck and strangled him and you didn't wake up?' says Harry. **'I didn't wake up',** she said after him. We must 'a looked as if we didn't see how that could be, for after a minute she said, **'I sleep sound'.** Harry was going to ask her more questions but I said maybe we ought to let her tell her story first to the coroner, or the sheriff, so Harry went fast as he could to Rivers' place, where there's a telephone.

COUNTY ATTORNEY: And what did Mrs. Wright do when she knew that you had gone for the coroner?

HALE: **She moved from that chair to this one over here [*Pointing to a small chair in the corner.*]** and just sat there with her hands held together and looking down. I got a feeling that I ought to make some conversation, so I said I had come in to see if John wanted to put in a telephone, and at that she started to laugh, and then she stopped and looked at me—scared. [*The COUNTY ATTORNEY, who has had his notebook out, **makes a note.***] I dunno, maybe it wasn't scared. I wouldn't like to say it was. Soon Harry got back, and then Dr. Lloyd came, and you, Mr. Peters, and so I guess that's all I know that you don't.

Activity 5 Focus on establishing characterisation: observing movement and gesture, and building momentum

1) What do we learn about characters through their communication (dialogue)?
2) What effect does interruption produce? (Note the dash at the end of a line of dialogue.)
3) What further can we learn about characters through gesture or action or blocking (positioning on stage)?
4) What do we learn that creates momentum (suspense, curiosity, engaged interest)?

Trifles by Susan Glaspell cont.

COUNTY ATTORNEY: [*Looking around.*] I guess we'll go upstairs first—and then out to the barn and around there. [*To the SHERIFF.*] You're convinced that there was **nothing important** here—nothing that **would point to any motive.**

SHERIFF: Nothing here but kitchen things.

[The COUNTY ATTORNEY, after again looking around the kitchen, opens the door of a cupboard closet. He gets up on a chair and looks on a shelf. Pulls his hand away, sticky.]

COUNTY ATTORNEY: Here's a nice mess.

[The women draw nearer.]

MRS. PETERS: [To the other woman.] Oh, her fruit; it did freeze. [To the LAWYER.] She worried about that when it turned so cold. She said the fire'd go out and her jars would break.

SHERIFF: Well, can you beat the women! Held for murder and worryin' about her preserves.

COUNTY ATTORNEY: I guess before we're through she may have something more serious than preserves to worry about.

HALE: Well, women are used to worrying over trifles.

[The two women move a little closer together.]

COUNTY ATTORNEY: [With the gallantry of a young politician.] And yet, for all their worries, what would we do without the ladies? [The women do not unbend. He goes to the sink, takes a dipperful of water from the pail and pouring it into a basin, washes his hands. Starts to wipe them on the roller-towel, turns it for a cleaner place.] Dirty towels! [Kicks his foot against the pans under the sink.] **Not much of a housekeeper, would you say, ladies?**

MRS. HALE: **[Stiffly.]** There's a great deal of work to be done on a farm.

COUNTY ATTORNEY: To be sure. And yet **[With a little bow to her.]** I know there are some Dickson county farmhouses which do not have such roller-towels. [He gives it a pull to expose its length again.]

MRS. HALE: Those towels get dirty awful quick. Men's hands aren't always as clean as they might be.

COUNTY ATTORNEY: Ah, loyal to your sex, I see. But you and Mrs. Wright were neighbors. I suppose you were friends, too.

MRS. HALE: [Shaking her head.] I've not seen much of her of late years. I've not been in this house—it's more than a year.

COUNTY ATTORNEY: And why was that? You didn't like her?

MRS. HALE: I liked her all well enough. Farmers' wives have their hands full, Mr. Henderson. And then—

COUNTY ATTORNEY: Yes—?

MRS. HALE: [Looking about.] It never seemed a very cheerful place.

COUNTY ATTORNEY: No—it's not cheerful. I shouldn't say she had the homemaking instinct.

MRS. HALE: Well, I don't know as Wright had, either.

COUNTY ATTORNEY: You mean that they didn't get on very well?

MRS. HALE: No, I don't mean anything. But I don't think a place'd be any cheerfuller for John Wright's being in it.

COUNTY ATTORNEY**: I'd like to talk more of that a little later.** I want to get the lay of things upstairs now. [He goes to the left, where three steps lead to a stair door.]

SHERIFF: I suppose anything Mrs. Peters does'll be all right. She was to take in some clothes for her, you know, and a few little things. We left in such a hurry yesterday.

COUNTY ATTORNEY: Yes, **but I would like to see what you take, Mrs. Peters,** and keep an eye out for anything that might be of use to us.

MRS. PETERS: Yes, Mr. Henderson.

Activity 6 Focus on character building: blocking and gesturing, verbal and dramatic irony, and building momentum

1) What do you learn about the characters through their actions, gestures, and dialogue?
2) What causes the momentum to continue to build?
3) What do you notice about gender roles and assumptions? What is the significance of the line, for example, 'Well, women are used to worrying over trifles'? Why do you think Glaspell chose this word as the title for her play?

Trifles by Susan Glaspell cont.

[*The women listen to the men's steps on the stairs, then look about the kitchen.*]

MRS. HALE: I'd hate to have men coming into my kitchen, snooping around and criticising.

[*She arranges the pans under sink which the LAWYER had shoved out of place.*]

MRS. PETERS: Of course it's no more than their duty.

MRS. HALE: Duty's all right, but I guess that deputy sheriff that came out to make the fire might have got a little of this on. [*Gives the roller-towel a pull.*] Wish I'd thought of that sooner. Seems mean to talk about her for not having things slicked up when she had to come away in such a hurry.

MRS. PETERS: [*Who has gone to a small table in the left rear corner of the room, and lifted one end of a towel that covers a pan.*] She had bread set. [*Stands still.*]

MRS. HALE: [**Eyes fixed on a loaf of bread beside the breadbox,** *which is on a low shelf at the other side of the room.* **Moves slowly toward it.**] She was going to put this in there [**Picks up loaf, then abruptly drops it.** *In a manner of returning to familiar things*] It's a shame about her fruit. I wonder if it's all gone. [*Gets up on the chair and looks.*] I think there's some here that's all right, Mrs. Peters. Yes—here; [*Holding it toward the window.*] This is cherries, too. [*Looking again.*] I declare I believe that's the only one. [*Gets down, bottle in her hand. Goes to the sink and wipes it off on the outside.*] She'll feel awful bad after all her hard work in the hot weather. I remember the afternoon I put up my cherries last summer.

[*She puts the bottle on the big kitchen table, center of the room. With a sigh, is about to sit down in the rocking-chair. Before she is seated realizes what chair it is; with a slow look at it, steps back. The chair which she has touched rocks back and forth.*]

MRS. PETERS: Well, I must get those things from the front room closet. [*She goes to the door at the right, but after looking into the other room, steps back.*] You coming with me, Mrs. Hale? **You could help me carry them.**

[*They go in the other room; reappear, MRS. PETERS carrying a dress and skirt, MRS. HALE following with a pair of shoes.*]

MRS. PETERS: My, it's cold in there.

[*She puts the clothes on the big table, and* **hurries to the stove**.]

MRS. HALE: [*Examining the skirt.*] Wright was close. I think maybe that's why she kept so much to herself. She didn't even belong to the Ladies Aid. I suppose she felt she couldn't do her part, and then you don't enjoy things when you feel shabby. She used to wear pretty clothes and be lively, when she was Minnie Foster, one of the town girls singing in the choir. But that—oh, that was thirty years ago. This all you was to take in?

MRS. PETERS: She said **she wanted an apron.** Funny thing to want, for there isn't much to get you dirty in jail, goodness knows. But I suppose just **to make her feel more natural.** She said they was in the top drawer in this cupboard. Yes, here. And then her little shawl that always hung behind the door. [*Opens stair door and looks.*] Yes, here it is.

[*Quickly shuts door leading upstairs.*]

MRS. HALE: [*Abruptly moving toward her.*] Mrs. Peters?

MRS. PETERS: Yes, Mrs. Hale?

MRS. HALE: Do you think she did it?

MRS. PETERS: [*In a **frightened voice**.*] Oh, I don't know.

MRS. HALE: Well, I don't think she did. Asking for an apron and her little shawl. Worrying about her fruit.

MRS. PETERS: [*Starts to speak, glances up, where footsteps are heard in the room above. In a low voice*] Mr. Peters says it looks bad for her. Mr. Henderson is awful sarcastic in a speech and he'll make fun of her sayin' she didn't wake up.

MRS. HALE: Well, I guess John Wright didn't wake when they was slipping that rope under his neck.

MRS. PETERS: No, it's strange. It must have been done awful crafty and still. They say it was **such a—funny way to kill a man, rigging it all up like that.**

MRS. HALE: That's just what Mr. Hale said. **There was a gun in the house.** He says that's what he can't understand.

MRS. PETERS: Mr. Henderson said coming out that what was needed for the case was a motive; something to show anger, or—sudden feeling.

MRS. HALE: [*Who is standing by the table.*] Well, I don't see any signs of anger around here. [*She puts her hand on the dish towel which lies on the table, stands looking down at table, **one half of which is clean, the other half messy.**] It's wiped to here. [**Makes a move as if to finish work, then turns and looks at loaf of bread outside the breadbox. Drops towel.** In that voice of coming back to familiar things*] Wonder how they are finding things upstairs. **I hope she had it a little more red-up up there.** You know, it seems kind of sneaking. Locking her up in town and then coming out here and trying to get her own house to turn against her!

MRS. PETERS: But Mrs. Hale, **the law is the law**.

MRS. HALE: I s'pose 'tis [*Unbuttoning her coat.*] Better loosen up your things, Mrs. Peters. You won't feel them when you go out.

[*MRS. PETERS takes off her fur tippet, goes to hang it on hook at back of room, stands looking at the under part of the small corner table.*]

MRS. PETERS: She was piecing a quilt.

[*She brings the large sewing basket and they look at the bright pieces.*]

MRS. HALE: It's log cabin pattern. Pretty, isn't it? I wonder if she was goin' to quilt it or just knot it?

[*Footsteps have been heard coming down the stairs. The SHERIFF enters followed by HALE and the COUNTY ATTORNEY.*]

SHERIFF: They wonder if she was going to quilt it or just knot it!

[*The men laugh, the women look abashed.*]

COUNTY ATTORNEY: [*Rubbing his hands over the stove.*] Frank's fire didn't do much up there, did it? Well, let's go out to the barn and get that cleared up. [*The men go outside.*]

Activity 7 Focus on characterisation building through dialogue, momentum, and irony

1) What effect does verbal and/or dramatic irony have in this section?
2) How are the two women differentiated in this section? To what extent are their **identities** established by physical action and dialogue?
3) What contributes to building momentum?

Trifles by Susan Glaspell cont.

MRS. HALE: [**Resentfully**.] I don't know as there's anything so strange, our takin' up our time with little things while we're waiting for them to get the evidence. [*She sits down at the big table smoothing out a block with decision.*] **I don't see as it's anything to laugh about.**

MRS. PETERS: [*Apologetically.*] Of course they've got awful important things on their minds.

[*Pulls up a chair and joins MRS. HALE at the table.*]

MRS. HALE: [*Examining another block.*] Mrs. Peters, look at this one. Here, this is the one she was working on, and look at the sewing! All the rest of it has been so nice and even. And look at this! It's all over the place! Why, it looks as if she didn't know what she was about!

[*After she has said this they look at each other, then start to glance back at the door. After an instant MRS. HALE has pulled at a knot and ripped the sewing.*]

MRS. PETERS: Oh, what are you doing, Mrs. Hale?

MRS. HALE: [*Mildly.*] Just pulling out a stitch or two that's not sewed very good. [*Threading a needle.*] Bad sewing always made me fidgety.

MRS. PETERS: [*Nervously.*] I don't think we ought to touch things.

MRS. HALE: I'll just finish up this end. [**Suddenly stopping and leaning forward**.] Mrs. Peters?

MRS. PETERS: Yes, Mrs. Hale?

MRS. HALE: What do you suppose she was so nervous about?

MRS. PETERS: Oh—I don't know. I don't know as she was nervous. I sometimes sew awful queer when I'm just tired. [*MRS. HALE starts to say something, looks at MRS. PETERS, then goes on sewing.*] Well I must get these things wrapped up. They may be through sooner than we think. [*Putting apron and other things together.*] I wonder where I can find a piece of paper, and string.

MRS. HALE: In that cupboard, maybe.

MRS. PETERS: [*Looking in cupboard.*] Why, here's a birdcage. [*Holds it up.*] Did she have a bird, Mrs. Hale?

MRS. HALE: Why, I don't know whether she did or not—I've not been here for so long. There was a man around last year selling canaries cheap, but I don't know as she took one; maybe she did. She used to sing real pretty herself.

MRS. PETERS: [*Glancing around.*] Seems funny to think of a bird here. But she must have had one, or why would she have a cage? I wonder what happened to it.

MRS. HALE: I s'pose maybe the cat got it.

MRS. PETERS: No, she didn't have a cat. She's got that feeling some people have about cats—being afraid of them. My cat got in her room and she was real upset and asked me to take it out.

MRS. HALE: My sister Bessie was like that. Queer, ain't it?

MRS. PETERS: [*Examining the cage.*] Why, look at this door. It's broke. One hinge is pulled apart.

MRS. HALE: [*Looking too.*] Looks as if someone must have been rough with it.

MRS. PETERS: Why, yes.

[*She brings the cage forward and puts it on the table.*]

MRS. HALE: I wish if they're going to find any evidence they'd be about it. I don't like this place.

MRS. PETERS: But I'm awful glad you came with me, Mrs. Hale. It would be lonesome for me sitting here alone.

MRS. HALE: It would, wouldn't it? [*Dropping her sewing.*] But I tell you what I do wish, Mrs. Peters. I wish I had come over sometimes when she was here. I—[*Looking around the room.*]—wish I had.

MRS. PETERS: But of course you were awful busy, Mrs. Hale—your house and your children.

MRS. HALE: I could've come. I stayed away because it weren't cheerful— and that's why I ought to have come. I—I've never liked this place. Maybe because it's down in a hollow and you don't see the road. I dunno what it is, but it's a lonesome place and always was. I wish I had come over to see Minnie Foster sometimes. I can see now—[*Shakes her head.*]

MRS. PETERS: Well, you mustn't reproach yourself, Mrs. Hale. Somehow we just don't see how it is with other folks until—something comes up.

MRS. HALE: Not having children makes less work—but it makes a quiet house, and Wright out to work all day, and no company when he did come in. Did you know John Wright, Mrs. Peters?

MRS. PETERS: Not to know him; I've seen him in town. They say he was a good man.

MRS. HALE: Yes—good; he didn't drink, and kept his word as well as most, I guess, and paid his debts. But he was a hard man, Mrs. Peters. Just to pass the time of day with him—[*Shivers.*] **Like a raw wind that gets to the bone.** [***Pauses, her eye falling on the cage.***] I should think she would 'a wanted a bird. But what do you suppose went with it?

MRS. PETERS: I don't know, unless it got sick and died.

[*She reaches over and **swings the broken door, swings it again,** both women watch it.*]

MRS. HALE: You weren't raised round here, were you? [*MRS. PETERS shakes her head.*] You didn't know—her?

MRS. PETERS: Not till they brought her yesterday.

MRS. HALE: She—come to think of it, she was kind of like a bird herself—real sweet and pretty, but kind of timid and—fluttery. How—she—did—change. [**Silence**; *then as if struck by a happy thought and relieved to get back to everyday things*] Tell you what, Mrs. Peters, why don't you take the quilt in with you? It might take up her mind.

MRS. PETERS: Why, I think that's a real nice idea, Mrs. Hale. There couldn't possibly be any objection to it, could there? Now, just what would I take? I wonder if her patches are in here—and her things.

[*They look in the sewing basket.*]

MRS. HALE: Here's some red. I expect this has got sewing things in it. [*Brings out a fancy box.*] What a pretty box. Looks like something somebody would give you. Maybe her scissors are in here. [*Opens box. Suddenly puts her hand to her nose.*] Why—[*MRS. PETERS bends nearer, then turns her face away.*] There's something wrapped up in this piece of silk.

MRS. PETERS: Why, this isn't her scissors.

MRS. HALE: [*Lifting the silk.*] Oh, Mrs. Peters—it's—[*MRS. PETERS bends closer.*]

MRS. PETERS: It's the bird.

MRS. HALE: [**Jumping up**.] But, Mrs. Peters—look at it! It's neck! Look at its neck! It's all—other side to.

MRS. PETERS: Somebody—wrung—its—neck.

[*Their eyes meet. A look of growing comprehension, of horror. Steps are heard outside. MRS. HALE slips box under quilt pieces, and sinks into her chair. Enter SHERIFF and COUNTY ATTORNEY. MRS. PETERS rises.*]

Activity 8 Focus on character building, silences, pauses, and momentum

1) What larger themes are introduced in this section?
2) What message is conveyed through pauses and/or moments of silence in this section?
3) How do the differing perspectives regarding Mrs Wright's actions contribute to characterisation?

Trifles by Susan Glaspell cont.

COUNTY ATTORNEY: [*As one turning from serious things to little pleasantries.*] Well ladies, have you decided whether she was going to quilt it or knot it?

MRS. PETERS: We think she was going to—knot it.

COUNTY ATTORNEY: Well, that's interesting, I'm sure. [*Seeing the birdcage.*] Has the bird flown?

MRS. HALE: [*Putting more quilt pieces over the box.*] We think the—cat got it.

COUNTY ATTORNEY: [*Preoccupied.*] Is there a cat?

[*MRS. HALE glances in a quick covert way at MRS. PETERS.*]

MRS. PETERS: Well, not now. They're superstitious, you know. They leave.

COUNTY ATTORNEY: [*To SHERIFF PETERS, continuing an interrupted conversation.*] No sign at all of anyone having come from the outside. Their own rope. Now let's go up again and go over it piece by piece. [*They start upstairs.*] It would have to have been someone who knew just the—

[*MRS. PETERS sits down.* **The two women sit there not looking at one another,** *but as if peering into something and at the same time holding back. When they talk now it is in the manner of feeling their way over strange ground,* **as if afraid of what they are saying***, but as if they cannot help saying it.*]

MRS. HALE: She liked the bird. She was going to bury it in that pretty box.

MRS. PETERS: [*In a whisper.*] When I was a girl—my kitten—there was a boy took a hatchet, and before my eyes—and before I could get there—[*Covers her face an instant.*] If they hadn't held me back I would have—[*Catches herself, looks upstairs where steps are heard, falters weakly.*]—hurt him.

MRS. HALE: [*With a slow look around her.*] I wonder how it would seem never to have had any children around. [*Pause.*] No, **Wright wouldn't like the bird—a thing that sang. She used to sing. He killed that, too.**

MRS. PETERS: [***Moving uneasily***.] We don't know who killed the bird.

MRS. HALE: I knew John Wright.

MRS. PETERS: It was an awful thing was done in this house that night, Mrs. Hale. Killing a man while he slept, slipping a rope around his neck that choked the life out of him.

MRS. HALE: His neck. Choked the life out of him.

[*Her hand goes out and rests on the birdcage.*]

MRS. PETERS: [**With rising voice**.] We don't know who killed him. We don't know.

MRS. HALE: [*Her own feeling not interrupted.*] If there'd been years and years of nothing, then a bird to sing to you, it would be awful—still, after the bird was still.

MRS. PETERS: [*Something within her speaking.*] **I know what stillness is.** When we homesteaded in Dakota, and my first baby died—after he was two years old, and me with no other then—

MRS. HALE: [*Moving.*] How soon do you suppose they'll be through, looking for the evidence?

MRS. PETERS: I know what stillness is. [**Pulling herself back**.] The law has got to punish crime, Mrs. Hale.

MRS. HALE: [*Not as if answering that.*] I wish you'd seen Minnie Foster when she wore a white dress with blue ribbons and stood up there in the choir and sang. [*A look around the room.*] Oh, I wish I'd come over here once in a while! **That was a crime! That was a crime! Who's going to punish that?**

MRS. PETERS: [*Looking upstairs.*] **We mustn't—take on.**

MRS. HALE: I might have known she needed help! I know how things can be—for women. I tell you, it's queer, Mrs. Peters. We live close together and we live far apart. We all go through the same things—it's all just a different kind of the same thing. [*Brushes her eyes, noticing the bottle of fruit, reaches out for it.*] If I was you, I wouldn't tell her her fruit was gone. Tell her it ain't. Tell her it's all right. Take this in to prove it to her. She—she may never know whether it was broke or not.

MRS. PETERS: [*Takes the bottle, looks about for something to wrap it in; takes petticoat from the clothes brought from the other room, very nervously begins winding this around the bottle.* **In a false voice.**] My, it's a good thing the men couldn't hear us. **Wouldn't they just laugh!** Getting all stirred up over a little thing like a—dead canary. As if that could have anything to do with—with—**wouldn't they laugh!**

[*The men are heard coming down stairs.*]

MRS. HALE: [*Under her breath.*] Maybe they would—maybe they wouldn't.

COUNTY ATTORNEY: No, Peters, it's all perfectly clear except a reason for doing it. But you know juries when it comes to women. If there was some definite thing. Something to show—something to make a story about—a thing that would connect up with this strange way of doing it—[*The women's eyes meet for an instant. Enter HALE from outer door.*]

HALE: Well, I've got the team around. Pretty cold out there.

COUNTY ATTORNEY: I'm going to stay here a while by myself [*To the SHERIFF.*] You can send Frank out for me, can't you? I want to go over everything. I'm not satisfied that we can't do better.

SHERIFF: Do you want to see what Mrs. Peters is going to take in?

[*The LAWYER goes to the table, picks up the apron, laughs.*]

COUNTY ATTORNEY: Oh, I guess they're not very dangerous things the ladies have picked out. [*Moves a few things about, disturbing the quilt pieces which cover the box. Steps back.*] No, Mrs. Peters doesn't need supervising. For that matter, a sheriff's wife is married to the law. Ever think of it that way, Mrs. Peters?

MRS. PETERS: Not—just that way.

SHERIFF: [*Chuckling.*] Married to the law. [*Moves toward the other room.*] I just want you to come in here a minute, George. We ought to take a look at these windows.

COUNTY ATTORNEY: [*Scoffingly.*] Oh, windows!

SHERIFF: We'll be right out, Mr. Hale.

[*HALE goes outside. The SHERIFF follows the COUNTY ATTORNEY into the other room. Then MRS. HALE rises, hands tight together, looking intensely at MRS. PETERS, whose eyes make a slow turn, finally meeting MRS. HALE's. A moment MRS. HALE holds her, then her own eyes point the way to where the box is concealed. Suddenly MRS. PETERS throws back quilt pieces and tries to put the box in the bag she is wearing. It is too big. She opens box, starts to take bird out, cannot touch it, goes to pieces, stands there helpless. Sound of a knob turning in the other room. MRS. HALE snatches the box and puts it in the pocket of her big coat. Enter COUNTY ATTORNEY and SHERIFF.*]

COUNTY ATTORNEY: [*Facetiously.*] Well, Henry, at least we found out that she was not going to quilt it. She was going to—what is it you call it, ladies?

MRS. HALE: [*Her hand against her pocket.*] We call it—knot it, Mr. Henderson.

CURTAIN

Activity 9 Focus on character and dialogue: momentum building and silence as 'speaking'

1) Which repeated actions or movements in the final scene have taken on symbolic meaning?
2) Which props have meaning beyond their literal function?
3) What are your final thoughts about the characters? Why does Mrs Peters lie to defend Mrs Wright? What changed her perspective?
4) Does Glaspell make use of specific dramatic strategies to create specific effects in the final scene? Consider how the dialogue between the two women changes in this scene. Do the stage directions contribute dramatically to what is not stated directly? Does character movement or positioning (blocking) add to the impact of the scene? Does 'silence' speak in this scene? When? What does it say?

Time and space considerations

For most of this section you've delved into Glaspell's play using the readers, writers, and texts area of exploration. This has given you the opportunity to practise your close-reading skills that are not only necessary for success in all IB Literature assessments, but also in decoding complex texts and situations. That said, shifting our lens for a brief moment to consider how the time and space area of exploration connects to Glaspell's play provides the opportunity to develop your knowledge even further.

Historical context

When she was a young woman, Susan Glaspell worked as a reporter for the *Des Moines Daily News* and wrote about the trial of Margaret Hossack, who was convicted of murdering her husband in his bed using an axe. Fifteen years later Glaspell wrote her one-act play, *Trifles*, and then rewrote the play one year later to be published in a magazine as a short story with a new title, *A Jury of Her Peers*. It's important to note that when Glaspell wrote *Trifles* and *A Jury of Her Peers* women did not have the right to vote nor could they serve as jurors. Indeed, professors of law and women's studies currently use Glaspell's literary texts to highlight issues of global significance, particularly regarding gender inequalities.

Collaborative comparisons – thematic, global, and Theory of Knowledge connections

1) In a small group, read the statements below regarding the Oscar-nominated short film based on Glaspell's work and construct a **global issue** from the ideas presented in one or both quotes:

Katharine T Bartlett, Professor at Duke University School of Law, called the 1980 film version of Glaspell's work, 'A gripping short drama that lays open some of the most basic differences between men's and women's lives, and the potential bearing of these differences on legal norms. A genuine classic.'

Andrea Friedman, of the History and Women's Studies department at Washington University says, 'How wonderful that [Glaspell's text] is again available… for provoking critical thought about gender and social institutions, as well as for exploring notions of women's voice, feminist perspective, and collective identity… From introduction to women's studies to feminist research methods, it never fails to get… students thinking in new ways about women, history, and justice.'

2) In terms of the text itself, consider the ethical implications of the crime. Who committed it? How do you know? To what extent is the crime justified? Is there ever a justification for murder?

3) Discuss how the assumptions regarding gender in this situation hinder *or* reveal knowledge. In other words, how do the men's and women's assumptions regarding gender frame their perspectives and lead them to an understanding of the crime. Which perspective is more accurate? Why?

4) Consider the topic of justice. What would be more just in this case, revealing the truth or keeping it hidden? Why? What does your discussion reveal about the connections between justice and truth?

Write notes from your discussion in your learner portfolio. Or, if such technology is available, you may want to work collaboratively on a shared document that you can copy and place in your portfolio for safekeeping.

Activity 10

Look up Patricia L Bryan and Thomas Wolf's prose non-fiction work, *Midnight Assassin* using the QR code.

What does this work imply about the connection between prose fiction and prose non-fiction? To what extent do literary works reflect and/or construct culture?

---

2) Time and space: an approach to Henrik Ibsen's *A Doll's House* (1879)

As we briefly touched on in *Trifles*, choosing the time and space lens to explore a text in any form considers the interaction between the text and the context in which it was produced and received. Nothing is created in a vacuum – and a play is no exception. Ibsen's time and place – its morality, its laws, and its social and cultural norms – inform the play he wrote and the play we experience.

For Ibsen's play that means researching secondary sources that can provide a fuller understanding of the primary text itself. Ibsen's **biography**, his economical and emotional foundations, both before and at the time of his writing, and the value systems of his culture and time period, may offer insights to both the characters and the situations on the stage.

To fully understand and offer insight and meaning to Ibsen's play, we must recognise that our modern perspective should be tempered through an appraisal of Ibsen's perspective as well as the perspective of his audience at that place and time. Ibsen admitted that is it natural for a 'reader [to] read his own feelings and sentiments' into a work of literature, but understanding the culture and context of a work provides us with knowledge and awareness that helps us establish our own interpretations with more depth and legitimacy.

A Doll's House, Ibsen's three-act 'well-made play', explores over a three-day period the changing dynamics between Nora and Torvald Helmer, their seriously ill, but devoted friend Dr Rank, and Mrs Linde, an old friend of Nora's, and Nils Krogstad, a former shamed associate of Torvald and blackmailer of Nora. In Act I, we watch as Nora vacillates between child and seductress, allowing Torvald free rein to dictate his desires, correcting and judging his wife as if she were a child. Nora believes that her husband's recent promotion will bode well for her with more expendable income, but Torvald clearly believes that money must be carefully managed, something he regards Nora as incapable of doing.

In Act I we see the entrance of Mrs Linde, clearly as a foil for Nora. She married not for love but for the financial advantages necessary to serve her elderly mother and children well. Now, with the death of that husband and mother, and her children raised, Kristine Linde wants to procure a job and has asked Nora to help her find work at Torvald's bank. Coincidentally, Nils Krogstag (Kristine's former love, who she rejected in marriage because he could not provide for her as well as Mr Linde could) appears.

Worried that Torvald might fire him for moral turpitude, Krogstag threatens Nora that he will divulge the nature of their financial relationship unless she helps him keep his job at the bank. He provided Nora with a loan several years ago so that she could pay for a vacation to Italy to save her husband whose health was suffering and who needed respite in a warmer climate. Nora forged her father's signature to obtain this loan from Krogstad who now threatens to use that information as blackmail – secure his job or pay the price. Nora puts him off, only to acknowledge to Kristine Linde that she has been paying Krogstad off over a period of time in installments and regrets none of her decisions. Act I ends with Torvald's condemnation of Krogstad as a forger, a morally depraved man who taints everyone who knows him, and so he will use his new position at the bank to fire him.

Act II opens with a worried Nora, who has taken Torvald's words concerning Krogstad's immorality and applied them to herself. She fears that she will be a corrupting influence on her children. Mrs Linde arrives and tells Nora to give up 'all this business' with Dr Rank, who she believes is the source of Nora's loan. Nora reassures her that he was not the source, but asks her friend to wait in another room when she sees Torvald returning. Nora continues to plead her case for Krogstad which infuriates her husband, who reveals that he intends to give the job to Mrs Linde. Nora frantically begs Torvald not to fire Krogstad, but Torvald dismisses her and heads off to his study. Dr Rank then arrives, and alludes to his rapidly degenerating health, implying that recent tests may reveal that he is not long for this world. Nora does not take his words seriously and instead begins to ask his advice about Torvald. At this point, Dr Rank sees opening to declare his love for her. Nora, shocked and uncomfortable with his declaration, ushers Dr Rank into Torvald's study.

Krogstad arrives, furious that he has received notice from the bank, and turns his fury on Nora, threatening to expose her crime (forgery) to Torvald unless Torvald creates a new position for him as his right-hand man. Nora defiantly tells him that will never happen.

Krogstad then leaves, stops at the letterbox, and deposits a letter. Kristine Linde re-enters to a frantic Nora who is rambling on about her sanity, her responsibility, and her belief that a miracle will occur. Kristine leaves to find Krogstad deciding that he will ask for the letter back before Torvald reads it.

Nora, with Dr Rank and Torvald watching her closely, decides that she needs them to help her practise the dance that she will perform the next evening at a party upstairs. She is terrified that her husband will go to the letterbox as was his custom at this time of day. She orders Dr Rank to play the piano while she practises, dancing frenetically around the room. Torvald watches in amazement then stops her, chastising Nora, telling her that she has forgotten everything he taught her about the dance – the tarantella – and that he will help his helpless little bird prepare herself.

Act III begins the following evening in the Helmer's apartment with the sound of dance music coming from upstairs. Mrs Linde and Krogstad talk about their former relationship and Kristine shocks Nils by declaring that they need each other and that she is willing to marry him and be a mother to his motherless children. The tarantella music begins, and Kristine's urging that everything must come out – that Torvald must know everything – drives Krogstad to leave. When the Helmers return downstairs from the party, Kristine whispers to Nora that everything must come out. Alone, Torvald claims that Nora is his most treasured possession and that he was filled with desire as he watched her dance. Nora rebuffs his advances and a knock on the door shifts their conversation. Dr Rank appears saying that he will be invisible at the next party, and then leaves.

Torvald checks the letterbox and finds two visiting cards from Dr Rank – one with a black cross that Torvald believes is an announcement of his death. Once again, Torvald turns his attention to Nora, embracing her and bidding her goodnight as he takes his other letters into his office to read. Torvald returns in full fury, Krogstad's letter in hand, and attacks Nora as a stupid, immoral woman who will no longer be able to care for her children since her influence on them would be corrupting. He rants and raves, condemning her and blaming her for jeopardising his whole future and happiness. The maid then enters with a note for Nora from Krogstad which Torvald reads with absolute joy as he is now 'saved' because Krogstad has returned Nora's IOU. Nora now takes control of the stage and their conversation. She asserts that she will leave him, that her first duty is to herself, and that she does not love him anymore. She returns his ring and takes back her own, saying that she does not believe in miracles anymore and that it would take a miracle for them to once again live as husband and wife. The final slamming of a door is Nora's final word.

Consider these observations by established critics of Ibsen's work

Michael Meyer, author of an outstanding biography, *Henrik Ibsen*, said that *A Doll's House* is not so much about women's rights as about the 'need of every individual to find out the kind of person he or she really is, and to strive to become that person'.

George Bernard Shaw stated in *The Quintessence of Ibsenism* that Ibsen's play is a reaction against preferred theatrical conventions including those of the Greek dramatists and Shakespeare. While we may understand and even identify with their characters and their motivations – jealousy, despair, self-hatred, revenge, pride, and arrogance, for example – we do not identify with the uncommon situations that prompt their motivations.

Consider Ibsen's observations

From his *Notes for the Tragedy of Modern Times* (19 October 1878) taken from the University Library, Oslo:

'There are two kinds of moral law, two kinds of conscience, one in man and a completely different one in woman. They do not understand each other; but in matters of practical living the woman is judged by man's law, as if she were not a woman but a man.'

'A woman cannot be herself in contemporary society, it is an exclusively male society with laws drafted by men, and with counsel and judges who judge feminine conduct from the male point of view.'

Ibsen's speech at the banquet of the Norwegian League for Women's Rights in Christiana, Oslo on 26 May 1898 (Ibsen and his wife were invited to the banquet given by the leading Norwegian feminist society):

'I am not a member of the Women's Rights League. Whatever I have written has been without any conscious thought of making propaganda. I have been more the poet and less the social philosopher than people generally seem inclined to believe. I thank you for the toast, but must disclaim the honor of having consciously worked for the

TOK

Do you agree with Ibsen's contention that because men and women embody 'two kinds of conscience' then 'there are two kinds of moral law'? Are men and women wired differently? And if so, should this have any bearing on morality?

What does Ibsen mean when he says 'the woman is judged by man's law'? What observations is he making about power structures in his society? To what extent is this argument a current-day global issue? Use examples to support your position.

women's rights movement. I am not even quite clear as to just what this women's rights movement really is. To me it has seemed a problem of mankind in general. And if you read my books carefully you will understand this. True enough, it is desirable to solve the woman problem, along with all the others; but that has not been the whole purpose. My task has been the description of humanity. To be sure, whenever such a description is felt to be reasonably true, the reader will read his own feelings and sentiments into the work of the poet. These are then attributed to the poet; but incorrectly so. Every reader remolds the work beautifully and neatly, each according to his own personality. Not only those who write but also those who read are poets. They are collaborators. They are often more poetical than the poet himself.'

Questions to consider

1) What is the significance of Ibsen using the word 'propaganda' in connection with women's rights issues?

2) Ibsen seems to separate the mission of the poet from the mission of the social philosopher (an individual who studies social behaviour and its moral and **cultural** implications). What does this reveal about his values, his intentions? Do you agree that these are two distinct roles? Why or why not?

3) What does Ibsen recognise about the connection between readers, writers, and texts? To what extent do you agree with his statements?

Reception details

Works written in Germany at this time were not copyrighted, and so theatres could stage and freely adapt Ibsen's works without his consent. When Ibsen heard that a German director was going to change the ending to a happy one, he decided that it would be better if he rewrote the ending himself. He called this ending 'a barbaric outrage'.

Ibsen's 'barbaric' happy ending

NORA: Where we could make a real marriage out of our lives together. Goodbye. [*Begins to go*.]

HELMER: Go then! [*Seizes her arm*.] But first you shall see your children for the last time!

NORA: Let me go! I will not see them! I cannot!

HELMER: [*Draws her over to the door, left*.] You shall see them. [*Opens the door and says softly*] Look, there they are asleep, peaceful and carefree. Tomorrow, when they wake up and call for their mother, they will be—motherless.

NORA: [*Trembling*.] Motherless...

HELMER: As you once were.

NORA: Motherless! [*Struggles with herself, lets her travelling bag fall, and says*] Oh, this is a sin against myself, but I cannot leave them. [*Half sinks down by the door*.]

HELMER [*Joyfully, but softly*.] Nora!

[*The curtain falls*.]

Activity 11

Compare and contrast the two endings of the play – the original and the 'happy' ending. What do the differing perspectives suggest?

Activity 12

Read the first act of *A Doll's House* by Ibsen. Observe the **cultural** context in the following scenes from Act I.

1) The opening scene between Nora and Torvald before guests arrive.
2) The scene between Nora and Mrs Linde.
3) The scene between Dr Rank, Nora, and Mrs Linde.
4) The scene between Torvald, Nora, and Mrs Linde.
5) The scene between Nora and Krogstad.
6) The scene between Nora and Torvald.

In a small group, review the scenes above and discuss them in reference to the following questions:

- What do we learn about what is valued in late 19th-century Norway?
- What do we learn about gender interactions?
- What do we learn about family structure, class, and work?

Activity 13 Group work and portfolio entries for Act I

Connecting characters to themes and dramatic conventions

1) Determine how Ibsen uses parallel characters – dramatic foils – such as Nora and Mrs Linde (power through submission/power through assertion) to create larger themes:
   a. Nora as Krogstad's 'shadow' (Torvald's comments about Krogstad are felt by Nora – the accusations and judgement of character and morality).
   b. Nora and Dr Rank (both sense impending doom and both believe that doom was not of their own making).
2) Select one of the following characters (Nils Krogstad, Nora Helmer, Torvald Helmer, Mrs Linde, or Dr Rank) and determine how that character:
   a. moves in relation to other characters; exits and enters on stage/in or out of rooms or the house; moves in relation to objects on the stage (the sofa, stove, letterbox)
   b. uses small gestures that imply attitudes (Nora often has her back to Torvald; Torvald knows that Nora is home, but doesn't come out of his office immediately to greet her).
   c. What does your character say that is self-revealing? Does your character use a tone of voice or style of speech differently with other characters?
   d. Do your observations about your character lead to revealing observations of another character?
   e. What conclusions can you draw about the motivation(s) behind your character's actions or lack of actions?

3) Intertextuality/connecting texts: an approach to August Strindberg's *The Father* (1887) translated by Michael Robinson

Choosing intertextuality as a lens allows you to focus on the connections between and among diverse literary texts, forms, traditions, creators, and ideas. One such play, Strindberg's *The Father*, has rich connections to Greek tragedy, Shakespearean tragedy, Ibsen, and Darwin. Direct and indirect **allusions** are one form of intertextuality which we will explore in this chapter. (We will also approach this area of exploration by analysing the three texts in this chapter in relation to each other.)

The plot of this tragedy revolves around the growing argument of where Bertha, the only daughter of Adolph and Laura, is to receive her education. Bertha's father, Captain Adolph, a military man/scientist, believes that it is his right to determine her education; he wants her to move into the town and study to be a teacher so that she can always support herself. Her mother, Laura, believes that she knows what is best for her daughter; she wants to keep her daughter at home where Bertha can pursue her gifts as an artist. The law of the time supports the captain's position. Married women have no rights – they sell their rights in agreeing to marry. The desperation that Laura feels prompts this battle of wills that ends tragically for the captain, the father.

The Father by August Strindberg (1887) translated by Michael Robinson

[*The PASTOR (Laura's brother) enters, takes a chair, and joins LAURA by the secretaire.*]

PASTOR: Good evening, Laura. I suppose you know I've been away all day; I've only just got back. This is a bad business.

LAURA: Indeed it is – the worst night and day I've ever been through.

PASTOR: Well, I see no harm has come to you, at all events.

LAURA: No, thank God, but just think what could have happened.

PASTOR: Tell me one thing, though, what started it? I've heard such different stories.

LAURA: It started with some wild fantasy about him not being Bertha's father, and ended with his throwing a burning lamp in my face.

PASTOR: But this is terrible! This is insanity, pure and simple. What's to be done now?

LAURA: We must try to prevent any further outbreaks. The Doctor's sent to the hospital for a straightjacket. In the meantime I've informed the Colonel and am now trying to make sense of our financial situation, which he's mismanaged in the most reprehensible way.

PASTOR: What a wretched business! But then I've always expected something of the kind. Fire and water – why, there's bound to be an explosion. What's all that in the drawer there?

LAURA [has pulled a drawer out of the desk]: Look what he's kept hidden away.

PASTOR: Oh, my God! That's your doll; and there's your christening cap; and Bertha's rattle; and your love letters; and your locket… [drying his eyes]. He must have loved you very much, Laura, all the same. I've never kept anything like that!

LAURA: I think he did love me once, but time – time changes so many things.

PASTOR: What's that paper there – the big one? – Why it's the deed to a grave! – Well, better a grave than the asylum! Laura! Tell me: are you quite blameless in all of this?

LAURA: Me? How am I to blame if a man goes mad?

PASTOR: Well, well! I shan't say anything. After all, blood is thicker than water!

LAURA: What do you mean by that?

PASTOR [looks her in the eye]: Listen!

LAURA: What?

PASTOR: Just listen to me! You can't deny all this fits in very nicely with your wanting to bring up your own child yourself.

LAURA: I don't understand.

PASTOR: I really can't help admiring you!

LAURA: Me? Hm!

PASTOR: And I shall be that freethinker's guardian! You know, I've always regarded him as a tare among our wheat.*

LAURA [with a brief, suppressed laugh; then quickly serious]: And you dare say this to me, his wife?

PASTOR: My God, you're strong, Laura! Unbelievably strong! Like a fox in a trap; you'd rather bite off your own leg than allow yourself to be caught! – Like a master thief: no accomplice, not even your own conscience. – Look in the mirror! You don't dare!

LAURA: I never use a mirror!

PASTOR: No, you daren't! – Let me see your hand! – Not one spot of blood* to give you away, not a trace of that insidious poison! An innocent little murder that the law can't touch; an unconscious crime – unconscious? What a marvelous idea! – Listen to him working away up there, though! – Just you watch out! If that man gets out, he'll saw you in two!

LAURA: You talk too much, as if you had a bad conscience. – Accuse me, if you can!

PASTOR: I can't!

LAURA: You see! You can't, and so – I'm innocent! – Now you take care of your ward, and I'll look after mine! – Here's the Doctor!

Activity 16 Intertextuality, ethics, and global issues

Each of the texts that we have studied in this chapter brings forth moral dilemmas that involve crimes and punishments. In *Trifles*, Mrs Wright is accused of murdering her husband; in *A Doll's House*, Nora forges her father's signature to illegally obtain funds in order to save her husband's life; and in *The Father*, Laura has managed to convince everyone that the captain has gone mad, thus relinquishing his rights to control her, their daughter, and their finances.

1) Discuss the various crimes in each of the texts and their punishments. To what extent are any of these crimes defendable? What punishments, if any, are warranted? Explain your rationale.
2) *Trifles*, *A Doll's House*, and *The Father* all connect to politics, power, and justice, one of the fields of inquiry that the IB Literature Guide suggests for the study of global issues.
    a. Discuss the following global issue in a small group: How does corruption function in any one of these works as a barrier to gender equality?
    b. As a group, discuss and select a specific passage from a text of your choice (other than drama) that you have already studied which illustrates this global issue.
    c. Present the issue to the class by acting out the passage and briefly explaining your rationale for your choice. Note: since the work you have selected is a different form, discuss how you will transform the lines in that work so that they can be acted out. In other words, how can you turn poetry or prose into a dramatic form? Which words will need to be put into dialogue? Which gestures will be visually presented but not spoken? How will you make use of props?
    d. Reflection: this activity asked you to work in a group, discuss, transform one form of text into another, and then perform it. Write a reflection in your learner portfolio in which you respond to one or more of the following questions: What is the value of considering the same global issue in texts from different forms? How does acting out a 'scene' help clarify the issue? What was the most valuable aspect of this exercise?

Activity 17 Considering style and audience

The way an audience reacts to a play is dependent on many aspects of theatre, but the staging choices that a playwright makes are certainly key. Consider George Bernard Shaw's comment about *A Doll's House*: 'Shakespeare had put ourselves on the stage but rarely our situations. Our uncles seldom murder our fathers and… marry our mothers. . . Ibsen. . . gives us not only ourselves, but ourselves in our own situations. The things that happen on his stage happen to us'.

While Glaspell, Ibsen, and Strindberg all provide detailed staging and scene descriptions, how we feel about individual characters varies substantially. Think back to the way each play in this chapter is represented. How does such representation affect how we feel about the characters and their situations? In order to answer this question you will need to do some close reading to make a chart that shows both similarities and differences in the presentation of characters, the movement of characters on and off the stage, and the function of silence and dialogue to reveal characters.

Select two plays that you feel show some interesting similarities and/or differences for this learner portfolio activity.

Nigerian writer Chimamanda Ngozi Adichie, New York, 2019.

Activity 18 More intertextual connections

In this activity you will listen to Chimamanda Ngozi Adichie's TED Talk, 'We Should all be Feminists', using the QR code, and apply it to your reading of *Trifles*, *A Doll's House*, and *The Father*.

Adichie's talk, which is based on her book of the same name, addresses the global issue of gender oppression in worldwide and local contexts. After you listen to the talk, consider the following:

1) According the Adichie, 'the problem with gender is that it prescribes how we should be rather than recognising how we are'. To what extent can this claim be applied to Nora from *A Doll's House*?
2) When Adichie considers history, it makes sense that men had occupied the top rung of the hierarchy because survival was dependent on physical strength. But now, '[t]he person more likely to lead is not the physically stronger person; it is the more creative person, the more intelligent person, the more innovative person, and there are no hormones for those attributes. A man is as likely as a woman to be intelligent, to be creative, to be innovative. We have evolved; but it seems to me that our ideas of gender had not evolved'. How do the women in *Trifles* exhibit this intelligence, creativity, and innovation? And to what extent do the men in the play demonstrate that their 'ideas of gender have not evolved'?
3) Adichie admits that '[g]ender is not an easy conversation to have. For both men and women, to bring up gender is sometimes to encounter almost immediate resistance.' And yet, she remains hopeful. 'Now imagine how much happier we would be,' Adichie says, 'how much freer to be our true individual selves, if we didn't have the weight of gender expectations.' Consider the three plays in this chapter in relation to this statement. To what extent have women in these plays been restricted from becoming their 'true individual selves' due to 'the weight of gender expectations'? What is the effect of this global issue within and between the texts?

Insights into drama

1. In stage directions, playwrights can establish full or partial descriptions of characters and state the way that actors should deliver specific lines. In addition, descriptions of costumes, facial expressions, and gestures enable a reader to have a clearer visual picture of the characters on stage. As a reader, you will have to imagine the tone of voice of a character with the help of specific stage directions.

2. While playwrights make use of **monologues**, soliloquies, and asides, the primary vehicle of expression on stage is dialogue. Pay attention to those moments when one character dominates the stage. Is that domination a result of the frequency of his or her speech or something else? Does the use of questioning have a significant function? Does the use of questioning establish tension? Is there a power struggle between one or more characters?

3. Reading and viewing a play are two very different experiences. Plays can be performed in all sorts of venues or even made into film versions. It's important to be aware of how your interpretation shifts according to the type of drama medium you experience.

4. Themes can emerge directly or indirectly. Characters can serve as the mouthpiece of the playwright. Without biographical insights, however, **denoting** a character as a mouthpiece is purely speculative. Remember, too, that themes develop and build as the play unfolds.

5. Irony, particularly dramatic irony, has a powerful function in drama. As a reader you must also be sensitive to those characters who use sarcasm or speak in asides.

6. Stage props can have symbolic value. While some symbols are traditional – darkness as a symbol of hopelessness, a cross as a symbol of Christianity, water as a symbol of rebirth, light as a symbol of insight or understanding – other symbols are particular to a text. Symbolic value is only established with the frequency and significance of use within the dramatic action of the play.

7. The events of the play and the ordering of those events determine the plot. Be aware that subplots often function in comparison or contrast to the main plot for purposes of character or thematic development.

8. The design of the stage set and the use of lighting and sound effects are all functional elements of the drama. Changes to the set in scene changes, the use of lighting or sound effects (including music) must be noted. The decision of the playwright to include these elements at a particular moment in the dramatic action is important. What effects are produced in the audience? How do these effects impact meaning or understanding?

Approaches to learning in poetry

1.3

When you read poetry, you are using your imagination, your senses, your intelligence, and your emotions. Poets **communicate** ideas through distilled, powerful language. Every word, every line, every space is purposeful. And this holds true for both 17th-century sonnet writers and modern-day rap lyricists whose intricate rhyming patterns can bring issues of social justice to light. The **approaches to learning**, which encourage us to communicate, think, **collaborate**, organise, and research, will be especially helpful as we study this multidimensional form.

Given the fluid nature of poetry, we have integrated our study of **areas of exploration** and **course concepts** with explanations of poetic conventions. Poetry lives and breathes both on and off the page, so from the beginning of the chapter you'll have the opportunity to study poetry through deep **inquiry**, collaborate with others through spoken word performances, and discuss **global issues** in various contexts. After you have become more familiar with poetic conventions, we will delve into each of the three areas of exploration in greater detail. We will conclude the chapter with **transformative** poetry exercises that will enable you to appreciate the form and prepare for assessments by fostering your **creative** writing and thinking skills. Enjoy the ride. Poetry can be inspirational, sometimes quirky, and often fun.

Activity 1 Definitions of poetry

There is no one set definition of poetry. Consider the quotes below about poetry.

- 'Poetry is the lifeblood of rebellion, revolution, and the raising of consciousness.' (Alice Walker)
- 'Yet, it is true, poetry is delicious; the best prose is that which is most full of poetry.' (Virginia Woolf)

- 'Poetry aims for an economy of truth – loose and useless words must be discarded, and I found that these loose and useless words were not separate from loose and useless thoughts.' (Ta-Nehisi Coates)
- 'Pure mathematics is, in its way, the poetry of logical ideas.' (Albert Einstein)
- 'Hip-hop is about the brilliance of pavement poetry.' (Michael Eric Dyson)
- 'Literature is a state of culture, poetry is a state of grace, before and after culture.' (Juan Ramon Jimenez)

Which definition most appeals to you? Why? Can you attribute a particular quote to a poem or song lyrics? What is your own definition of poetry?

Write down your responses to this exercise in your learner portfolio and share your thoughts with a partner or small group.

Poetry, like other literary forms, has its own particular set of conventions which set it apart. Your ability to recognise these conventions in any given poem is important, but you should not equate recognition with analysis. While you need to be able to observe a poet's use of specific conventions within a poem, analysis requires that you draw inferences about the effects that these textual features and/or authorial choices create. Through all three areas of exploration – **readers, writers, and texts**, **time and space**, and **intertextuality** – your observations will lead you to understand the effect of the poet's choices.

Like other works of art, poetry often evokes an emotional response. This is not simply because of the long history of love poems that have changed hands over the centuries. Poetry's compression, its ability to transform language into miniature worlds of sentiment, allows readers to uncover meanings that often remain hidden in other forms.

TOK

Consider Italian writer, literary critic, and philosopher, Umberto Eco's comment on the connection between poetry, emotion, and language: 'Poetry is not a matter of feelings, it is a matter of language. It is language which creates feelings.'

To what degree might each literary form be seen as having its own language? How do poems communicate feelings differently than novels, essays, or plays?

A closer look at textual features and authorial choices

Since poetry is written to be read aloud, sound is neither secondary nor incidental to meaning. Every poem has a sound all of its own – think of it as a kind of auditory 'fingerprint'. Pauses, **rhythms**, and rhymes all contribute to the sounds that words make when you read a poem aloud. Acoustical elements are even more deliberate in poetry written specifically for performance, such as poetic song lyrics and spoken word poetry. This poetry has an oral, musical nature often coupled with messages that tap into modern-day global issues, as you will see later in the chapter.

Apart from sound, however, what makes poetry, poetry? The appearance of poetry on the page – its physical arrangement, coupled with variations in rhyme and **metre** – reveals that this often compressed, creative form is not fixed. Its multiple **representations** evolve over time and space, and even vary between poems from the same period.

Poetry is perhaps the most transformative of all the literary forms.

Activity 2 Representation

1) Examine the spatial layout of the following poems. What do you *see* that is different in the visual representation of each?
2) Then, read them aloud, or in the case of Sarah Kay's poem, listen and watch as it is performed for you. What do you *hear* that makes one poem different from another?

'London' by William Blake (1794)

I wander through each chartered street,
Near where the chartered Thames does flow,
And mark in every face I meet
Marks of weakness, marks of woe.

In every cry of every man,
In every Infant's cry of fear,
In every voice, in every ban,
The mind-forged manacles I hear.

How the Chimney-sweeper's cry
Every black'ning Church appalls;
And the hapless Soldier's sigh
Runs in blood down Palace walls.

But most through midnight streets I hear
How the youthful Harlot's curse
Blasts the new-born Infant's tear,
And blights with plagues the Marriage hearse.

'We Wear the Mask' by Paul Laurence Dunbar (1896)

We wear the mask that grins and lies,
It hides our cheeks and shades our eyes,–
This debt we pay to human guile;
With torn and bleeding hearts we smile,
And mouth with myriad subtleties.

Why should the world be over-wise,
In counting all our tears and sighs?
Nay, let them only see us, while
        We wear the mask.

We smile, but, O great Christ, our cries
To thee from tortured souls arise.
We sing, but oh the clay is vile
Beneath our feet, and long the mile;
But let the world dream otherwise,
        We wear the mask!

'Requiem' by Bei Dao (2000)

(Translated from Chinese by Eliot Weinberger for Shanshan)

The wave of that year
flooded the sands on the mirror
to be lost is a kind of leaving
and the meaning of leaving
the instant when all languages
are like shadows cast from the west

life's only a promise
don't grieve for it
before the garden was destroyed
we had too much time
debating the implications of a bird flying
as we knocked down midnight's door

alone like a match polished into light
when childhood's tunnel
led to a vein of dubious ore
to be lost is a kind of leaving
and poetry rectifying life
rectifies poetry's echo

Using the QR code, watch Sarah Kay's spoken word poem, 'Hiroshima', which is embedded in her 2011 TED Talk, 'If I Should Have a Daughter'. The poem begins at 15:00.

The transcript of the poem is printed below, but the visual and acoustical effects are meant to be experienced through watching its performance.

'Hiroshima' by Sarah Kay

When they bombed Hiroshima, the explosion formed a mini-supernova, so every living animal, human or plant that received direct contact with the rays from that sun was instantly turned to ash. And what was left of the city soon followed. The long-lasting damage of nuclear radiation caused an entire city and its population to turn into powder. When I was born, my mom says I looked around the whole hospital room with a stare that said, 'This? I've done this before.' She says I have old eyes. When my Grandpa Genji died, I was only five years old, but I took my mom by the hand and told her, 'Don't worry, he'll come back as a baby.' And yet, for someone who has apparently done this already, I still haven't figured anything out yet. My knees still buckle every time I get on a stage. My self-confidence can be measured out in teaspoons mixed into my poetry, and it still always tastes funny in my mouth. But in Hiroshima, some people were wiped clean away, leaving only a wristwatch or a diary page. So no matter that I have inhibitions to fill all my pockets, I keep trying, hoping that one day I'll write a poem I can be proud to let sit in a museum exhibit as the only proof I existed. My parents named me Sarah, which is a biblical name. In the original story, God told Sarah she could do something impossible, and — she laughed, because the first Sarah, she didn't know what to do with impossible. And me? Well, neither do I, but I see the impossible every day. Impossible is trying to connect in this world, trying to hold onto others while things are blowing up around you, knowing that while you're speaking, they aren't just waiting for their turn to talk — they hear you. They feel exactly what you feel at the same time that you feel it. It's what I strive for every time I open my mouth — that impossible connection. There's this piece of wall in Hiroshima that was completely burnt black by the radiation. But on the front step, a person who was sitting there blocked the rays from hitting the stone. The only thing left now is a permanent shadow of positive light. After the A-bomb, specialists said it would take 75 years for the radiation-damaged soil of Hiroshima City to ever grow anything again. But that spring, there were new buds popping up from the earth. When I meet you, in that moment, I'm no longer a part of your future. I start quickly becoming part of your past. But in that instant, I get to share your present. And you, you get to share mine. And that is the greatest present of all. So if you tell me I can do the impossible — I'll probably laugh at you. I don't know if I can change the world yet, because I don't know that much about it — and I don't know that much about reincarnation either, but if you make me laugh hard enough, sometimes I forget what century I'm in. This isn't my first time here. This isn't my last time here. These aren't the last words I'll share. But just in case, I'm trying my hardest to get it right this time around.

American poet, Sarah Kay, is the founder and co-director of Project V.O.I.C.E., a group devoted to using the spoken word as a creative medium.

3) In examining each of these poems (of which one is meant to be performed), visual shape and sound are widely divergent. What accounts for the differences in these poems? And is there anything that we can say is a common feature of poetry?

Time and space

In some cases, it is helpful, or perhaps even necessary, to have knowledge of a time, place, or allusion to a literary or historical event when analysing a poem. This background information often helps convey a more accurate representation of truth, or carries a specific emotional meaning.

Activity 3 Considering context through course concepts

Look up some contextual information about each poem from Activity 2.

1) 'London': What is a chimney sweeper? What were the living conditions like for chimney sweepers in London during the late 18th century? How might this information affect your emotional response to the poem?
2) 'We Wear the Mask': Dunbar's poem is regarded as a presentation of the double nature of African-American experience in 1893 in the USA. What are the two **perspectives** that the poem addresses?
3) 'Requiem': What is the meaning of the word 'requiem'? Research the 4 June 1989 incident that occurred in Tiananmen Square in Beijing in response to student-led protests. How did your research contribute to your understanding of the writer's **culture** and perspective?
4) 'Hiroshima': Research Sarah Kay's lineage. How might knowledge of her background help you better understand how the concepts of **identity** and culture influence her poem?

Info box

For more detailed information about how fields of inquiry can help you develop a global issue, see pages 247–51 of the Individual oral chapter.

Global issues

Each of the poems above taps into global issues that cross several fields of inquiry including: culture, identity, and community; politics, power, and justice; and science, technology, and the environment. Work in small groups and discuss a global issue that emerges from any one of the poems.

Regardless of how you may define it, poetry, just like other literary forms, has a particular set of strategies, or conventions, which poets use to create meaning from experience. Poems are usually shorter than other forms of the literary imagination. The language of poetry is much more concentrated than the language of fiction, non-fiction, or drama. In poetry, experience is distilled into fewer words, and so those words must have more impact, more dimension, more potency.

Remember these points as you approach any poem for the first time.

- The subject matter of poetry is no different to any other form of literature. If a human being can have an experience, that experience can serve as the subject of a poem.

- Experiences translate into feelings. Some poets explore or confront feelings, rationalise feelings, or intellectualise feelings, but poetry is a vehicle for conveying emotion, either directly or indirectly.

- Think about the title and determine if it references the situation or the speaker, either directly or indirectly.

- In order to experience a poem you must be willing to experience the form. Read the poem aloud, if possible, several times. Read strictly according to the syntax (sentence structure). Let the punctuation of the poem determine your pauses and stops. The end of a line does not automatically signal a stop unless there is a full stop.

- If you don't know the meaning of a word, stop and look it up. Every word in a poem has been carefully chosen for a reason, so you need to understand them all.

- Think about the speaker of the poem and also about the situation that the speaker is referring to. What do you know about each?

Types of poetry: lyric, narrative, and dramatic

Narrative poems tell stories, and so, like fiction, contain plot, setting, characters, and point of view. The longest of these narrative poems, such as *The Odyssey* or *Beowulf*, are called **epics**. Shorter, highly rhythmic narratives often have repeated lines, like a refrain in a song, such as Edgar Allen Poe's 'The Raven'.

Dramatic poems have an invented speaker, or **persona**, who speaks in a dramatic **monologue** as a **soliloquy** or in a scene from a play. This type of poetry involves a highly emotive account that is composed in verse and meant to be recited. Robert Browning popularised this form in the 19th century with poems such as 'My Last Duchess' and 'Porphyria's Lover'.

Lyric poems were originally composed to be sung or chanted. Today, lyric poems are the largest group and include a highly personal, subjective, melodic reflection about ideas, abstractions, a person, or a place. **Odes** and **elegies** are considered specific types of lyric poems. An elegy is written on the occasion of someone's death, and an ode is typically a longer lyric which uses elevated language to describe a serious, often abstract, subject. John Milton's 'Lycidas' and Jorge Manrique's 'Coplas por la muerte de su padre (Couplets on the Death of his Father)' are well-known elegies.

Music lyrics can also be classified as poetry. The expanding definition of poetry now includes both classical and modern music verses. If you listen to music often, you may already know that it is a powerful medium with widespread appeal. Familiarising yourself with how to approach music **lyrics** as poetry will not only serve you well for IB literature assessments but will also enable you to recognise music lyrics as a creative and vital literary force that both represents and transforms culture.

Time and space considerations

Bob Dylan's lyrics are often formally analysed against the backdrop of global issues such as war, social justice, death, and religion. His infamous song, 'Blowin' in the Wind' captured the struggle between peace, war, and freedom during the 1960s American civil rights movement. The song has been recorded by hundreds of artists, and Dylan himself sang the anthem in the spring of 1963 during a voter registration demonstration in Greenwood, Mississippi, USA. When the famous folk trio, Peter, Paul and Mary,

July 1963: Bob Dylan singing at a civil rights gathering in Greenwood, Mississippi.

performed the lyrics at the Lincoln Memorial in Washington, DC, just hours before Martin Luther King delivered his infamous 'I have a dream' speech in the summer of 1963, the song quickly gained popularity as an anthem of the civil rights movement.

Professor Richard F Thomas, classics professor and author of *Why Bob Dylan Matters,* has been teaching a course on Bob Dylan at Harvard University since 2004. For Thomas, who lived in New Zealand in the 1960s, the human rights issues in 'Blowin' in the Wind' reached across the globe, beyond the American civil rights movement. On a personal level, Thomas participated in HART (Halt All Racist Tours), a student organisation that protested against the New Zealand rugby tours of South African apartheid. Indeed, Dylan's words, 'Yes, 'n' how many times can a man turn his head / Pretending he just doesn't see?' apply to multiple instances of social injustice.

TOK

Search the internet and find two different versions of Dylan's song being performed. To what extent do the different deliveries of the song affect your perception of its overall meaning? How do the acoustics of the song, its musical quality, coupled with the performance you viewed, affect your interpretation of it? What does this activity reveal about music lyrics as a literary form?

Activity 4 Why Dylan matters

1) Briefly research the background of the American civil rights movement so that you will better understand the context of Dylan's song when you read his lyrics.
2) Through an online source find the lyrics to Bob Dylan's iconic song, 'Blowin' in the Wind'.
3) Read the lyrics aloud (without music) and discuss in a small group how his lyrics speak to your own culture and context.
4) Write down some universal themes that Dylan's lyrics convey.
5) After briefly discussing one of these themes with your group, look more closely at the author's literary choices and consider the significance of the three sets of questions followed by the repeated responding couplet in the lyrics. How might these textual features help develop the theme your group discussed?
6) Record your responses in your learner portfolio.

Intertextual links between artists

Most of us experience music lyrics through listening. In this course, you are also encouraged to pay attention to the words themselves and how they function as poetry. Years before Bob Dylan won the 2016 Nobel Prize for Literature, a Wisconsin-based artist named Skye heightened this textual focus and began creating a large-scale

installation titled 'Shakespeare's in the Alley: A Tribute to Bob Dylan'. The text-based art exhibit features some of Dylan's most cherished songs reproduced on large fabric banners that hang from ceilings, enabling patrons to admire Dylan's work as they walk through a forest his of lyrics.

Interestingly, the title of the exhibit comes from a line in one of Dylan's songs, 'Stuck Inside of Mobile with the Memphis Blues Again'. The intertextual reference not only provides an authentic link to Dylan's own work, but also recognises him as a modern-day bard.

Skye calls her own exhibit 'a sanctuary of sorts, a place to be inspired by words and rhyme', where visitors can be 'immersed in an environment, perhaps moved to search out the music of a particular song lyric or write [their] own song or poem. The work is both historical and contemporary, abstract and literal. Enlarging words changes the effect of them. It is not the same to read the lyrics in a book as it is to read them on a 27-foot-long panel.'

Activity 5

Discuss the following questions with a small group and record your responses in your learner portfolio.

1) Consider Skye's comments about how enlarging words changes their effect. How can walking through a literal forest of words alter a perception of a work? What might be the advantage of viewing the work from this altered perspective?

2) Should the transformed work be considered an original work by the new artist? Why or why not? Consider how other artists borrow in this way (think of mash-ups where writers use lyrics from other, often older, musicians to create a new song). What does such remixing or borrowing reveal about how works are viewed over time?

3) More on time and space… In titling the exhibit 'Shakespeare's in the Alley. . .' Skye deliberately aligns Dylan with a classical artist whose works are still read centuries after his death. Do you think Dylan's lyrics will hold the same recognition centuries from now? Why or why not?

Structure and language

A word about translation

The process of translation is transformative. Translated poems are not identical to each other, nor are they replicas of the original. They are representations that attempt to capture the authenticity of an original form. Poems in translation will require you to understand that the artistry of the translator governs the choices he or she makes in translating specific words. A translator's understanding of the original language, with its nuance, its connotative, as well as denotative meaning, allows for a rendering of a poem. The fluid nature of language, as well as the translator's intentions, creates something new. The translator's artistry stands on its own merit.

Activity 6 Intertextual activity with TOK connections

Part 1

1) Use the QR codes to access two different translated versions of Pablo Neruda's 'Sonnet XVII' and read the poems. Consider how choices in punctuation, diction, and syntax affect tone and meaning.
2) What does this exercise reveal about translation? About language? About our ability to accurately convey meaning?

Part 2

The second version of the poem gives you the option to listen to the poem.

1) After completing Part 1, go back to the second link and *listen* to the video version of the poem.
2) How does listening to the poem affect your interpretation?
3) To what extent can an oral rendition of a text be considered another form of translation?

Speaker and persona

Speaker and persona – what's the difference? The difference relies upon the use of pronouns in a given poem. If an 'I' voice is used, we can assume that either the poet is speaking directly to us, as he or she would in a diary entry, or that the speaker is a character the poet has created with a singular personality and perspective.

It is problematic, and even dangerous, to assume that the 'I' voice of the poem is the poet. Such an assumption would mean that the poet is confessing their feelings, admitting their actions, or proclaiming an understanding in a completely self-conscious manner. To assume that the persona, the 'I' voice, is the poet, is the same as assuming that any first-person narrator is, in fact, the writer speaking directly to the reader. Only extensive biographical information could confirm that the 'I' voice is that of the poet speaking directly about his or her own experience. It is always best to assume that the persona is a voice created by the poet, to render the experience of the poem in a personal, immediate, and engaged manner.

Sometimes, the voice of the poem is termed *speaker*, despite the pronouns used in the poem. A voice that references 'he', 'she', 'it', or 'they' is called a speaker. This speaker functions in a similar way to a third-person narrator in prose fiction. This voice is less personal, less intimate, and less immediate than the voice of the persona.

Diction

Diction refers to the specific vocabulary used by a writer or speaker to express his or her point of view.

Flowery, ornate language has often been associated with poetry, but as a student of poetry, you will see that not all poems are written in **elevated language**. Many poems are expressed with simple, straightforward, even **colloquial language**. In some poems, you will often encounter **archaic** terms or phrasings that are unfamiliar. A dictionary is a necessity when you read poetry.

Another consideration of diction in poetry is the way in which poets use the connotation of a word. Connotations – implied meanings – are loaded with emotion. Poets use these emotional connotations to add impact and create intensity for the speaker or for the situation the speaker addresses.

Syntax

No matter how a poem may look on the page, as a reader, you must read the poem with full awareness of syntax. Poets often vary word order to change **rhyme schemes** or rhythm patterns, such as introducing metrical variations. The order of the words within sentences affects not only how the words sound, but also how we interpret meaning. This order can, therefore, alter our understanding of a poem. Inversion – reversing accepted syntactic patterns such as subject, verb, object – creates emphasis, or stress, on a particular word.

Briefly consider the poems we have already looked at in this chapter as examples of variations in syntax. 'London' has a regular and consistent syntactic pattern; each **stanza**, with four lines, contains a single sentence that works to enhance rhythm and rhyme. While Dunbar's poem, 'We Wear the Mask', has a clear rhyme pattern, the effect of the unrhymed final line in the second and third stanzas emphasises the unpredictable, thus stressing the unseen masks worn by African Americans as they struggled against the racist 'Jim Crow' laws of the late 19th century which maintained a kind of legalised social and political subjugation.

Sarah Kay's poem 'Hiroshima' is transcribed in prose rather than poetic form so the syntax is more difficult to analyse. The reader/viewer needs to listen to the poem to catch the syntactical flow of the text. Spoken word poetry often relies on the oral form for syntax cues, thereby making the acoustic aspect of this form even more significant. Dylan's syntax in 'Blowin' in the Wind' is rhythmic and regular with consistent patterns in word order, which is a characteristic of musical lyrics. This pattern works well with the repetition of the chorus; the lyrics build to a theme of understanding that holds universal relevance for each generation that studies the text.

Figurative language – metaphor, simile, personification

Figures of speech attempt to define something in terms of comparison to something else which is more familiar. Metaphor, simile, and **personification** are all useful to poets who are trying to convey meaning and emotion. In **similes**, the comparison is directly stated using the words 'like' or 'as'. Metaphors make the same comparison but without the comparative words. To say that 'his fist is a hammer' (metaphor) or 'his fist was like a hammer' (simile) conveys the same meaning. This meaning is produced through the comparison of two essentially unlike things expressed directly as a simile and indirectly as a metaphor.

Figurative language helps the reader create a picture within their mind's eye, and while that picture, or image, is most often visual, it can also be auditory or tactile. Instead of a picture, a sound or touch is conveyed. Figurative language becomes a way for us to imagine more clearly, more precisely. By using figurative language, poets enable their readers to access their senses more fully.

In personification, an abstraction is defined with human qualities. To say that 'love sat patiently by the door, waiting' works through a comparison of the animate and inanimate. Such a comparison creates a picture in the mind, but it also creates meaning. Abstract concepts are made concrete through such comparisons.

Sound: onomatopoeia, assonance, consonance, alliteration

As we noted at the beginning of this chapter, poems are meant to be read aloud, because the sound of the words is central to the poem's meaning. Sound devices, then, are significant and you must train your ear to *hear* them.

Onomatopoeia is a wonderful device where the word sounds like what it describes – 'splat', 'bubble', 'gurgle', and 'murmur' are all onomatopoeic words.

Assonance is the repetition of vowel sounds within a line or series of lines in a poem. Assonance creates a rhythmic effect, as when EE Cummings writes 'on a pr**ou**d r**ou**nd cl**ou**d in a wh**i**te h**i**gh n**i**ght.'

Consonance is the repetition of a consonant sound within a line of poetry, as can be seen in these lines from Emily Dickinson's poem 'Twas later when the summer went':

> 'Twas sooner when the cricket went
> Then when the winter came
> Yet that pathetic pendulum
> Keeps esoteric time

Alliteration in a line of poetry involves the repetition of the beginning consonant sound in a series of two or more words, such as in this line from George Wither's poem 'Shall I, Wasting in Despair':

> If she loves me, this believe,
> I will die ere she shall grieve;
> If she slight me when I woo,
> I can scorn and let her go;

Assonance, consonance, and alliteration are significant because the manipulation of sound creates an effect on the reading experience – words can be stressed and rhythms can either be intensified or broken.

Rhyme scheme

A rhyme scheme is the pattern of rhyme established by a poem, based on the sound at the end of each line. Looking across history, there are dozens of different formulaic rhyme schemes in use, some strictly laid down by the conventions of the type of poem. However, some poems will avoid a regular rhyme scheme altogether.

Rhyme schemes are commonly mapped out using a system of letters, each letter denoting a different rhyme sound. For example, here is John Donne's poem, 'Death be not Proud', with the rhyme scheme mapped out:

Death be not proud, though some have called thee	a
Mighty and dreadfull, for, thou art not soe,	b
For, those, whom thou think'st, thou dost overthrow,	b
Die not, poore death, nor yet canst thou kill mee	a
From rest and sleepe, which but thy pictures bee,	a
Much pleasure, then from thee, much more must flow,	b
And sooner our best men with thee doe goe,	b
Rest of their bones, and soules deliverie.	a
Thou art slave to Fate, Chance, kings, and desperate men,	c
And dost with poison, warre, and sicknesse dwell,	d
And poppie, or charmes can make us sleepe as well,	d
And better then thy stroake; why swell'st thou then?	c
One short sleepe past, wee wake eternally,	a
And death shall be no more; death, thou shalt die.	e

Remember, it is not enough in poetic analysis just to describe the rhyme scheme; you must also say what effect the rhyme scheme has, and how it contributes to meaning. Does the rhyme accent certain lines, and hence emphasise certain meanings? Does it produce a peaceful or a dissonant effect? Why does Donne break the rhyme in the final two lines? Does the lack of harmony in those final lines work to a purposeful effect? Reading the poem aloud will help you to sense the poetic effect more clearly.

Kendrick Lamar won the Pulitzer Prize for music in 2018 for his album *DAMN!*

A word about rhyme and rap

Originally regarded as street music, rap is now not only part of the musical mainstream, but also often considered poetry in its own right. Kendrick Lamar's album, *DAMN!* won the Pulitzer Prize for music in 2018. Known for their intricate, complex rhyming patterns, rap artists such as Lamar are exploring identity, influencing culture, and communicating across the globe to make their experiences palpable, raw, and relevant.

Like many rap artists, Lamar's lyrics are autobiographical; the line between persona and writer disappears. The difference between Lamar and many of his fellow MCs is that he is always able to find a new and worthwhile way to express his perceptions. In 'Swimming Pools', he delves into the mistakes of youth and why it is so easy to repeat the same blunders. In 'Fear', he expresses how a rapper now worth millions still fears losing everything – a holdover from a childhood full of violence and poverty. These lyrics are intensely personal, but relatable. Lamar reminds us that his experiences are not just about him. By providing us with a window into his life, he gives us a mirror for our own.

It is also important to understand that rap, like spoken word poetry, is meant to be performed, but there is an additional musical element that adds complexity. Music, and particularly rap music, doesn't simply rely on natural metric rhythms like a sonnet written in iambic pentameter. The beats in rap are unmistakably acoustic, greatly contributing to its meaning.

Before completing Activity **7**, watch Baba Brinkman's TED Talk, 'A Brief History of Rhyme: Wordplay Past and Present'.

In this podcast, rap artist Baba Brinkman legitimises rap music as an art form, showing that it is a type of innovative poetry that capitalises on linguistic complexity and playful rhyming patterns. Examples ranging from Eminem and Jay-Z to Chaucer and Tolkien reveal how the techniques rappers put into play have intertextual connections to poets across the globe and throughout time.

TOK

Reading and listening to lyrics are two different experiences. How would you describe the differences? To what extent do these separate experiences produce a different type of knowledge?

Activity 7 Rap as innovative poetry

Now that you have some background knowledge on intricate rhyme functions in rap, read the lyrics below from the song 'D.N.A.', in which Kendrick Lamar maintains that DNA shapes our identity through both biology and culture.

1) As you read the excerpt from the rap, consider not just the effects of rhyme, but also diction, alliteration, repetition, and figurative language.

'D.N.A.' by Kendrick Lamar

I got, I got, I got, I got
Loyalty, got royalty inside my DNA
Cocaine quarter piece, got war and peace inside my DNA
I got power, poison, pain and joy inside my DNA
I got hustle though, ambition, flow, inside my DNA
I was born like this, since one like this
Immaculate conception
I transform like this, perform like this
Was Yeshua's new weapon
I don't contemplate, I meditate...

2) To what extent do these lyrics reveal, as Brinkman argues, rap as 'an innovative poetry form rich with linguistic playfulness'?

3) Select a verse from a song of your choice (vintage or modern) and explain how the lyricist (poet) uses rhyme and one other textual feature to help communicate a theme in the text. Record your response in your learner portfolio.

Metre

Much like their rap artist counterparts, poets who do not set their words to music still use sound to create meaning and to elicit emotion in the reader. One way that poets create meaning is through the patterned arrangement of stressed and unstressed syllables in words. A stressed syllable has more emphasis, more sound, than an unstressed syllable, so if words are arranged in a set pattern of stressed and unstressed syllables, rhythm is created. **Scansion** is the process of scanning a line of poetry to determine this pattern of rhythm. By measuring the basic unit of a line, called a foot, we can describe the pattern. A foot consists of one stressed and one or two unstressed syllables, and they fall into the following categories:

- The **iamb** is an unstressed syllable followed by a stressed syllable: e.g. 'enough'.

- The **trochee** is a stressed syllable followed by an unstressed syllable: e.g. 'dearly'.

- The **anapest** is composed of two unstressed syllables followed by a stressed syllable: e.g. 'understand'.

- The **dactyl** is a stressed syllable followed by two unstressed syllables: e.g. 'desperate'.

- A **spondee** is formed by two stressed syllables: e.g. 'help me'.

A line is measured by the number of feet it contains:

- **monometer** – one foot

- **dimeter** – two feet

- **trimeter** – three feet

- **tetrameter** – four feet

- **pentameter** – five feet

- **hexameter** – six feet

- **heptameter** – seven feet

- **octameter** – eight feet.

As with rhyme, you should think about how the metre contributes to the overall **tone** and meaning of the poem. For example, does it make the poem rushed and breathless, or slow and steady? And how do these effects shape or emphasise the content of the poem? End-stopped lines, run-on lines, and enjambed lines also affect the rhythm of the poem.

> **Connections**
>
> The most common metre in English poetry is based on iambic feet. **Blank verse** (like all of Shakespeare's plays) is essentially unrhymed and is primarily written in iambic pentameter.

A word on sonnets

As with rhyme schemes and metre, poetry has, throughout its history, adopted several formulaic stanza forms. One particular form, the sonnet, continues to hold wide appeal through time and space. There are many variations of sonnets, including the English or Shakespearean sonnet and the Italian or **Petrarchan sonnet**. Both are 14 lines in length, but the difference is in structure. In the first, the sonnet divides into three units of four lines each (three **quatrains**) followed by a final two-line unit (rhyming **couplet**). In the second, the fundamental break is between the first eight lines (an **octave**) and the last six (a **sestet**). The rhyme scheme in the Shakespearean sonnet is typically abab, cdcd, efef, gg, while in the Petrarchan sonnet it is typically abbaabba cdecde. Traditional sonnets are written in iambic pentameter. A sonnet is a perfect form for arguing a point or an idea which is brought to conclusion at the end.

> **Activity 8 Collaborative spoken word poetry with Shakespeare's 'Sonnet 130'**
>
> 1) In a small group, read through 'Sonnet 130' and try to work out its message.
>
> ### 'Sonnet 130' by William Shakespeare (1609)
>
> My mistress' eyes are nothing like the sun;
> Coral is far more red than her lips' red;
> If snow be white, why then her breasts are dun;
> If hairs be wires, black wires grow on her head.
> I have seen roses damasked, red and white,
> But no such roses see I in her cheeks;
> And in some perfumes is there more delight
> Than in the breath that from my mistress reeks.
> I love to hear her speak, yet well I know

> That music hath a far more pleasing sound;
> I grant I never saw a goddess go;
> My mistress, when she walks, treads on the ground.
> And yet, by heaven, I think my love as rare
> As any she belied with false compare.

2) Once you have established an understanding of the text, decide how your group will 'act out' the poem for your peers, using sound, movement, and any props available.

3) Consider how the poetic devices contribute to the meaning of the poem and how your understanding of such literary effects informs your performance. For example, how will the metre and rhyme influence how you pace the performance? How will you use movement to express the figurative language?

4) After the activity, discuss how the multiple performance-based representations transform the poem.

5) Write a brief reflection in your learner portfolio explaining to what extent the differing perspectives helped you establish your own interpretation of the poem.

Connections

Understanding the type of poem may provide you with some quick insight as to the type of subject matter and tone. For example, a lyric, which by definition will have rhythm, will often be reflective, and will offer a highly emotional insight into an individual, an experience, or an event.

Poems written in **free verse** avoid regular metre and consequently have no obviously perceivable rhythm. These poems often have highly irregular line lengths, but may also use repetition of words or phrases.

Concrete poems often draw their meaning less from the words used in the poem and more from the physical arrangement or shape on the page. These shapes are visually recognisable.

Understanding the type of poem may provide you with some quick insight as to the type of subject matter and tone. For example, a lyric poem, by definition, will have rhythm, will often be reflective, and will offer a highly emotional insight into an individual, an experience, or an event.

Application of textual features and/or authorial choices and course concepts

As we complete this section you will be able see how the authorial choices that are referenced throughout the chapter apply to actual poems. The questions that follow each poem will help you focus on the effects of specific devices and course concepts.

Activity 9 Revisiting authorial choices, textual features, and course concepts

Read these poems and then answer the questions about them.

'Blood' by Naomi Shihab Nye (1986)

'A true Arab knows how to catch a fly in his hands,'
my father would say. And he'd prove it,
cupping the buzzer instantly
while the host with the swatter stared.

In the spring our palms peeled like snakes.
True Arabs believed watermelon could heal fifty ways.
I changed these to fit the occasion.

Years before, a girl knocked,
wanted to see the Arab.
I said we didn't have one.
After that, my father told me who he was,
'Shihab' – 'shooting star' –
a good name, borrowed from the sky.
Once I said, 'When we die, we give it back?'
He said that's what a true Arab would say.

Today the headlines clot in my blood.
A little Palestinian dangles a toy truck on the front page.
Homeless fig, this tragedy with a terrible root
is too big for us. What flag can we wave?
I wave the flag of stone and seed,
table mat stitched in blue.

I call my father, we talk around the news.
It is too much for him,
neither of his two languages can reach it.
I drive into the country to find sheep, cows,
to plead with the air;
Who calls anyone *civilized*?
Where can the crying heart graze?
What does a true Arab do now?

1) What can you infer about the speaker/persona?
2) What is the situation in this poem (time, place, occasion)?
3) Examine the use of punctuation in this poem. What effects are produced?
4) What is the speaker/persona's attitude toward the subject matter?
5) How is the concept of identity developed in this poem? To what effect?

'My Son, My Executioner' by Donald Hall (1955)

My son, my executioner,
    I take you in my arms,
Quiet and small and just astir,
    And whom my body warms.

Sweet death, small son, our instrument
    Of immortality,
Your cries and hungers document
    Our bodily decay.

We twenty-five and twenty-two,
    Who seemed to live forever,
Observe enduring life in you
    And start to die together.

6) Explain how the title could function metaphorically?
7) What is the tone of this poem?
8) What can you infer about the speaker/persona?
9) What is the effect of perspective (that of the first person) in this poem? Which words (diction) help you understand the speaker's state of mind?

'Of Love' by Ketty Nivyabandi

Falling in love
a flowering of the heart
an opening
a stretch out the world
a sunflower caught in the sky
two eyes closed
a tongue
searching for the sky
for a drop of rain
and the way it curls after finding it.

Falling out of love
a shedding of the heart
a soft wrinkling
a scar
the crisp cool air
that licks the musty room clean after a storm
a closing window too
which must be reopened
for the heart to breathe
all dying isn't sad
there is the dying that precedes the living
and that's the secret kind.

10) What do you know about the speaker of this poem?
11) What is the situation? (time, place, occasion)
12) What is the speaker's attitude toward this situation?
13) How would you describe the structure of the poem?
14) How do the two stanzas offer differing perspectives of love?

Info box

Sometimes poets use the technique of 'extended metaphor', when a metaphor is developed through the whole poem.

'How Everything Happens' by May Swenson (1967)

(Based on a Study of the Wave)

                  happen.
              to
           up
        stacking
      is   5
    something
When nothing is happening

When it happens
             something
                      pulls   10
                      back
                           not
                              to
                                 happen.

When   has happened.   15
        pulling back   stacking up
                 happens

        has happened   stacks up.
When it   something   nothing
                      pulls back while   20

Then nothing is happening.

                                 happens.
                        and
                    forward
                 pushes   25
              up
           stacks
        something
Then

15) Comment on the visual effect of this poem. Can you observe a pattern?
16) Does the shape/structure of the poem contribute to its meaning?
17) Think about the representation of this poem. Rearrange the words and transform them into another image. What is the effect of this transformation on meaning?

'A Lesson for this Sunday' by Derek Walcott (1962)

The growing idleness of summer grass
With its frail kites of furious butterflies
Requests the lemonade of simple praise
In scansion gentler than my hammock's swings
And rituals no more upsetting than a
Black maid shaking linen as she sings
The plain notes of some Protestant hosanna —
Since I lie idling from the thought in things —

Or so they should, until I hear the cries
Of two small children hunting yellow wings,
Who break my Sabbath with the thought of sin.
Brother and sister, with a common pin,
Frowning like serious lepidopterists.
The little surgeon pierces the thin eyes.
Crouched on plump haunches, as a mantis prays
She shrieks to eviscerate its abdomen.
The lesson is the same. The maid removes
Both prodigies from their interest in science.

The girl, in lemon frock, begins to scream
As the maimed, teetering thing attempts its flight.
She is herself a thing of summery light,
Frail as a flower in this blue August air,
Not marked for some late grief that cannot speak.

The mind swings inward on itself in fear
Swayed towards nausea from each normal sign.
Heredity of cruelty everywhere,
And everywhere the frocks of summer torn,
The long look back to see where choice is born,
As summer grass sways to the scythe's design.

18) What do you know about the speaker?
19) What is the situation?
20) Can you paraphrase this poem completely? If not, what lines defy paraphrase?
21) Examine the use of stanza. What is the progression in terms of subject matter and tone?
22) How do specific images work in this poem to intensify meaning?
23) What literary elements does the writer use to develop the concept of culture in this poem? To what effect?

Areas of exploration: analyse, evaluate, appreciate

Readers, writers, and texts: an approach to poetry

This area of exploration asks you to see the poem through the lens of a close reader. You are examining the poem in its detail – its shape, its sound, and its subject matter – closely noting 'what is there and what is not', as Morrison says in her essay, 'The Reader as Artist' (Chapter 1.1, Fiction). Every word counts in poetry. Think of it as a distillation, a kind of concentration of words, potent with meaning. The shape of a poem is equally powerful, as you will see in the poem which follows, for it too can contribute to meaning if you discover its patterns. In some sense, you must approach the poem as a mathematician or scientist might – observing, counting, noting nuances of chosen words, and then describing your findings in a logical, purposeful way. All of the poetic elements that you learned about earlier in this chapter come into play, but not all within the same poems. Each poem is a discrete example of the form and each will tell you how to read it – when to stop, pause, or quicken your pace of reading. The individuality of expression resonates through the sound, shape, and subject matter of every poem.

Guidelines for close reading poetry

The following list provides a kind of road map for reading poetry. You can use these guidelines to approach any poem as the first step in analysis.

1. Read the poem, preferably aloud, several times.

2. Pay attention to the title. Has your understanding of it changed as a result of reading the poem?

3. Is there a speaker or a persona? What do you know about him or her? Is their gender important? Does the speaker have personality or does he or she seem detached or disembodied? Do you respond personally to this voice? Does it engage you emotionally? Intellectually? Does the speaker address someone else in the poem? Can you determine their relationship to each other?

4. What is the situation in the poem? Does it take place at a specific time or place? Is location important?

5. How is imagery used in regard to defining both the situation and the speaker? What images strike you as particularly effective in terms of creating tone/attitude? Which of your senses are evoked through imagery – visual, auditory, tactile, olfactory, gustatory, kinesthetic, organic?

6. What tones are created? A few to consider include: reflective, nostalgic, playful, ironic, sad, bitter, humorous, sincere, objective, formal, informal, solemn, satiric, or serious.

7. What is the central purpose? To describe, to persuade, to tell a story, to reveal a moment in time, to reflect, to philosophise? Something else?

8. Does the poet draw your attention to a specific word, either through placement, repetition, allusion, or connotation? Do some words take on metaphorical or symbolic meaning?

9. What sound devices are used in the poem? Consider: onomatopoeia, alliteration, assonance, consonance, and rhyme. Is there a regular or irregular rhythm? If the rhythm is established through a metrical pattern, identify any breaks and/or shifts in that metrical pattern.

10. How does the shape of the poem, its structure, and its architecture work to underscore meaning? What effect does **enjambment** or punctuation produce? Does the physical structure of the poem reveal meaning?

Activity 10

Read the poems 'Patchwork' and 'Soap Suds' below and then observe how the features of each contribute to understanding on a literal level. Observe as well, those elements that contribute to the meaning (interpretation) in each. In your learner portfolio, keep a clear record of your observations of these two poems, noting similarities and differences in shape, sound, and subject matter that create effects that contribute to meaning or interpretation.

'Patchwork' by Eavan Boland

I have been thinking at random
on the universe,
or rather, how nothing in the universe
is random—

(there's nothing like presumption late at night.)*   5

My sumptuous
trash bag of colors
Laura Ashley cottons—
waits to be cut
and stitched and patched but   10

there's a mechanical feel
about the handle
of my secondhand sewing machine,
with its flowers,
and 'Singer' painted orange   15
and its iron wheel.

My back is to the dark.*
Somewhere out there
are stars and bits of stars
and little bits of bits,   20
and swiftnesses and brightnesses and drift—
but is it craft or art?*

I will be here
till midnight,
cross-legged in the dining room,   25
logging triangles and diamonds,
cutting and aligning,
finding greens in pinks
and burgundies in whites,
until I finish it.   30

There's no reason in it.*

Only when it's laid
right across the floor—
sphere on square
and seam to seam   35
in a good light—
will it start to hit me:

these are not bits
they are pieces
and the pieces fit.*   40

Examine each of the following and remark on their contribution to understanding
either the literal meaning or figurative/interpretive meaning of the poem.

bits and pieces   persona   causality   * syntax

randomness   punctuation   thinking

shapes   colours   dark/light

129

Go back to the guidelines for reading poetry above and follow along as each of the ten guidelines is addressed.

1) Read the poem aloud several times.
2) Note that the title is 'Patchwork', not 'A Patchwork', or 'The Patchwork', or 'Patchwork Quilt'. What is patchwork?
   - Find out about patchwork quilts: what they are made of, and when or why they are made.
3) What do you know about this persona?
   - Is gender important?
   - What effect do the parentheses in line 5 have?
   - Does the persona take themselves too seriously or not; how do you know?
   - What emotions does this persona reveal as the poem progresses?
4) Describe the situation of the poem: a house, at midnight, a task to be completed – what else?
   - Are the references to time important?
   - How does the concept of the universe come into play in this poem?
5) Which type(s) of imagery seem to dominate this poem?
   - To what effect?
   - Is a tone or attitude established through imagery?
6) What are the tones created by Boland?
   - Is the speaker solemn, playful, serious, or reflective?
7) Is this actually a poem about making a quilt?
   - Is there more to it?
   - What is the final revelation of the persona?
   - Is this revelation limited to the process of laying out a patchwork quilt?
   - Is this poem philosophical?
   - What is the message?
8) Is the term 'patchwork' a metaphor for the creative process?
   - Is Boland talking about her own process in this poem?
   - In what way does this poem seem like an observation about making poetry?
   - Think about the 'it' in this poem and what 'it' is made of – literally and figuratively.
   - Could the scraps of cloth represent 'bits' or 'pieces' of the poet's experience that she used to construct a poem?
9) Does this poem have a rhythm?
   - When you read the poem aloud, do you notice any sounds that draw attention to themselves?
   - In which stanza is this sound predominant?
   - Do you notice any other sounds?
   - Where? (assonance: short 'i', long 'i')
10) This poem has a seemingly 'random' shape. But you will need to carefully observe and note the external structure of the poem to determine if the shape is random or purposeful. To determine the external structure, you need to put on your mathematician's hat – count and measure in order to describe the shape of any poem.
    - How many stanzas?

- Are any of these stanzas enjambed? Remember that enjambment requires you to read some stanzas together as one unit of thought. Even though the stanza is set off from another with white space, if there is no end mark, then the stanzas are enjambed. Keep reading until you find an end mark. In Boland's poem, stanza 1 is enjambed with stanza 2, stanza 3 is enjambed with stanza 4, and stanza 8 is enjambed with stanza 9.
- What about end marks – where are they located? (Look at the asterisks.)
- How many total sentences make up this poem? Seven? The first sentence composes the first two stanzas. The second sentence composes the next two stanzas. The third sentence is a single line at the beginning of the fifth stanza. (Because this is the only single line sentence in the entire poem, Boland is asking us to pay attention to it. By breaking the pattern she established in the first four stanzas, she is telling us to pay attention to what the line says.)
- Is there other punctuation that is important to note? Look at the parentheses, the numerous dashes, the single question, and the colon – can you draw any conclusions as to the poet's use of these?
- Why is the fifth stanza a critical one in terms of meaning? Boland breaks patterns in that stanza: two sentences, one single lined sentence, one question mark, and assonance.

Examine each of the following and remark on their contribution to understanding either the literal meaning or the figurative/interpretive meaning of *Patchwork*.

bits and pieces   persona   causality   * syntax

randomness   punctuation   thinking

shapes   colours   dark/light

'Soap Suds' by Louis MacNeice (1964)

This brand of soap has the same smell as once in the big
House he visited when he was eight: the walls of the bathroom open

To reveal a lawn where a great yellow ball rolls back through a hoop
To rest at the head of a mallet held in the hands of a child.

And these were the joys of that house: a tower with a telescope;   5
Two great faded globes, one of the earth, one of the stars;
A stuffed black dog in the hall; a walled garden with bees;
A rabbit warren; a rockery; a vine under glass; the sea.

To which he has now returned. The day of course is fine
And a grown-up voice cries Play! The mallet slowly swings,   10
Then crack, a great gong booms from the dog-dark hall and the ball
Skims forward through the hoop and then through the next and then

Through hoops where no hoops were and each dissolves in turn
And the grass has grown head-high and an angry voice cries Play!
But the ball is lost and the mallet slipped long since from the hands   15
Under the running tap that are not the hands of a child.

Activity 11

Using the same ten guidelines/strategies for reading a poem, work with a partner in determining the guidelines that you believe are essential to understanding 'Soap Suds' literally. Then, once you have determined the literal meaning – the 'story' of the poem – offer three to five points to support a possible interpretation. How does flashback work as a device in this poem? Does it contribute directly to meaning?

Time and space in poetry

Approaching a poem through this lens, at least initially, requires students to delve into the background of the poet's world at the time the poem was written. Determining the situation that prompted the writing, whether it was directly or indirectly connected to the poet – through a specific time or place or the memory of such – is critical to understanding the poem literally as well as the subtleties of meaning embedded within it. To see the poem as a product of a person/poet living within a place at a particular time is to see the poem in terms of its time and space.

Sometimes the context, the time and space of a poem, is straightforward. Consider Anne Barney's poem, 'Another Moment' below as reflective of this type of poem written in response to a specific, solitary moment.

'Another Moment' by Anne Barney (2015)

Last night I woke up
too warm and in want
of a breeze.
I went to the window,
in a hurry to open it quickly,
to get back to sleep
before creatures began
to scurry in my thoughts.

I had left up the shade,
and looked forward to rising
early with the first light,
that gentle rousing
before the sun shouts over the mountain.
Raising the glass, I stared out,
into a night without moon,
a night of diamonds, just-cut.

One small bit of brilliance
shot through the sky, right then,
falling, it seemed, right
in front of me, and I
felt as my breath
left my body
for just a moment, a moment given to me

as a gift,
as all my moments are, a flash
of brilliance, or something
on which to wish,
out of a fathomless darkness
that holds so many,
and lets so many
go.

Activity 12

1) What is the situation that prompts the persona to rise from bed in the middle of the night?
2) Why did the persona leave the shade up? How does this simple action lead to a sudden and significant moment?
3) What realisation does the persona present in the final stanza? What meaning do you find in the comparison of a 'flash of brilliance' and a 'fathomless darkness'?

Other poems, such as 'Photograph from September 11' by Polish poet Wislawa Szymborska and translated by Clare Cavanagh (2005), hold more than personal significance, yet in this example, the moment of poetic creation was a moment of individual witnessing not unlike Barney's poem, 'Another Moment'. Follow the QR code to read 'Photograph from September 11'.

Activity 13

1) What is it about a photograph that encapsulates the lens of time and space? Does it create more distance or perhaps help provide focus for the situation?
2) Is the event the speaker describes more tragic because of the act that prompted it? In other words, how might the effect of this tragedy be altered if it were caused by a natural disaster rather than an act of terror?
3) The poem encapsulates a moment in time, but it taps into the global issue of how political conflict threatens individual peace and safety. How does Szymborska communicate this issue through her poem?
4) What is the significance of the last line? Why leave the poem unfinished?
5) Research John Keats's 'Ode to a Grecian Urn', a poem which also describes moments of stasis, where scenes are frozen in time. What connections can you draw between these two works?

Anna Akhmatova's poem 'Requiem'

Because 'Requiem' was written over a period of nearly 30 years, between 1935 and 1961, the context is richly extensive. Several historical points during this period in Russian history provide the context for the poet and her vision. Although written during this time period, Akhmatova believed that publishing the poem was too dangerous. The poem was not published until 1963 in Germany and 1987 in her own Soviet Union. Because of the oppression in Russia between 1935 and 1940, which technically sought to silence artists and those who would consider challenging the government, Akhmatova feared that the secret police would raid her rooms and recover the written poems, so she decided that no written record would be kept. She memorised the lines, and whispered them to her closest friends, who quickly memorised what they had heard. Akhmatova would then burn the scraps of paper on which she had written 'Requiem'.

Activity 14 Research activity

Because of the political/personal interplay in this poem, you must first do some research. Once you have this contextual foundation, you can read insightfully. Akhmatova's life at the time of writing informs every element of her poetry. Several contextual research details for this poem include: defining an elegy; learning about the differences between Acmeism vs Symbolism; understanding the historical references, including the 1917 Revolution, the Great Purge, and the Great Terror (Yezhov period); discovering how artists were regarded during this period of history; Leningrad prison/Kresty; and Lev Gumilev's (her son's) arrest.

Your teacher will direct you how to divide up these topics as you work with a partner or small group. Post your findings on a shared document and then present them with your peers.

Next, listen to the 4-minute NPR podcast titled 'An Unexpected Revival For A Beloved Russian Poet'. This provides more background information on Akhmatova and her poetry.

Now, search for Akhmatova's poem 'Requiem' on the Internet and read the beginning of the poem through the first section titled 'Dedication'.

Answer the questions below and record your responses in your learner portfolio.

1) How does Akhmatova's use of imagery (auditory as well as visual) recreate the situation and location of this poem?
2) How did the research activities in this section, which focus on time and space, help you better understand the poem's tone and theme? What might you have missed if you did not have any background information before reading it?
3) Is there ever a justification for reading a poem without context? If so, in what circumstances?

Global issue

How do artists create empathy in their audience for people in parts of the world who are experiencing emotional and physical hardships? How can artists move us to action?

Intertextuality: connecting texts in poetry

To approach poetry through the lens of intertextuality is to witness a poem in connection to another 'text' (form, tradition, artist, or idea). Sometimes the connection is directly stated in the poem, or in a prescript to a poem. Other times, the connection may be less obvious because the reader may not be familiar with the other, connecting text. In the poems which follow, you will see many variations of intertextuality:

- a poem written in response to an earlier poem

- a poem written in response to/or alluding to a painting

- a poem written in response to a myth or mythological figure

- a poem written in response to a particular time, place, or historical event

- a poem written with specific allusions to a person, place, or event.

Art and myth – example 1

In *Answering Back*, edited by Carol Ann Duffy (Picador, 2008), 50 poets were asked to choose a poem from the past and respond to it so as to 'speak to one another across the centuries'. The entire text is an exploration in intertextuality, allowing one poet's vision to be reframed by another.

WH Auden's poem, 'Musée des Beaux Arts' was chosen by contemporary poet, Billy Collins.

'Musée des Beaux Arts' by WH Auden (1938)

About suffering they were never wrong,
    The Old Masters: how well they understood
Its human position; how it takes place
While someone else is eating or opening a window or just walking dully along;
How, when the aged are reverently, passionately waiting
For the miraculous birth, there always must be
Children who did not specially want it to happen, skating
On a pond at the edge of the wood;

They never forgot
That even the dreadful martyrdom must run its course
Where the dogs go on with their doggy life and the torturer's horse
Scratches its innocent behind on a tree.

Art and myth – example 2

Scholars disagree on the extent to which Brueghel's paintings influenced Auden in the writing of this poem, but they do agree that Auden was influenced by a visit to a museum in Brussels, Belgium, in December of 1938. He saw in Brueghel's work a modern impulse to ignore the suffering of others in order to tend to selfish needs – an impulse of indifference which in 1938 allowed for man's inhumanity to man to flourish.

Brueghel's painting of *Landscape of the Fall of Icarus* is based on the myth of Daedalus and his son, Icarus, as told by Ovid in his *Metamorphoses*.

Brueghel's Landscape of the Fall of Icarus

Activity 15

Research this myth and examine its use in Brueghel's painting below.

This is Billy Collins' response to Auden's poem:

In Brueghel's *Icarus*, for instance: how everything turns away
Quite leisurely from the disaster; the ploughman may
Have heard the splash, the forsaken cry,
But for him it was not an important failure; the sun shone
As it had to on the white legs disappearing into the green
Water; and the expensive delicate ship that must have seen
Something amazing, a boy falling out of the sky,
Had somewhere to get to and sailed calmly on.

Activity 16

How would you characterise the differences in the tones of these two poems? Which poem seems more removed, more distant, from the painting's images? What is the significance of comparing these two poems? To what extent is Collins' response a different analysis of the same painting rather than a direct response to Auden's text? Both Auden and Collins analyse an aspect of Brueghel's painting. In what way is this similar to poets translating a poem from a different language as we explored with Neruda's 'Sonnet 1' earlier in the chapter?

Art and myth – example 3

Another poem which demonstrates the interconnectedness of art and myth and poetry is Sylvia Plath's poem, 'The Disquieting Muses', which shares an interconnection with Giorgio de Chirico's painting by the same name.

Take a close look at the painting, and in your learner portfolio, make a list of everything that you see in the painting. Note shade, shadows, objects, figures, colours, and positioning of objects in the foreground and background. Where would the sun be located based on the shadowing?

After making your list, research the artist, Giorgio de Chirico. What can you learn about his painting? When did he paint it? What was the context of this painting? Does de Chirico's painting present a picture of the world at the time of its painting?

Giorgio de Chirico's surrealist painting, *The Disquieting Muses*

In Plath's *Journal* and *Letters Home*, we learn that she took an art history course during her early years at Smith College in Northampton, Massachusetts, where she was introduced to de Chirico's work. Indeed, de Chirico's paintings profoundly influenced the Surrealists. His work, characterised as metaphysical, often included shadows, mannequins, Roman arcades, and long shadows which offer odd angles of perspective.

Now, read Sylvia Plath's poem of the same title:

'The Disquieting Muses' by Sylvia Plath (1957)

Mother, mother, what illbred aunt
Or what disfigured and unsightly
Cousin did **you so unwisely keep
Unasked to my christening**, that she
Sent these ladies in her stead
With **heads like darning-eggs** to nod
And nod and nod at foot and head
And at the left side of my crib?

In stanza 1: allusions to the 'Sleeping Beauty' myth and de Chirico's painting

Mother, who made to order stories
Of Mixie Blackshort the heroic bear,
Mother, whose **witches always, always,
Got baked into gingerbread**, I wonder
Whether you saw them, whether you said
Words to rid me of those three ladies
Nodding by night around my bed,
Mouthless, eyeless, with stitched bald head.

In stanza 2: allusions to 'Hansel and Gretel' and the painting

137

In the hurricane, when father's twelve
Study windows bellied in
Like bubbles about to break, you fed
My brother and me cookies and Ovaltine
And helped the two of us to choir:
'Thor is angry: boom boom boom!
Thor is angry: we don't care!'
But **those ladies broke the panes**.

Stanza 3: allusions to mythology of Thor as a protector-god and 'Sleeping Beauty'

When on tiptoe the schoolgirls danced,
Blinking flashlights like fireflies
And singing the glowworm song, I could
Not lift a foot in the twinkle-dress
But, **heavy footed, stood aside**
In the shadow cast by my dismal-headed
Godmothers, and you cried and cried:
And **the shadow stretched**, the lights went out.

Stanza 4: allusion to 'Sleeping Beauty' and the de Chirico painting

Mother, you sent me to piano lessons
And praised my arabesques and trills
Although each teacher found my touch
Oddly wooden in spite of scales
And the hours of practicing, my ear
Tone-deaf and yes, unteachable.
I learned, I learned, I learned elsewhere,
From muses unhired by you, dear mother.

Stanza 5: allusion to the painting and 'Sleeping Beauty'

I woke one day to see you, mother,
Floating above me in bluest air
On a green balloon bright with a million
Flowers and bluebirds that never were
Never, never, found anywhere.
But **the little planet bobbed away**
Like a soap-bubble as you called: Come here!
And I faced my traveling companions.

Stanza 6: allusions to 'The Little Prince'

Day now, night now, at head, side, feet,
They stand their vigil in gowns of stone,
Faces blank as the day I was born,

Stanza 7: Allusions to painting

Their shadows long in the setting sun
That never brightens or goes down.
And this is the kingdom you bore me to,
Mother, mother. But no frown of mine
Will betray the company I keep.

Plath seemed to believe that her own 'disquieting muses' were in some sense a curse that her mother created, consciously or not, that prohibited and often undermined her own sense of self-worth as a poet. Her 'muses' were 'disquieting', disturbing, unsettling, troubling. In some way the poem recounts her attempts at the 'arts' (song, dance, music) throughout her life, which she sees as all ending in failure and disappointment. She also alludes to her mother's forced optimism – nothing could harm you, there was nothing to fear – even in situations where the danger was real, like a hurricane. The world her mother created and 'bore her to' was like a fairy tale: her mother saw only happy endings while Plath was filled with disquietude.

Activity 17

The Grimm fairy tale, *Sleeping Beauty (Little Briar Rose)*, is another intertextual reference in Plath's poem. Research this connection by finding and reading the tale online.

Connections

In many ancient cultures there are myths of women, often three of them, referenced as 'the Fates'. These Fates literally spin the threads of mortals' lives and are equipped with supernatural capabilities. Their spindles determine the length of someone's life. In Greek mythology, the Fates are known collectively as the Moirai: Clothos, the spinner who spun the thread of life; Lachesis, the measurer, disposer of lots, who assigned each man to his destiny; and Atropos, the cutter of the thread of life. Together they determine the birth, life span, and death of an individual.

Sylvia Plath's poem borrows liberally from the de Chirico painting, the Sleeping Beauty myth, and several other references including another Grimm fairy tale and Antoine de Saint-Exupery's *The Little Prince*. (Note the bolded lines in 'The Disquieting Muses'.)

Activity 18

To what effect does Plath blend art, myth, and story? Does intertextuality work within a text to inform our reading in the same way that a metaphor might? Metaphors offer an understanding through comparison of two unlike things. Is the same effect achieved through intertextuality? In using multiple references and multiple texts does Plath's meaning become clearer, stronger, and more focused? Or does the use of multiple reference texts diminish, weaken, and blur that meaning? How does intertextuality function in determining an interpretation?

An intertextual blending of emerging silent voices

Carol Ann Duffy's poem, 'Medusa', from *The World's Wife* collection of poems published in 1999, like the other poems in this collection, is told from the perspective of the 'wives', or silenced, marginalised women, central to the stories of famous men in fairy tales, Greek mythology, popular culture, the Bible, and history.

'Medusa' by Carol Ann Duffy (1999)

A suspicion, a doubt, a jealousy
grew in my mind,
which turned the hairs on my head to filthy snakes,
as though my thoughts
hissed and spat on my scalp.

My bride's breath soured, stank
in the grey bags of my lungs.
I'm foul mouthed now, foul tongued,
yellow fanged.
There are bullet tears in my eyes.
Are you terrified?

Be terrified.
It's you I love,
perfect man, Greek God, my own;
but I know you'll go, betray me, stray
from home.
So better by far for me if you were stone.

I glanced at a buzzing bee,
a dull grey pebble fell
to the ground.
I glanced at a singing bird,
a handful of dusty gravel
spattered down.

I looked at a ginger cat,
a housebrick
shattered a bowl of milk.
I looked at a snuffling pig,
a boulder rolled
in a heap of shit.

I stared in the mirror.
Love gone bad
showed me a Gorgon.
I stared at a dragon.
Fire spewed
from the mouth of a mountain.

And here you come
with a shield for a heart
and a sword for a tongue
and your girls, your girls.
Wasn't I beautiful?
Wasn't I fragrant and young?

Look at me now.

In Edith Hamilton's *Mythology*, Medusa is associated with the story of Perseus, who, guided and protected by Hermes' winged sandals and Athena's polished bronze shield and a cap that made him invisible, vowed to kill her and return with her head. This was no small feat, as Medusa, like all three of her sisters, would turn to stone anyone or anything that met their gaze. Considered the most important of the three Gorgon sisters (because she alone could be killed), Perseus set out to find the great winged creatures whose wings and bodies were covered with golden scales and whose hair was a mass of twisting snakes. Using Hermes' winged sandals, Perseus hovered over the sleeping Gorgons, and looking only at the reflected image of Medusa in Athena's shield, he 'aimed a single stroke down at Medusa's throat' and cut off her head.

Ovid's rendition of Medusa describes her as a ravishing maiden with beautiful golden hair who had won the 'jealous admiration of many suitors', including Poseidon who raped her in Athena's temple. The enraged Athena, seeking revenge for this temple desecration, believed that Medusa deserved to be turned into an ugly Gorgon that no man or beast would ever want to lay eyes on, and so she aided Perseus in his quest to destroy Medusa.

Activity 19

1) How would you characterise the speaker of Duffy's poem?
2) Does Duffy manage to create sympathy? How does she do this?
3) Interestingly, two lines of this poem seem to be borrowed from Sylvia Plath's poem 'Medusa'. Read Plath's poem and remark on Duffy's use of those two lines.

Transformative poetry

This section on transformative poetry will enable you to hone your own creative writing skills as you delve into additional transformative and intertextual exercises. The idea is for you not simply to study, but to immerse yourself in the poetic world and experience this form from the inside out.

Activity 20 Transformative reflections

Poets often have keen observational skills: they watch others; they turn inward; they can create a world from memory. Seamus Heaney does just this in his poem, 'Digging' (1980).

For this activity, you will read Heaney's poem and then tap into memories of your own physical, tangible experiences – a creative process that will give you a chance to walk in a poet's shoes.

1) Read Seamus Heaney's poem, 'Digging'. Take note of the physical images in the poem. Which images resonate with you? How do they help you see his experience?

'Digging' by Seamus Heaney (1980)

Between my finger and thumb
The squat pen rests; snug as a gun.

Under my window, a clean rasping sound
When the spade sinks into gravelly ground:
My father, digging. I look down

Till his straining rump among the flowerbeds
Bends low, comes up twenty yards away
Stooping in rhythm through potato drills
Where he was digging.

The coarse boot nestled on the lug, the shaft
Against the inside knee was levered firmly.
He rooted out tall tops, buried the bright edge deep
To scatter new potatoes that we picked
Loving their cool hardness in our hands.

By God, the old man could handle a spade.
Just like his old man.

My grandfather cut more turf in a day
Than any other man on Toner's bog.
Once I carried him milk in a bottle
Corked sloppily with paper. He straightened up
To drink it, then fell to right away

Nicking and slicing neatly, heaving sods
Over his shoulder, going down and down
For the good turf. Digging.

The cold smell of potato mould, the squelch and slap
Of soggy peat, the curt cuts of an edge
Through living roots awaken in my head.
But I've no spade to follow men like them.

Between my finger and my thumb
The squat pen rests.
I'll dig with it.

2) Use your memory to recall specific physical experiences that stand out in your mind. Make a list of at least ten. Include a broad range of both everyday experiences (e.g. waiting tables in a busy restaurant, babysitting a toddler, painting a house) and the more remarkable ones (e.g. skiing down a mountain; rebuilding a community after a natural disaster, etc.). Don't think; just write.

3) Choose one memory from your list. This will be the focus of the next step.

4) Now reflect upon the experience without writing anything. Let it unfold in your mind. Steep yourself in the imagery: what did you see, hear, feel, smell, taste? Write down as much as you can recall from this experience. Include all details that come to mind.

5) Review your notes and write a poem that recreates this experience. Use words and phrases from your free writing. Your poem does not have to rhyme in a specific way, but it should be full of imagery. What details emerge that help you communicate your memory?

6) After you have completed your poem, reread Seamus Heaney's 'Digging' and write a response (a good-sized paragraph) comparing your experience and your poetry with Heaney's. Note any similarities and differences. This is a free association exercise. You can concentrate on any elements that come to mind: subject matter, poetic vision, length, use of stylistic and structural devices, etc.

Blackout poetry

Poets love to play with words. They love the musicality that comes with metre and rhymes; the multiple meanings that can be created with word compression; the beauty of a simplistic image. Rearranging words to transform one text into another is not a new concept, but in the early 21st century, writer Austin Kleon, with his blackout concept, turned the act of reading a newspaper into a hunt for poetic phrases. The idea was to identify a few key words or phrases in an article and then use a thick marker to black out the rest of the text. The result is a compressed poem that comes from another text but stands on its own as an original work. To watch Austin Kleon's newspaper blackout poetry in action, click on the QR code.

As a student of IB literature, you will read many types of forms including drama, prose fiction, and prose non-fiction. Your task here is to take one passage of no more than

30 lines from any form other than poetry and *black out* all but a handful of phrases that resonate with you.

For this exercise, feel free to choose your own passage or use the passage from Adichie's short story, 'Cell One', below.

TOK According to Austin Kleon, all art is inspired by ideas and works that already exist. Watch his TED Talk 'Steal Like an Artist', based on his book by the same name. To what extent is transformative art (art based on other works) a form of flattery or thievery? If, as Kleon maintains, all ideas stem from another source, can any work be considered original?

Activity 21 Blackout poetry

Depending on the passage you choose, you should narrow your focus regarding what phrases comprise your poem.

Leave words that (primarily):

- reveal a sense of place (setting)
- convey a character
- rhyme with each other
- appeal to the senses (imagery)
- convey action or motion
- appeal to you in some inexplicable way.

Once you've blacked out the remaining part of the passage, see what is left.

1) To what extent does it resemble or connect to the original passage?
2) How does it stand as a work on its own?
3) How does transforming one form into another help you better understand either form or the essence of the original passage?
4) Share your new poem with a partner and see if they can guess which text, or part of the text, you originally selected.
5) Record your reflections in your learner portfolio.

Excerpt from 'Cell One' by Chimamanda Ngozi Adichie

This is how it happened On a humid Monday, four cult members waited at the campus gate and waylaid a professor driving a red Mercedes. They pressed a gun to her head, shoved her out of the car, and drove it to the Faculty of Engineering, where they shot three boys who were coming out of the building. It was noon. I was in a class nearby, and when we heard the shots our lecturer was the first to run out the door. There was loud screaming, and suddenly the stairwells were packed with scrambling students unsure where to run. Outside, the bodies lay on the lawn. The Mercedes had already screeched away. Many students hastily packed their bags, and *okada* drivers charged twice the usual fare to take them to the motor park to get on a bus. The vice-chancellor announced that all evening classes would be canceled and everyone had to stay indoors after 9 p.m. This did not make much sense to me, since the shooting had happened in sparkling daylight, and perhaps it did not make sense to Nnamabia, either, because the first night of the curfew he didn't come home. I assumed that he had spent the night at a friend's; he did not always come home anyway. But the next morning a security man came to tell my parents that Nnamabia had been arrested at a bar with some cult boys and was at the police station. My mother screamed, 'Ekwuzikwana! Don't say that!' My father calmly thanked the security man. We drove to the police station in town, and there a constable chewing on the tip of a dirty pen said, 'You mean those cult boys arrested last night? They have been taken to Enugu. Very serious case! We must stop this cult business once and for all!'

We got back into the car, and a new fear gripped us all. Nsukka, which was made up of our slow, insular campus and the slower, more insular town, was manageable; my father knew the police superintendent. But Enugu was anonymous. There the police could do what they were famous for doing when under pressure to produce results: kill people.

Activity 22 Contracted poetry

A contracted poem distills a longer text down to its essential essence. Below is an excerpt from a famous contracted poem from Homer's *Odyssey*. Notice how Tennyson uses condensed language to convey Ulysses' (British name for Odysseus) passion for adventure.

'Ulysses' by Alfred, Lord Tennyson (1833)

It little profits that an idle king,
By this still hearth, among these barren crags,
Matched with an aged wife, I mete and dole
Unequal laws unto a savage race,
That hoard, and sleep, and freed, and know not me.
I cannot rest from travel; I will drink
Life to the lees. All times I have enjoyed
Greatly, have suffered greatly, both with those
That loved me, and alone; on shore, and when
Through scudding drifts the rainy Haydes
Vexed the dim sea. I am become a name;
For always roaming with a hungry heart
Much have I seen and known – cities of men
And manners, climates, councils, governments,
Myself not the least, but honored of them all
And drunk delight of battle with my peers,
Far on the ringing plains of windy Troy.
I am part of all that I have met…

1) Write and illustrate a contracted poem based on a full-length text in another form (prose fiction, prose non-fiction, or drama).
2) Your poem should be a minimum of 15 lines.
3) Use paper or a computer to construct your poem.
4) Once your poem is complete, illustrate it with physical tools (markers, coloured pencils, clippings from magazines, etc.) or online tools (computer images).

Activity 23 Transforming poetry through visual arts

In the Fiction chapter (1.1) you learned how visual literacy focuses on creating meaning from images. For this activity, you will transform flat text on a page into visual images that help you communicate your interpretation of a text. You must read the text closely to VISUALISE it – a process that sharpens your literary analysis skills.

Consider the first four lines of William Blake's poem, 'The Tyger'.

Tyger Tyger, burning bright,
In the forests of the night;
What immortal hand or eye,
Could frame thy fearful symmetry?

The language in Blake's poem, from his collection titled *Songs of Innocence*, is simple yet full of intricate images which create a complex tone. Look at the student-created panels below. Notice how the poem transforms once it is illustrated with visuals.

1) What does this graphic storyboard reveal about the student's interpretation of the poem?
2) What visuals did she use to convey the poem's tone and imagery?
3) How might illustrating a text through graphic panels help sharpen your literary interpretive skills?
4) Choose a section of one poem in this chapter to illustrate through graphic panels. (For more details on how to construct graphic panels see the graphic novel section in the Fiction chapter, 1.1.)
5) Share your illustrations with your peers and discuss what this activity reveals about the connection between visual art and language.

Viewing the world through colour

Won McIntosh writes poetry about New York City. Ten of her poems, each associated with a specific coloured object in the city, grace the entrance of New York City's Color Factory, an interactive pop-up museum that exhibits the works of writers, artists, and musicians. The Color Factory encourages patrons to immerse themselves in tactile colour experiences ranging from reading colour-inspired poems and tasting vividly coloured treats to viewing, drawing, and reflecting in a variety of contexts.

▲
The Color Factory encourages visitors to experience New York City through the lens of colour.

Won McIntosh's 'Pretzels' poem ▶

Visitors leave the museum with an interactive map that 'showcase[s] the colors and diverse stories that bring New York City to life, and encourage[s] visitors to consider how color can help define a place and contribute to our sense of togetherness'.

McIntosh's poems not only capture the culture and identity of the city, but also the 21st-century fascination with visual, tactile experiences. Indeed, poets have been writing about the connection between colour and setting for centuries, but the propensity to share internal reflections with the community at large has not always been the case, particularly with reclusive poets.

Activity 24 Observing nature through colour

Emily Dickinson was a prolific, yet reclusive 19th-century American writer who published only a handful of poems during her lifetime. In contrast to McIntosh's community-oriented city colour poems, consider Dickinson's nature-oriented colour poem below.

'Nature Rarer Uses Yellow' by Emily Dickinson (1896)

Nature rarer uses yellow
Than another hue;
Saves she all of that for sunsets, —
Prodigal of blue,

Spending scarlet like a woman,
Yellow she affords
Only scantly and selectly,
Like a lover's words.

1) How does Dickinson's connection between colours and the natural world contribute to the poem's meaning?
2) What do you notice about the structure of the poem? What is the effect of the punctuation?
3) What is the purpose of the two similes?
4) What is the significance of the title of the poem?

TOK

Consider how technology can help develop your knowledge. After completing Activity 24, use the QR code to access the Emily Dickinson Lexicon. Type words from the poem into the search feature and then reflect on how this new tool has helped reshape your understanding of the poem. Share your findings with a partner or a small group and write a brief reflection in your learner portfolio.

Postcard colour poetry

Won McIntosh puts a modern-day twist on her colour poems which appear on the walls of New York City's Color Factory and social media sites (see the picture on page 146) – they are also available for purchase as coloured postcards, the proceeds of which go to help non-profit work to prevent AIDS and homelessness. Modern poets in general are getting more traction on social media of late, but McIntosh's idea reveals how such platforms can connect the work of artists with humanitarian causes. As you complete Activity 25, consider how it might inspire a creative and meaningful CAS project.

McIntosh titled the ten poems in her exhibit: 'Subway Title', 'Asphalt', 'Scaffolding', 'Pretzels', 'Brownstone', 'Bodega Mums', 'F Train', 'Bike Lane', 'Taxi', and 'Manhattan Bridge'.

Activity 25 Creating your own colour postcard poem

Create a postcard poem or, if you are so inclined, create a series of them, as McIntosh did.

1) Read McIntosh's poem 'Pretzels' in the photo on page 146 to get a sense of how she interprets the world through coloured objects.
2) Select an object in your community that will be the focus and title of your poem.
3) Think about how the colour of the object helps you see the connection to the community. What images come to mind? Does your object create an idea? Tell a story? Share a secret?
4) Space is limited to the size of a postcard, so you need to compress your ideas into a short poem. Diction (word choice), syntax (word order), point of view, and punctuation all matter. Will you use figurative language? Will your poem rhyme?
5) Once you have written your poem, transfer it to a coloured postcard/paper that represents your object and share with your peers. Note that this activity can also be done using a digital device.
6) If the option is available, post your poem to a shared school site or a social media platform like Instagram® with the hashtag #pearsoncolorpoetry. Look for other poems with the same hashtag and see how your peers around the world share their communities through vivid colours and language.
7) Record your poem and reflections for the activity in your learner portfolio.

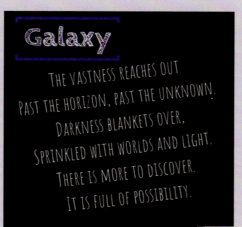

Galaxy

THE VASTNESS REACHES OUT
PAST THE HORIZON, PAST THE UNKNOWN.
DARKNESS BLANKETS OVER,
SPRINKLED WITH WORLDS AND LIGHT.
THERE IS MORE TO DISCOVER.
IT IS FULL OF POSSIBILITY.

Sp Adobe Spark

Student sample of a colour poem using Adobe Spark®.

Connections

For a more in-depth look at the effect of social media on the poetry form, read the article using the QR code in the margin ('How Instagram Saved Poetry') and consider the following questions:

- To what extent has social media helped revive interest in poetry as a literary form?
- Why might the compressed language of poetry appeal to modern-day readers and writers?
- To what extent have modern-day digital communications affected other literary forms (fiction, drama, prose non-fiction)?

Insights into poetry

Remember that poetry in its essence is pleasurable. Saying words, shaping them in your mouth, engages us on a very primal level. Consider the pleasure that children have in listening to the sounds of words. Rhymes amuse us as children listening to a story and continue to do so as we learn to read the words and make the sounds ourselves. Sound, then, lies at the heart of this form.

Other helpful insights as you explore this form include:

1. Initially, you need to determine all that you can about the speaker/persona and their tone of voice.

2. Consider that the tone of that voice reflects the speaker's attitude towards the situation of the poem.

3. Don't be afraid to look up a word you don't know or investigate a reference or allusion to a person, place, or event in history or myth. You must feel confident that you know what all the words mean, at least denotatively.

4. In much the same way, do not be afraid to empathise with the situation the poet presents or with the emotions which accompany it. Just as in other forms, be open to possibility, give yourself permission to think and to feel – consider this an opportunity to practise your emotional 'keyboard'.

5. Because of the many dimensions of the language of poetry and the vast number of poetic strategies/conventions that a poet has to use, accept that reading and rereading a poem many times has value. As you observe which strategies or conventions a poet uses, you can apply those observations to understand how the interaction of form and subject matter creates specific effects. To understand these effects and their functions within the poem is to produce analysis.

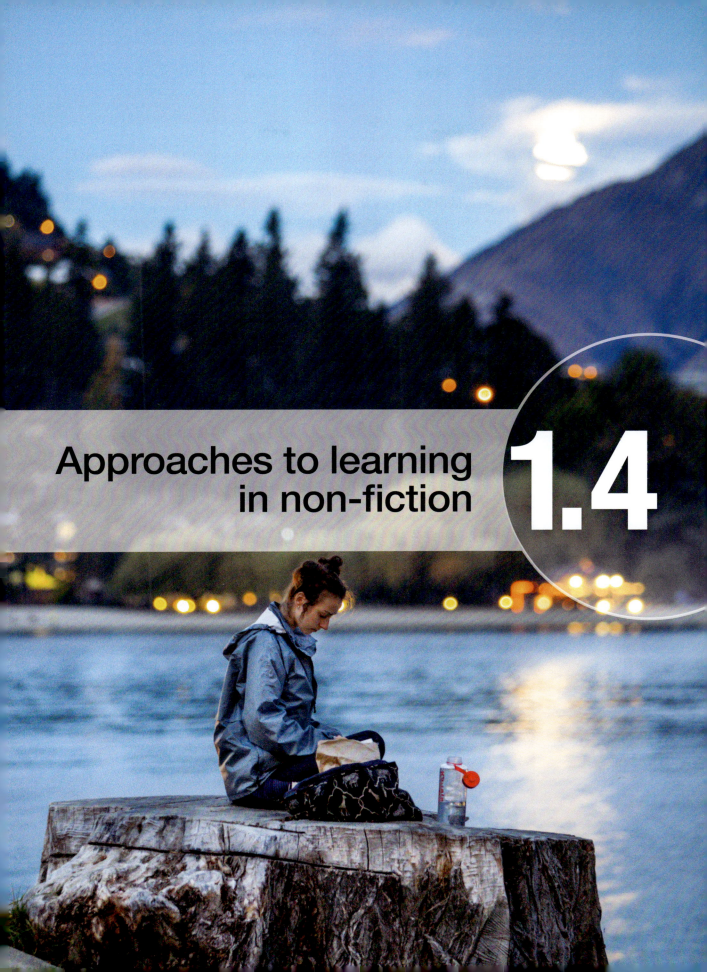

Approaches to learning in non-fiction

1.4

Learning objectives

In this chapter you will…
- connect non-fiction to approaches to learning, course concepts, and areas of exploration
- understand the difference between practical and literary non-fiction
- explore how literary terminology applies to non-fiction
- understand the significance of rhetorical appeals, audience, and purpose in non-fiction
- explore different types of non-fiction including letters, essays, speeches, memoirs, diaries, and travelogues
- communicate ideas through a variety of individual and collaborative activities
- analyse, evaluate and appreciate a range of non-fiction works through
  - readers, writers, and texts
  - time and space
  - intertextuality
  - global issues.

As you study non-fiction writers, it is important to remember that you too are a writer of non-fiction. In Language A: literature you will have opportunities not just to read different **representations** of non-fiction, but also to find your own academic voice. Your reflections may take the shape of a personal essay or memoir, and your analysis of **global issues** may morph into a speech or letter. Solid non-fiction writing is about **communication**; it is often shaped by purpose and audience, much like your assignments and assessments for your IB coursework.

This chapter will enable you to think like a non-fiction writer. We will begin with a definition of non-fiction and what studying it means for English A: literature specifically. You will learn about the conventions of non-fiction through an examination of literary and rhetorical terminology. As you explore different types of non-fiction, you will use your communication and social skills as you read and research texts. You will also work **collaboratively** with others to investigate how **culture**, **identity**, and **perspective** shape non-fiction works and their reception. Towards the end of the chapter, you will have the opportunity for deep inquiry as we connect **areas of exploration** to specific works. We will finish up with insights that will solidify your understanding of non-fiction, not just as a literary form but as a powerful means of shaping local and global contexts.

What is non-fiction?

Unlike fiction writers, who freely invent characters, places, and experiences, non-fiction writers are expected to deliver factually accurate prose about real events and people. Non-fiction is steeped in reflection, observation, and perceptions of recollected experience. Of course, facts, like fading memories, can become blurred over time, but for the most part non-fiction writers attempt 'to see things as they are, to find out true facts' (George Orwell, 'Why I write', 1946) – a trait that lends a sense of purpose and integrity to their works.

Broadly speaking, the non-fiction category covers a wide range of texts from the purely informational to the more literary. Because students will focus exclusively on literary texts in English A: literature, this chapter will focus on literary non-fiction. Memoirs, letters, autobiographies, personal essays, speeches, some types of journalism, and even travelogues all fall into this category. For non-fiction writer, Barrie Jean Borich, '[literary non-fiction] is a form that utilises memory, experience, observation, opinion, and all kinds of research'. The word 'literary' can refer to a way of reading and analysing a text or it can denote a type of text. Either way, some non-fiction texts are better suited for literary studies than others. In Activity 1, see if you can distinguish between practical and literary types of non-fiction.

Info box

Due to the nature of the English A: literature course, the type of non-fiction on your syllabus will include literary rather than practical non-fiction.

Activity 1 Practical vs literary non-fiction

Read the excerpts below from various non-fiction texts. Decide which texts are best suited for a literary study and which tend to convey practical, factual information. Label them (L) or (P).

- Even then my only friends were made of paper and ink. At school I had learned to read and write long before the other children. Where my school friends saw notches of ink on incomprehensible pages, I saw light, streets, and people. Words and the mystery of their hidden science fascinated me, and I saw in them a key with which I could unlock a boundless world, a safe haven from that home, those streets, and those troubled days in which even I could sense that only a limited fortune awaited me. My father didn't like to see books in the house. There was something about them – apart from the letters he could not decipher – that offended him. (Carlos Ruiz Zafón, *The Angel's Game*, 2008)

- Honey bees are hosts to the pathogenic large ectoparasitic mite Varroadestructor (Varroa mites). These mites feed on bee hemolymph (blood) and can kill bees directly or by increasing their susceptibility to secondary infection with fungi, bacteria or viruses. Little is known about the natural defenses that keep the mite infections under control. (Richard J. Sharpe and Lisa Heyden, 'Honey Bee Colony Collapse...', 2009)

- As the bomber flew toward them, they lay down. Phil pulled his knees to his chest and covered his head in his hands. Mac balled himself beside him. Louie took a last glance at them, then dropped into the water and swam back under the rafts.... The bullets showered the ocean in a glittering downpour. Looking up, Louie saw them popping through the canvas, shooting beams of intensely bright tropical sunlight through the raft's shadow. But after a few feet, the bullets spent their force and fluttered down, fizzing. Louie straightened his arms over his head and pushed against the bottom of one of the rafts, trying to get far enough down to be outside the bullets' lethal range. Above him, he could see the depressions formed by Mac and Phil's bodies. Neither man was moving. (Laura Hillenbrand, *Unbroken*, 2010)

- The mental consequences of our online info-crunching are not universally bad. Certain cognitive skills are strengthened by our use of computers and the Net. These tend to involve more primitive mental functions, such as hand-eye coordination, reflex response, and the processing of visual cues. One much-cited study of videogaming revealed that after just 10 days of playing action games on computers, a group of young people had significantly boosted the speed with which they could shift their visual focus between various images and tasks. (Nicholas Carr, 'The Web Shatters Focus, Rewires Brains', 2010)

- If I have said anything in this letter that overstates the truth and indicates an unreasonable impatience, I beg you to forgive me. If I have said anything that understates the truth and indicates my having a patience that allows me to settle for anything less than brotherhood, I beg God to forgive me.... I hope this letter finds you strong in the faith. I also hope that circumstances will soon make it possible for me to meet each of you, not as an integrationist or a civil-rights leader but as a

> fellow clergyman and a Christian brother. Let us all hope that the dark clouds of racial prejudice will soon pass away and the deep fog of misunderstanding will be lifted from our fear-drenched communities, and in some not too distant tomorrow the radiant stars of love and brotherhood will shine over our great nation with all their scintillating beauty. Yours for the cause of Peace and Brotherhood, Martin Luther King, Jr (Martin Luther King Jr, 'Letter from Birmingham Jail', 1963)
>
> - Of the sweets of adversity, and let me say that these are not numerous, I have found the sweetest, the most precious of all, is the lesson I learnt on the value of kindness. Every kindness I received, small or big, convinced me that there could never be enough of it in our world. To be kind is to respond with sensitivity and human warmth to the hopes and needs of others. Even the briefest touch of kindness can lighten a heavy heart. Kindness can change the lives of people. (Aung San Suu Kyi, 'Freedom of Fear', 1991)

Review your list and think about *why* you labelled a passage as practical or literary. In a small group, discuss and compare the reasons for your selections.

Next, choose **one** of the passages that you designated as literary (L) and think about how you would approach it using the questions below as a guide. Write your responses in your learner portfolio.

1) Imagery: Which images paint pictures in your mind?
2) Diction: Which words evoke an emotional response?
3) Syntax: What do you notice about word order?
4) Figurative language: To what effect does the author use similes, metaphors, or personification?
5) Audience and intention: What inferences can you make regarding the work's purpose and audience from the excerpt?

Studying literary non-fiction

Literary terminology

Non-fiction works may live and breathe in the world of real people and events, but as you may have noticed from Activity 1, analysing them as literary works means that the terminology from the other literary forms (fiction, poetry, and drama) will help you make meaning from non-fiction texts as well. As you study memoirs, essays, letters, and speeches, literary terms such as imagery, diction, figurative language, and point of view will help you evaluate how the writer brings factual events or information to life.

Audience and context

Unlike fiction, where in the majority of cases the reader is not known, many (though not all) non-fiction works have intended readers or viewers in mind. This type of writing is crafted with the objective of attracting and drawing in a specific reader or audience in some way. In terms of **time and space**, being aware of historical events taking place at the time, and knowing when a speech was made (and who exactly was being addressed) or when a letter was published, can give you important contextual background information.

Persuasion and intention

Another important convention of non-fiction is how writers attempt to persuade their audiences. For example, speeches or essays often function as arguments.

> **Connections**
>
> An awareness of **rhetoric**, or more simply, the tools writers use to communicate effectively, is key to analysing persuasive texts.

For the ancient Greeks, studying rhetoric was not just about awareness. It played an essential role in readying individuals to involve themselves in civic life, with activities such as taking part in public debates, serving on courtroom juries, and participating in military service. Learning the art of speaking and writing persuasively isn't simply about manipulating words and people. It's about understanding the power of language and its ability to shape our local and global communities.

> **Connections**
>
> Ancient Greeks who participated in debates and served on juries were knowledgeable communicators who freely participated in public service with open minds; they cared about their community. Not all individuals who used rhetoric, of course, were principled, but the study of it encouraged people to think about their larger role in contributing to their community. In this sense, ancient studies in rhetoric (academics) encouraged better citizenship, which is similar to how the IB connects course studies to the **learner profile** and CAS.

According to the Greek philosopher, Aristotle, there are three elements, or rhetorical appeals, that comprise the art of persuasion: ethos, pathos, and logos. Understanding how these appeals work can help you understand the significance of authorial choices and the effects such choices have on audiences across time and space.

Logos appeals provide logical reasons for the audience to be persuaded, such as facts, quotes from figures of authority, and specific evidence. In his spoken word essay, 'There is Such a Thing as Truth', Academy Award-winning documentary film-maker, Errol Morris reveals how some audiences are not willing to accept logos (logical thinking and facts) even in the face of compelling facts and evidence.

Ethos appeals centre on the credibility and/or reputation of the speaker. Arguments that are well organised and well informed create a positive ethos for the speaker, tacitly telling the audience, 'Trust me, believe me, I know what I'm talking about'. Ethos can also be established by reputation. When Nelson Mandela speaks of apartheid and injustice, for example, his credibility comes not just from his words, but also his well-known personal experience and policy work with this global issue.

Pathos appeals tap into the emotions of the audience and their sense of shared values. When an argument evokes empathy or anger or shared joy, this appeal is at work.

TOK

Listen to Errol Morris' short essay 'There is Such a Thing as Truth' using the QR code above and consider his claim that 'Truth is not relative. It's not subjective. It may be elusive or hidden. People may wish to disregard it. But there is such a thing as truth and the pursuit of truth.'

1) How does Morris use logos in his essay to support this claim?
2) Do you find his evidence convincing? Why or why not?
3) Are there circumstances where truth can be relative? If so, in what context?

Writers often use strong imagery, hyperbole (exaggeration), diction, and compelling symbolism to generate an emotional response from the audience.

When Chief Joseph and his Nez Perce Tribe were forced off their land by the United States Government in 1877, a series of violent encounters occurred between the Native Americans and the white settlers. In his pathos-inspired surrender speech, Chief Joseph appeals to the US Army's sense of humanity. His language is simple but powerful: 'It is cold, and we have no blankets; the little children are freezing to death. My people, some of them, have run away to the hills, and have no blankets, no food… I want to have time to look for my children, and see how many of them I can find. Maybe I shall find them among the dead. Hear me, my Chiefs! I am tired; my heart is sick and sad. From where the sun now stands I will fight no more forever.'

Using pathos can be highly effective and when combined with ethos and logos often creates a strong, multifaceted argument.

Activity 2 Analysing global issues and rhetorical appeals in letter writing

Read the following letter that Gandhi wrote to Adolf Hitler during World War II.

Letter to Adolph Hitler from MK Gandhi

As at Wardha,
December 24,
1940

DEAR FRIEND,

That I address you as a friend is no formality. I own no foes. My business in life has been for the past 33 years to enlist the friendship of the whole of humanity by befriending mankind, irrespective of race, colour or creed.

I hope you will have the time and desire to know how a good portion of humanity who have been living under the influence of that doctrine of universal friendship view your action. We have no doubt about your bravery or devotion to your fatherland, nor do we believe that you are the monster described by your opponents. But your own writings and pronouncements and those of your friends and admirers leave no room for doubt that many of your acts are monstrous and unbecoming of human dignity, especially in the estimation of men like me who believe in universal friendliness. Such are your humiliation of Czechoslovakia, the rape of Poland and the swallowing of Denmark. I am aware that your view of life regards such spoliations as virtuous acts. But we have been taught from childhood to regard them as acts degrading humanity. Hence we cannot possibly wish success to your arms.

But ours is a unique position. We resist British Imperialism no less than Nazism. If there is a difference, it is in degree. One-fifth of the human race has been brought under the British heel by means that will not bear scrutiny. Our resistance to it does not mean harm to the British people. We seek to convert them, not to defeat them on the battlefield. Ours is an unarmed revolt against the British rule. But whether we convert them or not, we are determined to make their rule impossible by non-violent non-co-operation. It is a method in its nature indefensible. It is based on the knowledge that no spoliator can compass his end without a certain degree of co-operation, willing or compulsory, of the victim. Our rulers may have our land and bodies but not our souls. They can have the former only by complete destruction of every Indian—man, woman and child. That all may not rise to that degree of heroism and that a fair amount of frightfulness can bend the back of revolt is true but the argument would be beside the point. For, if a fair number of men and women be found in India who would be prepared without any ill will against the spoliators to lay down their lives rather than bend the knee to them, they would have shown the way to freedom from the tyranny of violence. I ask you to believe me when I say that you will find an unexpected number of such men and women in India. They have been having that training for the past 20 years.

We have been trying for the past half a century to throw off the British rule. The movement of independence has been never so strong as now. The most powerful political organization, I mean the Indian National Congress, is trying to achieve this end. We have attained a very fair measure of success through non-violent effort. We were groping for the right means to combat the most organized violence in the world which the British power represents. You have challenged it. It remains to be seen which is the better organized, the German or the British. We know what the British heel means for us and the non-European races of the world. But we would never wish to end the British rule with German aid. We have found in non-violence a force which, if organized, can without doubt match itself against a combination of all the most violent forces in the world. In non-violent technique, as I have said, there is no such thing as defeat. It is all 'do or die' without killing or hurting. It can be used practically without money and obviously without the aid of science of destruction which you have brought to such perfection. It is a marvel to me that you do not see that it is nobody's monopoly. If not the British, some other power will certainly improve upon your method and beat you with your own weapon. You are leaving no legacy to your people of which they would feel proud. They cannot take pride in a recital of cruel deed, however skilfully planned. I, therefore, appeal to you in the name of humanity to stop the war. You will lose nothing by referring all the matters of dispute between you and Great Britain to an international tribunal of your joint choice. If you attain success in the war, it will not prove that you were in the right. It will only prove that your power of destruction was greater. Whereas an award by an impartial tribunal will show as far as it is humanly possible which party was in the right.

You know that not long ago I made an appeal to every Briton to accept my method of non-violent resistance. I did it because the British know me as a friend though a rebel. I am a stranger to you and your people. I have not the courage to make you the appeal I made to every Briton. Not that it would not apply to you with the same force as to the British. But my present proposal is much simple because much more practical and familiar.

During this season when the hearts of the peoples of Europe yearn for peace, we have suspended even our own peaceful struggle. Is it too much to ask you to make an effort for peace during a time which may mean nothing to you personally but which must mean much to the millions of Europeans whose dumb cry for peace I hear, for my ears are attended to hearing the dumb millions? I had intended to address a joint appeal to you and Signor Mussolini, whom I had the privilege of meeting when I was in Rome during my visit to England as a delegate to the Round Table Conference. I hope that he will take this as addressed to him also with the necessary changes.

I am,
Your sincere friend,
MK GANDHI

Write the responses to the questions below in your learner portfolio.

Readers, writers, and texts connections

1) What is the purpose of the letter? Explain how the purpose is connected to global issues.
2) Identify how Gandhi uses ethos (credibility of speaker), pathos (emotion), and logos (logic) in his letter to clarify his purpose and persuade his audience.
3) How do the literary elements such as imagery, figurative language, syntax, and diction help the writer develop the appeals?
4) Of the three appeals, which one, if any, do you consider most dominant (compelling)? Why?
5) What is the tone of the piece?

Gandhi wrote an initial letter to Hitler just before the start of World War II in 1939 and a second letter in 1940. Hitler never actually received the letters.

```
                                        As at Wardha
                                        C.P.
                                        India.
                                        23.7.'39.
Dear friend,

      Friends have been urging me to write to you for the sake
of humanity.  But I have resisted their request, because of
the feeling that any letter from me would be an impertinence.
Something tells me that I must not calculate and that I must
make my appeal for whatever it may be worth.

      It is quite clear that you are today the one person in
the world who can prevent a  war which may reduce humanity to
the savage state.  Must you pay that price for an object
however worthy it may appear to you to be ? Will you listen to
the appeal of one who has seliberately shunned the method of
war not without considerable success? Any way I anticipate
your forgiveness, if I have erred in writing to you.

Herr Hitler                       I remain,
Berlin                            Your sincere friend
Germany.
```

Intertextual connections

Now that you have analysed a letter that Gandhi wrote to Hitler in 1940 (during World War II), and read an earlier (and much shorter) letter that he wrote to Hitler in 1939 just before the war started:

6) What historical context may account for the differences in tone and content between the two letters?

7) To what extent do Gandhi's rhetorical strategies in the letters differ or overlap?
8) Is one letter more powerful or convincing than the other? Explain.
9) What is the significance of considering these letters in relation to each other rather than singly?

Considering time and space

10) Nearly a century has passed since these letters were written. How do you think Gandhi would regard modern-day global politics? To whom might he write? What would he say?
11) Using the letters you've just read as a guide, write a letter to a world leader that adopts Gandhi's rhetoric and sentiments. Share your letter with a small group and discuss how your various perspectives overlap or differ.

Different types of non-fiction

Letters

Perspective matters. As you can see from the example above, letters have a very clearly intended reader and are often written for one specific person. The Romans divided letters into two categories: private (*personalis*) and business letters or letters of affairs (*negotialis*). We can add to these a third category, which would be the open letter, written to the public at large.

Letters employ the first-person narrative to communicate their message. The essential elements to grasp when thinking of letters (or the **epistolary** form) is that they have an extremely loose structure, unlike speeches and essays, which we will discuss later in this chapter. Letters make use of context without necessarily feeling the need to explain situations in great detail to the uninformed reader, as they are written with the expectation that the events discussed will be known. Hence, the tone of letters tends to be very personal.

Connections

The epistolary form of literature focuses mostly on letters, though other types of documents, including diary entries, newspaper or article clippings, and in recent years, online blogs and emails, are also part of the genre. Earlier forms of the novel, such as Goethe's *The Sorrows of Young Werther* and Mary Shelley's *Frankenstein*, often included epistolary documents. Such inclusions allow the writers to tell their stories from different points of view without relying on an omniscient narrator. Letters also add a non-fictional quality to novels, making their fictional narratives seem more authentic.

Consider the personal tone of the letter on page 158 from Sullivan Ballou to his wife Sarah. Ballou, a soldier during the American Civil War, wrote the letter just a week before he was killed at the Battle of Bull Run.

Headquarters, Camp Clark
Washington, D.C., July 14, 1861

My Very Dear Wife:

Indications are very strong that we shall move in a few days, perhaps to-morrow. Lest I should not be able to write you again, I feel impelled to write a few lines, that may fall under your eye when I shall be no more...

I have no misgivings about, or lack of confidence in, the cause in which I am engaged, and my courage does not halt or falter. I know how strongly American civilization now leans upon the triumph of government, and how great a debt we owe to those who went before us through the blood and suffering of the Revolution, and I am willing, perfectly willing to lay down all my joys in this life to help maintain this government, and to pay that debt...

But, my dear wife, when I know, that with my own joys, I lay down nearly all of yours, and replace them in this life with care and sorrows, when, after having eaten for long years the bitter fruit of orphanage myself, I must offer it, as their only sustenance, to my dear little children, is it weak or dishonorable, while the banner of my purpose floats calmly and proudly in the breeze, that my unbounded love for you, my darling wife and children, should struggle in fierce, though useless, contest with my love of country...

Sullivan Ballou

Sarah, my love for you is deathless. It seems to bind me with mighty cables, that nothing but Omnipotence can break; and yet, my love of country comes over me like a strong wind, and bears me irresistibly on with all those chains, to the battlefield.

The memories of all the blissful moments I have spent with you come crowding over me, and I feel most deeply grateful to God and you, that I have enjoyed them so long. And how hard it is for me to give them up, and burn to ashes the hopes of future years, when, God willing, we might still have lived and loved together, and seen our boys grow up to honorable manhood around us.

I know I have but few claims upon Divine Providence, but something whispers to me, perhaps it is the wafted prayer of my little Edgar, that I shall return to my loved ones unharmed. If I do not, my dear Sarah, never forget how much I love you, nor that, when my last breath escapes me on the battle-field, it will whisper your name...

Sarah, do not mourn me dear; think I am gone, and wait for me, for we shall meet again...

Activity 3 A closer look at personal communications

Readers, writers, and texts connections

1) Identify the tone of Ballou's letter on page 158. How does the audience shape the tone?
2) How does Ballou blend ethos and pathos in his letter? What is the effect?
3) What does this letter reveal about the relationship between Ballou and his wife? His country? His cause? What do these relationships reveal about his character?
4) In the past, letter writing was a more popular form of literary non-fiction, but newer technologies have made it less popular. Do you think meaningful written communications between friends and family members have been reduced because letter writing is on the decline or have other, perhaps more technologically themed forms of communication simply taken their place? Is one form more effective than another? Explain.

How has technology changed the way we communicate with each other?

Activity 4 Combining intertextual and time and space connections

Compare the tone and purpose of Sullivan Ballou's letter to his wife, Sarah with either of Gandhi's letters to Hitler.

1) How does the form of this non-fiction category change according to the audience and reasons for writing?
2) To what extent is your knowledge and understanding of the letters dependent on culture and context?

Essays

The essay form is an older subgenre that harkens back to Montaigne's writings in 16th-century France where the word for essay (*essais*) means an 'attempt' or 'try'. Montaigne wrote in French but borrowed ideas and phrases from Greek, Latin, and Italian thinkers to craft his thoughts, which were more investigative or introspective journeys than structured arguments. The form thrives today in periodicals, blogs, anthologies, and stand-alone works. You may be writing your own personal essay during the university application process.

Essay writing can be personal and is often political. George Orwell, who is known for both his novels and essays, argues that politics, or more specifically the 'desire to push the world in a certain direction, to alter other peoples' idea of the kind of society that they should strive after', is the thrust behind all commendable writing. 'Good prose,' Orwell maintains, 'is like a windowpane… and looking back through my work, I see that it is invariably where I lacked a political purpose that I wrote lifeless books…' ('Why I Write').

But good writing is not just purposeful. In literary non-fiction 'words and their right arrangement' also matter: there is nothing quite like 'the firmness of good prose or the rhythm of a good story' (Orwell, 'Why I Write'). In this section, you will read George Orwell's essay 'A Hanging', which blends political purpose with literary-minded prose. The essay first appeared in 1931 in *The Adelphi*, a popular English literary and political magazine that published reviews, articles, and letters from 1922 to 1948.

Time and space considerations

During his early career, when much of India was under British rule, George Orwell worked in Burma (now Myanmar) as a British police officer. Young Orwell, then known as Eric Blair, was just 19 years old when he joined the British Imperial Police,

Burma – the location of George Orwell's non-fiction essay, 'A Hanging'.

a job he held for five years before returning to England, changing his name, and beginning his successful career as a writer.

After leaving Burma, Orwell wrote both fiction and non-fiction accounts of his time there. As you read the essay 'A Hanging', it is important to remember that the 'I' in this narrative is Orwell himself and the experience he recounts is his own reflection on an actual event that occurred many years before he wrote it down.

'A Hanging' by George Orwell (1931)

It was in Burma, a sodden morning of the rains. A sickly light, like yellow tinfoil, was slanting over the high walls into the jail yard. We were waiting outside the condemned cells, a row of sheds fronted with double bars, like small animal cages. Each cell measured about ten feet by ten and was quite bare within except for a plank bed and a pot of drinking water. In some of them brown silent men were squatting at the inner bars, with their blankets draped round them. These were the condemned men, due to be hanged within the next week or two.

One prisoner had been brought out of his cell. He was a Hindu, a puny wisp of a man, with a shaven head and vague liquid eyes. He had a thick, sprouting moustache, absurdly too big for his body, rather like the moustache of a comic man on the films. Six tall Indian warders were guarding him and getting him ready for the gallows. Two of them stood by with rifles and fixed bayonets, while the others handcuffed him, passed a chain through his handcuffs and fixed it to their belts, and lashed his arms tight to his sides. They crowded very close about him, with their hands always on him in a careful, caressing grip, as though all the while feeling him to make sure he was there. It was like men handling a fish which is still alive and may jump back into the water. But he stood quite unresisting, yielding his arms limply to the ropes, as though he hardly noticed what was happening.

Eight o'clock struck and a bugle call, desolately thin in the wet air, floated from the distant barracks. The superintendent of the jail, who was standing apart from the rest of us, moodily prodding the gravel with his stick, raised his head at the sound. He was an army doctor, with a grey toothbrush moustache and a gruff voice. 'For God's sake hurry up, Francis,' he said irritably. 'The man ought to have been dead by this time. Aren't you ready yet?'

Francis, the head jailer, a fat Dravidian in a white drill suit and gold spectacles, waved his black hand. 'Yes sir, yes sir,' he bubbled. 'All iss satisfactorily prepared. The hangman iss waiting. We shall proceed.'

'Well, quick march, then. The prisoners can't get their breakfast till this job's over.'

We set out for the gallows. Two warders marched on either side of the prisoner, with their rifles at the slope; two others marched close against him, gripping him by arm and shoulder, as though at once pushing and supporting him. The rest of us, magistrates and the like, followed behind. Suddenly, when we had gone ten yards, the procession stopped short without any order or warning. A dreadful thing had happened — a dog, come goodness knows whence, had appeared in the yard. It came bounding among us with a loud volley of barks, and leapt round us wagging its whole body, wild with glee at finding so many human beings together. It was a large woolly dog, half Airedale, half pariah. For a moment it pranced round us, and then, before anyone could stop it, it had made a dash for the prisoner, and jumping up tried to lick his face. Everyone stood aghast, too taken aback even to grab at the dog.

'Who let that bloody brute in here?' said the superintendent angrily. 'Catch it, someone!'

A warder, detached from the escort, charged clumsily after the dog, but it danced and gambolled just out of his reach, taking everything as part of the game. A young Eurasian jailer picked up a handful of gravel and tried to stone the dog away, but it dodged the stones and came after us again. Its yaps echoed from the jail wails. The prisoner, in the grasp of the two warders, looked on incuriously, as though this was another formality of the hanging. It was several minutes before someone managed to catch the dog. Then we put my handkerchief through its collar and moved off once more, with the dog still straining and whimpering.

It was about forty yards to the gallows. I watched the bare brown back of the prisoner marching in front of me. He walked clumsily with his bound arms, but quite steadily, with that bobbing gait of the Indian who never straightens his knees. At each step his muscles slid neatly into place, the lock of hair on his scalp danced up and down, his feet printed themselves on the wet gravel. And once, in spite of the men who gripped him by each shoulder, he stepped slightly aside to avoid a puddle on the path.

It is curious, but till that moment I had never realized what it means to destroy a healthy, conscious man. When I saw the prisoner step aside to avoid the puddle, I saw the mystery, the unspeakable wrongness, of cutting a life short when it is in full tide. This man was not dying, he was alive just as we were alive. All the organs of his body were working — bowels digesting food, skin renewing itself, nails growing, tissues forming — all toiling away in solemn foolery. His nails would still be growing when he stood on the drop, when he was falling through the air with a tenth of a second to live. His eyes saw the yellow gravel and the grey walls, and his brain still remembered, foresaw, reasoned — reasoned even about puddles. He and we were a party of men walking together, seeing, hearing, feeling, understanding the same world; and in two minutes, with a sudden snap, one of us would be gone — one mind less, one world less.

The gallows stood in a small yard, separate from the main grounds of the prison, and overgrown with tall prickly weeds. It was a brick erection like three sides of a shed, with planking on top, and above that two beams and a crossbar with the rope dangling. The hangman, a grey-haired convict in the white uniform of the prison, was waiting beside his machine. He greeted us with a servile crouch as we entered. At a word from Francis the two warders, gripping the prisoner more closely than ever, half led, half pushed him to the gallows and helped him clumsily up the ladder. Then the hangman climbed up and fixed the rope round the prisoner's neck.

We stood waiting, five yards away. The warders had formed in a rough circle round the gallows. And then, when the noose was fixed, the prisoner began crying out on his god. It was a high, reiterated cry of 'Ram! Ram! Ram! Ram!', not urgent and fearful like a prayer or a cry for help, but steady, rhythmical, almost like the tolling of a bell. The dog answered the sound with a whine. The hangman, still standing on the gallows, produced a small cotton bag like a flour bag and drew it down over the prisoner's face. But the sound, muffled by the cloth, still persisted, over and over again: 'Ram! Ram! Ram! Ram! Ram!'

The hangman climbed down and stood ready, holding the lever. Minutes seemed to pass. The steady, muffled crying from the prisoner went on and on, 'Ram! Ram! Ram!' never faltering for an instant. The superintendent, his head on his chest, was slowly poking the ground with his stick; perhaps he was counting the cries, allowing the prisoner a fixed number — fifty, perhaps, or a hundred. Everyone had changed colour. The Indians had gone grey like bad coffee, and one or two of the bayonets were wavering. We looked at the lashed, hooded man on the drop, and listened to his cries — each cry another second of life; the same thought was in all our minds: oh, kill him quickly, get it over, stop that abominable noise!

Suddenly the superintendent made up his mind. Throwing up his head he made a swift motion with his stick. 'Chalo!' he shouted almost fiercely.

There was a clanking noise, and then dead silence. The prisoner had vanished, and the rope was twisting on itself. I let go of the dog, and it galloped immediately to the back of the gallows; but when it got there it stopped short, barked, and then retreated into a corner of the yard, where it stood among the weeds, looking timorously out at us. We went round the gallows to inspect the prisoner's body. He was dangling with his toes pointed straight downwards, very slowly revolving, as dead as a stone.

The superintendent reached out with his stick and poked the bare body; it oscillated, slightly. '*He*'s all right,' said the superintendent. He backed out from under the gallows, and blew out a deep breath. The moody look had gone out of his face quite suddenly. He glanced at his wrist-watch. 'Eight minutes past eight. Well, that's all for this morning, thank God.'

The warders unfixed bayonets and marched away. The dog, sobered and conscious of having misbehaved itself, slipped after them. We walked out of the gallows yard, past the condemned cells with their waiting prisoners, into the big central yard of the prison. The convicts, under the command of warders armed with lathis, were already receiving their breakfast. They squatted in long rows, each man holding a tin pannikin, while two warders with buckets marched round ladling out rice; it seemed quite a homely, jolly scene, after the hanging. An enormous relief had come upon us now that the job was done. One felt an impulse to sing, to break into a run, to snigger. All at once everyone began chattering gaily.

The Eurasian boy walking beside me nodded towards the way we had come, with a knowing smile: 'Do you know, sir, our friend (he meant the dead man), when he heard his appeal had been dismissed, he pissed on the floor of his cell. From fright. — Kindly take one of my cigarettes, sir. Do you not admire my new silver case, sir? From the boxwallah, two rupees eight annas. Classy European style.'

Several people laughed — at what, nobody seemed certain.

Francis was walking by the superintendent, talking garrulously. 'Well, sir, all hass passed off with the utmost satisfactoriness. It wass all finished — flick! like that. It iss not always so — oah, no! I have known cases where the doctor wass obliged to go beneath the gallows and pull the prisoner's legs to ensure decease. Most disagreeable!'

'Wriggling about, eh? That's bad,' said the superintendent.

'Ach, sir, it iss worse when they become refractory! One man, I recall, clung to the bars of hiss cage when we went to take him out. You will scarcely credit, sir, that it took six warders to dislodge him, three pulling at each leg. We reasoned with him. 'My dear fellow,' we said, 'think of all the pain and trouble you are causing to us!' But no, he would not listen! Ach, he wass very troublesome!'

I found that I was laughing quite loudly. Everyone was laughing. Even the superintendent grinned in a tolerant way. 'You'd better all come out and have a drink,' he said quite genially. 'I've got a bottle of whisky in the car. We could do with it.'

We went through the big double gates of the prison, into the road. 'Pulling at his legs!' exclaimed a Burmese magistrate suddenly, and burst into a loud chuckling. We all began laughing again. At that moment Francis's anecdote seemed extraordinarily funny. We all had a drink together, native and European alike, quite amicably. The dead man was a hundred yards away.

1931

Activity 5 Readers, writers, and texts connections

1) **Form**: This is a non-fiction essay, but it may read more like fiction. Which aspects of the essay are 'story-like'?
2) **Point of view**: To what extent is Orwell a reliable narrator? Which aspects of the essay seems most credible? Why?
3) **Literary elements**: How does Orwell use imagery? Figurative language? Symbolism? How does the use of such devices develop the tone of the work?
4) **Transformation**: How might the effect of the narrative change if Orwell described the experience in a more factual (less literary) way?

TOK

Since Orwell wrote this essay many years after the event, it's unlikely that he could remember every detail and quote with accuracy, yet this work is still categorised as non-fiction. To what extent can we say that non-fiction accounts are true?

5) **Writer's impressions and audience assumptions:** How does Orwell feel about the man's hanging? How do you regard Orwell's actions as a police officer in Burma who participated in this event? To what extent should individuals be held personally responsible for actions initiated by a corrupt system?

6) **Essay vs journal/diary writing:** Why is it significant that Orwell decided to write about this event in an essay form rather than in a personal journal or diary?

Global issue

Orwell's essay raises several global issues about justice and power. How does he explore the effects of imperialism and capital punishment in 'A Hanging'? Discuss in a small group and write your responses in your learner portfolio.

Speeches

Speeches are spoken pieces of rhetoric used to raise awareness, make a statement, rally people around a cause, or inspire. They differ from numerous other types of non-fiction in that they are intended for an audience to hear rather than read.

The art of making speeches, using language for public verbal persuasion, was known traditionally as rhetoric and was one of the most important aspects of an education in the ancient world. Some of the famous speech-makers of the past include the Roman philosopher Cicero, Winston Churchill, and Adolf Hitler. Politicians are not the only ones to make speeches, though, and there are a host of examples of powerful speeches made by human rights activists, celebrities, CEOs, and even sports figures.

Activity 6 Analysing inspiring moments through speech

Arundhati Roy is a well-known writer who is perhaps best known for her first novel, *The God of Small Things*, which won the Man Booker Prize in 1997. Over the past two decades her non-fiction works have gained her notoriety as a fierce political activist who raises awareness for human rights and environmental causes.

In the speech below, which Roy delivered at the PEN World Voices Festival on 12 May 2019 in New York City, she discusses her experiences as a writer and humanitarian who continuously crosses literary forms and political borders.

Arundhati Roy, author and political activist

Here are excerpts from her lecture:

I remember sitting in a lecture hall in a college in Hyderabad in front of an audience of five or six hundred students. On my left, chairing the event, was the vice-chancellor of the university. On my right, a professor of poetry. The vice-chancellor whispered in my ear, 'You shouldn't spend any more time on fiction. Your political writing is the thing to concentrate on.' The professor of poetry whispered, 'When will you get back to writing fiction? That is your true calling. This other stuff you do is just ephemeral.'

I have never felt that my fiction and non-fiction were warring factions battling for suzerainty. They aren't the same certainly, but trying to pin down the difference between them is actually harder than I imagined. Fact and fiction are not converse. One is not necessarily truer than the other, more factual than the other, or more real than the other. Or even, in my case, more widely read than the other. All I can say is that I feel the difference in my body when I'm writing.

Sitting between the two professors, I enjoyed their contradictory advice. I sat there smiling, thinking of the first message I received from John Berger. It was a beautiful handwritten letter, from a writer who had been my hero for years: 'Your fiction and non-fiction — they walk you around the world like your two legs.' That settled it for me.

... I'm still here, standing on my two writing legs, speaking to you. But my lecturer friend is in jail, charged with participating in anti-national activity. India's prisons are packed tight with political prisoners — most of them accused of being either Maoist or Islamist terrorists.... In the latest batch of pre-election arrests, teachers, lawyers, activists, and writers have been jailed, charged with plotting to assassinate Prime Minister Modi. The plot is so ludicrous that a six-year-old could have improved on it. The fascists need to take some good fiction-writing courses...

Much of this has been the subject of my writing, fiction as well as non-fiction, for several years....

The God of Small Things, published in the summer of 1997, was the result of a search for a language and a form to describe the world I had grown up in, to myself and to people I loved, some of whom were entirely unfamiliar with Kerala. I had studied architecture, written screenplays, and now I wanted to write a novel. A novel that could only be a novel — not a novel that really wanted to be a film, or a manifesto, or sociological treatise of some kind.

In May 1998, less than a year after the publication of *The God of Small Things*... the prime minister at the time... fulfilled a longstanding dream... by conducting a series of nuclear tests. Pakistan responded immediately with tests of its own. The nuclear tests were the beginning of the journey toward the crazed rhetoric of nationalism that has become a normal form of public speech in India today. I was taken aback by the orgy of celebration that greeted the nuclear tests... That was when I wrote my first essay, 'The End of Imagination,' condemning the tests. I said that entering the nuclear race would colonize our imagination: 'If it's anti-Indian and anti-Hindu to have a nuclear bomb implanted in my brain,' I wrote, 'then I secede. I hereby declare myself a mobile republic.'

I will leave you to imagine the reaction that followed.

'The End of Imagination' was the first of what would turn out to be 20 years of writing non-fiction essays.... For each essay, I searched for a form, for language, for structure and narrative. Could I write as compellingly about irrigation as I could about love and loss and childhood? About the salinization of soil? About drainage? Dams? Crops? About structural adjustment and privatization? About the per unit cost of electricity? About things that affect ordinary peoples' lives? Not as reportage, but as a form of storytelling? Was it possible to turn these topics into literature? Literature for everybody — including for people who couldn't read and write, but who had taught me how to think, and could be read to?...

Almost every essay got me into enough trouble to make me promise myself that I wouldn't write another. But inevitably, situations arose in which the effort of keeping quiet set up such a noise in my head, such an ache in my blood, that I succumbed, and wrote....

Intertextual connections

1) Roy's speech and Orwell's essay focus on how issues of power and subjugation in India have global implications, but Orwell speaks from the position of an outsider who observes the events in a country that is not his own, while Roy observes what is happening in her own country and culture. What is the effect of putting these two different perspectives side by side? What do you notice?

2) Roy and Orwell are both fiction and non-fiction writers. Why do you think Roy spends the first part of her argument talking about these two forms of writing? How does her discussion of writing, particularly different forms of writing, connect to the global issues she explores?

3) How would you characterise the tone of each piece? What does this reveal about each author's intension?

4) Orwell presents his points through writing and Roy through speech. How do the different delivery methods affect the impact of their arguments?

5) Consider the following quote by Roy: 'For me my fiction and my non-fiction are both political. The fiction is a universe, the non-fiction is an argument.' Make a list of other writers to which this quote may apply. Explain your rationale for your choices and share them with a partner or small group.

Reading, listening, and comparing modes

6) Roy's speech is multilayered. She uses the form of speech to discuss the difference between writing about fiction and non-fiction. Reread her speech and imagine how she sounds. **Transform** the sound of the words in your mind. Which words would be emphasised? Where would she pause? At what point would she alter her pacing?

7) Go online and find a video of Roy's speech titled 'Come September'. Listen to the first two minutes of the speech. Compare the way she begins 'Come September' with the way she begins her address at the PEN Literary Festival as written above (**intertextuality**). What does her body language suggest? Her tone? Her persona?

8) What is the difference between watching and listening to a speech and reading it? What are the advantages and disadvantages of the two formats (representations)?

9) Share your findings with a partner or small group and write a brief reflection of your discussion in your learner portfolio.

Activity 7 Speech mash-ups: an intertextual activity

In music, a mash-up involves mixing the lyrics of two or more songs to create a new song. This type of transformation creates a new representation within the same form.

For this activity, you will research several of the speeches listed below and then create a new speech using the phrases from at least three speeches.

Emmeline Pankhurst, 'Freedom or Death'
Elizabeth I, 'Speech to the Troops at Tilbury'
Lou Gehrig, 'Farewell to Baseball Address'
Napoleon Bonaparte, 'Farewell to the Old Guard'
Winston Churchill, 'Never Give In'

Aung San Suu Kyi, 'Freedom From Fear'
Theodore Roosevelt, 'Strength and Decency'
Ronald Reagan, 'Address to the Nation on the Challenger'
Sojourner Truth, 'Ain't I A Woman'
Martin Luther King, 'I Have a Dream'
Douglas MacArthur, 'Duty, Honor, Country'
William Faulkner's Nobel Prize Acceptance Speech
Charles De Gaulle, 'The Appeal of 18 June'
Chief Joseph, 'Surrender Speech'
Socrates, 'Apology'
Mahatma Gandhi, 'Quit India'
Marcus Tullius Cicero, 'The First Oration Against Catiline'
Patrick Henry, 'Give Me Liberty or Give Me Death!'
Frederick Douglass, 'What to the Slave is the Fourth of July?'
Abraham Lincoln, 'The Gettysburg Address'
Martin Luther King Jr, 'I Have a Dream'

 Lou Gehrig

▲ Napoleon Bonaparte

▲ Aung San Suu Kyi

▲ Chief Joseph

1) Be sure to research the context and content of each speech as well as the background of the person who delivered it, so that you'll have some knowledge of the original texts when you construct your own.

2) Your mash-up will consist of words and phrases from existing speeches, but you are essentially creating a new text (representation) with a defined purpose and audience.

3) Feel free to add some of your own lines for transition or alter a word here or there as needed.

4) Once you have written your speech, prepare to present it. Consider body language, voice projection, pacing, eye contact, and inflection (the tone and pitch of your voice) as you prepare. Memorise the speech as best you can so that your delivery will be smooth and continuous. Alternatively, you could create a video or slideshow where your speech would function as a 'voiceover' as your multi-media visuals are presented.

5) Once you've completed the written or oral parts of this activity, write a short reflection in your learner portfolio. How did using the rhetoric from past speeches help you find your own voice?

Memoirs and autobiographies

The famous 18th-century British literary wit, Dr Samuel Johnson, is believed to have said that no man is better qualified to write his life than himself (although we could doubt this quite seriously). Autobiographies are accounts of a life written by that person. Memoirs differ from autobiographies in that their focus tends to be more on what the writer has observed than a chronological account of events that reveal character development. Memoir writers are less concerned with accuracy of dates than recreating the authenticity of experience. It is impossible to remember a conversation that occurred many years ago, but it is perfectly permissible, even encouraged, to include dialogue in memoirs because it captures the essence of the experience more thoroughly than description alone.

Jeannette Walls' memoir, *The Glass Castle*, was published in 2005 and by 2007 had sold over 2.7 million copies. Set in 20th-century America in the south-west, West Virginia, and New York City, the compelling narrative centres on Walls' impoverished childhood and dysfunctional family, with much focus on her abusive and alcoholic father. Despite parental neglect and rodent-infested living conditions, Walls also reveals moments of joy and connection, showing the complexities of familial bonds and the fortitude of the human heart.

Activity 8 Analysing the role of memory and emotion in knowledge

For this activity, you will read two separate passages from *The Glass Castle*. Directions will follow each passage.

The Glass Castle by Jeannette Walls (2005)

Passage 1

When I started sixth grade, the other kids made fun of Brian and me because we were so skinny. They called me spider legs, skeleton girl, pipe cleaner, two-by-four, bony butt, stick woman, bean pole, and giraffe, and they said I could stay dry in the rain by standing under a telephone wire. At lunchtime, when other kids unwrapped their sandwiches or bought their hot meals, Brian and I would get out books and read. Brian told everyone he had to keep his weight down because he wanted to join the wrestling team when he got to high school. I told people that I had forgotten to bring my lunch. No one believed me, so I started hiding in the bathroom during lunch hour. I'd stay in one of the stalls with the door locked and my feet propped up so that no one would recognize my shoes. When other girls came in and threw away their lunch bags in the garbage pails, I'd go retrieve them. I couldn't get over the way kids tossed out all this perfectly good food: apples, hard-boiled eggs, packages of peanut-butter crackers, sliced pickles, half-pint cartons of milk, cheese sandwiches with just one bite taken out because the kid didn't like the pimentos in the cheese. I'd return to the stall and polish off my tasty finds. There was, at times, more food in the wastebasket than I could eat. The first time I found extra food — a bologna-and-cheese sandwich — I stuffed it into my purse to take home for Brian. Back in the classroom, I started worrying about how I'd explain to Brian where it came from. I was pretty sure he was rooting through the trash, too, but we never talked about it. As I sat there trying to come up with ways to justify it to Brian, I began smelling the bologna. It seemed to fill the whole room. I became terrified that the other kids could smell it, too, and that they'd turn and see my overstuffed purse, and since they all knew I never ate lunch, they'd figure out that I had pinched it from the trash. As soon as class was over, I ran to the bathroom and shoved the sandwich back in the garbage can.

1) After reading the passage above, write a brief reflection in your learner portfolio. Don't think too long. Just write.
   - What words come to mind as you think about the speaker's experience?
   - What is her life like? Her attitude?
   - What emotions does this passage evoke in you?

Once you have finished your quick-write, read the next passage.

The Glass Castle by Jeannette Walls (2005)

Passage 2

I never believed in Santa Claus. None of us kids did. Mom and Dad refused to let us. They couldn't afford expensive presents and they didn't want us to think we weren't as good as other kids who, on Christmas morning, found all sorts of fancy toys under the tree that were supposedly left by Santa Claus.

Dad had lost his job at the gypsum, and when Christmas came that year, we had no money at all. On Christmas Eve, Dad took each one of us kids out into the desert night one by one.
'Pick out your favorite star,' Dad said.

'I like that one!' I said.

Dad grinned, 'that's Venus', he said. He explained to me that planets glowed because reflected light was constant and stars twinkled because their light pulsed.

'I like it anyway' I said.

'What the hell,' Dad said. 'It's Christmas. You can have a planet if you want.'
And he gave me Venus.

Venus didn't have any moons or satellites or even a magnetic field, but it did have an atmosphere sort of similar to Earth's, except it was super hot - about 500 degrees or more. 'So,' Dad said, 'when the sun starts to burn out and Earth turns cold, everyone might want to move to Venus to get warm. And they'll have to get permission from your descendants first.'

We laughed about all the kids who believed in the Santa myth and got nothing for Christmas but a bunch of cheap plastic toys. 'Years from now, when all the junk they got is broken and long forgotten,' Dad said, 'you'll still have your stars.'

2) Write a second reflection in your learner portfolio, this time focusing on the speaker's feelings connected with this moment. What emotions come to mind? Make a short list. What does this memory tell you about her family? About her father?

3) Briefly compare this passage with the passage above. What does reading them together tell you about the character's culture and identity that reading them singly does not?

4) Work with a partner or small group and share your responses.

Connections

Listening in… how personal stories connect to global issues

Since memoirs are personal and the 'I' in the memoir is the author, it's interesting to hear not just about the writer but *from* the writer. Using the QR code, listen to the PBS broadcast as Jeannette Walls discusses her experience writing *The Glass Castle*, and how sharing her story affected how others perceived her.

- How did listening to this podcast affect your perception of the passages above and the author herself?
- To what extent does personalising a global issue, such as homelessness, alter your understanding of it?

Write a reflection to the questions above in your learner portfolio or discuss them with a small group.

Activity 9 Writing a mini-memoir

Memoir writers often focus on a specific event and use literary language to transport their readers to that moment in time.

1) Think of a memory that is meaningful to you. It could involve something ordinary like cooking with a grandparent, or extraordinary like surviving a near-fatal accident.

2) In draft form, write down everything you remember, especially how you felt at the time. These can be sentences or just bullet points.

3) Transform your notes into a short memoir-like piece that includes details and dialogue from a singular experience. This is not a long assignment; you are focusing on a singular moment in time. Use your memory and **creativity** to communicate your moment, your perspective. Include your memoir in your learner portfolio.

TOK

As you read back over your memoir, reflect on the significance of truth in memoir writing. Even if the quotes and details are not fully accurate, to what extent did they help you present a more authentic representation of your experience?

What effect did the act of writing the mini-memoir have on you? In other words, what did you learn about the situation? About yourself? Write down your reflections in your learner portfolio.

Memoir writing captures the feelings behind memory.

Travel writing

'To travel is to make a journey, a movement through space', travel writer and scholar Carl Thompson points out. 'Possibly this journey is epic in scale, taking the traveler to the other side of the world or across a continent, or up a mountain; possibly, it is more modest in scope, and takes place within the limits of the traveler's own country or region, or even just their immediate locality.' People travel for different reasons, but travel writers choose to document their journeys with a perceptive eye, and use their pens to create a shared, connected experience.

Travel writing often challenges the imaginary or idealised rendering of a place.

There are many different styles and types of travel literature through the ages, but they all focus on a writer's perception of place and culture. Herodotus' *History of the Persian Wars*, Strabo's *Geographica*, or Pausanias' *Guide to Greece* comprise early accounts of travel literature dating all the way back to 440 BC. Well-known epics such as Homer's *Odyssey* or Dante's *Divine Comedy* use the fiction literary form to mix myth with journey, creating a framework for the non-fiction travelogues that would follow in later centuries. More recent texts such as Jack Kerouac's *On the Road* or Robert Pirsig's *Zen and the Art of Motorcycle Maintenance* demonstrate how the literal journey can be a path to self-discovery.

The focus and style of travel writing varies between time periods and cultures. Scottish historian and non-fiction writer, William Dalrymple, makes an interesting observation: 'If 19th-century travel writing was principally about place – about filling in the blanks of the map and describing remote places that few had seen – I think that some of the best 21st-century travel writing is about people: exploring the extraordinary diversity that still exists in the world beneath the veneer of globalisation.'

With Dalrymple's observation in mind, read the two travel-writing passages below that span these different time periods (19th and 21st centuries) and complete the activities that follow each passage.

19th-century travel literature often focused on the transformative power of idyllic settings.

Activity 10 Travel literature through time and space

Passage 1

Summer on the Lakes by Margaret Fuller (1843)

No heaven need wear a lovelier aspect than earth did this afternoon, after the clearing up of the shower. We traversed the blooming plain, unmarked by any road, only the friendly track of wheels which tracked, not broke the grass. Our stations were not from town to town, but grove to grove. These groves first floated like blue islands in the distance. As we drew nearer, they seemed fair parks, and the little log houses on the edge, with their curling smokes, harmonized beautifully with them.

1) As evidenced from the passage above, travel is often a visual experience that connects us to setting. It also enables us to practise the art of mindfulness, of being in the moment. Using Margaret Fuller's passage as inspiration, take a nature walk. Even if you are in a busy city, you can notice greenery, flower vendors, a bird in the background. What do you observe? What do you hear? See? Smell? Feel free to take pictures during the activity.
2) When you return from your walk, write a paragraph that conveys a sense of place. You can use your notes or pictures for inspiration.

Passage 2

Travels with Herodotus by Ryszard Kapuściński (2008)

I walked around the city, copying down signboards, the names of goods in stores, words overheard at bus stops. In movie theaters, I scribbled blindly, in darkness, the words on the screen, and noted the slogans and banners carried by demonstrators in the streets. I approached India not through images, sounds, and smells, but through words; furthermore, words not of the indigenous Hindi, but of a foreign, imposed tongue, which by then had so fully taken root here that it was for me an indispensable key to this country, almost identical with it. I understood that every distinct geographic universe has its own mystery and that one can decipher it only by learning the local language. Without it, this universe will remain impenetrable and unknowable, even if one were to spend entire years in it.

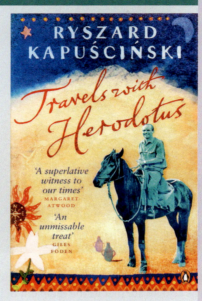

3) After reading this passage, go to a busy place like a café, museum, market, or any public area where you can observe language. Listen to the sound of it. It is best if you can observe a culture different than your own, but you can still do this within your own community. Listen. What do you hear? How is language conveyed through visual cues?

4) Write down what your observations reveal about the connection between language and culture. Use details. Transport your readers to a different place through a linguistic lens.

Kapuściński's *Travels with Herodotus* reveals how observing language and culture can provide insights into unknown places.

TOK

Research Margaret Fuller and Ryszard Kapuściński in terms of their culture and context. What additional contributions did they make to their professions? What interesting personal facts did you discover? Describe the culture and historical time in which they were writing. Who were their contemporaries? To what extent does this knowledge help you better understand, or perhaps even change, your perception regarding the passages your read for this exercise?

After considering these questions, write a short response in your learner portfolio.

Areas of exploration: analyse, evaluate, appreciate

Readers, writers, and texts in non-fiction: an approach to Toni Morrison's 'Nobel Prize Lecture' (1993)

On 7 December 1993, Toni Morrison stood before the members of the Swedish Academy, who days earlier had awarded her the Nobel Prize for Literature. The Academy noted that Morrison received this award because she was a writer 'who, in novels characterised by visionary force and poetic import, gives life to an essential aspect of American reality'.

Toni Morrison, winner of the 1993 Nobel Prize for Literature

As part of her acceptance of the award, Morrison was asked to address the members of the Academy. Her first words to this audience were as follows:

> Narrative has never been merely entertainment for me. It is, I believe, one of the principal ways in which we absorb knowledge. I hope you will understand, then, why I begin these remarks with the opening phrase of what must be the oldest sentence in the world, the earliest one we remember from childhood: 'Once upon a time…'

And then she followed with the lecture below. If you are able to do so, listen to Morrison read this lecture as you read along with her. Consider those lines, or even specific words, where Morrison seems to stress or direct her words to highlight their import to her audience. Her lecture was written for this specific audience, but she was also aware that as the recipient of literature's finest honour, her lecture would be heard, as well as read, by many lovers of literature from around the world.

As you read, also note that this lecture has been purposefully segmented to allow you the opportunity to observe the strategies that Morrison has used to address her audience. Her lecture requires close attention to language, perspective, and tone. Lines and phrases are underlined which require you to reflect on, question, discuss, and finally negotiate meaning.

Activity 11

Your initial questions to consider independently in your learner portfolio are these…

1) Why is this talk to the Swedish Academy referenced and titled as a 'lecture' as opposed to a 'speech'? What connotations are implicit in the term *lecture*? How do these connotations differ, or not, from the connotations of a *speech*?
2) Once you have completed these initial questions, share your ideas with your classmates and begin the reading of Morrison's Nobel Lecture.

'Nobel Prize Lecture' by Toni Morrison (1993)

'Once upon a time there was an old woman. Blind but wise.' Or was it an old man? A guru, perhaps. Or a griot soothing restless children. I have heard this story, or one exactly like it, in the lore of several cultures.

'Once upon a time there was an old woman. Blind. Wise.'

In the version I know the woman is the daughter of slaves, black, American, and lives alone in a small house outside of town. Her reputation for wisdom is without peer and without question. Among her people she is both the law and its transgression. The honor she is paid and the awe in which she is held reach beyond her neighborhood to places far away; to the city where the intelligence of rural prophets is the source of much amusement.

One day the woman is visited by some young people who seem to be bent on disproving her clairvoyance and showing her up for the fraud they believe she is. Their plan is simple: they enter her house and ask the one question the answer to which rides solely on her difference from them, a difference they regard as a profound disability: her blindness. They stand before her, and one of them says, 'Old woman, I hold in my hand a bird. Tell me whether it is living or dead.'

She does not answer, and the question is repeated. 'Is the bird I am holding living or dead?'

Still she doesn't answer. She is blind and cannot see her visitors, let alone what is in their hands. She does not know their color, gender or homeland. She only knows their motive.

The old woman's silence is so long, the young people have trouble holding their laughter.

Activity 12

What is their motive? Do the young people believe that the old woman's blindness is a sign of weakness? In what sense is it a 'profound disability'? Why do they laugh? What emotion is at the source of this laughter?

Finally she speaks and her voice is soft but stern. 'I don't know,' she says. 'I don't know whether the bird you are holding is dead or alive, but what I do know is that it is in your hands. It is in your hands.'

Her answer can be taken to mean: 'if it is dead, you have either found it that way or you have killed it. If it is alive, you can still kill it. Whether it is to stay alive, it is your decision. Whatever the case, it is your responsibility.'

For parading their power and her helplessness, the young visitors are reprimanded, told they are responsible not only for the act of mockery but also for the small bundle of life sacrificed to achieve its aims. The blind woman shifts attention away from assertions of power to the instrument through which that power is exercised.

Activity 13

1) What is important about the old woman's voice?
2) Is there logic in the old woman's reply?
3) What connotation does the word 'parading' have?
4) Why is the young people's question an 'act of mockery'?

Speculation on what (other than its own frail body) that bird-in-the-hand might signify has always been attractive to me, but especially so now thinking, as I have been, about the work I do that has brought me to this company. So I choose to read the bird as language and the woman as a practiced writer. She is worried about how the language she dreams in, given to her at birth, is handled, put into service, even withheld from her for certain nefarious purposes. Being a writer she thinks of language partly as a system, partly as a living thing over which one has control, but mostly as agency – as an act with consequences. So the question the children put to her: 'Is it living or dead?' is not unreal because she thinks of language as susceptible to death, erasure; certainly imperiled and salvageable only by an effort of the will. She believes that if the bird in the hands of her visitors is dead the custodians are responsible for the corpse. For her a dead language is not only one no longer spoken or written, it is unyielding language content to admire its own paralysis. Like statist language, censored and censoring. Ruthless in its policing duties, it has no desire or purpose other than maintaining the free range of its own narcotic narcissism, its own exclusivity and dominance. However moribund, it is not without effect for <u>it actively thwarts the intellect, stalls conscience, suppresses human potential</u>. Unreceptive to interrogation, <u>it cannot form or tolerate new ideas, shape other thoughts, tell another story, fill baffling silences.</u> Official language <u>smitheryed to sanction ignorance and preserve privilege</u> is a suit of armor polished to shocking glitter, a husk from which the knight departed long ago. Yet there it is: <u>dumb, predatory, sentimental</u>. Exciting reverence in schoolchildren, providing shelter for despots, summoning false memories of stability, harmony among the public.

Activity 14

1) How does the old woman define a 'dead' language? What is characteristic of such a language? What effects does this type of language have on humankind?
2) What does it mean to 'sanction ignorance' and 'preserve privilege'?

She is convinced that when language dies, out of carelessness, disuse, indifference and absence of esteem, or killed by fiat, not only she herself, but all users and makers are accountable for its demise. <u>In her country children have bitten their tongues off and use bullets instead to iterate the voice of speechlessness, of disabled and disabling language, of language adults have abandoned altogether as a device for grappling with meaning, providing guidance, or expressing love.</u> But she knows <u>tongue-suicide</u> is not only the choice of children. It is common among the infantile heads of state and power merchants whose evacuated language leaves them with no access to what is left of their human instincts for they speak only to those who obey, or in order to force obedience.

The systematic <u>looting of language</u> can be recognized by the tendency of its users to forgo its nuanced, complex, mid-wifery properties for menace and subjugation. <u>Oppressive language does more than represent violence; it is violence; does more than represent the limits of knowledge; it limits knowledge.</u> Whether it is obscuring state language or the faux-language of mindless media; whether it is the proud but calcified language of the academy or the commodity driven language of science; whether it is the malign language of law-without-ethics, or language designed for the estrangement of minorities, hiding its racist plunder in its literary cheek – it must be rejected, altered and exposed. It is <u>the language that drinks blood</u>, laps vulnerabilities, tucks its fascist boots under crinolines of respectability and patriotism as it moves relentlessly toward the bottom line and the bottomed-out mind. <u>Sexist language, racist language, theistic language – all are typical of the policing languages of mastery, and cannot, do not permit new knowledge or encourage the mutual exchange of ideas.</u>

Activity 15

1) Decipher the old woman's metaphor about 'tongue-suicide'. What does her metaphor of bullets substituted for language allude to?
2) What political message is at the heart of the 'policing languages of mastery'?

The old woman is keenly aware that no intellectual mercenary, nor insatiable dictator, no paid-for politician or demagogue; no counterfeit journalist would be persuaded by her thoughts. There is and will be <u>rousing language</u> to keep citizens armed and arming; slaughtered and slaughtering in the malls, courthouses, post offices, playgrounds, bedrooms and boulevards; <u>stirring</u>, <u>memorializing language to mask the pity and waste of needless death</u>. There will be more <u>diplomatic language</u> to countenance rape, torture, assassination. There is and will be more <u>seductive, mutant language</u> designed to throttle women, to pack their throats like paté-producing geese with their own unsayable, transgressive words; there will be more of the <u>language of surveillance</u> disguised as research; of politics and history calculated to render the suffering of millions mute; <u>language glamorized to thrill</u> the dissatisfied and bereft into assaulting their neighbors; <u>arrogant pseudo-empirical language</u> crafted to lock creative people into cages of inferiority and hopelessness.

Underneath the eloquence, the glamor, the scholarly associations, however stirring or seductive, the heart of such language is languishing, or perhaps not beating at all – if the bird is already dead.

Activity 16

How does the old woman describe the types of dead or dying language? What do these types of language have in common?

She has thought about what could have been the intellectual history of any discipline if it had not insisted upon, or been forced into, the waste of time and life that rationalizations for and representations of dominance required – lethal discourses of exclusion blocking access to cognition for both the excluder and the excluded.

The conventional wisdom of the Tower of Babel story is that the collapse was a misfortune. That it was the distraction, or the weight of many languages that precipitated the tower's failed architecture. That one monolithic language would have expedited the building and heaven would have been reached. Whose heaven, she wonders? And what kind? Perhaps the achievement of Paradise was premature, a little hasty if no one could take the time to understand other languages, other views, other narratives period. Had they, the heaven they imagined might have been found at their feet. Complicated, demanding, yes, but a view of heaven as life; not heaven as post-life.

She would not want to leave her young visitors with the impression that language should be forced to stay alive merely to be. The vitality of language lies in its ability to limn the actual, imagined and possible lives of its speakers, readers, writers. Although its poise is sometimes in displacing experience it is not a substitute for it. It arcs toward the place where meaning may lie. When a President of the United States thought about the graveyard his country had become, and said, 'The world will little note nor long remember what we say here. But it will never forget what they did here,' his simple words are exhilarating in their life-sustaining properties because they refused to encapsulate the reality of 600,000 dead men in a cataclysmic race war. Refusing to monumentalize, disdaining the 'final word', the precise 'summing up', acknowledging their 'poor power to add or detract', his words signal deference to the uncapturability of the life it mourns. It is the deference that moves her, that recognition that language can never live up to life once and for all. Nor should it. Language can never 'pin down' slavery, genocide, war. Nor should it yearn for the arrogance to be able to do so. Its force, its felicity is in its reach toward the ineffable.

Activity 17

What does it mean to say that 'language can never live up to life… Nor should it'?

Be it grand or slender, burrowing, blasting, or refusing to sanctify; whether it laughs out loud or is a cry without an alphabet, the choice word, the chosen silence, unmolested language surges toward knowledge, not its destruction. But who does not know of literature banned because it is interrogative; discredited because it is critical; erased because alternate? And how many are outraged by the thought of a self-ravaged tongue?

Word-work is sublime, she thinks, because it is generative; it makes meaning that secures our difference, our human difference – the way in which we are like no other life.

We die. That may be the meaning of life. But we do language. That may be the measure of our lives.

Activity 18

Paraphrase the two underlined paragraphs above.

'Once upon a time, …' visitors ask an old woman a question. Who are they, these children? What did they make of that encounter? What did they hear in those final words: 'The bird is in your hands'? A sentence that gestures towards possibility or one that drops a latch? Perhaps what the children heard was 'It's not my problem. I am old, female, black, blind. What wisdom I have now is in knowing I cannot help you. The future of language is yours.'

They stand there. Suppose nothing was in their hands? Suppose the visit was only a ruse, a trick to get to be spoken to, taken seriously as they have not been before? A chance to interrupt, to violate the adult world, its miasma of discourse about them, for them, but never to them? Urgent questions are at stake, including the one they have asked: 'Is the bird we hold living or dead?' Perhaps the question meant: 'Could someone tell us what is life? What is death?' No trick at all; no silliness. A straightforward question worthy of the attention of a wise one. An old one. And if the old and wise who have lived life and faced death cannot describe either, who can?

But she does not; she keeps her secret; her good opinion of herself; her gnomic pronouncements; her art without commitment. She keeps her distance, enforces it and retreats into the singularity of isolation, in sophisticated, privileged space.

Nothing, no word follows her declaration of transfer. That silence is deep, deeper than the meaning available in the words she has spoken. It shivers, this silence, and the children, annoyed, fill it with language invented on the spot.

'Is there no speech,' they ask her, 'no words you can give us that helps us break through your dossier of failures? Through the education you have just given us that is no education at all because we are paying close attention to what you have done as well as to what you have said? To the barrier you have erected between generosity and wisdom?'

'We have no bird in our hands, living or dead. We have only you and our important question. Is the nothing in our hands something you could not bear to contemplate, to even guess? Don't you remember being young when language was magic without meaning? When what you could say, could not mean? When the invisible was what imagination strove to see? When questions and demands for answers burned so brightly you trembled with fury at not knowing?

'Do we have to begin consciousness with a battle heroines and heroes like you have already fought and lost leaving us with nothing in our hands except what you have imagined is there? Your answer is artful, but its artfulness embarrasses us and ought to embarrass you. Your answer is indecent in its self-congratulation. A made-for-television script that makes no sense if there is nothing in our hands.

Activity 19

What is it that the young people want to know from the old woman? Why do they seem angry at her? What does she represent for them? How has she failed them?

'Why didn't you reach out, touch us with your soft fingers, delay the sound bite, the lesson, until you knew who we were? Did you so despise our trick, our modus operandi you could not see that we were baffled about how to get your attention? We are young. Unripe. We have heard all our short lives that we have to be responsible. What could that possibly mean in the catastrophe this world has become; where, as a poet said, 'nothing needs to be exposed since it is already barefaced.' Our inheritance is an affront. You want us to have your old, blank eyes and see only cruelty and mediocrity. Do you think we are stupid enough to perjure ourselves again and again with the fiction of nationhood? How dare you talk to us of duty when we stand waist deep in the toxin of your past?

'You trivialize us and trivialize the bird that is not in our hands. Is there no context for our lives? No song, no literature, no poem full of vitamins, no history connected to experience that you can pass along to help us start strong? You are an adult. The old one, the wise one. Stop thinking about saving your face. Think of our lives and tell us your particularized world. Make up a story. Narrative is radical, creating us at the very moment it is being created. We will not blame you if your reach exceeds your grasp; if love so ignites your words they go down in flames and nothing is left but their scald. Or if, with the reticence of a surgeon's hands, your words suture only the places where blood might flow. We know you can never do it properly – once and for all. <u>Passion is never enough; neither is skill. But try</u>. For our sake and yours forget your name in the street; tell us what the world has been to you in the dark places and in the light. Don't tell us what to believe, what to fear. Show us belief's wide skirt and the stitch that unravels fear's caul. <u>You, old woman, blessed with blindness, can speak the language that tells us what only language can: how to see without pictures</u>. Language alone protects us from the scariness of things with no names. Language alone is meditation.

Activity 20

What is meant by the statement that only language can show the young people how to see without pictures? Is this a definition of imagination? Explain.

'<u>Tell us</u> what it is to be a woman so that we may know what it is to be a man. What moves at the margin. What it is to have no home in this place. To be set adrift from the one you knew. What it is to live at the edge of towns that cannot bear your company.

'<u>Tell us</u> about ships turned away from shorelines at Easter, placenta in a field. <u>Tell us</u> about a wagonload of slaves, how they sang so softly their breath was indistinguishable from the falling snow. How they knew from the hunch of the nearest shoulder that the next stop would be their last. How, with hands prayered in their sex, they thought of heat, then sun. Lifting their faces as though it was there for the taking. Turning as though there for the taking. They stop at an inn. The driver and his mate go in with the lamp leaving them humming in the dark. The horse's void steams into the snow beneath its hooves and its hiss and melt are the envy of the freezing slaves.

'The inn door opens: a girl and a boy step away from its light. They climb into the wagon bed. The boy will have a gun in three years, but now he carries a lamp and a jug of warm cider. They pass it from mouth to mouth. The girl offers bread, pieces of meat and something more: a glance into the eyes of the one she serves. One helping for each man, two for each woman. And a look. They look back. The next stop will be their last. But not this one. This one is warmed.'

It's quiet again when the children finish speaking, until the woman breaks into the silence.

'Finally', she says, 'I trust you now. I trust you with the bird that is not in your hands because you have truly caught it. Look. How lovely it is, this thing we have done – together.'

Activity 21

For the final exercise, break into small groups and discuss one of the following questions. Present your ideas.

1) According to Morrison, what is the writer's job? What must they do? What does the gift of language require of them?
2) How can a writer fail in their responsibility?
3) Is this lecture an extended metaphor about the relationship of reader, writer, and text? Or perhaps, a parable?
4) What 'stories' do the young people want to hear? Why is the old woman's silence an offence to them?
5) What have the young people 'caught' and why is the result something 'lovely' that has been created together?
6) The word 'margin' is used in the first paragraph of this last section. What does that word mean in context, literally? What other meanings could the word 'margin' have in the context of life experience?

Time and space in non-fiction: an approach to Nelson Mandela's 'I Am Prepared to Die' speech (1964)

Just as Toni Morrison had a specific audience for her Nobel Prize Lecture, so did Nelson Mandela. This speech was delivered at the opening of his defence case, on charges of sabotage, at the Supreme Court of South Africa, Pretoria, 20 April 1964. In some sense, Mandela is offering his 'testimony' to the court and the world.

Nelson Mandela

The time and place of this speech, and the historical and social contexts referenced within it, are critical to understanding this testimonial. Mandela is aware that he will be sent to prison on Robben Island, but he also realises that this is a moment to set the record straight regarding the political environment and his crimes against that environment. What he offers is a kind of historical summary of injustice, the reactions of African peoples against such injustice – the progression from non-violent strategies to violent strategies – and what a new, free, democratic society would look and feel like. Above all, Mandela specifies all of the ways, both legislated and insidious, that Africans are denied human dignity.

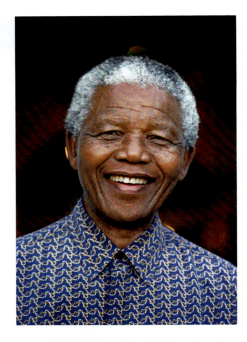

Info box

It was in 1964 at the Rivonia Trial that Nelson Mandela made his famous 'I am Prepared to Die' speech before being sentenced to prison, where he spent 27 years, making the world turn apartheid-based South Africa against its laws of racial discrimination.

Activity 22

Prior to reading Mandela's speech, do some research on the bolded items within the speech. Understanding the details of these points of reference is part of the task of a close reading. And when the context of a close reading is instrumental in constructing meaning, details matter!

Be sure to annotate your research findings in your learner portfolio.

'I am Prepared to Die' speech by Nelson Mandela (1964)

I am the first accused. I hold a bachelor's degree in arts and practised as an attorney in Johannesburg for a number of years in partnership with Oliver Tambo. I am a convicted prisoner serving five years for leaving the country without a permit and for inciting people to go on strike at the end of May 1961.

[...]

Some of the things so far told to the court are true and some are untrue. I do not, however, deny that I planned sabotage. I did not plan it in a spirit of recklessness, nor because I have any love of violence. I planned it as a result of a calm and sober assessment of the political situation that had arisen after many years of tyranny, exploitation, and oppression of my people by the whites.

I admit immediately that I was one of the persons who helped to form **Umkhonto we Sizwe**. I deny that Umkhonto was responsible for a number of acts which clearly fell outside the policy of the organisation, and which have been charged in the indictment against us. I, and the others who started the organisation, felt that without violence there would be no way open to the African people to succeed in their struggle against the principle of white supremacy. All lawful modes of expressing opposition to this principle had been closed by legislation, and we were placed in a position in which we had either to accept a permanent state of inferiority, or to defy the government. We chose to defy the law.

We first broke the law in a way which avoided any recourse to violence; when this form was legislated against, and then the government resorted to a show of force to crush opposition to its policies, only then did we decide to answer violence with violence.

The **African National Congress** (ANC) was formed in 1912 to defend the rights of the African people, which had been seriously curtailed. For 37 years – that is, until 1949 – it adhered strictly to a constitutional struggle. But white governments remained unmoved, and the rights of Africans became less instead of becoming greater. Even after 1949, the ANC remained determined to avoid violence. At this time, however, the decision was taken to protest against apartheid by peaceful, but unlawful, demonstrations. More than 8,500 people went to jail. Yet there was not a single instance of violence. I and 19 colleagues were convicted for organising the campaign, but our sentences were suspended mainly because the judge found that discipline and non-violence had been stressed throughout.

[...]

In 1960 there was the **shooting at Sharpeville**, which resulted in the declaration of the ANC as an unlawful organisation. My colleagues and I, after careful consideration, decided that we would not obey this decree. The African people were not part of the government and did not make the laws by which they were governed. We believed in the words of the Universal Declaration of Human Rights, that 'the will of the people shall be the basis of authority of the government', and for us to accept the banning was equivalent to accepting the silencing of the Africans for all time. The ANC refused to dissolve, but instead went underground.

In 1960 the government held a referendum which led to the establishment of the republic. Africans, who constituted approximately 70% of the population, were not entitled to vote, and were not even consulted. I undertook to be responsible for organising the national stay-at-home called to coincide with the declaration of the republic. As all strikes by Africans are illegal, the person organising such a strike must avoid arrest. I had to leave my home and family and my practice and go into hiding to avoid arrest. The stay-at-home was to be a peaceful demonstration. Careful instructions were given to avoid any recourse to violence.

The government's answer was to introduce new and harsher laws, to mobilise its armed forces, and to send Saracens, armed vehicles, and soldiers into the townships in a massive show of force designed to intimidate the people. The government had decided to rule by force alone, and this decision was a milestone on the road to Umkhonto. What were we, the leaders of our people, to do? We had no doubt that we had to continue the fight. Anything else would have been abject surrender. Our problem was not whether to fight, but was how to continue the fight.

We of the ANC had always stood for a non-racial democracy, and we shrank from any action which might drive the races further apart. But the hard facts were that 50 years of non-violence had brought the African people nothing but more and more repressive legislation, and fewer and fewer rights. By this time violence had, in fact, become a feature of the South African political scene.

There had been **violence in 1957 when the women of Zeerust were ordered to carry passes**; there was **violence in 1958 with the enforcement of cattle culling in Sekhukhuneland**; there was **violence in 1959 when the people of Cato Manor protested against pass raids**; there was **violence in 1960 when the government attempted to impose Bantu authorities in Pondoland**. Each disturbance pointed to the inevitable growth among Africans of the belief that violence was the only way out — it showed that a government which uses force to maintain its rule teaches the oppressed to use force to oppose it.

I came to the conclusion that as violence in this country was inevitable, it would be unrealistic to continue preaching peace and non-violence. This conclusion was not easily arrived at. It was only when all else had failed, when all channels of peaceful protest had been barred to us, that the decision was made to embark on violent forms of political struggle. I can only say that I felt morally obliged to do what I did.

Four forms of violence were possible. There is sabotage, there is guerrilla warfare, there is terrorism, and there is open revolution. We chose to adopt the first. Sabotage did not involve loss of life, and it offered the best hope for future race relations. Bitterness would be kept to a minimum and, if the policy bore fruit, democratic government could become a reality. The initial plan was based on a careful analysis of the political and economic situation of our country. We believed that South Africa depended to a large extent on foreign capital. We felt that planned destruction of power plants, and interference with rail and telephone communications, would scare away capital from the country, thus compelling the voters of the country to reconsider their position. **Umkhonto had its first operation on December 16 1961, when government buildings in Johannesburg, Port Elizabeth and Durban were attacked**. The selection of targets is proof of the policy to which I have referred. Had we intended to attack life we would have selected targets where people congregated and not empty buildings and power stations.

[…]

Another of the allegations made by the state is that the aims and objects of the ANC and the Communist party are the same. The creed of the ANC is, and always has been, the creed of African nationalism. It is not the concept of African nationalism expressed in the cry, 'Drive the white man into the sea.' The African nationalism for which the ANC stands is the concept of freedom and fulfilment for the African people in their own land. The most important political document ever adopted by the ANC is the **'freedom charter'**. It is by no means a blueprint for a socialist state. It calls for redistribution, but not nationalisation, of land; it provides for nationalisation of mines, banks, and monopoly industry, because big monopolies are owned by one race only, and without such nationalisation racial domination would be perpetuated despite the spread of political power. Under the freedom charter, nationalisation would take place in an economy based on private enterprise.

As far as the Communist party is concerned, and if I understand its policy correctly, it stands for the establishment of a state based on the principles of Marxism. The Communist party sought to emphasise class distinctions whilst the ANC seeks to harmonise them. This is a vital distinction.

It is true that there has often been close cooperation between the ANC and the Communist party. But cooperation is merely proof of a common goal – in this case the removal of white supremacy – and is not proof of a complete community of interests. The history of the world is full of similar examples. Perhaps the most striking is the cooperation between Great Britain, the United States and the Soviet Union in the fight against Hitler. Nobody but Hitler would have dared to suggest that such cooperation turned Churchill or Roosevelt into communists. Theoretical differences amongst those fighting against oppression is a luxury we cannot afford at this stage.

What is more, for many decades communists were the only political group in South Africa prepared to treat Africans as human beings and their equals; who were prepared to eat with us; talk with us, live with us, and work with us. They were the only group which was prepared to work with the Africans for the attainment of political rights and a stake in society. Because of this, there are many Africans who, today, tend to equate freedom with communism. They are supported in this belief by a legislature which brands all exponents of democratic government and African freedom as communists and bans many of them (who are not communists) under the Suppression of Communism Act. Although I have never been a member of the Communist party, I myself have been imprisoned under that act.

I have always regarded myself, in the first place, as an African patriot. Today I am attracted by the idea of a classless society, an attraction which springs in part from Marxist reading and, in part, from my admiration of the structure of early African societies. The land belonged to the tribe.

There were no rich or poor and there was no exploitation. We all accept the need for some form of socialism to enable our people to catch up with the advanced countries of this world and to overcome their legacy of extreme poverty. But this does not mean we are Marxists.

[...]

I have been influenced in my thinking by both west and east. I should tie myself to no particular system of society other than of socialism. I must leave myself free to borrow the best from the west and from the east.

Our fight is against real, and not imaginary, hardships or, to use the language of the state prosecutor, 'so-called hardships'. Basically, we fight against two features which are the hallmarks of African life in South Africa and which are entrenched by legislation. These features are poverty and lack of human dignity, and we do not need communists or so-called 'agitators' to teach us about these things. South Africa is the richest country in Africa, and could be one of the richest countries in the world. But it is a land of remarkable contrasts. The whites enjoy what may be the highest standard of living in the world, whilst Africans live in poverty and misery. Poverty goes hand in hand with malnutrition and disease. Tuberculosis, pellagra and scurvy bring death and destruction of health.

The complaint of Africans, however, is not only that they are poor and the whites are rich, but that the laws which are made by the whites are designed to preserve this situation. There are two ways to break out of poverty. The first is by formal education, and the second is by the worker acquiring a greater skill at his work and thus higher wages. As far as Africans are concerned, both these avenues of advancement are deliberately curtailed by legislation.

The government has always sought to hamper Africans in their search for education. There is compulsory education for all white children at virtually no cost to their parents, be they rich or poor. African children, however, generally have to pay more for their schooling than whites.

Approximately 40% of African children in the age group seven to 14 do not attend school. For those who do, the standards are vastly different from those afforded to white children. Only 5,660 African children in the whole of South Africa passed their junior certificate in 1962, and only 362 passed matric.

This is presumably consistent with the policy of **Bantu education** about which the present prime minister said: 'When I have control of native education I will reform it so that natives will be taught from childhood to realise that equality with Europeans is not for them. People who believe in equality are not desirable teachers for natives. When my department controls native education it will know for what class of higher education a native is fitted, and whether he will have a chance in life to use his knowledge.'

The other main obstacle to the advancement of the African is the industrial colour-bar under which all the better jobs of industry are reserved for whites only. Moreover, Africans who do obtain employment in the unskilled and semi-skilled occupations open to them are not allowed to form trade unions which have recognition. This means that they are denied the right of collective bargaining, which is permitted to the better-paid white workers.

The government answers its critics by saying that Africans in South Africa are better off than the inhabitants of the other countries in Africa. I do not know whether this statement is true. But even if it is true, as far as the African people are concerned it is irrelevant.

Our complaint is not that we are poor by comparison with people in other countries, but that we are poor by comparison with the white people in our own country, and that we are prevented by legislation from altering this imbalance.

The lack of human dignity experienced by Africans is the direct result of the policy of white supremacy. White supremacy implies black inferiority. Legislation designed to preserve white supremacy entrenches this notion. Menial tasks in South Africa are invariably performed by Africans.

When anything has to be carried or cleaned the white man will look around for an African to do it for him, whether the African is employed by him or not. Because of this sort of attitude, whites tend to regard Africans as a separate breed. They do not look upon them as people with families of their own; they do not realise that they have emotions - that they fall in love like white people do; that they want to be with their wives and children like white people want to be with theirs; that they want to earn enough money to support their families properly, to feed and clothe them and send them to school. And what 'house-boy' or 'garden-boy' or labourer can ever hope to do this?

Pass laws render any African liable to police surveillance at any time. I doubt whether there is a single African male in South Africa who has not had a brush with the police over his pass. Hundreds and thousands of Africans are thrown into jail each year under pass laws.

Even worse is the fact that pass laws keep husband and wife apart and lead to the breakdown of family life. Poverty and the breakdown of family have secondary effects. Children wander the streets because they have no schools to go to, or no money to enable them to go, or no parents at home to see that they go, because both parents (if there be two) have to work to keep the family alive. This leads to a breakdown in moral standards, to an alarming rise in illegitimacy, and to violence, which erupts not only politically, but everywhere. Life in **the townships** is dangerous. Not a day goes by without somebody being stabbed or assaulted. And violence is carried out of the townships [into] the white living areas. People are afraid to walk the streets after dark. Housebreakings and robberies are increasing, despite the fact that the death sentence can now be imposed for such offences. Death sentences cannot cure the festering sore.

Africans want to be paid a living wage. Africans want to perform work which they are capable of doing, and not work which the government declares them to be capable of. Africans want to be allowed to live where they obtain work, and not be endorsed out of an area because they were not born there. Africans want to be allowed to own land in places where they work, and not to be obliged to live in rented houses which they can never call their own. Africans want to be part of the general population, and not confined to living in their own ghettoes.

African men want to have their wives and children to live with them where they work, and not be forced into an unnatural existence in men's hostels. African women want to be with their menfolk and not be left permanently widowed in the reserves. Africans want to be allowed out after 11 o'clock at night and not to be confined to their rooms like little children. Africans want to be allowed to travel in their own country and to seek work where they want to and not where the labour bureau tells them to. Africans want a just share in the whole of South Africa; they want security and a stake in society.

Above all, we want equal political rights, because without them our disabilities will be permanent. I know this sounds revolutionary to the whites in this country, because the majority of voters will be Africans. This makes the white man fear democracy. But this fear cannot be allowed to stand in the way of the only solution which will guarantee racial harmony and freedom for all. It is not true that the enfranchisement of all will result in racial domination. Political division, based on colour, is entirely artificial and, when it disappears, so will the domination of one colour group by another. The ANC has spent half a century fighting against racialism. When it triumphs it will not change that policy.

This then is what the ANC is fighting. Their struggle is a truly national one. It is a struggle of the African people, inspired by their own suffering and their own experience. It is a struggle for the right to live. During my lifetime I have dedicated myself to this struggle of the African people. I have fought against white domination, and I have fought against black domination. I have cherished the ideal of a democratic and free society in which all persons live together in harmony and with equal opportunities. It is an ideal which I hope to live for and to achieve. But if needs be, it is an ideal for which I am prepared to die.

Activity 23

Examine the ethos appeals in Mandela's speech. Find five specific references within the speech that reinforce his credibility as a voice of the ANC (African National Congress).

Activity 24

Examine the pathos appeals in Mandela's speech. What direct references does Mandela use in the speech to offer his audience a sense of shared values? What are these shared values? How does Mandela use hyperbole, emotionally charged language/diction, and/or powerful symbolism to generate an emotional response from his audience?

Activity 25

Examine the logos appeals in Mandela's speech. How does Mandela appeal to logic in his speech? Do facts and specific references influence the effectiveness of his speech? What facts and references make the greatest influence in terms of his argument?

Activity 26

What do you believe that Mandela intended to accomplish with this speech? His guilt was not in doubt as he admits readily that he committed sabotage. What is the nature of his argument?

Intertextuality: connecting texts in non-fiction: an approach to Sylvia Plath's *Letters Home* (1975) and *The Journals of Sylvia Plath* (1982)

According to Margaret Atwood in *Negotiating with the Dead, A Writer on Writing* (2002), 'The private diary is about as minimalist as you can get, in the writer-to-reader department, because writer and reader are assumed to be the same. It is also about as intimate, as a form. Next comes, I suppose, the private letter: one writer, one reader, and a shared intimacy.'

These two forms of non-fiction – the private diary/journal and the private letter – are at the centre of this intertextual approach. Both texts were posthumously published and both were heavily edited. The question of who has rights to publish such personal and private writing will long be argued about, but the point that they are published, even in part, allows us an interesting perspective of the differences and similarities between two texts, two forms, and two specific audiences/readers – self and mother.

Sylvia Plath, poet

The American poet and author Sylvia Plath's *Letters Home*, primarily written to her mother, Aurelia Plath, and a few other family members, was published in 1975 by her mother, who had saved 696 letters written from the time of Plath's college years in the UK in 1950 until her death early in February 1963. The *Journals of Sylvia Plath* was not published until 1982. The primary content of the journals includes entries from 1957–59.

Sylvia Plath: Selections from Plath's *Journals* and *Letters Home*

The first text is from a journal entry dated 25 February 1956. The second is a letter to her mother, also dated 25 February 1956.

Journal entry, 25 February 1956, by Sylvia Plath

Went to psychiatrist this morning and like him: attractive, calm and considered, with that pleasant feeling of age and experience in a reservoir; felt: Father, why not? Wanted to burst out in tears and say Father, Father, comfort me. I told him about my break-up and found myself complaining mainly about not knowing mature people here: that's it, too! There is not one person I know here whom I admire who is older than I! In a place like Cambridge, that is scandalous. It means that there are many fine people I have not met; probably many young dons and men are mature. I don't know (and, I always ask, would they want to know me?). But at Newnham there isn't one don I admire *personally*. The men are probably better, but there is no chance of getting them for supervisors, and they are too brilliant to indulge in that friendly commerce which Mr [Al] Fisher, Mr [Alfred] Kazin and Mr [George] Gibian were so dear about.

Well, I shall look up Dr Beuscher's friend, and plan to see the Carabuts at Easter. I can give them youth, enthusiasm and love to make up for the ignorances. Sometimes I feel so very stupid; yet, if I were, would I not be happy with some of the men I have met? Or is it because I am stupid that I'm not; hardly. I long for someone to blast over Richard; I deserve that, don't I, some sort of blazing love that I can live with. My God, I'd love to cook and make a house, and surge force into a man's dreams, and write, if he could talk and walk and work and passionately want to do his career. I can't bear to think of this potential for loving and giving going brown and sere in me. Yet the choice is so important, it frightens me a little. A lot...

What I fear most, I think, is the death of the imagination. When the sky outside is merely pink, and the rooftops merely black: that photographic mind which paradoxically tells the truth, but the worthless truth, about the world. It is that synthesizing spirit, that 'shaping' force, which prolifically sprouts and makes up its own worlds with more inventiveness than God which I desire. If I sit still and don't do anything, the world goes on beating like a slack drum, without meaning. We must be moving, working, making dreams to run toward; the poverty of life without dreams is too horrible to imagine: it is that kind of madness which is worst: the kind with fancies and hallucinations would be a Bosch-ish relief.

I listen always for footsteps coming up the stairs and hate them if they are not for me. Why, why can I not be an ascetic for a while, instead of always teetering on the edge of wanting complete solitude for work and reading, and, so much, so much, the gestures of hands and words of other human beings. Well, after this Racine paper, this Ronsard purgatory, this Sophocles, I shall write: letters and prose and poetry, toward the end of the week; I must be stoic till then.

Letters Home, 25 February 1956, by Sylvia Plath

Dearest Mother,

I felt that after the wailing blast of the last letter, I owed you a quick follow-up to tell you that it is a new day; bright, with sun, and a milder aspect, and my intense physical misery is gone, and with it, my rather profound despair.

I had a complete physical exam last week (having had a chest x-ray) and was pronounced fine, but they suggested that I might see their psychiatrist to fill in the details of my breakdown, and so I would know in case the stress of completely new circumstances made me feel I wanted to talk to him. Well, I went over to see him this morning and really enjoyed talking to him. He is a pleasant, keen middle-aged man, and I felt a certain relief in telling someone here a little about my past. In a way, it makes me feel a certain continuity. Well, I found myself telling him about my opinions of life and people in Cambridge, and as I went on, I realized that what I miss most is the rich intellectual and emotional contact I had with *older* people at home and at college. I am literally *starved* for friends who are older, wiser, rich with experience, to whom I can look up, from whom I can learn.

... I know there are, no doubt, brilliant dons here at Cambridge, and many men who are mature and integrated emotionally and intellectually, but I just haven't met them. The best ones we get on the lecture platform, but our women supervisors in Newnham are, as I have so often said, bluestocking grotesques, who know about life second-hand. As a woman, my position is probably more difficult, for it seems the Victorian age of emancipation is yet dominant here: there isn't a woman professor I have that I admire personally! I am not brilliant enough to invade the professors at the men's colleges (the biggest ones only teach research students, and the dons supervise the men in their own colleges), but there is no medium for the *kind* of rapport I had at Smith. I realized with a shock this morning that there isn't one person among my friends here or in Europe who is more mature than I! All the girls and boys I know are younger or barely equal (however brilliant they may be in their subjects), and I am constantly being sister or mother. Only when I am sick, it seems... can I be the depended one...

I feel that while I am ignorant and untutored in much, I *can* give some of my native joy of life to older people and balance our relation this way. I also am going to look up that couple whose address Dr. B. gave me. I've put it off and off... I really need deep contact with the mellowness and perspective of older people which the orientals do so well to reverence...

Tonight I am going to a party celebrating the publication of a new literary review, which is really a brilliant counteraction to the dead, uneven, poorly written two literary magazines already going here, which run on prejudice and whim... This new one is run by a combination of Americans and Britons, and the poetry is really brilliant, and the prose, taut, reportorial, and expert... I must admit I feel a certain sense of inferiority, because what I have done so far seems so small, smug, and *little*. I keep telling myself that I have a vivid, vital, good life, and that it is simply that I haven't learned to be tough and disciplined enough with the form I give it in words which limits me, not the life itself.

... I could never be either a complete scholar or a complete housewife or a complete writer: I must combine a little of all, and thereby be imperfect in all. Although I would like to concentrate on writing in intense spurts when I feel like it... Do know that I am really happy, and it is not a contradiction to say that at the same time I am debating inwardly with problems. That is just life, and I am ready to take it and wrestle with it to the end of my days. I love you very much, and hope you will understand my present frankness and know that it has made me feel much better just to know that you are listening.

Your own loving Sivvy

Activity 27 Compare and contrast the two texts

Consider:
- content similarities and differences (perspective of self, men, friends)
- tone towards self in the journal entry/tone towards mother in letter
- diction, imagery, sentence structure differences.

> ### Activity 28
>
> What insights can you draw from the relationship of one text to the other? Is the idea of a writer's voice dependent on audience?

> ### Activity 29
>
> Try your hand at creating two voices for yourself. Write a short diary account about an event that you witnessed – a film, a sporting event, a family gathering – and then choose another audience for retelling the same event. The new 'reader' could be someone you know well, or someone that you know only superficially. Explain who is this reader is and why you chose them.

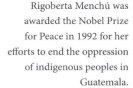
Rigoberta Menchú was awarded the Nobel Prize for Peace in 1992 for her efforts to end the oppression of indigenous peoples in Guatemala.

Sample study of the three areas of exploration in non-fiction: readers, writers, and texts; time and space; and intertextuality: connecting texts

The following three chapters are taken from the memoir of Rigoberta Menchú, who was awarded the Nobel Prize for Peace in 1992 for her efforts to end the oppression of indigenous peoples in Guatemala. Her memoir, *I, Rigoberta Menchú*, published in 1983,

was edited and introduced by Venezuelan anthropologist Elisabeth Burgos-Deray, and translated from the Spanish by Ann Wright. This memoir serves as a moving account of the social and political experience of a 23-year-old Quiché Indian woman who is, according to Burgos-Deray, 'a privileged witness of the genocide that destroyed her family and community, and who is stubbornly determined to break the silence and to confront the systematic extermination of her people. She refuses to let us forget. Words are her only weapons. That is why she resolved to learn Spanish and break out of the linguistic isolation into which the Indians retreated in order to preserve their culture.'

I, Rigoberta Menchú: An Indian Woman in Guatemala was initiated as a series of taped interviews over a period of a week. Burgos-Debray then had the task of transcribing all of the tapes (a total of 24 hours) and determining a form. The form she selected was that of a monologue, one continuous narrative, which was then divided into chapters organised around themes.

As Quiché Indians, one of several indigenous tribes descended from the ancient Mayan civilisation, Menchú's family lived in the mountainous region of north-western Guatemala. Her memoir not only reveals the horrors of the civil war where thousands of Indians were brutally attacked, 'disappeared', or executed, but it also captures the cultural beliefs and traditions of the Quiché people. The three chapters that you have here – 'The Family', 'The Nahual', and 'Exile' – are representative of the cultural, political, and personal journey of the Guatemalan Indians in the last half of the 20th century.

In chapter 1, 'The Family', italicised terms are important to understand, as many of them are repeated throughout the memoir. These are the terms and their definitions:

Ladino/mestizo: Today, any Guatemalan – whatever his economic position – who rejects, either individually or through his cultural heritage, Indian values of Mayan origin. It also implies mixed blood.

Mimbre: Type of willow, used for making cane baskets, furniture, etc.

Caballeria: Agrarian measurement equivalent to 64 manzanas, i.e. 45 hectares (= 2.471 acres).

Finca: Plantation, estate. Can be coffee, sugar, cotton, etc.

Altiplano: Name given to the mountainous region in the north-west of Guatemala where the majority of the Indian population live.

Centavo: Monetary unit. 100 *centavo*s = 1 quetzal.

Activity 30

Read the short chapter on 'The Family' and describe the kind of life that Rigoberta was born into. What is important to the Indian community? What products are cultivated? Is the life of her family and community tied to the land? If so, in what ways? Is the Indian family structure like or unlike your own? What are the similarities and differences?

I, Rigoberta Menchú, Chapter 1, 'The Family'

My name is Rigoberta Menchú. I am twenty-three years old. This is my testimony. I didn't learn it from a book and I didn't learn it alone. I'd like to stress that it's not only my life, it's also the testimony of my people. It's hard for me to remember everything that's happened to me in my life since there have been many very bad times but, yes, moments of joy as well. The important thing is that what has happened to me has happened to many other people too: my story is the story of all poor Guatemalans. My personal experience is the reality of a whole people.

I must say before I start that I never went to school, and so I find speaking Spanish very difficult. I didn't have the chance to move outside my own world and only learned Spanish three years ago. It's difficult when you learn just by listening, without any books. And, well, yes, I find it a bit difficult. I'd like to start from when I was a little girl, or go back even further to when I was in my mother's womb, because my mother told me how I was born and our customs say that a child begins life on the first day of his mother's pregnancy.

There are twenty-two indigenous ethnic groups in Guatemala, twenty-three including the *mestizos*, or *ladinos* as we call them. Twenty-three groups and twenty-three languages. I belong to one of them – the Quiché people – and I practise Quiché customs, but I also know most of the other groups very well through my work organizing the people. I come from San Miguel Uspantán, in the north-western province of El Quiché. I live near Chajul in the north of El Quiché. The towns there all have long histories of struggle. I have to walk six leagues, or twenty-four kilometres, from my house to the town of Uspantán. The village is called

Chimel, I was born there. Where I live is practically a paradise, the country is so beautiful. There are no big roads, and no cars. Only people can reach it. Everything is taken down the mountainside on horseback or else we carry it ourselves. So, you can see, I live right up in the mountains.

My parents moved there in 1960 and began cultivating the land. No-one had lived up there before because it's so mountainous. But they settled there and were determined not to leave no matter how hard the life was. They'd first been up there collecting the *mimbre* that's found in those parts, and had liked it. They'd started clearing the land for a house, and had wanted to settle there a year later but they didn't have the means. Then they were thrown out of the small house they had in the town and had no alternative but to go up into the mountains. And they stayed there. Now it's a village with five or six *caballerias* of cultivated land.

They'd been forced to leave the town because some *ladino* families came to settle there. They weren't exactly evicted but the *ladinos* just gradually took over. My parents spent everything they earned and they incurred so many debts with these people that they had to leave the house to pay them. The rich are always like that. When people owe them money they take a bit of land or some of their belongings and slowly end up with everything. That's what happened to my parents.

My father was an orphan, and had a very hard life as a child. He was born in Santa Rosa Chucuyub, a village in El Quiché. His father died when he was a small boy, leaving the family with a small patch of maize. But when that was finished, my grandmother took her three sons to Uspantán. She got work as a servant to the town's only rich people.

Her boys did jobs around the house like carrying wood and water and tending animals. But as they got bigger, her employer said she didn't work enough for him to go on feeding such big boys. She had to give away her eldest son, my father, to another man so he wouldn't go hungry. By then he could do heavy work like chopping wood or working in the fields but he wasn't paid anything because he'd been given away. He lived with these *ladinos* for nine years but learned no Spanish because he wasn't allowed in the house. He was just there to run errands and work, and was kept totally apart from the family. They found him repulsive because he had no clothes and was very dirty. When my father was fourteen he started looking around for some way out. His brothers were also growing up but they weren't earning anything either. My grandmother earned barely enough to feed them. So my father went off to find work on the *fincas* near the coast. He was already a man and started earning enough money to send to my grandmother and he got her away from that family as soon as he could. She'd sort of become her employer's mistress although he had a wife. She had to agree because she'd nowhere else to go. She did it out of necessity and anyway there were plenty more waiting to take her place. She left to join her eldest son in the coastal estates and the other boys started working there as well.

We grew up on those *fincas* too. They are on the south coast, part of Escuintla, Suchitepequez, Retalhuleu, Santa Rosa, Jutiapa, where coffee, cotton, cardamom and sugar are grown. Cutting cane was usually men's work and the pay was a little higher. But at certain times of the year, both men and women were needed to cut cane. At the beginning things were very hard. They had only wild plants to eat, there wasn't even any maize. But gradually, by working very hard, they managed to get themselves a place up in the *Altiplano*.

…

That's when my father met my mother and they got married. They went through very difficult times together. They met in the *Altiplano* since my mother was from a very poor family too. Her parents were very poor and used to travel around looking for work. They were hardly ever at home in the *Altiplano*.

That's how they came to settle up in the mountains. There was no town there. There was no-one. They founded a village up there. My village has a long history – a long and painful history. The land up there belonged to the government and you had to get permission to settle there. When you'd got permission, you had to pay a fee so that you could clear the land and then build your house. Through all my parents' efforts in the *fincas*, they managed to get enough money together to pay the fee, and they cleared the land. Of course, it's not very easy to make things grow on land that's just been cleared. You don't get a good yield for at least eight or nine years. So my parents cultivated the land and eight years later, it started to produce. We were growing up during this period. I had five older brothers and sisters. I saw my two eldest brothers die from lack of food when we were down in the *fincas*. Most Indian families suffer from malnutrition. Most of them don't even reach fifteen years old. When children are growing and don't get enough to eat, they're often ill, and this… well… it complicates the situation.

So my parents stayed there. My mother found the trees and our amazing mountains so beautiful. She said that they'd get lost sometimes because the mountains were so high and not a single ray of light fell through the plants. It's very dense. […]

I was born there. My mother already had five children, I think. Yes, I had five brothers and sisters and I'm the sixth. My mother said that she was working down on a *finca* until a month before I was born. She had just twenty days to go when she went up to the mountains, and she gave birth to me all on her own. My father wasn't there because he had to work the month out on the *finca*.

Most of what I remember is after I was five. We spent four months in our little house in the *Altiplano* and the rest of the year we had to go down to the coast, either in the Boca Costa where there's coffee picking and also weeding out the coffee plants, or further down the south coast where there's cotton. […] So we'd work in the *fincas* for eight months and in January we'd go back up to the *Altiplano* to sow our crops. Where we live in the mountains – that is, where the land isn't fertile – you can barely grow maize and beans. The land isn't fertile enough for anything else. But on the coast the land is rich and you can grow anything. After we'd sown our crops, we'd go down to the coast again until it was time to harvest them, and then we'd make the journey back again. But the maize would soon run out, and we'd be back down again to earn some money. From what my parents said, they lived this harsh life for many years and they were always poor.

Activity 31

Read the short Chapter 3, 'The Nahual', below and discuss how secrets form a significant aspect of Rigoberta's Indian culture. What does the connection to animal and plant life seem to say about the values of their culture?

I, Rigoberta Menchú, Chapter 3, 'The Nahual'

Every child is born with a nahual. The nahual is like a shadow, his protective spirit who will go through life with him. The nahual is the representative of the earth, the animal world, the sun and water, and in this way the child communicates with nature. The nahual is our double, something very important to us. We conjure up an image of what our nahual is like. It is usually an animal. The child is taught that if he kills an animal, that animal's human double will be very angry with him because he is killing his nahual. Every animal has its human counterpart and if you hurt him, you hurt the animal too.

Our days are divided into dogs, cats, bulls, birds, etc. There is a nahual for every day. If a child is born on a Wednesday, his nahual is a sheep. The day of his birth decides his nahual. So for a Wednesday child, every Wednesday is special. Parents know what a child's behaviour will be from the day of the week he is born. Tuesday is a bad day to be born because the child will grow up badtempered. That is because Tuesday's nahual is a bull and bulls are always angry. The child whose nahual is a cat will like fighting with his brothers and sisters.

We have ten sacred days, as our ancestors have always had. These ten days have their nahual. They can be dogs, cats, horses, bulls, but they can also be wild animals, like lions. Trees can be nahuals too: trees chosen by our ancestors many centuries ago. A nahual is not always only one animal. With dogs, for example, nine dogs represent a nahual. Or in the case of horses, three. It can vary a lot. You don't know how many in fact, or rather, only the parents know the number of animals which go to make the nahuals of these ten special days. For us the meekest days are Wednesday, Monday, Saturday and Sunday. The nahuals are sheep, or birds or animals which don't harm other animals.

All this is explained to young people before they get married so that when they have children they know which animal represents each day. One very important thing they have to remember is not to tell the child what his nahual is until he is grown up. We are only told what our nahual is when our personalities are formed and our parents see what our behaviour is normally. Otherwise a child might take advantage of his nahual. For example, if his nahual is a bull, he might like fighting and could say, 'I behave like this because I'm such and such an animal and you must put up with me'. If a child doesn't know his nahual he cannot use it as an excuse. He may be compared to the animal, but that is not identifying him with his nahual. Younger children don't know the nahual of their elder brothers and sisters. They are only told all this when they are mature enough and this could be at any age between ten and twelve. When this happens the animal which is his nahual is given to him as a present. If it is a lion, however, it is replaced by something else. Only our parents, or perhaps other members of the community who were there when we were born, know the day of our birth. People from other villages don't know and they are only told if they become close friends.

A day only has a special meaning if a child is born on it. If no baby is born on any one Tuesday, it is of no interest to anyone. That is, there is no celebration. We often come to love the animal which is our nahual even before we know what it is. Although we love all the natural world, we are often drawn to one particular animal more than to the others. We grow to love it. Then one day we are told that it is our nahual. All the kingdoms which exist on this earth are related to man. Man is part of the natural world. There is not one world for man and one for animals, they are part of the same one and lead parallel lives. We can see this in our surnames. Many of us have surnames which are the names of animals. *Quej*, meaning horse, for example.

We Indians have always hidden our identity and kept our secrets to ourselves. This is why we are discriminated against. We often find it hard to talk about ourselves because we know we must hide so much in order to preserve our Indian culture and prevent it being taken away from us. So I can only tell you very general things about the nahual. I can't tell you what my nahual is because that is one of our secrets.

Chapter 34, 'Exile' has one important italicised term. Here is the definition:

Compañero/compañera: Name widely used in Latin America to mean friend or companion, in general terms, and more specifically 'comrade' in political terms. Here it is used toward the beginning to refer to the inhabitants of the village who participate in the life of the community. Towards the end it becomes used in a more political sense for the militants of the CUC (Comité de Unidad Campesina – Committee for Peasant Unity).

Activity 32

Read the short chapter, 'Exile', on pages 193–195, and draw conclusions about Rigoberta's journey to leadership in the CUC and what that leadership role now means in terms of her family relationships. What cause now defines her life? What do the final few lines of this chapter (and this memoir) say about Rigoberta's Indian identity – the secret of that identity? What is the meaning of the final line of the text? To what aspect of her culture is Rigoberta fully committed?

I, *Rigoberta Menchú*, Chapter 34, 'Exile'

And so the time came for me to leave there. I was happy, but, at the same time, something happened that I would never have believed possible. The *compañeros* got me out on a plane to Mexico, and I felt a shattered, broken woman, because I'd never imagined that one day those criminals would force me to abandon my country. All the same, I also hoped to come back very soon and carry on working. I didn't want to interrupt my work for a single moment, because I know that I can only hold my parents' banner high if I dedicate myself to the struggle that they left half finished.

I went to different parts of Mexico, but I didn't know what to do there. Poor people never dream of travelling abroad, we don't even dream of travelling anywhere. Because we can't. But, well... I left, I went to other places, got to know other people. I was with many people who love me very much and I've received the same affection from them as from my loved ones. I remember that they asked for my testimony about the situation in Guatemala and I was very moved.

[...]

Later I was told that some people were coming to visit me and that I'd be together with *compañeros* coming out of Guatemala. I was happy. It didn't matter which *compañeros* they were, men or women, because I loved all my people, and for me they're all brothers and sisters whoever they are. And soon afterwards I had the wonderful surprise of seeing my little sisters, and I felt so happy. And it doesn't really matter that we (not only myself but all my brothers and sisters) don't know the whereabouts of the grave of my brothers who died in the *finca*, nor the grave of my little brother who was tortured, nor that of my father, nor my mother. But after my parents' death, I hadn't heard anything about my brothers and sisters, yet I hoped and hoped that they were alive. When we were separated, my littlest sister was helping my mother. The other one had gone into the mountains with our *compañeros*, the guerrillas. The two of them had left the country simply because my sister who was in the mountains felt that she had to go and help the other one, to accompany her and see that everything went smoothly. My little sister had opted for the armed struggle; she was eight when she joined the guerrillas. She thought like an adult, she felt like a woman, especially when it came to defending her people. Well, anyway, she went into the mountains. It was perhaps because she'd got to know the guerrillas before I did. I'd begun leaving our community and going off to others, so I'd begun to move away from the mountains to other more populated towns where they don't have the wonderful mountains we have. It wasn't because the guerrillas came to our village, but because when my sister went down to work in the Brol's *finca*, she found that most of the Brol's labourers were guerrillas. So my sister had contact with them, but she knew how to keep all her secrets. She never told my parents that she had direct contact because she thought it could mean death for my parents. She'd be risking everything. She thought of my parents' lives and her own life, so she kept it all secret. When we realised that my sister had disappeared, we started investigating immediately and went looking for her. But people told us: 'Oh yes, she was in touch with the guerrilla army, so it's obvious she's gone off to the mountains.' But we weren't sure. We thought that perhaps she'd got lost, or been kidnapped, or anything, because they'd threatened that if they couldn't kill one of my parents, they'd kill one of us, I only knew for certain in 1979, when my sister came down from the mountains once and we met. She said: 'I'm happy. Don't worry about me. Even if I suffer hunger, pain and long marches through the mountains, I'm doing it with love and I'm doing it for you.' It was in a village where she'd been given permission to hear mass and go to communion. She'd come down to the village and by pure chance we were at the mass.

[...]

We went back to Guatemala and my sisters each chose an organisation to work in. The *compañeros* told us to choose the best one for us, where we could contribute most. Well, me, I love the CUC. I love it because that's where I realized the importance of the people's revolutionary war, that we had to fight our enemies, and at the same time, fight for change, as a people. I'd no doubt about that. So I said: 'I want to work with the people, even though it means running a lot of risks.' I was very worried about my youngest sister because she grew up in the mountains, she grew up in our village which was very high up in the mountains, and she loved the mountains, the greenery, all the natural world, and I thought that she would opt for a task which was even harder than mine. And it was true. She said: 'I can only honour my mother's banner by taking up arms. For me, there's no other choice.' She made her decision clearly and responsibly. She said: 'I'm a grown-up woman. I am a *compañera*.' My other sister told her: 'Sister, from now on we are comrades in arms. I'm a *compañera* like you and you are a *compañera* like me.' Then they had to find ways of reaching their organizations because we were out of touch with everything.

My sisters went up to the mountains and I stayed to organize the people. I thought a lot about whether to go back to the CUC , but I decided that the CUC had enough leaders, enough peasant members, and also many women taking on responsibilities in the organization. So, because of my Christian background, I opted for the 'Vicente Menchú' Revolutionary Christians. I didn't choose it because it bore my father's name, but because, as a Christian, it was my duty to work with the people. My task was to educate the Christian *compañeros* whose faith brings them into the organisation.

[...]

We all came to important conclusions by studying the Bible. All our *compañeros* did. We discovered that the Bible has been used as a way of making us accept our situation, and not to bring enlightenment to the poor. The work of revolutionary Christians is above all to condemn and denounce the injustices committed against the people.

[...]

We also denounce the stance of the Church hierarchy because it is so often hand in glove with the government. This is actually something I have thought about a lot. Well, because they call themselves Christians, yet they are often deaf to the suffering of the people.

[...]

Well, my role is now that of a leader. This is mostly because the enemy knows me. My job is above all carrying papers into the interior or to the towns, and organising the people, at the same time practising with them the light of the Gospel. My life does not belong to me. I've decided to offer it to a cause. They can kill me at any time, but let it be when I'm fulfilling a mission, so I'll know that my blood will not be shed in vain, but will serve as an example to my compañeros. The world I live in is so evil, so bloodthirsty, that it can take my life away from one moment to the next. So the only road open to me is our struggle, the just war. The Bible taught me that. I tried to explain this to a Marxist *compañero*, who told me she wanted to fight the revolution as a Christian. I told her that the whole truth is not found in the Bible, but neither is the whole truth in Marxism, and that she had to accept that. We have to defend ourselves against our enemy but, as Christians, we must also defend our faith within the revolutionary process. At the same time, we have to think about the important work we have to do, after our victory, in the new society. I know that no-one can take my Christian faith away from me. Not the government, for fear, not weapons. And this is what I have to teach my people: that together we can build the people's Church, a true Church. Not just a hierarchy, or a building, but a real change inside people. I chose this as my contribution to the people's war. I am convinced that the people, the masses, are the only ones capable of transforming society. It's not just another theory. I chose to stay in the city among the people, instead of choosing to take up arms, as I said. We all contribute in different ways, but we are all working for the same objective.

That is my cause. As I've already said, it wasn't born out something good, it was born out of wretchedness and bitterness. It has been radicalized by the poverty in which my people live. It has been radicalized by the malnutrition which I, as an Indian, have seen and experienced. And by the exploitation and discrimination which I've felt in the flesh. And by the oppression which prevents us performing our ceremonies, and shows no respect for our way of life, the way we are. At the same time, they've killed the people dearest to me, and here I include my neighbors from my village among my loved ones. Therefore, my commitment to our struggle knows no boundaries or limits. This is why I've travelled to many places where I've had the opportunity to talk about my people. Of course I'd need a lot of time to tell you all about my people, because it's not easy to understand just like that. And I think I've given some idea of that in my account. Nevertheless, I'm still keeping my Indian identity a secret. I'm still keeping secret what I think no-one should know. Not even anthropologists or intellectuals, no matter how many books they have, can find out all our secrets.

Activity 33

In many chapters throughout this text, there is a quote attributed to Popol Vuh. Research this name. Who or what is it? Look at the prescripts below for the two chapters you have read, 'The Family' and 'Exile'. What significance do the quotations have for the content or context of the chapter?

'The Family'

'We have always lived here: we have the right to go on living where we are happy and where we want to die. Only here can we feel whole; nowhere else would we ever feel complete and our pain would be eternal.'
Popol Vuh

'Exile'

'We are the avengers of death. Our race will never be extinguished while there is light in the morning star.'
Popol Vuh

Activity 34

Argue that each of the three areas of exploration – readers, writers, and texts; time and space; and intertextuality: connecting texts – would offer an appropriate approach to this memoir.

Insights into non-fiction

All non-fiction informs and brings some truth to light, but some non-fiction takes on a literary designation when the writer assumes some of the same conventions as fiction writers. Conventions like imagery, figurative language, syntax, and diction contribute to producing emotional and intellectual effects in the reader/audience. These effects, from outrage to empathy, can be agents of change in our world.

Unlike fiction writers, however, many non-fiction writers have an intended audience or reader who they seek to persuade. The persuasion may be subtle, producing a kind of understanding that opens the world of the reader to new knowledge, or it may require more of the reader, exposing some dark underbelly of our world, challenging the reader to initiate some cultural or political change (global issues). Whatever the intention, regardless of the who or the what, the where or the when, the non-fiction writer has one measure of success – response from their reader or listener.

Below are other points that contribute to your understanding of the non-fiction form:

1. Three types of rhetoric used to persuade the reader, or audience, in the case of a speech are pathos, logos, and ethos. These strategies are often used in speeches.

2. Memoirs/autobiographies, letters, diaries/journals, essays, speeches, and travelogues are all considered types of literary non-fiction.

3. The tone of any non-fiction piece is directly suited to the intended audience as well as the intended response/effect the writer wishes to achieve.

4. Memoir and **autobiography** are differentiated by intention. Autobiography is often more chronologically focused while memoir is less so, often referencing time in general, rather than specific terms.

5. Letters are intimate and highly personal reflections, written to a specific person for a specific reason.

6. Diaries/journals are even more intimate forms. Most often, diary and journal entries were never written for any other reader. The audience is the self and so these reflections offer great insight into the psyche of the writer.

7. Essays are formally structured to reveal a logical, systematic presentation of ideas, philosophical and/or personal in nature.

8. Travel writers choose to document their journeys with a perceptive eye and use their pens to create a shared, connected experience. Past travel writing tended to focus on setting, but more current forms centre on the writer's interactions with people and language, a shift that suggests the significance of understanding the connections between place, culture, and context.

9. Speeches are perhaps the most persuasive form of non-fiction. Rhetorical strategies are essential in this form. Because a speech is intended to be heard, it is important to listen to a recording of the speech, if possible, in order to notice the nuance of the delivery: pauses, pacing, and body language are used as rhetorical strategies.

Paper 1: Guided literary analysis (HL/SL)

2.1

In this chapter you will...
• understand the requirements for exam paper 1
• explore the specifics of a guided literary analysis
• review the textual features and/or authorial choices of the four literary forms
• examine the relationship between the learner portfolio and exam paper 1
• understand the assessment criteria
• evaluate sample exam paper 1 passages and guiding questions.

The nature of exam paper 1 (HL and SL)

Paper 1 is a summative evaluation that takes place at the end of your two-year course in Language A: literature, during the May or November exam period. Both SL and HL students take paper 1. If you are an SL student, the duration of the exam is 1 hour and 15 minutes. If you are a HL student, the duration is 2 hours and 15 minutes. For both SL and HL students, your paper 1 exam is weighted at 35%.

You will be asked to write one (SL students) or two (HL students) guided literary analyses. A guided literary analysis is an exploration of a passage supported by a guiding question which asks you to consider a technical or formal aspect of the passage.

Both SL and HL students will have the same exam paper with two previously unseen passages. HL students will write guided literary analyses **on each of the two passages**, while SL students will **choose only one** of the passages on which to write a guided literary analysis. The primary difference is HL students must be careful to use the time judiciously, writing for approximately half of the 2 hours and 15 minutes on each passage (i.e. 1 hour and 7 minutes).

The passages could be taken from any of the four literary forms: prose fiction, literary non-fiction, drama, poetry. Each of the passages will be from a different literary form, so it is critical that you have had close reading practice of each of the four forms throughout your two-year course. A little later in this chapter you will see how your close reading activities in your learner portfolio prepare you for this task.

Literary analysis vs literary commentary

The guiding question will help you focus your literary analysis.

The essential difference between a literary commentary and a guided literary analysis is one of organisation and the development of ideas, as opposed to the nature of the analysis. In both tasks, you are asked to demonstrate an understanding of the thought and feeling within the passage, as well as to show an appreciation for the ways in which a writer shapes meaning through specific choices of language, structure, technique, and style. An analysis is an investigation into a passage, supported by a guiding question that serves as the entry point of your analysis. You are not expected to elaborate on every literary feature of the passage. Instead, the guiding question will narrow the focus of your analysis.

The connection between guided literary analysis and literary form

The form of the passage will also determine your approach to the analysis. Prose fiction, drama, poetry, and literary non-fiction all have distinct literary features. When we speak of the 'hand of the writer', the 'writer's strategies', or the 'literary techniques that the writer uses', we are acknowledging that writers make purposeful choices to **create** meaning. And, as readers of these forms, we contribute to and are **transformed** by the experience of reading. Meaning is created through a collaborative process between the conventions of the form, the hand of the writer, and the reader.

It is important to remember that the form of the passage will determine the approach and the language of your analysis.

Prose fiction (the novel, the short story)

The language and focus of your analysis could include:

- plot, setting (geography, topography, location)

- time (historical, contextual, flashback)

- character function/development (major/minor/foil/parallel/protagonist/antagonist)

- theme (implicit or explicit/lesson about human nature)

- structure (chaptering, sectioning)

- point of view (first person, second person, third-person limited or omniscient).

Poetry

The language and focus of your analysis could include:

- structure, shape, form (stanzas, lines, enjambment, free verse, lyric, narrative)

- sound (onomatopoeia, alliteration, assonance, consonance)

- rhyme (patterns, end rhyme, eye rhyme)

- subject matter

- tone, occasion

- speaker/persona

- irony

- diction and syntax.

Info box

Graphic novels and memoirs are subcategories of prose fiction and literary non-fiction, so you should be prepared to respond to literary texts with visual components. Music lyrics are a subcategory of poetry, but if music lyrics appear on exam paper 1, you will not have to address music features of the text. Please see Chapters 1.1 (Fiction) and 1.3 (Poetry) for more details on analysing visual literary texts and music lyrics respectively.

Drama

The language and focus of your analysis could include:

- entries, exits, and blocking

- staging – lighting, props, music, costumes

- irony – verbal, situational, dramatic

- character – gesture, voice, visual appearance

- time (passage of and historical)

- momentum

- sound (other than music) and silence

- character function/development

- dialogue

- structure.

Literary non-fiction

The language and focus of your analysis could include:

- audience (familiar, unfamiliar)

- register (technical, formal, informal, colloquial)

- persuasive strategies (rhetoric, pathos, logos, ethos)

- form (essay, memoir, letter, speeches, autobiography, biography)

- authenticity.

Info box

The paper 1 passages themselves can be complete pieces of writing or extracts from longer pieces. Whenever possible, writers listed on the *Prescribed reading list* will not have their works used as sample passages.

Info box

A guiding question provides an entry point for your analysis of a passage.

Responding to the guiding question

- For each passage, one guiding question will be provided on a central technical or formal element that may provide an interesting point for your entry into the text.

- Although it is not compulsory to answer the guiding question, you should be aware that it is expected that your analysis will focus on a particular aspect of the text.

- So, if you decide not to use the guiding question provided, be sure that you clearly propose an alternative entry point to the text.

- Some technical or formal element must provide a focus for your analysis. The 'guide' in a guided literary analysis is the guiding question – the one proposed, or the one you propose in its place.

What follows is a series of sample passages for exam paper 1: guided literary analysis. The sample passages include complete poems and extracts taken from larger works in the forms of prose fiction, drama, and literary non-fiction. Reading through the passages and completing the accompanying activities will enable you to build skills for guided literary analysis.

Sample poetry passage for exam paper 1: guided literary analysis

With a partner, read the poem out loud and follow the directions below the poem.

'Words Don't Die of Cold' by Kedarnath Singh

Words don't die of cold
they die from a lack of courage
Words often perish
because of humid weather

I once met   5
a word
that was like a bright red bird
in the swamp along the riverbank in my village
I brought it home
but as soon as we reached the wooden door-frame   10
it gave me
a strangely terrified look
and breathed its last

After that I started fearing words
If I ran into them I beat a hasty retreat   15
if I saw a hairy word dressed in brilliant colours
advancing towards me
I often simply shut my eyes

Slowly after a while
I started to enjoy this game   20
One day for no reason at all
I hit a beautiful word with a stone
while it hid
like a snake in a pile of chaff

I remember its lovely glittering eyes   25
down to this day

With the passage of time
my fear has decreased
When I encounter words today
we always end up asking after each other   30

Now I've come to know
many of their hiding-places
I've become familiar with
many of their varied colours
Now I know for instance   35
that the simplest words
are brown and beige
and the most destructive
are pale yellow and pink

Most often the words we save   40
for our saddest and heaviest moments
are the ones
that on the occasions meant for them
seem merely obscene

And what shall I do now   45
with the fact that I've found
perfectly useless words
that wear ugly colours
and lie discarded in the garbage
to be the most trustworthy
in my moments of danger   50

It happened just yesterday –
half a dozen healthy and attractive words
suddenly surrounded me
in a dark street
I lost my nerve –   55

For a while I stood before them
speechless
and drenched in sweat
Then I ran
I'd just lifted my foot in the air   60
when a tiny little word
bathed in blood
ran up to me out of nowhere panting
and said –
'Come, I'll take you home'   65

Possible guiding questions

While only one question is provided on the exam paper, consider the variety of questions that could be posed:

- What do we know about the persona/speaker of this poem?

- How does figurative language contribute to its meaning?

- How are words personified and to what effect?

Activity 1 Analysing and constructing guiding questions for poetry

1) Select one of the guiding questions above and list, in your learner portfolio, the conventions of this poetic form as well as your observations about choices that the poet made which are unusual or striking to the eye or ear.
2) Create two additional guiding questions for this poem with a partner. Once you have created your questions, share them with another group and justify why your questions would be helpful as an entry point for an analysis.
3) Record your responses in your learner portfolio.

Prose analysis: practice with guiding questions and introductory paragraphs

Read the sample passage below from Mariama Bâ's epistolary novel, *So Long a Letter*. Answer the guiding question below the extract and complete the activities that follow.

Context of the extract: In this epistolary novel (a novel written as a series of letters), *So Long a Letter*, Ramatoulaye writes to her childhood friend, Aissiatou, with the news of her husband's death as well as his decision to 'take another wife', a co-wife, five years prior. Ramatoulaye writes to her friend finding consolation in their shared early memories but questioning the role of fate, destiny, health, and the futility of understanding her husband's decision.

An epistolary novel is one written as a series of letters.

Sample prose fiction passage for exam paper 1: guided literary analysis

From *So Long a Letter* by Mariama Bâ

When I stopped yesterday, I probably left you astonished by my disclosures.

Was it madness, weakness, irresistible love? What inner confusion led Modou Fall to marry Binetou?

To overcome my bitterness, I think of human destiny. Each life has its share of heroism, an obscure heroism, born of abdication, or renunciation and acceptance under the merciless whip of fate.

I think of all the blind people the world over, moving in darkness. I think of all the paralysed the world over, dragging themselves about. I think of all the lepers the world over wasted by their disease.

Victims of a sad fate, which you did not choose, compared with your lamentations, what is my quarrel, cruelly motivated, with a dead man who no longer has any hold over my destiny? Combining your despair, you could have been avengers and made them tremble, all those who are drunk on their wealth; tremble, those upon whom fate has bestowed favours. A horde powerful in its repugnance and revolt, you could have snatched the bread that your hunger craves.

Your stoicism has made you not violent or subversive but true heroes, unknown in the mainstream of history, never upsetting established order, despite your miserable condition.

I repeat, beside your visible deformities, what are moral infirmities from which in any case you are not immune! Thinking of you, I thank God for my eyes which daily embrace heavens and earth. If today moral fatigue makes my limbs stiff, tomorrow it will leave my body. Then, relieved, my legs will carry me slowly and I shall again have around me the iodine and the blue of the sea. The star and white cloud will be mine. The breath of wind will again refresh my face. I will stretch out, turn around, I will vibrate. Oh, health, live in me. Oh, health...

My efforts cannot for long take my mind off my disappointment. I think of the suckling baby, no sooner born than orphaned. I think of the blind man who will never see his child's smile. I think of the cross the one-armed man has to bear. I think… But my despair persists, but my rancor remains, but the waves of an immense sadness break in me.

Madness or weakness? Heartlessness or irresistible love? What inner torment led Modou Fall to marry Binetou?

And to think that I loved this man passionately, to think that I gave him thirty years of my life, to think that twelve times over I carried his child. The addition of a rival to my life was not enough for him. In loving someone else, he burned his past, both morally and materially. He dared to commit such an act of disavowal.

And yet, what didn't he do to make me his wife!

Guiding question: To what effect is punctuation used in this passage?

A guiding question should provide an entry point to your analysis.

Activity 2 Analysing and constructing guiding questions for prose fiction

1) Consider how the prose form helps you respond to the guiding question above. How might the punctuation function differently in prose than it does in poetry?
2) With a partner, create two additional guiding questions for this passage. Once you have created your questions, share them with another group and justify why your questions would be helpful as an entry point for an analysis.
3) Record your responses in your learner portfolio.

Sample paper 1 response – introductory paragraph to the guiding question with thesis

This passage from Mariama Bâ's *So Long a Letter* reveals a deeply distressed Ramatoulaye, who questions why her husband would choose a second wife, and how in grief is it possible for her to reconcile her feelings of 'disavowal' with those of a grieving widow. She is, in a sense, blinded by her husband's choices and searches for a sense of herself without him. She seeks an identity beyond 'wife'. Questions and responses to those questions are scattered through this passage, but their placement is not random. Through question marks, exclamation points, and ellipses, Ramatoulaye reflects on herself, her rival, and her victimisation. Her questions act as demonstrations of her active search for answers and for peace.

Activity 3 Analysing an opening paragraph

Using the introductory sample paragraph on page 204 as a guide, go back to the extract from Bâ's epistolary novel and note the claims made in the student sample. Then, select and highlight specific examples from the text to support those claims. A clean copy of the passage is available in the eBook.

Sample drama passage for exam paper 1: guided literary analysis

Friends, a tragicomedy in 13 scenes, was first performed in Tokyo in 1967. This is the opening scene of the play.

Friends by Kōbō Abe, translated by Donald Keene

Scene One

The curtain rises to the sweetly seductive melody of 'The Broken Necklace' (music by Inomata Takeshi).

> Night time in the big city –
> Now that the string is broken, the beads of the necklace
> Scatter here and scatter there
> In every direction.
> Poor broken necklace, where is the breast that warmed you once?
> When did you leave it, where has it gone?
> Little lost beads, little lost beads.

Two large, partition-like walls meet in a 'V' at the middle of the stage. Shadows of human figures, four each from left and right, appear on the walls and, to the rhythm of the music, gradually grow larger, until in the end they seem to loom like giants over the audience.

As the music comes to an end, the owners of the shadows reveal themselves from the wings on both sides. The composition of this family of eight could hardly be more average, but one senses something peculiar about its members. They move mechanically, nobody as yet showing any expression on his face.

MIDDLE DAUGHTER [*steps forth from the group and advances to the center of the stage. The music should continue, but without words.*]

MIDDLE DAUGHTER [*taking up the words of the song that has been heard, her voice pleading and romantic*]: But we can't just leave them to their fate. We'll gather up those poor little beads. Yes, we'll gather them up and run a new string through them. [*She turns to* GRANDMOTHER.] We can do it, Grandma, can't we?

GRANDMOTHER [*in a completely matter of fact tone*]: Of course we can. That's our job, isn't it?

MIDDLE DAUGHTER [*turning back to the audience and continuing her previous remarks*]: It's wrong for there to be lost children and lonely people. It's all wrong. But you can't make a necklace without running a string through the beads. [*She turns to* FATHER.] We'll be the string for the necklace. Won't we, Father?

FATHER [*with a look of having heard this before*]: Don't you think I know it already, that being a string is our job?

MIDDLE DAUGHTER [*singing to the music*]:

> Where is the breast that warmed you once?
> When did you leave it, where has it gone?
> Little lost beads, little lost beads.

YOUNGEST DAUGHTER [*suddenly gives a loud sneeze that stops the music.*]

MOTHER: My poor darling. [*To the others, reproachfully.*] If we don't settle down somewhere soon, it'll be ten o'clock before we know it.

YOUNGER SON: That's right. [*He yawns ostentatiously.*] I for one have had enough of this gabbing.

ELDER SON [*sharply*]: Don't talk like a fool. It's our job, isn't it?

ELDEST DAUGHTER [*without expression*]: That's right. It's our job.

[*The music begins again.*]

MIDDLE DAUGHTER [*resuming her exalted tone*]: And that's why we must go on. We must search out all the lonely people and offer them our love and friendship. We are the messengers of love who can heal their loneliness. We must sniff out the faint wisps of sadness that escape like drops of starlight from the windows of the city, and go there with our gift of joy. [*She spreads her arms open as if introducing the family to the audience.*] Yes, we are the angels of broken necklaces.

Each member of the family simultaneously shines a flashlight from below on his face and smiles timidly. The contrast with the mood of what has preceded should be as strong as possible.
Blackout.

Guiding question: How do the stage directions reinforce this play as a tragicomedy? (A tragicomedy combines elements of both tragedy and comedy.)

When analysing drama passages, think about the reactions that an audience might experience.

Activity 4 Analysing the significance of stage directions

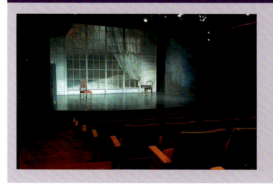

With a partner or small group, examine the function of repetition, blocking (character movement on stage), and sound in this opening scene. What is the effect of each? Then, in your learner portfolio, make a list of reactions that an audience might experience if they were to witness this scene on stage.

Activity 5 Composing guiding questions for drama

With a different partner or group configuration, compose at least one guiding question for each of the conventions of drama that you evaluated above in Activity 4 (repetition, blocking, and sound). Record your guiding questions in your learner portfolio.

Sample literary non-fiction passage for paper 1: guided literary analysis

Buckeye by Scott Russell Sanders (1995)

Years after my father's heart quit, I keep in a wooden box on my desk the two buckeyes that were in his pocket when he died. Once the size of plums, the brown seeds are shriveled now, hollow, hard as pebbles, yet they still gleam from the polish of his hands. He used to reach for them in his overalls or suit pants and click them together, or he would draw them out, cupped in his palm, and twirl them with his blunt carpenter's fingers, all the while humming snatches of old tunes.

'Do you really believe buckeyes keep off arthritis?' I asked him more than once.

He would flex his hands and say, 'I do so far.'

My father never paid much heed to pain. Near the end, when his worn knee often slipped out of joint, he would pound it back in place with a rubber mallet. If a splinter worked into his flesh beyond the reach of tweezers, he would heat the blade of a knife over a cigarette lighter and slice through the skin. He sought to ward off arthritis not because he feared pain but because he lived through his hands, and he dreaded the swelling of knuckles, the stiffening of fingers. What use would he be if he could no longer hold a hammer or guide a plow? When he was a boy he had known farmers not yet 40 years old whose hands had curled into claws, men so crippled up they could not tie their own shoes, could not sign their names.

'I mean to tickle my grandchildren when they come along,' he told me, 'and I mean to build doll houses and turn spindles for tiny chairs on my lathe.'

So he fondled those buckeyes as if they were charms, carrying them with him when our family moved from Ohio at the end of my childhood, bearing them to new homes in Louisiana, then Oklahoma, Ontario, and Mississippi, carrying them still on his final day when pain a thousand times fiercer than arthritis gripped his heart.

The box where I keep the buckeyes also comes from Ohio, made by my father from a walnut plank he bought at a farm auction. I remember the auction, remember the sagging face of the widow whose home was being sold, remember my father telling her he would prize that walnut as if he had watched the tree grow from a sapling on his own land. He did not care for pewter or silver or gold, but he cherished wood. On the rare occasions when my mother coaxed him into a museum, he ignored the paintings or porcelain and studied the exhibit cases, the banisters, the moldings, the parquet floors.

I remember him planing that walnut board, sawing it, sanding it, joining piece to piece to make foot stools, picture frames, jewelry boxes. My own box, a bit larger than a soap dish, lined with red corduroy, was meant to hold earrings and a pin, not buckeyes. The top is inlaid with pieces fitted so as to bring out the grain, four diagonal joints converging from the corners toward the center. If I stare long enough at those converging lines, they float free of the box and point to a center deeper than wood.

Activity 6 Developing guiding questions for literary non-fiction

The terms listed below are often used to describe the technical aspects of literary non-fiction. Choose three that you believe are significant to Sanders' memoir excerpt and create a guiding question for each. Record your guiding questions in your learner portfolio:

- cinematic scene
- specificity and detail
- dialogue
- image and metaphor
- telling truth/finding authenticity.

Connections between exam paper 1 and the learner portfolio

As is true for all of the summative assessments in this course, the learner portfolio may well be the most important tool to help you prepare for paper 1.

You will need to practise writing a guided literary analysis frequently throughout your course. In some instances, you will practise using passages or extracts from works that you are studying in class. But even more importantly, you will need to practise writing a guided literary analysis on passages (poems and extracts from novels, plays, and literary non-fiction) that you have never read before. Be sure to practise writing about each form, because you may have passages on exam paper 1 from any of the four genres.

Keep in mind that your analysis skills will develop over time. Your learner portfolio will provide you with 'real time' examples of the progress you have made over the two years of this course. Use your observations of your strengths and weaknesses to focus on what skills you need to improve upon so that you are confident in your abilities when you sit the exam.

Be aware as you develop your close reading skills how insights into one literary form can inform another. For example, if you have an extract from a novel written in a first-person point of view, and a poem with a specific persona, you might find it interesting to compare the common effects produced by each: an engaging voice, or witness, who seems to be speaking directly to the reader in the present. Do you find you have more sympathy with, or understanding of, a first-person point of view or persona as opposed to a third-person narrator or speaker? These are the kinds of comparative analytical observations that contribute to your skills as a reader of an unfamiliar passage in any form.

You will also need to become familiar with the assessment criteria and make sure that you can comfortably assess the strengths and weaknesses of guided literary analyses.

The assessment criteria for Paper 1: Guided literary analysis

Activity 7 Breaking down the assessment criteria

Work with a partner or a small group to analyse both assessment criteria tables listed below. The first table specifically lays out the expectations for each criterion in the form of questions. The second table is more detailed and indicates the student level of achievement from 1–5 (the markband) for each criterion.

Look closely at criteria A–D in Table 1 below.
- What do you need to do in order to achieve high marks for each criterion?
- Make a list of terms that are specific to this assessment.
- How will your knowledge of these terms help you better understand the requirements of the assessment?
- Record your responses in your learner portfolio.

Info box

A markband determines the range of points available to students, based on specific criteria.

Table 1: Guided literary analysis criteria SL/HL (Paper 1)

Criterion A: Understanding and interpretation	5 marks
• How well does the candidate demonstrate an understanding of the text and draw reasoned conclusions from implications in it? • How well are ideas supported by references to the text?	
Criterion B: Analysis and evaluation	**5 marks**
• To what extent does the candidate analyse and evaluate how textual features and/or authorial choices shape meaning?	
Criterion C: Focus and organisation	**5 marks**
• How well organised, coherent, and focused is the presentation of ideas?	
Criterion D: Language	**5 marks**
• How clear, varied, and accurate is the language? • How appropriate is the choice of register and style? ('Register' refers, in this context, to the candidate's use of elements such as vocabulary, tone, sentence structure, and terminology appropriate to the analysis.	
TOTAL	**20 marks**

NOTE: Each essay is worth 20 marks. Since HL students write two essays, the total marks possible for HL students is 40.

Activity 8

Look closely at criteria A–D and the markband range (1–5) in Table 2.
- Which words in Table 2 distinguish the highest band for each criterion?
- What strategies will help you achieve top marks in each criterion?

Compare your findings with other groups and write a reflection about scoring expectations for guided literary analysis in your learner portfolio.

NOTE: Keep these tables handy. You will come back to them later in the chapter when you read and analyse student sample assessments.

Table 2: Guided literary analysis (Paper 1)

Criteria	0	1	2	3	4	5
Criterion A: Understanding and interpretation	The work does not reach a standard described by the descriptors.	The response demonstrates little understanding of the literal meaning of the text. References to the text are infrequent or are rarely appropriate.	The response demonstrates some understanding of the literal meaning of the text. References to the text are at times appropriate.	The response demonstrates an understanding of the literal meaning of the text. There is a satisfactory interpretation of some implications of the text. References to the text are generally relevant and mostly support the candidate's ideas.	The response demonstrates a thorough understanding of the literal meaning of the text. There is a convincing interpretation of many implications of the text. References to the text are relevant and support the candidate's ideas.	The response demonstrates a thorough and perceptive understanding of the literal meaning of the text. There is a convincing and insightful interpretation of larger implications and subtleties of the text. References to the text are well chosen and effectively support the candidate's ideas.
Criterion B: Analysis and evaluation	The work does not reach a standard described by the descriptors.	The response is descriptive and/or demonstrates little relevant analysis of textual features and/or authorial choices.	The response demonstrates some appropriate analysis of textual features and/or authorial choices, but is reliant on description.	The response demonstrates a generally appropriate analysis of textual features and/or authorial choices.	The response demonstrates an appropriate and at times insightful analysis of textual features and/or authorial choices. There is a good evaluation of how such features and/or choices shape meaning.	The response demonstrates an insightful and convincing analysis of textual features and/or authorial choices. There is a very good evaluation of how such features and/or choices shape meaning.
Criterion C: Focus and organisation	The work does not reach a standard described by the descriptors.	Little organisation is apparent in the presentation of ideas. No discernible focus is apparent in the analysis.	Some organisation is apparent in the presentation of ideas. There is little focus in the analysis.	The presentation of ideas is adequately organised in a generally coherent manner. There is some focus in the analysis.	The presentation of ideas is well organised and mostly coherent. The analysis is adequately focused.	The presentation of ideas is effectively organised and coherent. The analysis is well focused.
Criterion D: Language	The work does not reach a standard described by the descriptors.	Language is rarely clear and appropriate; there are many errors in grammar, vocabulary, and sentence construction and little sense of register and style.	Language is sometimes clear and carefully chosen; grammar, vocabulary, and sentence construction are fairly accurate, although errors and inconsistencies are apparent; the register and style are to some extent appropriate to the task.	Language is clear and carefully chosen, with an adequate degree of accuracy in grammar, vocabulary, and sentence construction despite some lapses; register and style are mostly appropriate to the task.	Language is clear and carefully chosen, with a good degree of accuracy in grammar, vocabulary, and sentence construction; register and style are consistently appropriate to the task.	Language is very clear, effective, carefully chosen, and precise, with a high degree of accuracy in grammar, vocabulary, and sentence construction; register and style are effective and appropriate to the task.

Colour-marking and exam paper 1

Info box

Colour-marking is a strategy for identifying image patterns, motifs, and other authorial choices which contribute to meaning.

As you prepare for exam paper 1, **colour-marking** is an effective strategy to observe and categorise the types of literary features that create meaning. But, before we look at the specifics of the colour-marking process, we should define a few terms:

- **Image**: a word (or words) appealing to at least one of our senses, and thereby generating a response in the reader. Of our five senses (visual, auditory, olfactory, tactile, and gustatory), the visual is generally the strongest.

- **Image patterns**: the repetition of these images, not necessarily in uninterrupted succession.

- **Motif**: a repeated pattern of any type within a text. Note that an image pattern is a motif, but a motif is not always an image pattern. An image pattern is a repeated reference to a particular sense, and, since a motif is a repeated pattern, we can say that an image pattern is a motif. We cannot, however, say that the reverse is true. Any repeated pattern, say a repetition of references to time, is indeed a motif. But although we have senses of sight, sound, smell, etc., we do not have a sense called 'time'. Our understanding of time is, however, perceived through many of our senses – the ticking of a clock or the rising of the sun. (Note also that motif is defined variously in reference sources.) When the term is used in this course, use the above definition.

Activity 9 Colour-marking close reading exercise

Now, we'll look through a literary microscope at a passage in order to understand the writer's strategies, whether they be narrative (as in prose fiction), poetic, or dramatic. The process below applies to all forms: poetry and prose.

The process with seen (studied in class) and unseen (not studied) passages is as follows:

1) Choose any passage or poem from one of the previous activities (or choose one from your own programme) and mark with different colours each type of image/image pattern/motif noted in the given passage. If the text is an extract from a larger work that you have studied, think about the context surrounding the extract and how that helps you clarify its meaning.

2) Based on your colour-marking, ask these questions:
   - Is one colour predominant? Why?
   - Is there some progression of imagery/motif, from one type to another? Is the progression logical in terms of the content of the passage? Why?
   - How do the imagery/motifs reinforce and/or illustrate the content of the passage? If you prefer, what is the relationship of the scene to the imagery/motifs used to describe it? Imagery reinforces content by giving it emphasis, by making it fresh through an unusual or **creative** use of imagery, and/or by adding irony (imagery appears to contradict the content or describe it in terms of its opposite qualities).
   - Is a specific tone or mood created by the marked material?

3) Based on your answers to these questions and any others you think appropriate, code each colour-marked passage with inferences you draw about the use of that image/image pattern/motif.

4) Share your responses with a small group and see where your ideas differ or overlap.

5) Now consider the following poem by Robert Druce and colour-mark the poem before looking at our sample beneath it. A clean copy of the poem is available in the eBook.

6) How did your colour-marking differ from ours? What did the process help you to understand about the effects of the authorial choices?

7) Record your observations in your learner portfolio.

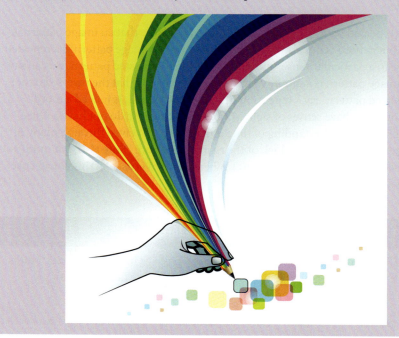

'Child and Insect' by Robert Druce (1980)

He cannot hold his hand huge enough.
How can he cage the sudden clockwork fizz
he has snatched from the grassblades?
He races back, how quick he is,
look! to his mother   5
through the shrieking meadow.
But kneeling at her side
finds only a silence in his fearful clutch.
Revealed, the grasshopper
lies broken on his palm.   10

       It is
nothing now: its dead struts snapped
even the brittle lidless eyes
crushed into the tangle.

                    Sunlight   15
and the landscape flood away
in tears.
For horror he dare not
look at what is cradled in his fingers
and will not be comforted.   20
                    O,
will not.

Yet quick and now
as if by magic the undead insect
with a flick re-   25
assembles itself
            throbs
and is latched to a leaf a yard away.
And once again incredibly it skirls unspoilt
its chirruping music.   30
He weeps, sick with relief and rage.
'There now, my love. It wasn't hurt at all.'
His mother laughs and puts an arm
around him.
            Tearfully   35
he shakes her off.
He will not rejoice (in time he may
but that is not yet certain) after
such betrayal of his grief.
            He must not   40
have tears torn from him
by petty trickery.
Before his mother's eyes he would not care
to do it (and perhaps not ever)
but gladly in this instant he   45
could snatch the creature up and
shatter it
for leaving him so naked.

Colour-marked text

'Child and Insect' by Robert Druce (1980)

He cannot hold his hand huge enough.
How can he cage the [sudden clockwork fizz]
he has snatched from the grassblades?
He races back, how quick he is,
look! to his mother   5
through the (shrieking meadow).
But kneeling at her side
finds only [a silence] in his fearful clutch.

*Note the word/line placement/erratic extensions.

Revealed, the grasshopper
lies broken on his palm.   10

            *It is
nothing now: [its dead struts snapped]
even the [brittle lidless eyes
crushed] into the tangle,
                *Sunlight   15
and the landscape flood away
in tears.
For horror he dare not
look at what is cradled in his fingers
and will not be comforted.   20
                *O,
will not.

Yet quick and now
as if by magic the undead insect
with a flick re-   25
assembles itself
            * throbs
and is [latched to a leaf a yard away.
And once again incredibly it skirls unspoilt
its chirruping music.]   30
He weeps, sick with relief and rage.
'There now, my love. It wasn't hurt at all.'
His mother laughs and puts an arm
around him.
            * Tearfully   35
he shakes her off.
He will not rejoice (in time he may
but that is not yet certain) after
such betrayal of his grief.
            * He must not   40
Have (tears torn) from him
by petty trickery.
Before his mother's eyes he would not care
to do it (and perhaps not ever)
but gladly in this instant he   45
could snatch the creature up and
shatter it
for leaving him so naked.

Colour-marking key:

Body parts motif
Kinesthetic imagery/motion image pattern

Visual/auditory imagery
Anger motif
Grief motif
Vulnerability
Time progression/cause and effect
[ ] Metaphor
( ) Personification

Analysing student samples

In this section you will read and analyse student samples. The first sample is based on the preceding colour-marked poem and includes examiner comments. You will also have the opportunity to reflect upon this essay's strengths and weaknesses and review examiner feedback. The second sample is designed for you to read and practise your scoring using the assessment criteria for the guided literary analysis.

Read the samples below and complete the activities that follow.

First sample student exam paper 1: guided literary analysis of a poem

Guiding question: Discuss the appropriateness of the title.

Student response:

The poem 'Child and Insect' by Robert Druce is loaded with emotion. The reader is thrust into the world of the poet's imagination through attention to detail. It is impossible not to sympathise with the young boy in the poem because his emotions are direct and evocative. The title sets in motion the confrontation that we know must come to pass. Druce seems to believe that any child and any insect will do. They are in opposition from the very start — almost to suggest that the scene and the emotions that unfold are perfectly natural. The child will possess the insect and will have power over it. The child's rage, in part, seems to come from the fact that he thinks that he has accidentally killed it. The insect wasn't supposed to die. And, when he see the insect 'undead' and it 'reassembles itself' in front of him, he feels tricked, betrayed by his own belief, his own visual evidence that the insect was dead.

The title really doesn't indicate any of the emotional impact that is to come in the poem. It is matter of fact, simple, a naming only. What shocks the reader in this poem is that the mother and her child, like the child and the insect, do not understand the violence that betrayal triggers. As the mother pulls her child close and laughs a knowing, somewhat sympathetic little laugh, the child's rage builds. His true thoughts are hidden. His tears are not what they seem.

Druce uses sensory imagery to entice the reader with a detailed, familiar world. The world of the poem, like our own, is filled with fields of grass, young children, and grasshoppers. The poet, however, attributes a certain emotional aspect to each description in the poem. The fields are 'shrieking' in line 16. This shrieking mirrors the wild joy that the boy feels when he captures the insect — perhaps for the first time in his life.

It is the 'petty trickery' of the insect that leaves the boy 'naked' at the poem's end. The final word of the poem strikes the reader to the bone. The unprotected vulnerability of the child's nakedness leaves the reader feeling sympathetic. The boy tries to show his joyful love of the insect, yet it deceives him. He drops his emotional walls in front of his mother, weeping openly, 'sick with relief and rage'. The reference to relief is straightforward enough. The child in some sense is relieved that the insect is not dead. The child did not accidentally kill the insect by grasping it too tightly in his small fist. The insect did not die as the child ran shrieking to show his mother what he had captured. The reference to rage, however, is where the poem's meaning takes a turn. This is not simply a poem about gaining experience or losing innocence. The poem seems to consider the possibility that this child, this young boy, has the potential for violence, for destruction, for murder, within him. Ironically, it is his pride that triggers these emotions — emotions far older than the child, emotions programmed from our ancient drives. Druce seems to be saying that the impulse for violence lies dormant within us all, and even more ironically, loss, coupled with pride, triggers the impulse.

Activity 10 Analysing sample 1

Work with a partner or small group and discuss the following:

1) Criterion A: Understanding and interpretation
   - How well does the candidate demonstrate an understanding of the text and draw reasoned conclusions from implications in it?
   - How well are ideas supported by references to the text?

2) Criterion B: Analysis and evaluation
   - To what extent does the candidate analyse and evaluate how textual features and/or authorial choices shape meaning?
   - How well are ideas supported by references to the text?

3) Criterion C: Focus and organisation
   - How well organised, coherent, and focused is the presentation of ideas?

4) Criterion D: Language
   - How clear, varied, and accurate is the language?
   - How appropriate is the choice of register and style? ('Register' refers, in this context, to the candidate's use of elements such as vocabulary, tone, sentence structure, and terminology appropriate to the analysis.)

5) Read the examiner's comments below and compare them to your own responses.

6) Record your notes in your learner portfolio.

Examiner's comments:

This sample of a guided literary analysis demonstrates a keen understanding of both the content and the feeling expressed in the poem. The essay's attempt to show an appreciation of the writer's stylistic choices, and how those choices shape meaning, however, are not adequate. In balance, the language is clear and effective, and the ideas are well organised and coherent.

Second sample student exam paper 1: guided literary analysis of a prose passage

Work in groups or pairs when looking at the assessment criteria.

Activity 11 Analysing sample 2 and applying the assessment criteria

Read the excerpt, the guiding question, and the student response below, and complete the questions that follow.

From *O Pioneers!* by Willa Cather (1913)

She was almost through with her figures when she heard a cart drive up to the gate, and looking out of the window she saw her two older brothers. They had seemed to avoid her ever since Carl Linstrum's arrival, four weeks ago that day, and she hurried to the door to welcome them. She saw at once that they had come with some very definite purpose. They followed her stiffly into the sitting-room. Oscar

5 sat down, but Lou walked over to the window and remained standing, his hands behind him.

'You are by yourself?' he asked, looking toward the doorway into the parlor.

'Yes. Carl and Emil went up to the Catholic fair.'

For a few moments neither of the men spoke.

Then Lou came out sharply. 'How soon does he intend to go away from here?'

10 'I don't know, Lou. Not for some time, I hope.' Alexandra spoke in an even, quiet tone that often exasperated her brothers. They felt that she was trying to be superior with them.

Oscar spoke up grimly. 'We thought we ought to tell you that people have begun to talk,' he said meaningly.

Alexandra looked at him. 'What about?'

15 Oscar met her eyes blankly. 'About you, keeping him here so long. It looks bad for him to be hanging on to a woman this way. People think you're getting taken in.'

Alexandra shut her account-book firmly. 'Boys,' she said seriously, 'don't let's go on with this. We won't come out anywhere. I can't take advice on such a matter. I know you mean well, but you must not feel responsible for me in things of this sort. If we go on with this talk it will only

20 make hard feeling.'

Lou whipped about from the window. 'You ought to think a little about your family. You're making us all ridiculous.'

'How am I?'

'People are beginning to say you want to marry the fellow.'

25 'Well, and what is ridiculous about that?'

Lou and Oscar exchanged outraged looks. 'Alexandra! Can't you see he's just a tramp and he's after your money? He wants to be taken care of, he does!'

'Well, suppose I want to take care of him? Whose business is it but my own?'

'Don't you know he'd get hold of your property?'

30   'He'd get hold of what I wished to give him, certainly.'

Oscar sat up suddenly and Lou clutched at his bristly hair.

'Give him?' Lou shouted. 'Our property, our homestead?'

'I don't know about the homestead,' said Alexandra quietly. 'I know you and Oscar have always expected that it would be left to your children, and I'm not sure but what you're right. But

35   I'll do exactly as I please with the rest of my land, boys.'

'The rest of your land!' cried Lou, growing more excited every minute. 'Didn't all the land come out of the homestead? It was bought with money borrowed on the homestead, and Oscar and me worked ourselves to the bone paying interest on it.'

'Yes, you paid the interest. But when you married we made a division of the land, and you were

40   satisfied. I've made more on my farms since I've been alone than when we all worked together.'

'Everything you've made has come out of the original land that us boys worked for, hasn't it? The farms and all that comes out of them belongs to us as a family.'

Alexandra waved her hand impatiently. 'Come now, Lou. Stick to the facts. You are talking nonsense. Go to the county clerk and ask him who owns my land, and whether my titles are good.'

45   Lou turned to his brother. 'This is what comes of letting a woman meddle in business,' he said bitterly. 'We ought to have taken things in our own hands years ago. But she liked to run things, and we humored her. We thought you had good sense, Alexandra. We never thought you'd do anything foolish.'

Alexandra rapped impatiently on her desk with her knuckles. 'Listen, Lou. Don't talk wild. You

50   say you ought to have taken things into your own hands years ago. I suppose you mean before you left home. But how could you take hold of what wasn't there? I've got most of what I have now since we divided the property; I've built it up myself, and it has nothing to do with you.'

Oscar spoke up solemnly. 'The property of a family really belongs to the men of the family, no matter about the title. If anything goes wrong, it's the men that are held responsible.'

55   'Yes, of course,' Lou broke in. 'Everybody knows that. Oscar and me have always been easygoing and we've never made any fuss. We were willing you should hold the land and have the good of it, but you got no right to part with any of it. We worked in the fields to pay for the first land you bought, and whatever's come out of it has got to be kept in the family.'

Oscar reinforced his brother, his mind fixed on the one point he could see. 'The property of

60   a family belongs to the men of the family, because they are held responsible, and because they do the work.'

Alexandra looked from one to the other, her eyes full of indignation. She had been impatient before, but now she was beginning to feel angry. 'And what about my work?' she asked in an unsteady voice.

65   Lou looked at the carpet. 'Oh, now, Alexandra, you always took it pretty easy! Of course we wanted you to. You liked to manage round, and we always humored you. We realize you were a great deal of help to us. There's no woman anywhere around that knows as much about business as you do, and we've always been proud of that, and thought you were pretty smart. But, of course, the real work always fell on us. Good advice is all right, but it don't get the weeds out of the corn.'

70   'Maybe not, but it sometimes puts in the crop, and it sometimes keeps the fields for corn to grow in,' said Alexandra dryly. 'Why, Lou, I can remember when you and Oscar wanted to sell this homestead and all the improvements to old preacher Ericson for two thousand dollars. If I'd consented, you'd have gone down to the river and scraped along on poor farms for the rest of your lives.'

Guiding question: How does the writer establish the tension in this passage?

Student response:

The opening paragraph of this passage initially provides exposition where we learn that the sister, Alexandra, is working on her 'account book' at a window in her sitting room when her two older brothers, Lou and Oscar, arrive suddenly after four weeks of avoidance, which she attributes to her involvement with Carl Lindstrom. We learn that Alexandra 'hurries to the door' to welcome them and that the brothers enter purposefully, if not 'stiffly', and follow her back into the sitting room. Lou positions himself in front of the window, looking outward with his hands behind his back, while Oscar sits. Awkwardly tense, this detailed scene setting is significant as Cather sets the stage for the interaction that is to follow, providing insight into the relationship that exists between these siblings. Point of view, along with elements of dialogue and tone, establish the conflict at the root of the brothers' 'very definite purpose' in visiting their sister and the tension which accompanies this conflict.

That purpose, we learn, is to interrogate their younger sister as to the nature of her relationship with Carl Lindstrom — a man they regard as a 'tramp', who they believe is 'after her money'. Lou's initial question, asking Alexandra if she is alone, while his back is to her, implies that what they have to discuss is personal and perhaps unpleasant, and that he is clearly in charge. A few moments of silence only increases the tension.

When Lou speaks again, he speaks 'sharply', wanting to know when Carl is leaving while Oscar adds 'grimly' that people are 'talking . . . about [her] getting taken in'. Alexandra's response is characteristically calm and unflustered, speaking in 'an even, quiet tone that exasperates her brothers'. As she 'shuts her account book', she asserts that they are 'not responsible' for her in matters of the heart and to discuss it further would create 'hard feelings', but they press on. The tension builds as they, 'outraged' and 'shouting', question her intentions to marry Carl and let him 'get hold of [her] property'.

The pace of the dialogue, as well as the tension, increases when Lou quips that Alexandra 'should think a little about [her] family' because she is 'making [them] look ridiculous'. What follows is a kind of bantering between the siblings with her brothers accusing and questioning not only Carl's intentions but Alexandra's as well. Lou 'clutches his hair' and Oscar '[sits] up suddenly' as Alexandra responds to their barrage of questions 'quietly'. Alexandra matches the intensity of their emotional outrage with a quiet assertion that she will 'do exactly as [she] please[s]' with her land, her property.

This declaration of ownership, and subsequent entitlement, raises the conflict even higher. While Lou is growing 'more excited' by the minute, boasting that the land Alexandra owns is actually part of the homestead that they, the 'boys', laboured to pay the interest on, their sister does not dispute this fact, but counters that the profits she has made on her 'agreed to' piece of the homestead has far exceeded what they accomplished earlier, making 'more on [her] farms' on her own, as opposed to when they 'worked together'.

This implication that she is a better, more shrewd business person than her two brothers, cuts to their core and the tone and content of the passage shifts once again. The argument has become personal for the brothers. Their egos bruised, they now try to gain the upper hand through guilt, familial obligation and gender hierarchy.

Ironically, the tension increases after line 50, when the brothers stop questioning (they asked thirteen questions prior to this point in the passage) and take the position that they, as men, are entitled to all of the homestead, including Alexandra's titled land, because 'the property of a family belongs to the men of the family because they do the work'. She has overstepped her place in the family and in the world by asserting her rights to her own land. They 'humored' her, gave her a share of the homestead, but now they see that was 'foolish'. She may be 'pretty smart' for a woman and no other woman 'knows as much about business' as she does, but only men do 'the real work'.

Their patronising tone, coupled with a total disregard of Alexandra's contributions to the success of their homestead, prompts her anger. After line 50 there are only two questions posed and they are both Alexandra's. Her final question, 'And what about my work?' may be delivered with an 'unsteady voice', but she has one more card to play. Her 'advice' may not 'get the weeds out of the corn', according to her brothers, but her final reminder to her brothers deflates the tension. She was the one who saved the homestead when they foolishly wanted to sell it for a pittance of its worth. Her 'work' created their success.

Activity 12

Discuss the following in a small group:

1) Use the IB assessment criteria (Table 2, page 210) to assign a score to the essay. Start with the highest-level markband for each criterion and see if the descriptors in each box fit. If the level in the markband is not reached, move down to the next markband until you've found the descriptor that best fits the assessment. Do this for each of the four criteria until you have arrived at a total score.

2) How would you score this essay? What does the student do well? What could be improved?

3) How does this essay compare to the first student sample?

4) Record your responses in your learner portfolio.

Insights into Paper 1: Guided literary analysis

1. Exam paper 1 contains two passages from two different forms. SL students choose one passage for their guided literary analysis, while HL students must write a guided literary analysis on both of the passages.

2. A guided literary analysis demonstrates an understanding of the thought and feeling of a passage as well as how meaning is created through textual features and/or a authorial choices.

3. The duration for SL students is 1 hour and 15 minutes; for HL, it is 2 hours and 15 minutes.

4. HL students must use the time judiciously so that each passage receives equal treatment.

5. Any of the four forms listed on the *Prescribed reading list* can provide passages for paper 1.

6. Each of the passages has a guiding question. Students need to address the guiding question provided, or provide an alternative guiding question as the focal point of their analysis.

7. The guided literary analysis requires frequent close reading practice, including close reading passages from works not read in class.

8. The learner portfolio is a critical tool for developing the necessary skills to be successful with this summative assessment.

9. Students must be aware of the conventions and textual strategies used in each of the four forms.

Paper 2:
Comparative essay
(HL/SL)

2.2

Learning objectives

In this chapter you will…
- understand the requirements for exam paper 2
- appreciate how intertextuality/connecting texts relate to exam paper 2
- understand the assessment criteria
- appreciate the connection between the learner portfolio and paper 2
- explore strategies for a comparison/contrast essay response
- address the requirements of the question in exam paper 2
- practise writing comparative responses
- evaluate sample paper 2 responses.

The nature of exam paper 2 (HL and SL)

This exam paper is written during the summative written exams in May or November at the end of the two-year course. The paper will consist of four questions of a general nature. You will select **one** question only and will write a comparative essay referring only to **two** works studied during the course.

The format, questions, assessment criteria, and length of this exam paper will be identical for HL and SL students in the literature course as well as for students taking the language and literature course. The only difference is in the weight of the exam paper 2. At the HL, the weight is 25%; at the SL, the weight is 35%.

Exam paper 2 is written under exam conditions, meaning that you will have no access to the works you have studied in the course. You will write a comparative essay based on two works that you have studied at some point during the two-year course. You are free to select any work as long as you have not used that work in any other summative assessment, including the HL essay or the individual oral.

Preselecting texts for your paper 2 essay means that you will be able to use your time more effectively.

It is highly recommended that you preselect three texts in preparation for this assessment, either individually, or in conjunction with your teacher. By preselecting, you will be able to use your time more effectively in determining which question to select and which two texts to use in response to that question. In this way, you can pay more attention to the relevance of the question you select and the appropriateness of the two works that you choose to support it. You are expected to make **detailed** references to the two texts; however, you are not expected to include quotations from those texts.

Intertextuality – the heart of exam paper 2: comparative essay

Throughout the two-year course in Language A: literature you have examined texts using the '**intertextuality**: connecting texts' approach. With this approach, you thought comparatively, examining how different texts compared and contrasted with each other, seeing similarities and differences in terms of **cultural** ideas, themes, character presentation, stylistic features, etc. So, in a sense, you have been preparing for exam paper 2 from the first text you read in your first year of the course. Paper 2 is testing the skills you've been developing over the course in terms of seeing one text of any form in the context of another.

Comparing texts that have the same form can produce interesting insights into the text as well as the form, but comparing texts regardless of form offers another kind of analytical opportunity. The conceptual focus of the course allows you, if you'd like, to compare and contrast any two texts from any two forms on this exam paper. Texts can be grouped for comparison by form, but also by ideas or issues, or any of the seven **course concepts** such as **culture**, **identity**, or **perspective**.

Comparing and contrasting involves strategic, analytical, and creative thinking.

If you revisit any of the four form chapters – fiction, poetry, drama, and non-fiction – you will see that you have been practising intertextual activities in each of these chapters: comparing and contrasting an aspect of one play with another, the poetic vision of two poets, the effect of cultural context in two non-fiction pieces, or determining the variations of irony in two fiction samples. But you will also see that many of these works share similar and yet distinctly different points of analysis, from gender identity and power to cultural roles and expectations of the individual within a community. Exam paper 2 is an exercise in comparison and contrast – perhaps you are finding difference within similarity (the role of women and cultural power) or similarity within difference (public trauma and personal loss or gain).

Addressing the requirements of the question

The four questions that you can choose from are general in nature. What does the term 'general' imply? It implies that the questions will focus on generic aspects of literary study rather than those features that are specific to a particular form. Some questions could be related to theme, or broader textual choices that authors writing in any form might make. Or, these questions could focus on one or more of the seven **concepts** underpinning the course – **communication**, **identity**, **culture**, **perspective**, **transformation**, **representation**, and **creativity**. Rather than specific to form, these concepts are applicable to any text studied in the course, from any form or genre, so that you can use two texts from any form to address the question in a comparative essay response. You could choose a work of drama to compare with a work of prose fiction, or a work of poetry to compare with a work of literary non-fiction. Works may be in translation or written in the language of the course. The works may have come from the *Prescribed reading list* or may have been freely chosen. Any work studied in the two-year course is acceptable as long as it has not been used in another summative assessment (HL essay or individual oral).

In determining the three preselected works to use for exam paper 2, you should list the works that you have studied but *not* used for the HL essay and the individual oral. The works selected should offer the best combination for the comparative essay. These works should provide opportunities for a wide range of possible connections between the works including conceptual, thematic, stylistic, or formal comparisons. Intertextual explorations have been stressed throughout the course, so any activities in your learner portfolio and/or class discussions which focus on the connections between the works and the seven concepts will also help you to determine your three preselected works.

Take a look at these sample questions for exam paper 2, comparative essay:

1) Identify some of the forms intolerance can take, and discuss how its effects on both the victims and the intolerant are presented in **two** of the works you have studied.

2) To what effect is contrast and/or juxtaposition used in **two** of the works you have studied?

3) Discuss whether or not the endings/conclusions of **two** of the works you have studied are satisfactory.

4) Analyse the role that non-human elements play in **two** of the works you have studied.

5) How and why might **two** of the works you have studied be considered inspirational?

6) Explore the presentation and significance of jealousy in **two** works you have studied.

7) How do **two** of the writers you have studied foreshadow events or ideas to come later in their works, and what is the effect of such foreshadowing?

8) Pride can lead to failure and self-destruction, or to accomplishment and self-fulfillment. Discuss the presentation of pride, and its consequences, in **two** of the works you have studied.

9) Examine the presentation of male and female views of the central concerns or issues in **two** works you have studied, and discuss the ways in which these views differ.

10) Tension often builds to a critical point in a piece of literature. How is tension created in **two** of the works you have studied and for what purpose?

Activity 1

Examine each of the 10 sample exam paper 2 questions above and on page 224 and identify the **general** subject matter at the heart of each question.

For example, look at the fourth question listed above: *Analyse the role non-human elements play in two of the works you have studied.*

The general subject matter in this question is non-human elements. Non-human elements in drama could include props, costumes, lighting, or music. In a work of fiction, a non-human element could be an animal, a building, the weather, or some topographical feature like water or mountains.

Activity 2

Choose four of the sample questions above and on page 224 and select two works from your own course of study that could be used as texts to develop a comparative essay in response to each question.

Make sure that these texts have not been used in previous summative assessments like the HL essay or the internal assessment/individual oral.

Make a copy of the table below in your learner portfolio to record your ideas.

Question	Works

Activity 3

Are there texts you have studied that could be used in any other questions? If so, which texts and which questions? Are there any texts which you have studied in a previous summative assessment that you have not yet used?

Make a copy of the table below in your learner portfolio to record your ideas.

Questions not used in previous activity	Works that would pair well with this question

Activity 4

One very important consideration in determining which question to choose, and which works to use as the focus of your comparative essay, is to remember that even though the question may not overtly or directly address the analysis of formal features, an exploration of *how* authorial choices create meaning is a key feature of exam paper 2. This is evaluated in criterion B: analysis and evaluation.

With this point in mind, go back to Activity 2 and create a table for each of the four questions you have selected, along with the two works that you would use to address each of the questions. You can create your own table or use the one below. Be sure to include in your table the specific authorial choices that you believe create meaning with regard to that specific question.

These are the authorial choices for each form:

- **For a work of fiction**: point of view, plot (momentum, subplots), conflict (external and internal), major and minor characters (foils), time (historical and passing of), setting, symbol, style, or theme.
- **For a work of poetry**: speaker and tone, diction (denotation/connotation/figurative language), sound effects, structure and form, or theme.
- **For a work of drama**: plot and momentum, time, staging (props, lighting, music, blocking), major and minor characters (foils), conflict (external and internal), audience, dramatic irony, and theme.
- **For a work of literary non-fiction**: persuasive techniques, rhetorical strategies, authenticity, creating empathy, philosophical or psychological truths.

Question	Works	Effects of authorial choices

The learner portfolio and the comparative essay

One of the primary functions of the learner portfolio is that it provides opportunities for developing comparative strategies with every text that is studied in this two-year course. The intertextual approach used in the course should ensure that there are plenty of comparative activities between texts and even within texts. With frequent practice, you will begin to 'think' comparatively as you read a new text. Asking yourself questions about your own reading process lies at the heart of the comparative process. For example:

- Even if both characters are despicable in some sense, why am I more sympathetic to one character than the other?

- Is there a scene in two different texts that made me feel the same (repulsed, angry, sad, etc.)?

With frequent practice you will begin to think comparatively as you read texts.

- Are there characters in two different works that remind me of each other? Why?

- Which text did I find the most complex? Which text would I classify as straightforward? Why?

- Are there two works that I found inspirational in some way? Why?

- What aspect of two different works did I find surprising or shocking? Why?

- Which part of a text seemed to move very slowly? Which part of a text read very quickly?

- Are there two texts where I felt as if the narrator was talking directly to me? Which voice did I like better?

- Which two texts had the most satisfying endings? Why?

- Which two texts had the most engaging beginnings? Why?

Asking these kinds of questions and recording your responses as you read will contribute to your ability to produce an interesting and valid comparative analysis.

Asking yourself questions lies at the heart of the comparative process.

The following learner portfolio activities can help you develop your skills in comparative analysis.

- Group the works you have studied according to a common theme or issue and explore their similarities and differences.

- Develop awareness of the differences between literary forms and how these differences may have a bearing on how different works approach one theme or issue.

- Consider which combinations of works might be the most productive to address a variety of questions you might encounter in exam paper 2.

- Inquire into connections between works studied, the **areas of exploration**, and the central concepts to gain awareness of the multiplicity of lenses that can be used in studying a work, and the essay questions these might potentially lead to.

- Compare your successive practices of paper 2 with the first one you did and monitor the evolution of their overall performance on paper.

Activity 5 Comparing the openings of four different novels

The opening of a novel typically introduces characters, locations, and/or critical situations, and establishes an initial tone that may be maintained throughout the novel. Read the five novel openings below before continuing with the questions that follow them.

1. *A Mercy* by Toni Morrison (2008)

Don't be afraid. My telling can't hurt you in spite of what I have done and I promise to lie quietly in the dark – weeping perhaps or occasionally seeing the blood once more – but I will never again unfold my limbs to rise up and bare teeth. I explain. You can think what I tell you a confession, if you like, but one full of curiosities familiar only in dreams and during those moments when a dog's profile plays in the steam of a kettle. Or when a corn-husk doll sitting on a shelf is soon splaying in the corner of a room and the wick of how it got there is plain. Stranger things happen all the time everywhere. You know. I know you know. One question is who is responsible? Another is can you read? If a pea hen refuses to brood I read it quickly, and sure enough, that night I see a minha mae standing hand in hand with her little boy, my shoes jamming the pocket of her apron. Other signs need more time to understand. Often there are too many signs, or a bright omen clouds up too fast. I sort them and try to recall, yet I know I am missing much, like not reading the garden snake crawling up to the door saddle to die. Let me start with what I know for certain.

2. *The Awakening* by Kate Chopin (1899)

A green and yellow parrot, which hung in a cage outside the door, kept repeating over and over: 'Allez vous-en! Allez vous-en! Sapristi! That's all right!'

He could speak a little Spanish, and also a language which nobody understood, unless it was the mocking-bird that hung on the other side of the door, whistling his fluty notes out upon the breeze with maddening persistence.

Mr. Pontellier, unable to read his newspaper with any degree of comfort, arose with an expression and an exclamation of disgust. He walked down the gallery and across the narrow 'bridges' which connected the Lebrun cottages one with the other. He had been seated before the door of the main house. The parrot and the mocking-bird were the property of Madame Lebrun, and they had the right to make all the noise they wished. Mr. Pontellier had the privilege of quitting their society when they ceased to be entertaining.

He stopped before the door of his own cottage, which was the fourth one from the main building and next to the last. Seating himself in a wicker rocker which was there, he once more applied himself to the task of reading the newspaper. The day was Sunday; the paper was a day old. The Sunday papers had not yet reached Grand Isle. He was already acquainted with the market reports, and he glanced restlessly over the editorials and bits of new which he had not had time to read before quitting New Orleans the day before.

Mr. Pontellier wore eye-glasses. He was a man of forty, of medium height and rather slender build; he stooped a little. His hair was brown and straight, parted on one side. His beard was neatly and closely trimmed.

3. *Bleak House* by Charles Dickens (1852)

London. Michaelmas Term lately over, and the Lord Chancellor sitting in Lincoln's Inn Hall. Implacable November weather. As much mud in the streets, as if the waters had but newly retired from the face of the earth, and it would not be wonderful to meet a Megalosaurus, forty feet long or so, waddling like an elephantine lizard up Holborn Hill. Smoke lowering down from chimney-pots, making a soft black drizzle, with flakes of soot in it as big as full-grown snowflakes – gone into mourning, one might imagine, for the death of the sun. Dogs, undistinguishable in mire. Horses, scarcely better; splashed to their very blinkers. Foot passengers, jostling one another's umbrellas, in a general infection of ill-temper, and losing their foot-hold at street-corners, where tens of thousands of other foot passengers have been slipping and sliding since the day broke (if the day ever broke), adding new deposits to the crust upon crust of mud, sticking at those points tenaciously to the pavement, and accumulating at compound interest.

Fog everywhere. Fog up the river, where it flows among green aits and meadows; fog down the river, where it rolls defiled among the tiers of shipping and the waterside pollutants of a great (and dirty) city. Fog on the Essex marshes, fog on the Kentish heights. Fog creeping into the cabooses and collier-brigs, fog lying out on the yards, and hovering in the rigging of great ships; fog drooping on the gunwales of barges and small boats. Fog in the eyes and throats of ancient Greenwich pensioners, wheezing by the firesides of their wards; fog in the stem and bowl of the afternoon pipe of the wrathful skipper, down in his close cabin; fog cruelly pinching the toes and fingers of his shivering little 'prentice boy on deck. Chance people on the bridges peeping over the parapets into a nether sky of fog, with fog all round them, as if they were up in a balloon, and hanging in the misty clouds.

4. *Out Stealing Horses* by Per Petterson, translated by Anne Born (2005)

Early November. It's nine o'clock. The titmice are banging against the window. Sometimes they fly dizzily off after the impact, other times they fall and lie struggling in the new snow until they can take off again. I don't know what they want that I have. I look out the window at the forest. There is a reddish light over the trees by the lake. It is starting to blow. I can see the shape of the wind on the water.

I live here now, in a small house in the far east of Norway. A river flows into the lake. It is not much of a river, and it gets shallow in the summer, but in the spring and autumn it runs briskly, and there are trout in it. I have caught some myself. The mouth of the river is only a hundred metres from here. I can just see it from my kitchen window once the birch leaves have fallen. As now in November. There is a cottage down by the river that I can see when its lights are on if I go out onto my doorstep. A man lives there. He is older than I am, I think. Or he seems to be. But perhaps that's because I do not realise what I look like myself, or life has been tougher for him than it has been for me. I cannot rule that out. He has a dog, a border collie.

I have a bird table on a pole a little way out in my yard. When it is getting light in the morning I sit at the kitchen table with a cup of coffee and watch them come fluttering in. I have seen eight different species so far, which is more than anywhere else I have lived, but only the titmice fly into the window. I have lived in many places. Now I am here.

5. *Purple Hibiscus* by Chimamanda Adichie (2003)

Things started to fall apart at home when my brother, Jaja, did not go to communion and Papa flung his heavy missal across the room and broke the figurines on the etagere. We had just returned from church. Mama placed the fresh palm fronds, which were wet with holy water, on the dining table and then went upstairs to change. Later, she would knot the palm fronds into sagging cross shapes and hang them on the wall beside our gold-framed family photo. They would stay there until next Ash Wednesday, when we would take the fronds to church, to have them burned for ash. Papa, wearing a long, gray robe like the rest of the oblates, helped distribute ash every year. His line moved the slowest because he pressed hard on each forehead to make a perfect cross with his ash-covered thumb and slowly, meaningfully enunciated every word of 'dust and unto dust you shall return'.

Papa always sat in the front pew for Mass, at the end beside the middle aisle, with Mama, Jaja, and me sitting next to him. He was first to receive communion. Most people did not kneel to receive communion at the marble altar, with the blond life-sized Virgin Mary mounted nearby, but Papa did. He would hold his eyes shut so hard that his face tightened into a grimace, and then he would stick his tongue out as far as it could go. Afterward, he sat back on his seat and watched the rest of the congregation troop to the altar, palms pressed together and extended, like a saucer held sideways, just as Father Benedict had taught them to do.

Respond to the following questions for each of the opening texts in your learner profile:

1) Place – where is this? How do we know? Clues to time and setting/location?
2) Perspective – what is the narrative point of view? First, second, third (full or limited omniscience).
3) Voice – what is the narrator like as a person? Telling details (age, gender, race, social status, cultural values)?
4) Character – which characters are introduced? Is one character presented in deeper detail/focus?
5) Tone – what situation is described? Is there tension? What specific words or phrases signal tension to you? What single word would you use to characterise the opening?

Activity 6 Extending observation notes to a written paragraph

Once you have completed Activity 5, read the information about 'Finding your focus/thesis', which is included in 'Strategies for writing the comparative essay' below. Then, work with a partner to create a comparative paragraph that focuses on any two of the openings in Activity 5.

Your paragraph should begin with an assertion (your thesis) on one of the comparative points above and how that point is developed in each text. Determine similarity and difference using at least three points of comparison.

Share paragraphs with your classmates, either electronically or orally.

Once all of the comparison paragraphs have been shared, write a reflection in your learner portfolio about how individuals can maintain and support various perspectives in the same opening passage. Then, in a separate entry in your learner portfolio, offer a comparison of any two openings from the works in your own two-year programme, or any of the samples provided in the chapters on drama, prose non-fiction, and poetry. For poetry, consider the first stanza or the first half of the poem as an 'opening'.

Strategies for writing the comparative essay

Finding your focus/thesis

The comparison/contrast essay encourages you to make connections between texts and ideas, engage in critical thinking, and go beyond mere summary or description to create an interesting analysis. When you reflect on similarities and differences, you gain a deeper understanding of the texts you are comparing and of what is most important about them. When you select one of the four questions on exam paper 2, you are choosing a focus for your comparison and contrast. This focus becomes the subject of your comparative essay.

For example, if you select this question – 'Explore the presentation and significance of jealousy in two works you have studied' – *jealousy* becomes the focus or subject of your essay.

Your thesis, however, is very important. It can help you create a focused argument about your subject in relation to two texts, as well as providing a kind of road map for your reader.

> Your thesis provides a kind of road map for your reader.

Info box

A thesis is an arguable assertion about an idea that can be supported with textual evidence. The resulting written or oral product is called an 'interpretation'.

For example, your thesis might read: 'While both text A and text B use jealousy as the *motivation behind* character action, text A's character reveals the positive influence of social stereotype while text B's character represents the inherent destruction within social stereotype.'

Organising your comparison/contrast essay

Two of the most common methods used to organise and structure your essay are subject by subject or point by point.

A subject-by-subject structure is a logical choice if you are writing what is sometimes called a 'lens' comparison, in which you use one subject to better understand another. For example, you might compare a poem that you have studied extensively with one that you have just read. It would make sense to give a brief summary of your main ideas about the first poem (your 'lens' subject) and then spend most of your paper discussing how those points are similar to, or different from, your ideas about the second poem.

You could organise your essay subject by subject.

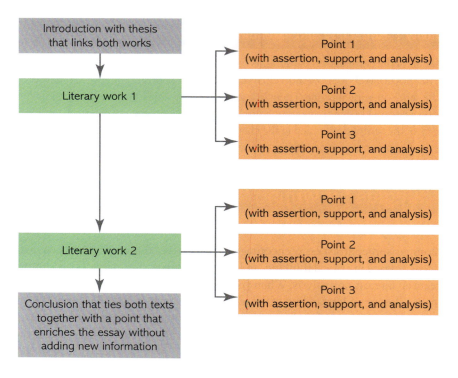

A point-by-point structure differs because instead of addressing one subject at a time, you may wish to talk about one point of comparison at a time. If you have a little to say about each subject you are comparing, you might in a single paragraph discuss how a certain point of comparison or contrast relates to all the items you are discussing.

You might prefer to organise your essay point by point.

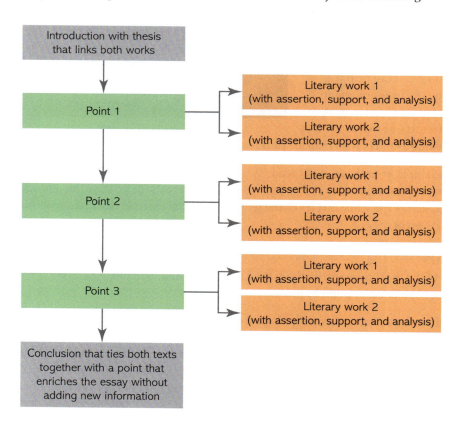

If you have a bit more to say about the items you are comparing/contrasting, you might devote an entire paragraph to how each point relates to each item.

There are no hard and fast rules about organising a comparison/contrast essay; just be sure not to confuse your reader with the placement of different points. One way to help your reader keep track of where you are in a comparative essay is to make sure that your transitions and topic sentences are strong and clear. Your thesis will give your reader an idea of the points that you'll be making and the organisation you'll be using, but you can help your reader by providing cues to transitioning between the works. The following transition words help your reader maintain focus: like, similar to, unlike, similarly, in the same way, likewise, again, compared with, in contrast, on the contrary, however, although, yet, even though, still, but nevertheless, conversely, at the same time, regardless, despite, while, on the one hand, on the other hand.

If you are writing a comparison/contrast in service of an argument, keep in mind that the last point you make is the one you are leaving your reader with. If you think that the differences between the texts are most important, you'll want to end with the differences – and vice versa if the similarities seem most important to you.

Evaluation overview

The assessment requires you to show knowledge and understanding of two works, as well as develop an interpretation of the implications of these works and their similarities and differences in connection with a given focus.

The assessment expects you to write a comparative analysis and evaluation of the two texts in terms of the demands of the question.

The assessment requires you to write a formal essay which is well organised, offers a balanced comparison between the two works, and is clearly focused on a given question.

Elaboration of assessment criteria

Since the assessment criteria are stated in generic language, it is important to verify and validate what skill levels are anticipated.

Criterion A: Knowledge, understanding, and interpretation

- How much knowledge and understanding of the works does the candidate show?
- To what extent does the candidate make use of knowledge and understanding of the works to draw conclusions about their similarities and differences in relation to the question?

Students show **knowledge** of the texts by providing well-chosen and detailed references to the texts rather than vague generalisations about the texts; **understanding** is evaluated through the degree to which the student shows that they understand the demands of the question, and use appropriate works to answer it; **interpretation** is shown by the student comparing and contrasting the content of both texts in relation to the question.

Table 1: External assessment – paper 2: comparative essay SL/HL (2021 onwards)

Criteria	0	1–2	3–4	5–6	7–8	9–10
Criterion A: Knowledge, understanding, and interpretation	The work does not reach a standard described by the descriptors.	There is little knowledge and understanding of the works in relation to the question answered. There is little meaningful comparison and contrast of the works used in relation to the question.	There is some knowledge and understanding of the works in relation to the question answered. There is a superficial attempt to compare and contrast the works used in relation to the question.	There is satisfactory knowledge and understanding of the works and an interpretation of their implications in relation to the question answered. The essay offers a satisfactory interpretation of the similarities and differences between the works used in relation to the question.	There is good knowledge and understanding of the works and a sustained interpretation of their implications in relation to the question answered. The essay offers a convincing interpretation of the similarities and differences between the works used in relation to the question.	There is perceptive knowledge and understanding of the works and a persuasive interpretation of their implications in relation to the question answered. The essay offers an insightful interpretation of the similarities and differences between the works in relation to the question.
Criterion B: Analysis and evaluation	The work does not reach a standard described by the descriptors.	The essay is descriptive and/or demonstrates little relevant analysis of textual features and/or the broader authorial choices.	The essay demonstrates some appropriate analysis of textual features and/or broader authorial choices, but is reliant on description. There is a superficial comparison and contrast of the authors' choices in the works selected.	The essay demonstrates a generally appropriate analysis of textual features and/or broader authorial choices. There is an adequate comparison and contrast of the authors' choices in the works selected.	The essay demonstrates an appropriate and at times insightful analysis of textual features and/or broader authorial choices. There is a good evaluation of how such features and/or choices shape meaning. There is a good comparison and contrast of the authors' choices in the works selected.	The essay demonstrates a consistently insightful and convincing analysis of textual features and/or broader authorial choices. There is a very good evaluation of how such features and/or choices contribute to meaning. There is a very good comparison and contrast of the authors' choices in the works selected.
	0	**1**	**2**	**3**	**4**	**5**
Criterion C: Focus and organisation	The work does not reach a standard described by the descriptors.	The essay rarely focuses on the task. There are few connections between ideas.	The essay only sometimes focuses on the task, and treatment of the works may be unbalanced. There are some connections between ideas, but these are not always coherent.	The essay maintains a focus on the task, despite some lapses; treatment of the works is mostly balanced. The development of ideas is mostly logical; ideas are generally connected in a cohesive manner.	The essay maintains a mostly clear and sustained focus on the task; treatment of the works is balanced. The development of ideas is logical; ideas are cohesively connected.	The essay maintains a clear and sustained focus on the task; treatment of the works is well balanced. The development of ideas is logical and convincing; ideas are connected in a cogent manner.
Criterion D: Language	The work does not reach a standard described by the descriptors.	Language is rarely clear and appropriate; there are many errors in grammar, vocabulary and sentence construction and little sense of register and style.	Language is sometimes clear and carefully chosen; grammar, vocabulary and sentence construction are fairly accurate, although errors and inconsistencies are apparent; the register and style are to some extent appropriate to the task.	Language is clear and carefully chosen with an adequate degree of accuracy in grammar, vocabulary and sentence construction despite some lapses; register and style are mostly appropriate to the task.	Language is clear and carefully chosen, with a good degree of accuracy in grammar, vocabulary and sentence construction; register and style are consistently appropriate to the task.	Language is very clear, effective, carefully chosen and precise, with a high degree of accuracy in grammar, vocabulary and sentence construction; register and style are effective and appropriate to the task.
Total Marks						30

Criterion B: Analysis and evaluation

- To what extent does the candidate analyse and evaluate how the choices of language, technique, and style, and/or broader authorial choices, shape meaning?
- How effectively does the candidate use analysis and evaluation skills to compare and contrast both works?

Students **explore** each writer's chosen strategies and bring together these ideas in terms of an overall reading of the text and the effects produced; students do not evaluate the texts in terms of the competence of the writer or whether or not they liked the text.

To **evaluate** is defined as 'making an appraisal by weighing the strengths and limitations'. Evaluation will show that the student has engaged with the texts, demonstrating the ability to see how or why something works in a text as well as showing an understanding of the effect created.

Criterion C: Focus and organisation

- How well-structured, balanced, and focused is the presentation of ideas?

The focus should be made clear in the first paragraph of the analysis, with the following paragraphs maintaining the line of argument initially proposed.

Criterion D: Language

- How clear, varied, and accurate is the language?
- How appropriate is the choice of register and style? ('Register' refers, in this context, to the candidate's use of elements such as vocabulary, tone, sentence structure, and terminology appropriate to the essay.)

Student uses the formal language of analysis.

Sample paper 2 evaluations

Using Table 1 on page 234, 'External assessment paper 2: Comparative essay SL/HL, Criteria (2021 onwards)', evaluate each the following sample exam paper 2 comparative essays (A, B, and C). You may work alone or with a partner or small group. Offer specific comments to support your evaluation of each criterion in your learner portfolio.

You must use the assertion/support/analysis model (see page 284 in the HL essay chapter) to evaluate sample A. This helpful model will allow you see the assertions, support, and analysis more specifically, thus enabling you to evaluate the strengths and weaknesses of this comparison and contrast essay.

Sample A

Question: How do the writers of two of the works you have studied convey a sense of place to their readers, and to what purpose?

Student response:

In both Jean Rhys's *Wide Sargasso Sea* and Arundhati Roy's *The God of Small Things*, the sense of place is a crucial part of the text's development. In *The God of Small Things*, the setting in Ayemenem, India, begins in the monsoon season then flashes back to a period of weeks during a summer twenty-three years ago. The chapters are juxtaposed, with the present time of the novel in the odd-numbered chapters and the past in the even-numbered chapters. Everything in the present setting — the emotionally broken characters as well as the devastation of their once beautiful natural world — is chronicled through the juxtaposed events of the past.

In *Wide Sargasso Sea*, the structure of the novel also influences our understanding of the relationship of place and character. The novel is structured into three parts with three distinct narrative voices. Part one is told through Antoinette's perspective, part two through Rochester's, and part three from Bertha's/ Antoinette's point of view while locked in a tower room at Rochester's home in the English countryside. While Roy uses the interplay of past and present to add depth to our understanding of the characters, Rhys uses the interplay of voice and perspective to add to our understanding of the characters and their relationship to place/setting. In both novels, the settings contribute to the building of tension in character relationships and advancement of plot while also serving to facilitate each author's social commentary.

In *Wide Sargasso Sea*, the key setting Rhys uses is the Windward Islands of the Caribbean. Antoinette spends various parts of her childhood in different parts of the islands and after her marriage lives in Granbois with her husband (implied to be Rochester of Bronte's Jane Eyre). This setting is crucial to the building of tension in the novel and their marriage. As Rochester is thrust into this strange new world of the Caribbean, he suffers from sensory overload and the 'alien and disturbing' feel of everything he is encountering. Rochester has spent his entire life in England and is now surprised to find that everything is 'too much' for him in this new and foreign place. He feels overwhelmed with the jungle-like vegetation. The exotic plants are overgrown and menacing. The people who work for and are closest to Antoinette, Christophine and Baptiste, are equally threatening. Their silence, their laughing, and their stares unnerve him. This threatening feeling contributes to the reader's sense that tension is building and everything, including Rochester, is ready to explode.

In a similar fashion, Arundhati Roy uses a setting of heightened tension from the first page of *The God of Small Things*. The reader learns immediately that Ayemenem is a 'hot, brooding' place and the city is 'suffused with sloth'. This fetid, stifling climate adds to the slowly building tension implicit in the stagnant atmosphere of the place. Roy depicts Ayemenem as a way to foreshadow the conflict and 'The Terror' of the social system that we experience in the later portions of the novel. The caste system and the laws that determine who can be loved and by whom is what forces Vellya Paapen to tell Mammachi the story of Ammu and Velutha standing together in the moonlight in a lover's embrace. Their love sparks Mammachi's fury resulting in the shattered lives of not only Ammu and Velutha but of Ammu's children as well. We learn that to defy centuries of tradition requires a very steep price.

Rhys, too, uses the settings of her novel to foreshadow Antoinette's tragic demise in *Wide Sargasso Sea*. Unlike Roy's work, however, where the conflict rises from the desires of the main characters clashing with society as a whole, *Wide Sargasso Sea* examines a single character in a setting where he is a stranger and, as a result, lashes out against not only the setting but the characters native to it. Rochester hated the place, particularly Granbois, and this seems to bring about his disdain for Antoinette. From the moment he first laid eyes on the place, he was overly suspicious of the island and its inhabitants. When he learns from Daniel Conwy's letter that Antoinette is 'mad', he projects his own disconnection and paranoia onto her. His fear materialises as a condescending attitude towards the place and all who live there.

This condescension that Rochester feels for the people of the Caribbean is a key part of Rhys' social commentary. Rhys appears to condemn the patronising nature of the colonial attitude that most of the British characters seem to possess with regard to the people of the Islands. Rochester even goes so far as to tell Antoinette that he thinks of her as Bertha, and so, Bertha she will be. His renaming of her exemplifies his control and ownership of her, treating her as a slave to be named as he desires. She has lost her identity to a man whose prejudice against a place has extended to its people.

Setting possesses a similar relevance in Roy's *The God of Small Things*. Roy uses Ayemenem to criticise the caste system but also globalisation, of which she is an ardent opponent. Roy portrays Western culture as an evil force, polluting the culture of India, and uses the setting to symbolise this. Twenty-three years after the Terror occurred, Ammu's children, Rahel and Esta, return to their childhood home which is now epitomised by waste and corruption. The quickly moving river of their childhood is now transformed into a thick, toxic, polluted sludge primarily because Western hotels are exploiting the town for tourist purposes. The Terror of the caste system has been replaced by what Roy sees as the Terror of Western culture.

Both authors expose and explore the corruption of a social system through the interplay of place and identity. In each text, the manipulation of the structures of both novels helps to reveal the liberating and destructive force that place can assume in any text.

General evaluation questions to ask yourself after reading Sample A:

Does this comparison/contrast essay:

1) offer an arguable thesis/interpretation based on a question using two works

2) offer a balanced treatment of the works? Do the works contribute equally in the essay

3) provide knowledge and insight of each of the texts

4) offer a clearly focused structure that is logically developed

5) provide both similarities and differences in the analysis

6) support an interpretation with convincing textual evidence

7) provide clear and precise language and accurate grammar?

Sample B

Question: In what ways have two writers explored the role of the individual within society, and what conclusions might be drawn from these explorations?

Student response:

History teaches us that oppression is a road that splits into two paths: rebellion and submission. This trend holds true for Kate and Nora from William Shakespeare's *The Taming of the Shrew* and Henrik Ibsen's *A Doll's House*. Although their behaviours are polar opposites, both women go through the same radical change to cope with the oppression their society inflicts upon them as individuals.

Both women have had the role and image of a doll superimposed upon them by their societies, especially by their fathers. In *The Taming of the Shrew*, Baptista favoured Bianca over Kate because Bianca was quiet, obedient, and beautiful: she was the paragon of a woman and everything Kate refused to be. Nora was raised in a similar fashion. Her father pampered and coddled her like a child, giving her little pet names and calling her his precious 'doll baby'. Ultimately, both women were raised for the single purpose of being married off to the man who chose her.

Kate rebelled against the constraints imposed upon her by being a shrew. She acts out violently against those who try to subjugate her, as evident in the scene where she hits Hortensio with the lute. Kate also has no problems vocalising her grievances. She scolds her father for what he said about her in public and warns Petruchio to avoid her 'sting'. To Kate, the only way to cope with a society that would not accept her is to rebel against it. Women who comply with society's whims are fools because they are afraid to resist these social constraints.

Nora, on the other hand, chose to play out the role given to her by society. She puts on a façade to convince everyone — including herself — that she is a cheerful, childlike woman. Unlike Kate, Nora lets Torvald dominate her and offers no verbal or physical resistance whatsoever until the end of the play. While Kate fumed at Petruchio for calling her bonny Kate and super-dainty Kate, instead of Katherine, Nora never complained when Torvald called her his lark, his squirrel, and his little wastrel. However, Nora is not totally submissive to Torvald. She claims her right to power by deceiving Torvald, first by forging her father's name on a loan, and second by secretly managing her household money and doing needlework to repay the loan to Krogstad. By pretending to be an obedient doll, Nora is able to satisfy both society's need for her to fulfil her role as a woman and her own desire to have a secret power that she can keep to herself. Kate, on the other hand, does not have this privilege. In order to keeps her ideals, Kate must push aside her need for a loving husband and a family and continue to reject the oppressive ideals of her society.

Both Kate and Nora know their limitations as women, but neither is fully aware of the limitations they place upon themselves. Kate, in order to retain her own individualism, refuses to let down her guard and therefore prevents anyone from understanding her. The internal struggle for power and love in Kate fuels all of her actions. When Petruchio shows up late for the wedding, Kate is left vulnerable and deeply hurt. She lets down her guard when she entreats Petruchio to stay for the after-wedding dinner. When Petruchio rebukes her attempt at compromise, Kate reverts to her shrewish defensiveness. Her emotions are black and white without any shades of grey in between. Because of her inability to compromise with her own emotions, Kate traps herself in the role of a shrew.

Nora is more complex than Kate when it comes to managing her own temperament. She knows that she must perform certain duties before she can get a reward. By playing out the role expected of her, Nora is able to hide and protect her inner self from a society that would never accept it. Although Nora thinks there is absolutely nothing wrong with a wife saving her husband's life, she knows that she must squirrel away this secret because it would be embarrassing and humiliating for Torvald. Nora prides herself in having this secret because it gave her power over Torvald. She knew something that he did not know, and having this secret made her feel almost like a man. Nora, however, is the only one who knows this secret until she shares it with Kristine Linde. Kristine believes that Nora's actions are unwise and indefensible. It is as if there are two sides to Nora, the internal Nora who exerts her power on society and the external Nora, the overgrown child, who defers to social norms of what a woman should be. This disparity causes Nora tremendous stress, and ultimately leads to her final break with Torvald. Unlike Kate, Nora does not know which side of herself is the real self. She has lived with lies for so long that she realises that a new truth, a new Nora, can only be found outside of her 'doll's' house. Her 'make-believe' has to come to an end. While Kate longs for someone to understand her, Nora hopes to understand herself. Both women need to find a self that can live within the constraints of society without destroying that self.

The power wielded by both women is their capacity for change. Once she has been married to Petruchio and killed with kindness, Kate learns the art of compromise. Since the idea of a woman having more power than a man is unheard of in Kate's patriarchal society, the only way for her to have any power at all is through deception. When Kate obeyed her husband's orders, she ended up winning him his bet as well as the respect of all the men present. Bianca, on the other hand, is scolded by Lucentio for making him lose the bet. The pattern is not hard to see. Kate's sudden metamorphosis does not mean that she has been tamed or broken. She merely knows how to adapt and twist the situation to her own advantage.

Nora already knows how to lie and adapt to a situation. She has been taught to lie all of her life, so much so that she no longer knows her true self. Like Kate near the ending of *The Taming of the Shrew*, Nora obeys Torvald and gets what she wants through deception. While Kate learns to use deception for her own advantage, Nora has always hoped that some wonderful miracle would happen to save her from her deceptions. She remains in her role as a doll-wife to wait for the wonderful moment when Torvald would defend her against society's judgements. When the moment arrives, Torvald is not the least bit interested in saving anyone but himself. This realisation prompts her decision to leave, slamming the door on her doll life.

The differences are subtle in the characterisation of each woman. Kate is strong in her ability to adapt to her society and survive. Nora is strong in her determination and will to survive on her own. It is impossible to judge which of the two is stronger because they each possess essentially the same qualities. The only certain thing is that both 'dolls' succumb to society's pressures, only to break the roles set upon them with their yielding strengths.

Sample C

Question: Explore the presentation and significance of corruption in two works you have studied.

Student response:

Whether the result of government power, or lack thereof, corruption has existed in communities since the beginning of time. At its heart is a destructive power that victimises the corrupt as well as the innocents that fall prey to it. No one seems immune from corruption either in intent or deed. We all feel its sting. Two works which speak of destructive power and the victims that either lie in its wake or stand in its path are Chimamanda Ngozi Adichie's novel, *Purple Hibiscus*, and the lyrics of Bob Dylan. While these writers use different forms to present the nature of corruption in their work, they share many ideas about the victims of power and the personal and political harm that grows from the seeds of corruption.

In her novel, *Purple Hibiscus*, Adichie's corruption is both personal and political. Family dynamics and government institutions share in her vision of corruption. The novel's narrator, 15-year-old Kambili, and her older brother, Jaja, and their mother, Beatrice, suffer under the cruelty of their father, Papa Eugene, whose religious fanaticism and repressive control creates physical and emotional abuse for the entire family. Ironically, Papa Eugene is idolised outside his family compound for his generosity to the community. And, as an editor of a pro-democracy newspaper and factory owner, he is highly respected by the community for his commitment to exposing the tyrannical rule of the current Nigerian military government which suppresses freedom of speech through intimidation and violence. It's as if Papa Eugene is two different men — compassionate and cruel — a dichotomy serving hope for his community and desperation for his family.

Bob Dylan's lyrics also reference government corruption on a large scale. In 'Hurricane' and 'Blowin' in the Wind' he attacks how racial intolerance, instituted by governmental regulation and supported by the judicial system, has corrupted the fabric of American culture, and by extension the helpless victims of political corruption, the young and the disillusioned. Dylan's poems, in varying rhythms and subject matter, also speak of the lies and deceit on which corruption is established. In 'Masters of War', the persona declares that he 'can see through [the] masks' of those who hide behind their money, their titles, and their mansions. The poem serves as a reckoning of the day 'When your death takes its toll/ [and] All the money you made/Will never buy back your soul.' 'Blowin' in the Wind' almost reads like a plea rather than a condemnation to those same individuals whose power is built on corrupt values and institutions. Dylan asks what victims of corruption must do to survive in such a world. He pleads for an end to war, for protections of our natural world, and for recognition that all human beings are created equal. But, in 'Hurricane', the plea becomes an attack on a corrupt legal system which, along with law enforcement, 'falsely tried' Rubin Carter, a black prize fighter who was framed for murder 'in a land/Where justice is a game'.

Dylan's tribute to Rubin Carter is deeply personal. The corruption, and the language Dylan uses to describe it, is angry and straightforward. While he attests to the victimisation of Rubin 'Hurricane' Carter, he presents how others are made part of the corrupt judicial system. Corruption seems to beget corruption.

In Adichie's novel, however, the corruption of a family where safety and care should be fully realised is chronicled in the journey of the victims. Kambili and Jaja and their mother survive, not without cost, but at the end of the novel, Kambili's words hint of a future of opportunity and renewal. Kambili dreams that she and Jaja will join Aunty Ifeoma in America where they will plant orange trees and purple hibiscus will bloom again. Her language is lyrical and uplifting.

As the narrator, Kambili has not always used such lyrical language. In describing the tortures that she and other members of her family endure, her language is matter of fact, almost journalistic in its straightforward description of horrific acts. She describes her father pouring boiling water over her feet as she stands in the shower with tactile precision devoid of emotion. It is only later, after she and Jaja live for a time with their Aunty Ifeoma that Kambili finds her voice and, subsequently, her strength. It is at this point that she becomes Adichie's mouthpiece. Her retrospective narration traces what came before the opening scene where her father throws his missal at Jaja, because he refused to go to Palm Sunday service, and ends up breaking her mother's deeply loved figurines. In retrospect, she is fully capable of thinking and speaking for herself once she sees herself as something more than her father's silent daughter, her father's victim.

Both Dylan and Adichie speak to the destructive power of corruption in both the individual and the community. Governments, like families, are powerful institutions. Each is formed with the intent to serve and protect, to provide safety and care. The corruption that occurs with an imbalance of power is both merciless and menacing, attacking the individual through control and suppression. Each writer, the lyricist and the novelist, uses their chosen form as a voice of hope and defiance. Victimhood is challenged in their writings.

Applying what you've learned about exam paper 2: comparative essay

Choose **one** of the following sample exam paper 2 essay questions below and write a sample comparative essay using the short story, *Cell One*, by Chimamanda Ngozi Adichie (included in its entirety in Chapter 1.1 Fiction) and Susan Glaspell's play, *Trifles* (included in its entirety in Chapter 1.2 Drama). Afterwards, participate in a peer review and provide feedback to each other. Finally, write a reflection in your learner portfolio about the writing and scoring process.

Choose one of the following questions:

> 1) Tension often builds to a critical point in a piece of literature. How is tension created in two of the works you have studied and for what purpose?
>
> 2) How are challenges to authority presented in two of the works you have studied, and what impact have such challenges had on readers or audiences?
>
> 3) What techniques did two of your writers use to convey the 'thoughts' of their characters, narrators, or speakers, and to what effect?
>
> 4) Discuss whether or not the endings/conclusions of two of the works you have studied are satisfactory.
>
> 5) Many works are concerned with human suffering. How has this concern been expressed in a way that engages audiences of various times and/or places in two of the works you have studied?
>
> 6) Analyse the role non-human elements play in two of the works you have studied and to what effect.

Insights to Paper 2: Comparative essay

1. The exam paper 2 is written under exam conditions.

2. You will select one of four questions to answer.

3. You will have preselected three works to use on paper 2, but will use only two in response to one of the four questions provided. The works selected may or may not be the same form.

4. Any work may be preselected as long as it has not been used in another summative assessment (HL essay and the individual oral).

5. The paper 2 response will compare and contrast two texts in relation to the question selected.

6. The learner portfolio provides comparative strategies on works studied in the course.

7. Point by point and subject by subject are common organisational strategies for a comparison/contrast essay.

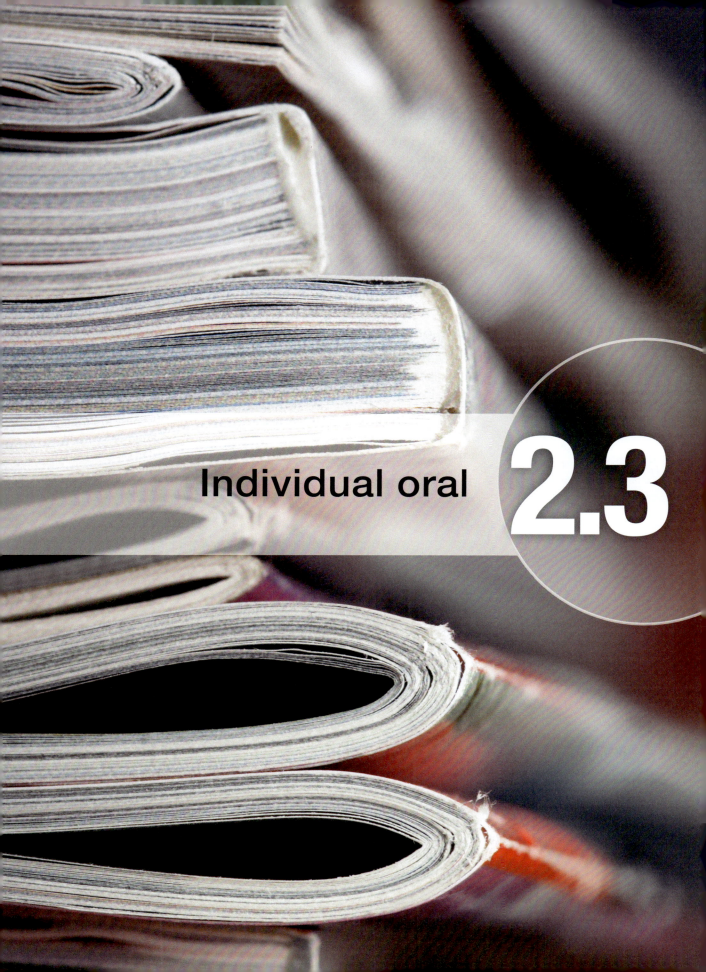

Individual oral

2.3

In this chapter you will…
• understand the requirements for the individual oral
• appreciate the connection between literary studies and global issues
• determine the relationship of the learner portfolio to the individual oral
• explore strategies for refining your global issue and developing a solid outline
• examine the individual oral assessment criteria
• prepare to deliver a practice individual oral
• review and analyse sample individual oral assessments
• participate in peer consensus scoring.

What is the individual oral?

• The individual oral (also known as the IO) is a required internal assessment for both standard level (SL) and higher level (HL) students.

• For this assessment, you will be required to deliver an oral response to a prompt, using two extracts from two different works (one must be in translation), and examine how one **global issue** of your choosing is presented in each text.

• The task is the same for both HL and SL students, but it is weighted 20% in the HL programme and 30% in the SL programme.

What is the link between literary studies and global issues?

An IB education involves more than taking a series of courses that fulfil academic requirements. One of the **approaches to learning** focuses on *learning that is developed in local and global contexts.* Your English A: literature course involves reading a range of texts that vary in form from different places and time periods so that you can appreciate diverse literature and cultures that connect us.

Global issues are part of this connection, as they are present in every subject area and throughout the IB core. For example, you may explore global issues related to gender inequalities in several classes or through a CAS project. Examining global issues in different contexts makes learning more meaningful and connected. As you study characters who are subjugated by class, gender, or race, who face political strife, or who engage with advances in technology, you immerse yourself in topics that matter both inside and outside the course.

Global issues offer a pathway towards understanding the meaning of an **international-minded** education. Your participation in the individual oral is a step towards this goal.

Global issues offer a pathway towards understanding the meaning of an international-minded education.

Overview of the requirements for the individual oral

Prompt	• The individual oral is based on a response to the following prompt: 'Examine the ways in which the global issue of your choice is presented through the content and form of two of the works that you have studied.'
Global issue	• You will select one global issue as a focus for the discussion of the two works. • During your assessment you must discuss how the global issue is expressed through both form and content. *Content* refers to the subject matter of the text. *Form* refers to authorial choices that comprise the text.
Authorial choices	• Authorial choices **represent** the form itself (drama, fiction, non-fiction, poetry) and the structural and stylistic textual features that authors use to express the global issue. This means that you will select a global issue and discuss it through a literary lens.

Works	• The assessment is based on two works studied: one translated and one in the original language of the course. • The works selected for the individual oral cannot be used for any other assessment including the HL essay or paper 2. • You will choose two extracts (one from each work, of no more than 40 lines each) and examine how the global issue is present in the extracts and throughout the texts.
Extracts and student outlines (to be used during the exam)	• On the day of the exam you may bring unannotated copies of the extracts and one prepared outline of no more than ten bullet points into the exam room. The IB will provide you with a form for this outline. • As part of the planning process, you will select your texts and extracts and prepare your outline under the guidance of your teacher. Keep in mind that your teacher is a guide and will not select works or extracts for you, nor can they edit your outline. • You must provide your teacher with final copies of your extracts and outline at least one week in advance of the assessment. • It is important to note that the outline should not be a script. Rather, it should include touchpoints to help you generate an organised, cohesive delivery. • The extracts can also help you demonstrate how authorial choices in structure and style develop the global issue. • Think of each extract as a springboard that enables you to connect the global issue in the passage to the work as a whole.
Delivery	• Your delivery time is 10 minutes, followed by 5 minutes of questioning by your teacher. • The entire assessment is 15 minutes. • The oral will be audio recorded for moderation by the IB.

Guidance and authenticity

Teacher support

- Your teacher will guide and support you through your IO process by familiarising you with:
  - the requirements of the IO
  - the standards for academic integrity
  - the assessment criteria.

- Your teacher cannot select the texts or extracts for you, but they can provide:
  - guidance on the two works and extracts you use to address your global issue
  - advice on the suitability of your global issue to the two works
  - feedback on your outline.

- You can practise the IO process with global issues other than the one you have selected for your assessment, but you may not rehearse your actual IO with your teacher.

Academic integrity

- It is important that you adhere to the standards of academic integrity in preparing for and presenting the IO.

- You will be required to confirm that all IO materials are your own authentic work.

- Teachers are also part of this process and must authenticate the work of their students.

IB fields of inquiry

The IB has designed five **fields of inquiry** that can help you think about literary texts in global terms. The fields of inquiry listed below are not exhaustive, nor are they actual global issues. They are starting points from which you can refine and develop your specific global issue.

Activity 1 Brainstorming literary texts that align with fields of inquiry

As you review the five fields of inquiry below, work with a small group and make lists of texts from your course that align with the descriptions of each field. Record your findings in your learner portfolio. You will find a downloadable MS Word version of this table in the eBook.

	Fields of inquiry	
1	**Culture, identity, and community**	**Literary texts that align with this field**
	  Students might focus on the way in which works explore aspects of family, class, race, ethnicity, nationality, religion, gender, and sexuality, and the way these impact on individuals and societies. They might also focus on issues concerning migration, colonialism, and nationalism.	

2	Beliefs, values, and education	Literary texts that align with this field
	 Students might focus on the way in which works explore the beliefs and values nurtured in particular societies, and the ways in which they shape individuals, communities, and educational systems. They might also explore the tensions that arise when there are conflicts of beliefs and values, and ethics.	
3	Politics, power, and justice	Literary texts that align with this field
	 Students might focus on the ways in which works explore aspects of rights and responsibilities, as well as the workings and structures of governments and institutions. They might also investigate hierarchies of power, the distribution of wealth and resources, the limits of justice and the law, equality and inequality, human rights, and peace and conflict.	

4	Art, creativity, and the imagination	Literary texts that align with this field
	Students might focus on the ways in which works explore aspects of aesthetic inspiration, creation, craft, and beauty. They might also focus on the shaping and challenging of perceptions through art, and the function, value, and effects of art in society.	
5	Science, technology, and the environment	Literary texts that align with this field
	Students might focus on the ways in which works explore the relationship between humans and the environment, and the implications of technology and media for society. They might also consider the idea of scientific development and progress.	

Activity 2 From fields of inquiry to global issues

The table on page 250 includes the five fields of inquiry, each with two sample global issues. Effective global issues are broad enough to include a range of texts, places, and times periods, but specific enough to demonstrate knowledge of the texts and the presentation of the issue within the timeframe of the assessment.

For this activity, you will identify each global issue below as **Broad (B)**, **Effective (E)**, or **Narrow (N)**. Justify each choice in the column to the right. For each pairing, there will be one effective choice and one that is either too narrow or too broad. You will find the answers and a downloadable MS Word version of this table in your eBook. Once you have completed the activity, discuss your selections and justifications with a partner.

Field of inquiry	Sample global issues	Broad (B) Effective (E) Narrow (N)	For each pairing below, justify your rationale for the global issue you identified as effective
Culture, identity, and community	What is the connection between dysfunctional families and dysfunctional societies?		
	What is culture?		
Beliefs, values, and education	How do the values of the Igbo tribe in Africa affect the way individuals in that community are educated?		
	To what extent do societal expectations and values impact an individual's transformation?		
Politics, power, and justice	How does the use and abuse of power affect individual rights?		
	What were the effects of the Warsaw Pact on Western Europe prior to 1990?		
Art, creativity, and imagination	To what extent do works of art give us insight into the human condition?		
	The role of art in creativity.		
Science, technology, and the environment	The pros and cons of exchanging individual freedoms for public safety.		
	How is technology related to science?		

Activity 3 Creating a global issue from the United Nations' Sustainable Development Goals

Another way that you can develop your global issue is by reviewing the United Nations' (UN) Sustainable Development Goals (SDG). Study the graphic on page 251. Is there a goal that interests you? Perhaps one of the SDGs is the focus of your CAS project, or you are addressing the goal in another subject area. If so, feel free to develop your literary-focused individual oral around this goal.

The UN's 17 Sustainable Development Goals

As an example, Goal 1: 'No poverty' may pair particularly well with Jeannette Walls' memoir, *The Glass Castle*, and Friedrich Dürrenmatt's play, *The Visit*. Both focus on the issue of poverty as a driving force for character motivations and actions. Your global issue in this case could be: *How does poverty affect the motivations and actions of individuals?*

Complete the following with a partner or a small group and write your responses in your learner portfolio.

1) Use the QR code to view the three-minute UN Video, 'We the people for the global goals', and brainstorm which global issues in literature you are studying overlap with the SDGs expressed in the video.
2) How does viewing the video and reviewing the SDG graphic above help you better understand the international-minded aspect of the individual oral?
3) Why might focusing on a global issue be more meaningful than simply tracing a common theme through two texts?

Connections

Exploring an SDG through a literary lens will deepen your knowledge and understanding of its global significance.

The individual oral and the learner portfolio

Reviewing the activities in your learner portfolio will help you identify works and global issues as you develop ideas for your individual oral. The list below is not exhaustive, but useful portfolio entries could include any of the following:

- direct or indirect writings or discussions on global issues

- reflections

- close readings and literary analyses on specific passages or poems

- preparation for role playing or recorded role playing

Your leaner portfolio will help you identify works and global issues.

- links to podcasts and videos

- in-class writings

- reactions to **transformed** versions of texts (like film versions of plays or novels)

- group assignments

- creative projects

- practice assessments

- CAS portfolio entries

- TOK connections.

Even if a learner portfolio entry does not seem to have a direct link to a global issue, as you can see from Activity 1, global issues derive from broad fields of inquiry that are present in literature across **time and space**. A simple roleplay in which students act out a scene where one character dominates another by virtue of their class or gender status can tap into the 'Culture, identity, and community' field of inquiry.

In Shakespeare's *Hamlet*, for example, Polonius exhibits **gender bias** when he treats his daughter, Ophelia, more harshly than his son, Laertes, even using Ophelia as a pawn at times. The siblings clearly live by two different sets of rules. A reflective assignment in your portfolio may inspire a way to develop this idea into a more specific global issue.

It is important to keep the global issue quite broad initially, i.e. until you select the second text for your individual oral. Since *Hamlet* was originally written in the language of the course (English), the paired work must be a translated text. You might select Nora from Ibsen's *A Doll's House* as a character who also experiences gender bias. Next, you would review your portfolio entries from both works that focus on this issue. As you look more closely at Ophelia's interactions with her brother and Hamlet, and Nora's interactions with her husband and Krogstad, the following global issue may emerge: *To what extent does gender bias reflect and/or construct cultural values?*

Connections

Learner portfolios are as unique as the ways that students select texts and develop global issues for the individual oral. Some students will begin with texts and develop the global issue from their selection; other students may begin with the global issue and then select texts that aptly present it. In any case, your learner portfolio will play a valuable role in the planning process for the individual oral.

Different pathways towards developing a global issue

The IB suggests several ways to develop global issues. Your approach may include one or a combination of the following:

- **Inductive:** study several works and identify a common global issue.

- **Deductive:** start with your global issue and then select works in which the issue is expressed.

- **Retrospective:** use your portfolio as a starting point. Make connections among portfolio entries, works, and the global issues that emerge from your inquiry.

- **External:** connect your CAS experiences and your learning outcomes or discussions in another course, such as TOK, to a global issue that has relevance to texts you are studying in English A: literature.

- **Internal:** begin with your fields of inquiry and then decide which works connect with the field. Pare down the field and develop a global issue that connects your works.

There are several ways to identify and develop global issues.

Activity 4 Developing global issues

This activity mixes several of the modes above.

1) Review your learner portfolio (**retrospective** approach) and use the table below to help you develop two distinct global issues.
   Two approaches:
   - Start by selecting two fields of inquiry or one field of inquiry and one sustainable development goal (SDG) (**internal** approach) OR
   - Select works first and develop your global issue by finding common fields of inquiry or SDGs in works and building a global issue with the works as the starting point (**inductive** approach).
2) In the last column write notes that explain the links between the works and the global issue.
3) Transfer your ideas from your table to your learner portfolio. By the end of this exercise you should have two solid global issues along with well-paired texts. If your IO is not for some time, you can keep coming back to develop more ideas for your internal assessment. Eventually, you will narrow your selection to one global issue and two texts.
4) You will find a downloadable MS Word version of this table in your eBook.

Field of inquiry/SDG (Choose 2)	Global issue	Suggested works (one in language of course and one in translation)	Notes about the works that link to global issue
Culture, identity, and community			
Beliefs, values, and education			
Politics, power, and justice			
Art, creativity, and the imagination			
Science, technology, and the environment			
Sustainable Development Goal (SDG) – choose one goal from the UN's SDG chart			

Connecting global issues to literary forms and authorial choices

While it may seem sufficient to discuss a global issue during your individual oral as you would in another course such as TOK, history, or environmental science, it is important to remember that the individual oral is a literary assessment. This means that you will need to be familiar not only with how the global issue is expressed through content, but also through a literary lens.

The table below contains common features of each literary form. It is certainly not exhaustive, but it will keep your analysis of the global issue rooted in literary aspects of the texts. The idea is for you to consider how the authorial choices associated with each form help convey the global issue you selected.

Activity 5 Making literary connections to global issues

1) Examine the two global issues that you developed in Activity 4.
2) Using the table below, and your literary knowledge in general, extend your connection between the works and the global issue by explaining how the literary forms and authorial choices in each work help present your global issue.
3) Write you findings in your learner portfolio.

Literary form	Common features to consider
Fiction	point of view, plot (momentum, subplots), major and minor characters (foils), time, setting, symbol, style, structure, or theme
Poetry	speaker and tone, diction (denotation/connotation/figurative language), sound effects, structure and form, or theme
Drama	plot and momentum, time, staging (props, lighting, costumes, music, blocking), major and minor characters (foils), conflict (internal and external), audience, dramatic irony, and theme
Non-fiction	persuasive techniques, rhetorical strategies (ethos, pathos, logos), literary elements to support authenticity of narrative, direct connection between author and audience, and multiple forms (letters, diaries, essays, memoirs, speeches) and their complex connection to truth

Unpacking the assessment criteria

The individual oral is worth 40 marks at both the HL and SL level but in terms of overall weight, it is weighted 30% for SL students and 20% for HL students towards the composite score for IB English A: literature. While the assessment criteria are standardised across all English A: literature assessments, the *application* of the assessment criteria is individualised for each assessment.

This means that examiners are trained to apply the assessment criteria in specific ways for each assessment. For example, the HL essay does not focus on global issues so examiners will not assess how well you present a global issue in that assessment. Because the individual oral is an internal assessment, your teacher will score your assessment and outside IB examiners will moderate randomly selected samples from your school.

The activity below will help you determine exactly what IB examiners (and your teacher) are assessing when they score the individual oral.

Activity 6 Breaking down the assessment criteria, part 1

Work with a partner or a small group to analyse both assessment criteria tables below. The first table specifically lays out the expectations for each criterion in the form of questions. The second table is more detailed and indicates the student level of achievement from 1–10 (the markband) for each criterion.

Look closely at criteria A–D in Table 1 below.

1) What do you need to do in order to achieve high marks for each criterion?
2) Make a list of terms that are specific to this assessment.
3) How will your knowledge of these terms help you better understand the requirements of the assessment?
4) Record your responses in your learner portfolio.

Info box

A markband determines the range of points available to students, based on specific criteria.

Table 1: Individual oral assessment criteria SL/HL

Criterion A: Knowledge, understanding, and interpretation	10 marks
• How well does the candidate demonstrate knowledge and understanding of the extracts, and of the works/texts from which they are taken? • To what extent does the candidate make use of knowledge and understanding of the extracts and works/texts to draw conclusions in relation to the global issue? • How well are the ideas supported by references to the extracts and to the works/texts?	
Criterion B: Analysis and evaluation	**10 marks**
• How well does the candidate use his or her knowledge and understanding of each of the extracts and their associated works/texts to analyse and evaluate the ways in which authorial choices present the global issue?	
Criterion C: Focus and organisation	**10 marks**
• How well does the candidate deliver a structured, well-balanced, and focused oral? • How well does the candidate connect ideas in a cohesive manner?	
Criterion D: Language	**10 marks**
• How clear, accurate, and effective is the language?	
TOTAL	**40 marks**

Table 2: Individual oral assessment criteria (SL/HL)

Criteria	0	1–2	3–4	5–6	7–8	9–10
Criterion A: Knowledge, understanding, and interpretation	The work does not reach a standard described by the descriptors.	There is little knowledge and understanding of the extracts and the works/texts in relation to the global issue. References to the extracts and to the works/texts are infrequent or are rarely appropriate.	There is some knowledge and understanding of the extracts and the works/texts in relation to the global issue. References to the extracts and to the works/texts are at times appropriate.	There is satisfactory knowledge and understanding of the extracts and the works/texts and an interpretation of their implications in relation to the global issue. References to the extracts and to the works/texts are generally relevant and mostly support the candidate's ideas.	There is good knowledge and understanding of the works/texts and a sustained interpretation of their implications in relation to the global issue. References to the extracts and to the works/texts are relevant and support the candidate's ideas.	There is excellent knowledge and understanding of the extracts and of the works/texts and a persuasive interpretation of their implications in relation to the global issue. References to the extracts and to the works/texts are well chosen and effectively support the candidate's ideas.
Criterion B: Analysis and evaluation	The work does not reach a standard described by the descriptors.	The oral is descriptive or contains no relevant analysis. Authorial choices are seldom identified and, if so, are poorly understood in relation to the presentation of the global issue.	The oral contains some relevant analysis, but it is reliant on description. Authorial choices are identified and/or only partially treated and/or understood in relation to the presentation of the global issue.	The oral is analytical in nature, and evaluation of the extracts and their works/texts is mostly relevant. Authorial choices are identified and reasonably understood in relation to the presentation of the global issue.	Analysis and evaluation of the extracts and their works/texts are relevant and at times insightful. There is a good understanding of how authorial choices are used to present the global issue.	Analysis and evaluation of the extracts and their works/texts are relevant and insightful. There is a thorough and nuanced understanding of how authorial choices are used to present the global issue.
Criterion C: Focus and organisation	The work does not reach a standard described by the descriptors.	The oral rarely focuses on the task. There are few connections between ideas.	The oral only sometimes focuses on the task, and treatment of the extracts and of the works/texts may be unbalanced. There are some connections between ideas, but these are not always coherent.	The oral maintains a focus on the task, despite some lapses; treatment of the extracts and works/texts is mostly balanced. The development of ideas is mostly logical; ideas are generally connected in a cohesive manner.	The oral maintains a mostly clear and sustained focus on the task; treatment of the extracts and works/texts is balanced. The development of ideas is logical; ideas are cohesively connected in an effective manner.	The oral maintains a clear and sustained focus on the task; treatment of the extracts and works/texts is well balanced. The development of ideas is logical and convincing; ideas are connected in a cogent manner.
Criterion D: Language	The work does not reach a standard described by the descriptors.	The language is rarely clear or accurate; errors often hinder communication. Vocabulary and syntax are imprecise and frequently inaccurate. Elements of style (for example, register, tone, and rhetorical devices) are inappropriate to the task and detract from the oral.	The language is generally clear; errors sometimes hinder communication. Vocabulary and syntax are often imprecise with inaccuracies. Elements of style (for example, register, tone, and rhetorical devices) are often inappropriate to the task and detract from the oral.	The language is clear; errors do not hinder communication. Vocabulary and syntax are appropriate to the task but simple and repetitive. Elements of style (for example, register, tone, and rhetorical devices) are appropriate to the task and neither enhance nor detract from the oral.	The language is clear and accurate; occasional errors do not hinder communication. Vocabulary and syntax are appropriate and varied. Elements of style (for example, register, tone, and rhetorical devices) are appropriate to the task and somewhat enhance the oral.	The language is clear, accurate, and varied; occasional errors do not hinder communication. Vocabulary and syntax are varied and create effect. Elements of style (for example, register, tone, and rhetorical devices) are appropriate to the task and enhance the oral.

The connection between literary analysis and global issues

Below is a sample passage from Shakespeare's *Hamlet* along with literary analysis questions to show how developing a global issue from a literary text is often an inductive process. Notice how the questions move from the specific (focusing on textual features) to the more general (focusing on characterisation, themes, and global issues).

Claudius' prayer passage from *Hamlet*, Act 3.3

King. Thanks, dear my lord. [Exit POLONIUS]
O, my offence is rank, it smells to heaven;
It hath the primal eldest curse upon 't,
A brother's murder. Pray can I not,
Though inclination be as sharp as will.   (5)
My stronger guilt defeats my strong intent,
And, like a man to double business bound,
I stand in pause where I shall first begin,
And both neglect. What if this cursed hand
Were thicker than itself with brother's blood,   (10)
Is there not rain enough in the sweet heavens
To wash it white as snow? Whereto serves mercy
But to confront the visage of offence?
And what's in prayer but this twofold force,
To be forestalled ere we come to fall,   (15)
Or pardoned being down? Then I'll look up.
My fault is past. But, O, what form of prayer
Can serve my turn? 'Forgive me my foul murder'?
That cannot be, since I am still possessed
Of those effects for which I did the murder,   (20)
My crown, mine own ambition, and my queen.
May one be pardoned and retain th' offence?
In the corrupted currents of this world
Offence's gilded hand may shove by justice,
And oft 'tis seen the wicked prize itself   (25)

Buys out the law. But 'tis not so above.
There is no shuffling; there the action lies
In his true nature; and we ourselves compelled,
Even to the teeth and forehead of our faults,
To give in evidence. What then? What rests? (30)
Try what repentance can. What can it not?
Yet what can it when one cannot repent?
O wretched state! O bosom black as death!
O limed soul, that struggling to be free,
Art more engaged! Help, angels! Make assay. (35)
Bow, stubborn knees, and heart with strings of steel,
Be soft as sinews of the newborn babe!
All may be well. [He kneels]

Hamlet literary analysis questions – Claudius praying in chapel:

1. The passage is located in Act _____ Scene _____.

2. Briefly contextualise the passage. In other words, what happens directly before and after the passage?

3. To what allusion does Claudius refer when he says that his offence '… hath the primal eldest curse upon 't'? Why might Claudius use this allusion in his opening prayer to God? What connection does it have to his own circumstances?

4. What literary devices are at work in the following lines: 'What if this cursed hand/Were thicker than itself with brother's blood,/Is there not rain enough in the sweet heavens/To wash it white as snow?' What is the effect?

5. According to Claudius what are the two ('twofold force') purposes of prayer? Are these the only reasons for prayer? Explain.

6. What conclusion does Claudius come to in lines 19–20? What must he do in order to be forgiven by God?

7. Paraphrase the following lines: 'In the corrupted currents of this world/Offence's gilded hand may shove by justice,/And oft 'tis seen the wicked prize itself/Buys out the law' (23–26). What are some modern day examples of 'gilded hand[s]' who 'shove by justice' and 'buy out the law'? What connection is Shakespeare making between wealth and corruption?

8. In line 23 mentioned above, what are the possible meanings of the word 'currents'? What is the effect?

9. What is the effect of the punctuation in lines 30–37? What does it reveal about Claudius' state of mind?

10. Shakespeare has very few stage directions in his plays. Explain the significance of the stage direction in the last line of this passage.

11. What does Claudius say nearly 30 lines after this passage? (Hint: famous couplet). What is the effect?

12. Describe the tone of the passage. Is it consistent throughout or does it change? Explain.

13. What does this passage reveal about Claudius?

14. List the major themes expressed in this passage.

15. Review your responses to the questions above and develop a global issue based on this passage.

Activity 8 The mini individual oral: a practice presentation

For this activity, you will present a mini individual oral to your peers. You will select a passage from a literary work that is not listed in your two-year course syllabus and use close-reading analysis to develop a global issue. If you already have a literary analysis of a specific passage in your portfolio, feel free to use it for this activity.

How to begin:

Step 1: Select a passage of no more than 40 lines from a literary work.

Step 2: Look closely at how the structure and style of the passage point towards a specific global issue.

Step 3: Once you have completed your analysis, design a short presentation that:
- states the global issue in your passage
- explains how textual features and/or authorial choices in the passage help express the global issue
- explains how the global issue is expressed in the work as a whole.

Step 4: Create a notecard with no more than five bullet points. The notecard will provide brief talking points about how your global issue is linked to your passage, the authorial choices, and the text as a whole.

Step 5: Present your mini IO in front of a group of peers. You may refer to your bullet points as you present, but they should not be a script.

Step 6: Follow the mini IO checklist:
- ✓ Your mini oral should: demonstrate your knowledge of the extract and work with respect to the global issue; provide relevant insights related to how the authorial choices express the global issue; and develop your ideas in a logical and convincing manner.

Info box

As this activity is a practice individual oral, you cannot use the same global issue and work that you will use for your actual IO. However, the experience will help familiarise you with the process.

✓ Remember to speak clearly and use language that is accurate and appropriate to the task.

✓ Delivery time: 4–5 minutes.

Assessment: The mini IO can be assessed with the IB assessment criteria using peer feedback, teacher feedback, or both.

Reflection: After you have received feedback, write a reflection in your portfolio about how this experience helped prepare you for your actual IO. What did you do well? What adjustments will you make to prepare for your IO assessment?

Activity 9 The next step: organising ideas for the IO outline

In this chapter you have:

- learned about the IO process
- constructed global issues from lines of inquiry and/or sustainable development goals
- explored ways to make the discussion literary
- unpacked the assessment criteria
- practised a mini individual oral.

You are now ready to move on to the outline phase of your individual oral. The IB will provide you with a form for you to organise your presentation. You are allowed to write or type up to ten bulleted points on the form, which you can bring into the exam room along with your extracts. For this activity you will begin by organising a more detailed outline than the one required by the IB.

You are now ready to move on to outlining your individual oral.

Connections

Creating a longer, more detailed outline and then distilling it into ten bulleted points will help you organise your final product into a literary-focused, text-based examination of a specific global issue.

The questions in the box on page 261 will help you develop the points of your individual oral. You are not creating a script, but rather constructing an argument that follows an **assertion → support → analysis** pattern. Following this pattern, will align your planning materials with the assessment criteria and serve you well as you deliver your individual oral.

Use the box below as a checklist and a guide to prepare a detailed outline for your individual oral, which you will eventually pare down to no more than ten bullet points.

Preliminary outline (detailed)

Both works

- Which works have you selected for this assessment?
- Is one work in the original language of the course and the other in translation?
- Have you used either of the works for another IB assessment?
- What is the global issue you are exploring?
- Why is this issue worthy of investigation?
- How will the literary form and authorial choices (textual features, structure, and style) of each work help you develop your analysis of the global issue within the work?

Points for work #1

- What ==assertions== will help you develop your discussion?
- How will you ==support== your assertions? (Use specific examples from the extract and work as a whole.)
- How will you ==analyse== and ==evaluate== your examples?
- NOTE: Don't forget to link your global issue to the literary form and authorial choices.

Points for work #2

- What ==assertions== will help you develop your discussion?
- How will you ==support== your assertions? (Use specific examples from the extract and work as a whole.)
- How will you ==analyse== and ==evaluate== your examples?
- NOTE: Don't forget to link your global issue to the literary form and authorial choices.

Conclusion:

- Pull your points together regarding your position on this global issue and how it plays out in each work.

Now, distill this longer outline into ten or fewer bullet points. You are now ready to share your condensed outline with your teacher.

Analysing student samples

Below are transcriptions of two sample individual orals. The first sample is highlighted with points of ==assertion==, ==support==, and ==analysis==, so that you can review the strengths and weaknesses of the response with regards to the assessment criteria. You will also have the opportunity to reflect upon the first assessment and review examiner feedback.

The second sample is designed for you to read and practise your scoring using the assessment criteria for the individual oral.

Read each transcribed sample with its accompanying extracts and complete the activities that follow.

Marjane Satrapi's *Persepolis* ▶

Student sample #1

Global issue: The connections between dysfunctional families and dysfunctional societies in Shakespeare's *Hamlet* and Marjane Satrapi's *Persepolis*.

Extract #1: From *Persepolis* (70–71)

Extract #2: From *Hamlet* (Act 1, Scene 5)

Ghost

Ay, that incestuous, that adulterate beast,
With witchcraft of his wit, with traitorous gifts, –
O wicked wit and gifts, that have the power
So to seduce! – won to his shameful lust
The will of my most seeming-virtuous queen:
O Hamlet, what a falling-off was there!
From me, whose love was of that dignity
That it went hand in hand even with the vow
I made to her in marriage, and to decline
Upon a wretch whose natural gifts were poor
To those of mine!
But virtue, as it never will be moved,
Though lewdness court it in a shape of heaven,
So lust, though to a radiant angel link'd,
Will sate itself in a celestial bed,
And prey on garbage.
But, soft! methinks I scent the morning air;
Brief let me be. Sleeping within my orchard,
My custom always of the afternoon,
Upon my secure hour thy uncle stole,
With juice of cursed hebenon in a vial,
And in the porches of my ears did pour
The leperous distilment; whose effect
Holds such an enmity with blood of man
That swift as quicksilver it courses through
The natural gates and alleys of the body,
And with a sudden vigour doth posset
And curd, like eager droppings into milk,
The thin and wholesome blood: so did it mine;
And a most instant tetter bark'd about,
Most lazar-like, with vile and loathsome crust,

All my smooth body.
Thus was I, sleeping, by a brother's hand
Of life, of crown, of queen, at once dispatch'd:
Cut off even in the blossoms of my sin,
Unhousel'd, disappointed, unanel'd,
No reckoning made, but sent to my account
With all my imperfections on my head:
O, horrible! O, horrible! most horrible!

Language A: literature internal assessment student outline form

---

Global issue: the connections between dysfunctional families and dysfunctional societies.

Works chosen

Work in translation: Marjane Satrapi's *Persepolis*

Work in language A: Shakespeare's *Hamlet*

Notes for the oral (maximum of 10 bullet points)
- There is a connection between dysfunctional families and dysfunctional societies
- Dysfunction in Hamlet's family mirrors that of Danish society
- Imagery in passage drives Hamlet to revenge (betrayal)
- Hamlet & society mourn king (Hamlet lost father; guards lost leader and protector)
- Claudius corrupted Gertrude and in turn will corrupt entire kingdom
- Fortinbras and Hamlet are linked (foils); dysfunction in family leads to death. Without strong leaders everything falls apart.
- *Persepolis* is about young girl who grows up during Islamic Revolution
- Marjane was religious but this changed when her uncle was murdered by government
- Marjane lost faith and identity. (Passage). Also lost faith when she was sent to Vienna
- Without a strong foundation or a strong sense of identity that comes from being together and communicating there is dysfunction in families and in societies

NOTE: For the ten-minute student delivery portion of the assessment, ==assertions are highlighted in yellow==; support is highlighted in blue; and ==analysis is highlighted in pink==.

Student sample #1: Individual oral (transcription):

My global issue will focus on the connections between dysfunctional families and dysfunctional societies in Shakespeare's *Hamlet* and Marjane Satrapi's *Persepolis*.

My passage from *Hamlet* is from Act 1 scene 5 where the ghost of Old Hamlet confronts young Hamlet and asks his son to avenge his murder. Through detailed imagery the ghost reveals the gruesome way in which he was murdered by Claudius and drives Hamlet to avenge his father's death. When Claudius pours the 'leperous distillment' into old King Hamlet's ear, the King's body began to rot from the inside out. Hamlet's sadness turns to anger when he hears that his father's death is due to a family betrayal. This dysfunction in the form of corruption drives the plot of the play.

Backing up a little, from the first scene of the first act in *Hamlet*, Denmark is on edge. Everyone, including the guards and Hamlet himself, feels anxious or threatened by the death of Old King Hamlet and his brother Claudius' ascension to the throne. The dysfunction in Hamlet's family mirrors that of Danish society. When the family unit does not work together cohesively, it is often difficult for a society, which is essentially a network of these smaller family units, to function well.

Old Hamlet brought direction to both the kingdom and to his family. In the opening lines of the play, one of the guards mentions that he is 'sick at heart'. Old Hamlet ruled for over 30 years, giving the Danes a sense of peace and security, and when he died, the people of Denmark were feeling really lost and confused just like Hamlet is feeling. The guards are also uneasy about the possible military threat to the kingdom at this time when they've just lost their leader and even question Horatio about why so much military preparation is happening seven days a week. Hamlet may be wearing the 'inky cloak' but the kingdom is still in deep mourning and is nervous as well, showing how the dysfunction at the family level affects the kingdom as a whole.

In the Act 1, scene 5 passage I selected, the ghost characterises Claudius as an 'incestuous, adulterate beast'. He describes how Claudius seduced Gertrude and how Gertrude herself was once 'seeming virtuous' but Claudius corrupted her and ruined her and now she becomes animal-like and 'preys on garbage'. With the 'garbage' comment, it seems that everything Claudius touches including Gertrude and the Old King Hamlet begins to rot, which goes back to the rotting motif. Later in Act 1 one of the guards says that 'something is rotten in the state of Denmark'. Claudius's act of murder didn't corrupt just Gertrude, but also stands to corrupt the entire kingdom. The dysfunction in Hamlet's family is linked to the dysfunction of society at large. In this case the ghost's revenge is not just personal. If Claudius can corrupt a virtuous queen, imagine what he will do to the entire kingdom. Gertrude has been corrupted and 'seduced'. The only way to save Denmark is to kill Claudius.

Hamlet feels trapped by the ghost's request to avenge his death. Being a skeptic, he cannot just kill Claudius; he needs proof. He cannot trust Gertrude, who betrayed her husband by marrying Claudius. Many of the struggles that Hamlet is going through, especially his distrust of everyone around him is similar to what the people in Denmark feel because of the military threat from Norway. There is a tension between all these unstable feelings. Fortinbras is a threat to Denmark but in many ways he is a lot like Hamlet. Both men have lost their fathers and want to avenge their fathers' deaths. Losing a father causes a sort of dysfunction, but these men are very high profile and so their pain has consequences for society as well. Fortinbras is trying to find a way to take over Denmark. He's a threat to the whole Danish society whereas Hamlet's threat is personal and he is only trying to take out his revenge against Claudius. But so many people get drawn into the dysfunction. When Hamlet kills Polonius it sets off a chain of events that leads to Laertes's anger, Ophelia's madness and suicide, Gertrude's death. All of these people die, including Hamlet. Families need a strong foundation, with bonds of love and trust to keep them from falling apart. Countries are much the same. They require strong leaders who are trustworthy and have a deep love for the people they represent. Without these things, everything falls apart.

And so moving onto *Persepolis*, the passage I have chosen is a series of panels immediately after Marjane Satrapi's uncle died. Marjane grew up in Iran during the Islamic Revolution and at a young age moved to Vienna when her country started to become really unsafe. This separation caused a lot of dysfunction in her own family, but even before that we can see the dysfunction between her and her parents and her uncle. Marjane's uncle died because he didn't agree with the regime that had taken over Iran during this time and he was executed for what the regime perceived to be his crimes. His death really affected Marjane. When she was a young child Marjane really cared about her religion. There are a lot of panels about her talking to God holding her in his arms. She had a really close relationship with God. She even wanted to be a prophet but when her uncle dies that dysfunction within her family causes her to feel lost. She loses her strong ties to her religion. In the passage I selected Marjane says to God, 'shut up you. Get out of my life. I never want to see you again!' The exclamation points emphasise her frustration but the visual pointing of her finger in two separate panels pointing away from her, shows how adamant she is about rejecting God. Her eyebrows are furrowed and the text bubble includes sharp, angular edges, making her anger even more noticeable. We can see here this inverse relationship between Marjane's own faith and the Islamic faith in her country. There is an extreme version of Islam that seems to be shifting the focus away from the original origins of the religion to one that is more fundamentalist during this time. And Marjane is rejecting these changes and her own religion which gave her so much comfort. Her family crisis combines with this societal crisis or dysfunction and causes Marjane to lose faith.

Later in the memoir she moves to Vienna to escape the regime and the regime continues to get worse and more violent. Islam as a religion is a non-violent. There is no part of the Quran which promotes meaningless violence. We can see a disconnect between what the Islamic faith teaches versus what the Islamic regime in Iran was preaching and doing. This idea is linked again to Marjane and her own journey. When she was in Vienna she was feeling further disconnected from her own faith and her own identity as she grew up in Europe. She was still a very young girl at this time so you can imagine how lost and alone she must have felt without that link to her family and to her own identity. There really wasn't a way for her to stay grounded while she was without her own family. There is a scene or a panel where her mum comes to visit her several years after she's been living on her own and it shocks her because her mum looks completely different to how she remembers her and you can see how distant she's become from her family. It's like that distance between her and her family has created a rift between herself and her own identity to her own faith. Similarly in Iranian society there is a rift between the Islamic faith and the regime that is in power. Without a strong foundation or a strong sense of identity that comes from being together and communicating there is dysfunction in families and in societies. Like in *Hamlet*, the dysfunction at the family level mirrors the dysfunction in society. They are not separate.

Teacher question #1: You spent some time discussing how Marjane's identity and faith are linked to your global issue. How do you think that Hamlet's identity and faith are linked to the dysfunction in families and societies?

Student response: I think Hamlet was profoundly affected by his father's death and I think that his skepticism of 'Is this really my father's ghost and can I trust what he's saying and how do I deal with it if it is true?' is the driving force of the entire play. This whole process consumes him throughout the play. We don't really know what Hamlet is like without that dysfunction. That dysfunction is his whole being. His whole focus is how to deal with the revenge: 'Should I avenge my father's death? Was it a murder? What really happened?'

Teacher question #2: How does the form of each work (graphic memoir and play) affect the way your global issue is expressed?

Student response: With the memoir being a graphic novel you can really see what Marjane is feeling and how she's expressing it. So for example, in the passage that I selected you can see her floating in a sea of black and there's some space and planets and stars around this little girl floating all by herself. I think that seeing that visually really helps you understand how she was feeling and her lack of identity. In earlier panels she was in the arms of God and now she's just floating by herself, so I think that this contrast helps readers understand the dysfunction she experiences, and how it created her lack of faith and identity, better than if it were just written. As for the play, I think that even though plays are written, they are meant to be performed so people are going to see the story unfold in front of them. This play has more soliloquies than any other Shakespeare play, so we don't get the same background information we do with a novel, but we still get to understand a character's true inner thoughts through this device.

Teacher question #3: In the passage that you selected specifically for *Hamlet*, who is speaking and why is this significant?

Student response: This passage is a monologue where the ghost is speaking and Hamlet is reacting to what the ghost is telling him. It shows how Hamlet is the puppet of his father. He's skeptical himself but you can see the influence that his father has on him and how close their relationship was and how his loss affects Hamlet.

Teacher question #4: In terms of both Marjane and Hamlet, what is the end result of the connection between familial and societal dysfunction?

Student response: I think the ending of *Hamlet* is terrible. Everyone basically dies. So there is really no resolution. The dysfunction never gets solved for Hamlet. It never gets better. You could argue that Fortinbras is starting with a clean slate, without dysfunction, but Hamlet got drawn into a dysfunctional situation that cost him his life and the life of others. There's no satisfaction in that. With Marjane, she does figure out who she is. She goes to school and now she's an activist. She wrote this book, this memoir of what happened to her, so I think that she definitely did resolve her own dysfunction and she's finding her own way in life. I think this shows that dysfunction can but doesn't have to define us in negative ways. We can learn and grow from dysfunctional situations whether they are in our families or societies. Or both. We have choices.

Teacher: *Ok, and that's all we have time for. Thank you very much.*

Activity 10 Group discussion and analysis questions

Discuss the following with a small group:

1) After reading through the response, take note of the highlighted points of assertion, support, and analysis. What do you notice? Which points are particularly strong? What could be improved?
2) How well did the student respond to the teacher's questions? To what extent do you think the responses improved the overall quality of the IO? Explain.
3) Short checklist:
   - To what extent did the student establish and address a viable global issue?
   - How well was the discussion of the global issue sustained?
   - To what extent did the student focus on both the extracts and the works as a whole?
   - How effectively did the student keep the focus on content as well as form (authorial choices)?
   - Was the discussion organised and well developed? Justify your response.
   - Was the language clear and precise with proper use of terminology? Justify your response.
4) Read the examiner comments below and compare them with your own responses.

Examiner comments for this assessment

Criterion A: Knowledge, understanding, and interpretation

The candidate demonstrates knowledge and understanding of both texts and extracts in relation to the global issue, though the knowledge and interpretation is stronger for Persepolis than for Hamlet. The references to the text mostly support the candidate's assertions.

Criterion B: Analysis and evaluation

The analysis and evaluation are sustained throughout the individual oral. While the Hamlet discussion is not fully developed, the candidate connects the global issue to the author's literary choices. For example, she links familial and societal dysfunction to corruption that becomes the 'driving force of the play', points to the motif of rotting, and speaks of dramatic tension, though these ideas could be explored in more depth. The analysis of the passage seems to get lost in the discussion of the play as a whole.

In terms of Persepolis, the candidate connects concepts of identity of self with identity of country and links them back to her global issue. She analyses the graphic memoir aptly, pointing to specifics in her extract, both in the initial delivery and in the questioning section, that support her points regarding Marjane's loss of faith and identity. The responses to the questions further develop the discussion and offer additional insights, particularly the last comment which reveals how Marjane, unlike Hamlet, was able to resolve the dysfunction she faced through memoir writing and activism.

Criterion C: Focus and organisation

There is sustained focus on the global issue throughout and although the Hamlet discussion is a bit longer than the *Persepolis* discussion, the candidate aptly connects Marjane's loss of identity and faith with her personal and political struggles. This connection allows her to develop a cohesive discussion that is clearly linked to the global issue. The familial and societal connections are also woven together in the *Hamlet* portion, though not as cohesively. There could be more attention to the passage in the *Hamlet* portion of the discussion, though the candidate does connect the global issue to several examples throughout the work.

Criterion D: Language

The language is mostly clear, accurate, and precise. There are some minor lapses, but these do not impede meaning.

Student sample #2

Global issue: How is the use and abuse of power reflected in individuals and societies in *Hamlet* and *A Doll's House*?

Extract #1: From *Hamlet* (Act 2, Scene 1)

Ophelia reports Hamlet's erratic behaviour to her father, Polonius.

OPHELIA

O, my lord, my lord, I have been so affrighted!

LORD POLONIUS

With what i' the name of God?

OPHELIA

My lord, as I was sewing in my closet,
Lord Hamlet, with his doublet all unbraced;
No hat upon his head; his stockings foul'd,
Ungarter'd, and down-gyved to his ancle;
Pale as his shirt; his knees knocking each other;
And with a look so piteous in purport
As if he had been loosed out of hell
To speak of horrors, – he comes before me.

LORD POLONIUS

Mad for thy love?

OPHELIA

My lord, I do not know;
But truly, I do fear it.

LORD POLONIUS

What said he?

OPHELIA

He took me by the wrist and held me hard;
Then goes he to the length of all his arm;
And, with his other hand thus o'er his brow,
He falls to such perusal of my face
As he would draw it. Long stay'd he so;
At last, a little shaking of mine arm
And thrice his head thus waving up and down,
He raised a sigh so piteous and profound
As it did seem to shatter all his bulk
And end his being: that done, he lets me go:
And, with his head over his shoulder turn'd,
He seem'd to find his way without his eyes;
For out o' doors he went without their helps,
And, to the last, bended their light on me.

LORD POLONIUS

Come, go with me: I will go seek the king.
This is the very ecstasy of love,
Whose violent property fordoes itself
And leads the will to desperate undertakings
As oft as any passion under heaven
That does afflict our natures. I am sorry.
What, have you given him any hard words of late?

OPHELIA

No, my good lord, but, as you did command,
I did repel his fetters and denied
His access to me.

LORD POLONIUS

That hath made him mad.

Extract #2: From *A Doll's House* (Act 1)
Krogstad directs Nora to help him secure his job at the bank.

KROGSTAD [*changing his tone*]: Mrs Helmer, you will be so good as to use your influence on my behalf.

NORA: What? What do you mean?

KROGSTAD: You will be so kind as to see that I am allowed to keep my subordinate position in the Bank.

NORA: What do you mean by that? Who proposes to take your post away from you?

KROGSTAD: Oh, there is no necessity to keep up the pretence of ignorance. I can quite understand that your friend is not very anxious to expose herself to the chance of rubbing shoulders with me; and I quite understand, too, whom I have to thank for being turned off.

NORA: But I assure you –

KROGSTAD: Very likely; but, to come to the point, the time has come when I should advise you to use your influence to prevent that.

NORA: But, Mr Krogstad, I have no influence.

KROGSTAD: Haven't you? I thought you said yourself just now –

NORA: Naturally I did not mean you to put that construction on it. I! What should make you think I have any influence of that kind with my husband?

KROGSTAD: Oh, I have known your husband from our student days. I don't suppose he is any more unassailable than other husbands.

NORA: If you speak slightingly of my husband, I shall turn you out of the house.

KROGSTAD: You are bold, Mrs Helmer.

NORA: I am not afraid of you any longer. As soon as the New Year comes, I shall in a very short time be free of the whole thing.

KROGSTAD [controlling himself]: Listen to me, Mrs Helmer. If necessary, I am prepared to fight for my small post in the Bank as if I were fighting for my life.

NORA: So it seems.

KROGSTAD: It is not only for the sake of the money; indeed, that weighs least with me in the matter. There is another reason – well, I may as well tell you. My position is this. I daresay you know, like everybody else, that once, many years ago, I was guilty of an indiscretion.

NORA: I think I have heard something of the kind.

KROGSTAD: The matter never came into court; but every way seemed to be closed to me after that. So I took to the business that you know of. I had to do something; and, honestly, I don't think I've been one of the worst. But now I must cut myself free from all that. My sons are growing up; for their sake I must try and win back as much respect as I can in the town. This post in the Bank was like the first step up for me – and now your husband is going to kick me downstairs again into the mud.

NORA: But you must believe me, Mr Krogstad; it is not in my power to help you at all.

KROGSTAD: Then it is because you haven't the will; but I have means to compel you.

Student sample #2: Individual oral (transcription)

Today I will discuss how the use and abuse of power is reflected in individuals and societies. I will explore this global issue in both William Shakespeare's *Hamlet* and Henrik Ibsen's *A Doll's House*. For *Hamlet* I would like to focus on how the corruption, specifically of the crown, is reflected in the mental decline of those closest to the problem, as well as the increasing tension between Norway and Denmark.

I would like to begin with an excerpt from Act 2 Scene 1 that focuses on a conversation between Ophelia and Polonius. The audience knows that Hamlet is pretending to be mad but Ophelia is 'affrighted' as she says in the passage, by Hamlet's coming to her 'as if he had been loosed out of hell to speak of horrors'. Polonius wastes no time in bringing his daughter's information about Hamlet's state of mind straight to King Claudius. This action shows the corruption in the relationship between Polonius and Ophelia because it shows how Polonius uses a private conversation he has with his daughter to get into the good graces of the king. Later in the play in Act 3 Ophelia agrees to have Polonius and King Claudius spy on a conversation she has with Hamlet. Ophelia is clearly being used a pawn. Fathers are supposed to protect their children but in this case Polonius puts his political ambition over his loyalty to his family and is clearly abusing his power.

Polonius doesn't only abuse his power with his daughter but he also does so with his son when he asks Reynaldo to spy on Laertes when he was in France. Polonius obviously doesn't trust his children and cares about his position in the court. Ophelia simply does what she is told — she returns Hamlet's love tokens and follows her father's orders 'denying his access' to her, but this sets up confrontations between Ophelia and Hamlet and degrades her mental state. He yells 'get thee to a nunnery' and continues to 'affright' Ophelia as he did in the passage where he lets out a sigh that seems to 'shatter all his bulk'. In this case, it's not just Polonius that abuses his power, but also Hamlet. Hamlet knows that Ophelia is an obedient daughter. When he acted mad in the passage I selected Hamlet knew that she would be obedient and tell her father, who in turn would tell Claudius and the Queen about his madness. Hamlet went to Ophelia and acted mad and used her disposition and her relationship with her father to convey his antic disposition. The difference between Hamlet and Polonius is that Hamlet is trying to uncover the truth and find out if Claudius murdered his father while Polonius is simply trying to get into the good graces of the King. Polonius's attempts to get Ophelia to leave Hamlet and to spy on him caused Hamlet to act rashly, both scaring and scarring her as we see in her mental decline and her eventual drowning. Either way, both men are purposely manipulating Ophelia, and not only does this show that innocent characters are impacted by corrupt decisions but it also shows that the society in which these characters live is also affected.

The use and abuse of power in individuals is also projected in society as is demonstrated by the strained relations between Norway and Denmark. Young Fortinbras threatens Denmark specifically after Claudius abused his power and killed his own brother in cold blood. Claudius was able to get close enough to Old King Hamlet to kill him while he was sleeping. And he furthered this abuse of power by marrying his brother's wife, Gertrude, so that he could ascend to the throne. Old King Hamlet was not only the King of Denmark, but its protector. When Claudius killed his brother, he left Denmark vulnerable to Fortinbras who assumed that the kingdom was weak since Old King Hamlet was no longer in charge. Fortinbras feared Old King Hamlet, but now that he is gone, he has nothing to fear from the Danes. His threats against the Danish lands and his desire to take back the property that had once belonged to his father mirror the internal strife Denmark was now facing after the sudden death of their beloved king. Even though Fortinbras represents a threat to Denmark, he has strong ties to Hamlet. Both men lost their fathers and they are both seeking some sort of vengeance. These foils show the strife caused by the abuses of power not only affected the royal family of Denmark, but also other countries. This gives Claudius's specific act of deception more of a global context and shows how far one act can spread.

Now I will be moving on to how the use and abuse of power affected individuals and societies in *A Doll's House*. My passage is from the interaction between Nora and Krogstad in Act 1 in which he attempts to blackmail Nora into getting his job back. Specifically when Krogstad says, 'I have the means to make you' as well as 'I will fight to keep my job' this shows his abuse of power over Nora because he knew her secret concerning her taking out a loan to protect her husband. This abuse of power specifically causes the decay of Nora's own familial relationships as well as her mental health and eventually leads to her breaking away from her family to live on her own. This specific extract in the play classifies Krogstad as the villain and threatens Nora and destroys her family relationships.

But Krogstad is not the only character who abuses power. Nora's relationship with Torvald begins to become strained because the stress of getting Krogstad his job back begins to become too much for her. Nora has always been classified as a little childish and a little unstable and although she was never close with her children she begins to become more estranged from them. The climax of her mental health decline can be seen when Krogstad sends a letter to Torvald and it's sitting in his mailbox and to distract him from this letter she begins to dance for him, almost in a manic fashion. Ibsen uses this degradation of mental health not only to make the audience feel sympathy for Nora but also to show the importance of telling the truth. She never thought she would have to worry about the consequences of being dishonest and her dance becomes the physical manifestation of the 'influence' that she and Krogstad speak of in the passage I selected. It's Nora's desperate attempt to manipulate Torvald so that he won't find out the truth.

Another character that also shows the abuse of power is Miss Linde because she uses Krogstad's affections for her to influence his actions against Nora and against Torvald. She makes it seem as though she's going to ask Krogstad to rescind his letter that he had written to Torvald about Nora's unlawful actions, but she told Krogstad not to take back the letter until after Torvald had seen it. The momentum of the play builds here as this action is linked to the fight that Torvald and Nora have which results in Torvald's attempt to force Nora away from her own children and leads to Nora's abandonment of her family. Again, this all goes back to the idea of 'influence' from my passage. Krogstad encourages Nora to use her influence, but other characters do this as well, creating a momentum in the play that leads to explosive results.

Torvald attempts to control Nora by telling her that she is an unfit mother. This abuse of power, however, completely backfired on Torvald as Nora throughout the play was becoming more and more annoyed with other people using her for their own gain and she decided to instead leave her family and go off and live her own life ultimately taking power away from everyone else and putting it in her own hands. In the end, she decided to direct the influence she had towards herself. The abuse of power wielded by Krogstad, her husband, Mrs Linde and society's norms led to Nora breaking free from her those trying to control her.

Activity 11

Discuss the following in a small group:

1) Identify (through highlighting or by writing down notes) the assertions, support, and analysis in this oral response. What do you notice? How do these points compare with the first student sample? You will find a printable PDF version of the text in your eBook.

2) Use the IB assessment criteria (Table 2 on page 256) to assign a score to the oral response. Start with the highest level markband for each criterion and see if the descriptors in each box fit. If the level in the markband is not reached, move down to the next markband until you find the descriptors that best fit the assessment. Do this for each of the four criteria until you have arrived at a total score.

3) How would you score this individual oral assessment? What does the student do well? What could be improved?

4) Design three teacher questions that would help fill 'gaps' in the student's assessment. How would effective responses to these questions help improve the individual oral?

5) Share your total scores and responses with other groups and discuss.

Final reflections

- Think back to the activities that you completed in this chapter. Which activity was the most useful? Why?

- What is the purpose of addressing global issues in literary works? How is this purpose connected to the aims of English A: literature and the IB philosophy of international-mindedness? (See pages 6 and 7 in the 'Detailed overview' chapter).

- After reading this chapter, what do you now understand about the individual oral that you did not know before?

- If you could provide one piece of advice to another student regarding the individual oral, what would it be?

Insights into the individual oral

1. The individual oral is a required internal assessment for both standard level (SL) and high level (HL) programmes where students deliver an oral response to a prompt, using two extracts from two different works, and examine how one global issue of their choosing is presented in each text.

2. You will explore a global issue through a literary lens, a process which will enable you to understand, analyse, and evaluate literature within local and global contexts.

3. You are also encouraged to use the five fields of inquiry along with the UN's Sustainable Development Goals to develop your global issue.

4. The assessment is based on two works studied: one translated and one in the original language of the course. The works selected for the individual oral cannot be used for any other assessment including the HL essay or paper 2.

5. Your teacher will play an important guiding role as you prepare for this assessment. They cannot assign works or extracts, but they can provide valuable feedback on the works and extracts that you select and the outlines you construct.

6. You may bring two extracts of no more than 40 lines each and a brief outline of no more than 10 bullet points into the exam room. The extracts and outlines can assist you in the delivery of the individual oral, but points should not be memorised or treated as a script.

7. The delivery time of the individual oral is 10 minutes followed by 5 minutes of questioning by the teacher. The entire assessment is 15 minutes.

8. The learner portfolio plays a valuable role in the planning process for the individual oral. It can be used retrospectively to help you select works/extracts for the assessment and develop your global issue.

9. Part of the planning process also includes preparing an outline that focuses on how the global issues are expressed in content and form in the selected extracts and works. Creating a more detailed outline which can later be distilled to 10 or fewer specific points encourages a more focused and developed delivery.

10. The individual oral is comprised of four assessment criteria: A) knowledge, understanding, and interpretation; B) analysis and evaluation; C) focus and organisation; and D) language.

11. You are encouraged to practise your scoring and presentation skills to prepare for the assessment. While practice IOs on various works and global issues are permissible, you cannot practise your actual IO with your teacher.

12. The individual oral with its focus on global issues is directly linked to the aims for IB English A: literature and the IB philosophy of international-mindedness.

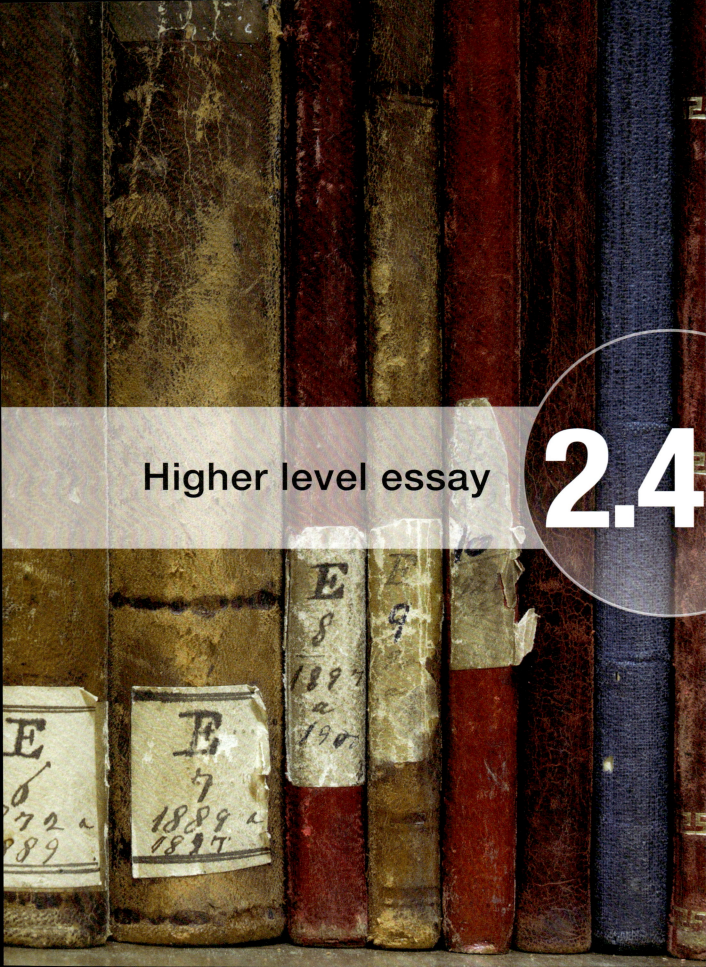

Higher level essay

2.4

In this chapter you will…
- understand the requirements for the higher level (HL) essay
- develop strategies for selecting a work and topic for the essay
- develop brainstorming techniques
- understand the importance of academic integrity
- determine the relationship of the learner portfolio to the essay
- explore pre-writing strategies to arrive at a workable/arguable/effective thesis
- understand the stages of the writing process
- explore rules for documentation and manuscript form
- review sample essays
- examine the assessment criteria for the HL essay.

The nature of the HL essay

As a higher level (HL) student in the Language A: literature course, 20% of your final course mark is determined by your successful writing of a formal essay (1200–1500 words) on one work previously studied in class. You will follow your own **line of inquiry** on a topic, and, with the help of your teacher, will refine your ideas into a focused, analytical argument. Any work may be selected as long as you have not used it for the internal assessment, nor plan to use it in paper 2. The essay offers you the opportunity to demonstrate that you are an 'independent, critical, and creative reader, thinker, and writer by exploring a literary topic over an extended period of time, refining your ideas through the process of planning, drafting, and re-drafting' (Language A: literature guide).

Strategies for getting started

Selecting a work and topic: how areas of exploration and course concepts can help

The Language A: literature guide states that a student needs to use a 'broader literary perspective' rather than a narrowly focused commentary in the selection of their topic for their essay. But what is the difference between a broad versus narrow perspective? A stylistic commentary is a type of essay that typically focuses on a passage of 20–30 lines within a text. The analysis of the selected passage or extract focuses only on those specific lines and does not focus on the work as a whole, and so it would be considered a 'narrow' perspective. Focusing on how a symbol functions in two specific passages of a novel or play would also be too narrow. The idea is to start with a broad inquiry question such as those connected to the **areas of exploration** and **course concepts**. The broader perspective considers the entire text in determining the focus of your topic as well as the line of inquiry that your argument will grow from.

Selecting one work only for your HL essay is certainly a viable option. For example, you may be interested in how characters negotiate power when they are subjugated by gender, class, or government in a singular substantial text, such as Isabel Allende's *The House of the Spirits*. This particular approach is derived from the following inquiry question that falls under the **readers, writers, and texts** area of exploration: '*How do literary texts offer insights and challenges?*'

If you are drawn to an individual short literary text, or if the **intertextuality** area of exploration appeals to you, you may want to consider aspects of an author's work that go beyond an individual short literary text studied in class. The importance is not the number of works you use, but the approach. For example, if you studied *The Metamorphosis* in class, you may want to explore an aspect of Kafka's text, say, the function of doors, in another text, e.g. *The Trial*, to see if the image is used in a different context with similar function, i.e. as a representation of the insulating and isolating features of the central character's world. This speaks to the broader intertextual concept of 'how diverse literary texts share points of similarity'.

Info box

When a text is a collection of short stories, poems, or song lyrics, or a short literary work, you may opt to focus on more than one text if you need to achieve a broader literary investigation.

Course concepts ▶

Another way to develop a topic from a broad literary perspective is to consider your chosen text in relation to one of the seven central concepts of the course: **identity**, **culture**, **creativity**, **communication**, **transformation**, **perspective**, and **representation**. While it is not necessary for you to trace your essay topic back to one of these concepts, working with these concepts allows you to question a work using the concept as a springboard for refining your ideas and narrowing your argument. Below, you will find broad inquiry questions for three of the seven concepts. The remaining concepts and corresponding inquiry questions are listed on pages 12–15 of the Detailed overview chapter.

Identity

- Consider the identity of the writer. How might knowledge of the writer's culture and context (**time and space**) inform our understanding of a text?

- What about the identity of the characters? How are these identities established?

- What textual features help us understand how characters identify with each other and themselves?

- How does your own identity affect the way you interpret meaning from a text?

Communication

- How is communication between readers and writers established through literary texts?

- How do authorial choices and/or textual features affect this communication?

- To what extent does the time and space in which a text is created, and the culture and context in which a reader resides, influence the process of communication?

- How can researching an author's culture, context, and literary style help you better understand what the author is trying to communicate?

- How can communicating about a literary work with peers help build knowledge of the text?

Representation

- What is the definition of literary **representation**?

- How does the representation (physical format) of a work affect how it is interpreted?

- How are such representations expressed across the literary forms?

- How does the representation of a drama or a poem as a written piece of text transform once it is performed?

The importance of literary form and conventions

While the HL essay requires a broad perspective, it is important to note that this perspective must include a literary lens. Below are some ideas that can help you develop a broad investigation that maintains a literary focus.

Your essay must maintain a literary focus.

- If you choose a work of **fiction** for your HL essay, you might decide to focus on one of the following narrative strategies: point of view, plot (momentum, subplots), major and minor characters (foils), time, setting, symbol, style, or theme.

- If you select **poetry**, your focus might include: speaker and tone, diction (denotation/connotation/figurative language), sound effects, structure and form, or theme.

- If you select **drama**, you could focus on one of the following elements: plot and momentum, time, staging (props, lighting, costumes, music, blocking), major and minor characters (foils), conflict (internal and external), audience, dramatic irony, or theme.

- If you select a work of **literary non-fiction**, possible elements of your focus could include: persuasive techniques, rhetorical strategies, authenticity, creating empathy, and philosophical and psychological truths.

Activity 1 Connection between course concepts and literary forms

For this activity, you will consider how course concepts and literary forms and conventions connect to works you have studied.

1) Select at least two works for this activity and fill out the table below. You can align each work to one or more concepts. The full listing of the seven course concepts is on pages 12–15 of the Detailed overview chapter. You will need to review that section to complete this activity.
2) You will find a downloadable version of the table in your eBook. Fill out the table moving from left to right until you have developed some potential topic ideas for your HL essay.
3) Keep a copy of this table in your learner portfolio for reference and add to it as needed.

Work and author	Concept	Notes from concept questions	Notes about literary form and conventions	Potential topic ideas

The importance of the learner portfolio

Depending on the form of the text that you select – drama, poetry, fiction, or literary non-fiction – another starting point to find a topic and line of inquiry that maintains a broader perspective is through examining the entries in your learner portfolio. Throughout the course, you have investigated a number of works from a variety of critical perspectives, lines of inquiry, and the three areas of exploration – readers, writers, and texts, time and space, and intertextuality: connecting texts. Your learner portfolio is literally a rich collection of ideas and approaches that can foster an engaging topic for analysis. Just remember that the work you choose must be substantial enough to support a developed, focused, analytical argument.

Brainstorming/establishing a line of inquiry

A mind map will help you narrow down your ideas to find a line of inquiry.

Keep in mind that this assessment for HL students in Language A: literature serves as a cumulative assessment of your ability to logically and systematically argue a point of understanding or an insight about a text you have studied carefully in class over a period of time. Depending on the timeline that your teacher sets for this assessment, you may have as many as six or seven works to choose from. Determining which text to write about may take some time, but once you have selected your text and have a general topic in mind, you can begin the process of narrowing that topic to find a line of inquiry or argument. You can use various brainstorming activities to narrow the topic, including mind mapping or other visual thinking routines such as free-writing, clustering/webbing, listing, or asking 'What?', 'So what?', or 'Now what?'

The intention of any brainstorming activity is to provide you with a way to move from a straightforward understanding of the literal meaning of a work to a separate, more synthesised or analysed understanding of that work. 'Thinking' about a work implies a process of sorting, comparing, or speculating about the work in such a way that leads to new perceptions, understanding, questions, or reactions to that work. This kind of thinking can be further developed through class discussions, individual and group projects, and learner portfolio assignments which may move your initial understandings of the work to more complex, logical interpretations. Sometimes, however, you may find it difficult to move to this level of response. Brainstorming can provide opportunities to create visuals that will help you see the relationships between your initial ideas through generating, sorting, and arranging. Ideally, this brainstorming process will lead you to an assertion about the work that can be argued systematically and convincingly with relevant textual evidence.

What are some of these brainstorming strategies?

Mind mapping is organised around a central idea and works like the branches of a tree. Ideas and then subsequent ideas that are associated with the main idea branch off from the central idea. As the tree 'grows' in size, so does the number of ideas about the subject and the specificity of ideas.

Free-writing is a timed activity where you choose a topic, idea, or question that you want to explore – a broad concept or a specific detail – and write non-stop for a designated period of time, say 3–5 minutes, on that topic. Spelling, grammar, and punctuation do not matter. The idea is to generate as many ideas as you can in that time period. Your writing doesn't have to make sense to anyone but you.

Free-writing involves generating as many ideas as possible on a specific topic, idea, or question in a short period of time.

If you run out of ideas, you should ask yourself 'What else?' about one or more of the ideas that you have generated. This process may help you discover something that you have not thought of about your topic, and move you closer to finding a line of inquiry for that topic.

Clustering/webbing is also a timed activity. Put a word in the centre of a piece of paper and draw a circle around it. As fast as you can, on any part of the page, jot down free-association words (words that you believe are associated with the centre word). If you get stuck, go back to the centre word and go in another direction. Speed is important, and quantity is the aim in this activity. When the time period ends, examine the seemingly random list of words all over the page and find some that can be grouped together (use a colouring system). The connections may lead you to a line of inquiry: an assertion that is arguable.

Asking 'What?', 'So what?', or 'Now what?' is a brainstorming activity that requires you to write a one-page answer to the question, *'What do I want to explore?'* After reading what you have written, ask *'So what?'* and write a one-page response to that question. Finally, ask *'Now what?'* and consider where you might go forward with your idea.

Take a look at the two brainstorming examples below. One is a clustering activity while the other is a mind map.

A mind-mapping activity for *The Great Gatsby*

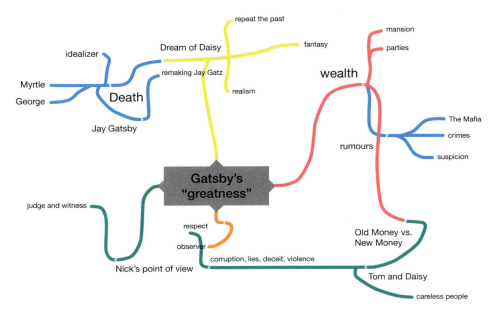

A clustering activity for *The Great Gatsby*

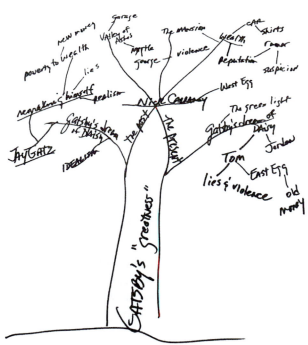

Narrowing your line of inquiry

Whatever topic you select to construct your line of inquiry/thesis/argument, remember that the purpose of this essay is to write an argument about some aspect of the text, not a description of the aspect. Your analysis will be grounded in a thesis statement that is valid and interesting and adds to our understanding of the text. Such a thesis avoids an obvious or self-evident claim – which means it won't argue a conclusion that many readers could determine on their own simply from reading the text. It also means that the main points are supported with strong evidence from the text. And, finally, an arguable thesis uses careful reasoning to show how textual evidence supports the main points of the argument.

Activity 2 Thesis statements

Below you will see paired examples of thesis statements about a given text. Based on your reading of this chapter so far, which sample would meet the standard of an *arguable* thesis – a thesis that can be argued – rather than a purely *descriptive* thesis that can only be developed by 'retelling' parts of the text?

Consider the following pairs of potential thesis statements. Which is clearly descriptive and which is arguable?

1) Dalene Matthee uses fog in *Fiela's Child* whenever Benjamin is confused about himself, his situation, or others.

   The motif of fog in Matthee's *Fiela's Child* functions to underscore Benjamin's journey from ignorance to truth.

2) The train in Dürrenmatt's *The Visit* progresses from an essentially comic device to a symbolic representation of the losses to humanity that come with progress.

   The sound of the rushing train in Dürrenmatt's *The Visit* interrupts the conversations of the townspeople at critical moments.

3) Senghor's use of rhyme in his poetry works to underscore his questioning of Western values.

   Senghor's poetry reveals his questioning of Western values and ideals.

4) The concepts of beauty and order in Jean Rhys's *Wide Sargasso Sea* allow for a deeper understanding of Rochester's need for power and control over Antoinette.

   Rochester and Antoinette define beauty differently throughout *Wide Sargasso Sea*.

5) In Arundhati Roy's *The God of Small Things*, the evils of the caste system are explored.

   Roy's choice to structure *The God of Small Things* in two distinct time frames serves to intensify the reader's sympathy for Rahel and Esta.

Activity 3 Thesis statements in more detail

Are there any specific words in the 'arguable' thesis statements that you identified above that signalled an assertion that could be argued? What are these words? Why are they considered argumentative?

Narrowing your topic and thesis: an example

In this example, a student is interested in exploring the concept of identity in her two favourite texts, *The Great Gatsby* and *The House of the Spirits*. She finds it interesting that in both novels a major character had varying, if not contrasting, presentations. She wondered how a reader knew which perspective to believe. Is Jay Gatsby, in *The Great Gatsby*, a victim of his own heart or a mysterious, unscrupulous man who thinks he can buy anything, including Daisy? Or, is Esteban Trueba in *The House of the Spirits* a ruthless, selfish, and cruel man whose love can never be trusted because he loves only himself?

To help her select one of the texts, she then returned to an exercise in her learner portfolio which explored the function of point of view to reveal and conceal information. In that activity she and her peers were tasked with determining the value of a single, first-person narrator as compared with a third-person limited or omniscient narration. Her notes led her to select *The Great Gatsby* as her text and the effects of first-person narration as her topic. The question she then asked herself was 'How can a first-person narrator provide multiple understandings of a protagonist?' And her second question was 'What function does point of view have in interpretation?'

Once she decides on the text and the topic of her investigation, she will pursue her line of inquiry through brainstorming, mind mapping, listing, asking questions, and creating visible thinking routines which will help narrow her topic and establish a clear argument or thesis. (See the two brainstorming examples that were provided earlier in this chapter.)

Now consider some questions that arise from her visual thinking routine:

- What is 'romantic' about the relationship between Gatsby and Daisy?

- Who is Tom a foil for?

- Is there any character in this novel that is not corrupt in some way?

- What role does innocence play in this novel?

- Why is Nick the ideal narrator? What does he alone possess that enables him to judge Gatsby as 'great'?

Remember that her goal is to write a clearly focused, analytical argument, examining the work from a broad literary perspective where she adheres to the formal framework of the academic essay, using citations and references.

Her narrowed, analytical thesis reads:

> *As the narrator of* The Great Gatsby, *Nick Carraway ultimately judges Jay Gatsby as 'great' man. To validate his judgement, Nick provides numerous perspectives of Gatsby from other characters, but his function in the text is ultimately to filter and refine those opinions so that we believe and accept his pronouncement of the 'great' Gatsby. Nick Carraway is not an unbiased narrator.*

Use your learner profile to help you develop ideas.

Activity 4 Exploring the pre-writing process

Using **two** texts of your own choice not studied in your IB Language A: literature course, apply these pre-writing steps:

1) Begin with a short list of potential texts to use in this activity and then decide on **two** texts that you can use either because of a *question* you have about your understanding of the text, or an *observation* on some aspect of the work that is at the heart of your interpretation of it.
2) Then, ask yourself questions (who, what, where, why, or significance) that address your initial question and/or observation for each text.
3) Now, determine which text offers the most interesting questions and use that **one** text for the remainder of this activity. Can you identify a topic or establish a line of inquiry?
4) Brainstorm your topic using a visual thinking routine or mind mapping.
5) From this brainstorming activity, can you determine some aspect of the topic that you believe is important to explore? Write a few questions that arise from your brainstorming activity. Could one of these questions be turned into an assertion or a claim that you could argue?
6) Write down your thesis (your claim or assertion that can be argued).

Activity 5 Finding textual evidence

The pre-writing process above also requires that you find textual support within your primary text which can sustain your argument and provide evidence to support your thesis. This evidence should be convincing and contribute to the persuasiveness of your essay. If you cannot find enough direct textual evidence, then you more than likely have a topic or an argument that is superficial, primarily descriptive, or lacks a clear understanding of the text.

Using the texts you selected in Activity 4, find 8–10 textual references that you could cite as evidence to support your thesis. Be sure to pare your citations down into shorter phrases that would be easier to incorporate into your own sentences. Be sure to include a page number for each citation in parentheses.

The writing process

Stages, deadlines, and academic integrity

Even though you will select the text and topic for your essay independently, consulting with your teacher is an essential aspect of the writing process. Your teacher will review your topic to make sure that it is a suitably broad literary investigation – one that can be focused into a reasoned argument that can be purposefully arranged into a convincing, textually supported analysis. Your teacher will monitor your progress by establishing timelines for different parts of the essay development and will provide feedback on your initial plans for the essay. The help, guidance, and support that your teacher provides will include advice on the appropriateness of your ideas, questioning to help you clarify your position, and suggestions that might lead you to adjust your approach to your topic. Your teacher will **not** assign the text or the topic, nor will they edit or correct your work – so don't even ask. They will, however, give you advice on your text selection, topic, and thesis, as well as on your first draft. Your teacher can make these suggestions through the form of marginal annotations on your paper – notes or questions that suggest how your essay could be improved. Your teacher will not, however, make those changes for you. This essay is, after all, your own, and it is extremely important that you remind yourself of this point throughout all of the stages of this writing process. The concept of academic integrity extends to every classroom activity as well as to those assessments that you create, in part or wholly, outside the classroom.

> ### Connections
>
> In practising academic integrity, you acknowledge that the academic world is built upon ideas and words. The IB learner profile lists 'principled' as one of ten attributes valued by IB World Schools. To be principled is to 'act with integrity and honesty, with a strong sense of fairness and justice, and with respect for the dignity and rights of people everywhere. We take responsibility for our actions and their consequences.'

At its core, academic integrity assumes a belief in the integrity of ideas and a respect for the words that comprise those ideas. The academic world at all levels – primary, secondary, collegiate, and beyond – is built upon this belief. Ideas and words are the currency of academia and those who participate in it must acknowledge this fact. Plagiarism (taking ideas or words from another source without crediting the source) in academia is theft. Always cite your source material – primary sources (the literary texts themselves) and secondary sources (published critical writings about those texts).

You are expected to make detailed references to your chosen primary text in the HL essay, using direct citations and paraphrased references to support your argument. Citing this textual evidence, showing direct support from the text to persuade your reader that your argument is valid, is central to the effectiveness of your essay – well-chosen, textual evidence moves your essay from generally adequate to the level of convincing and insightful. Secondary sources are not mandatory, but all sources should be cited using the standard for your school. Be sure to use correct manuscript form, incorporating your cited material seamlessly into your own sentences where possible, while correctly placing quotation marks, commas, and end marks (periods/ full stops, question marks, exclamation points) within those sentences. See examples of internal parenthetical citations using the MLA (Modern Language Association) style sheet below:

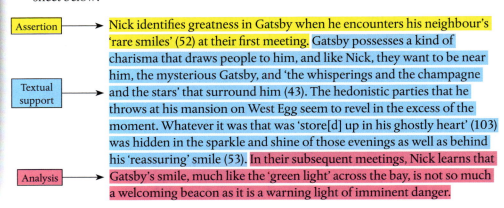

Assertion → Nick identifies greatness in Gatsby when he encounters his neighbour's 'rare smiles' (52) at their first meeting. Gatsby possesses a kind of charisma that draws people to him, and like Nick, they want to be near him, the mysterious Gatsby, and 'the whisperings and the champagne **Textual support** → and the stars' that surround him (43). The hedonistic parties that he throws at his mansion on West Egg seem to revel in the excess of the moment. Whatever it was that was 'store[d] up in his ghostly heart' (103) was hidden in the sparkle and shine of those evenings as well as behind his 'reassuring' smile (53). In their subsequent meetings, Nick learns that **Analysis** → Gatsby's smile, much like the 'green light' across the bay, is not so much a welcoming beacon as it is a warning light of imminent danger.

Note that the effective incorporation of textual citations is a 'seamless' effort that blends well with the writer's own assertion and analysis. Sentences flow smoothly with grammatical precision. In fact, the incorporation is so smooth that there is little consideration of which words belong to the writer of the essay and the text itself. The citations themselves are embedded within the sentences without calling attention to themselves.

Strategies for developing an arguable thesis

In Chapter 1.2 Approaches to learning in drama, you saw a variety of approaches to Ibsen's play, A Doll's House. What follows are responses based upon those activities. You will note that the process from learner portfolio activity to student essay seldom proceeds in a direct line. Activities in the learner portfolio are opportunities to establish a topic or lines of inquiry about a particular text, either individually or with peers. And, as such, these different approaches to lines of questioning and topic selection can take off in many directions – sometimes blending and merging ideas, sometimes abandoning an initial direction or interpretation, and other times seeing that an initial observation was biased and could not be defended through the textual evidence itself.

Allowing yourself to ask questions about questions will enable you to narrow your topic significantly and at the same time help you generate more and more textual evidence to support your argument. Questions are like springboards into ideas and observations that you have about a text. With each question you enter the surface of the text, and each answer becomes the subject of a subsequent question. As you dive even deeper into the text with this question/answer/question process, you are also narrowing and refining your initial observation. On the surface, this approach may seem flawed, but it isn't. How can expanding your questions about a text, a topic, or an observation lead you to a more narrowed argument or thesis? You will see an example of this narrowing strategy later in this chapter.

In the following section, you will be examining the thinking practice behind essay writing.

Let's assume that you are in the planning stages for writing your Language A: literature HL essay. You know that you want to write about Henrik Ibsen's A Doll's House, but you do not have a topic in mind initially. So, you decide to take a look at the work you did on A Doll's House in your learner portfolio, focusing on the prompts and specific questions. Sometimes, the prompts themselves can lead you to consider a topic that you can narrow into an argument. Understand, too, that often the format of exercises provided for the study of one text can be used for other texts as well. This point reinforces why your learner portfolio is such a valuable tool in generating topics and lines of inquiry for the HL essay.

The learner portfolio activities listed below are modified from those of pages 100–101 in Chapter 1.2, Approaches to learning in the conventions of drama. Re-examining these activities will be helpful in developing an arguable thesis for a HL essay on some aspect of Ibsen's A Doll's House.

The following activities are steps in a process that can be used for the analysis of any text.

Activity 6 *A Doll's House* oral presentation

1) Read the first act of *A Doll's House* by Ibsen before moving on to the next part of this activity.
2) Look back at your learner portfolio, to the exercises you completed on pages 100–101 of the drama chapter (1.2), and examine your individual responses to Activity 12, numbers 1–6, as well as your earlier group responses to the three bullet points.
3) Now, in a different group configuration, discuss your observations about those same three bullet points. Feel free to modify any of your earlier assumptions about these points.
4) Then, individually, select one of the six scenes that you believe reflects one or more of the three bullet points and prepare a two minute presentation that convincingly argues your position.

Activity 7 A debate

After the two-minute oral presentations, in teams of four or five prepare **one** of the following in a debate format:
- Are values, ideals, and truths synonymous? Do they change over time? Are they culturally or personally defined?
- Ask yourself what values, ideals, and truths you have? Do these values get challenged very often? How or why would this happen? What results from these challenges?
- Are ideals personal or social constructs designed as a measure to judge behaviours? Where do they come from? Can an ideal ever be reached?

Activity 8 Exploring dualities within *A Doll's House*

Choose one set of dualities and develop a visible thinking routine for one character:
- fear and secrets
- self and other
- responsibility and risk
- truth and power
- perpetrator and victim.

Activity 9 Complementary characters

1) What are the differences between the values, ideals, and truths of these characters: Nora Helmer, Torvald Helmer, Kristine Linde, Nils Krogstad, and Dr Rank?
2) Briefly note what you believe each of these characters would say is the most important character trait and/or moral belief that they have.
3) Can you make a case for two characters that you see as 'complementary' to each other in terms of their beliefs? Remember that 'complementary' characters need

not be opposites – though they could be. Complementary implies connection, balance, working together (in some sense) to make a point that the playwright believes is important. Do you believe that one of these characters functions as the playwright's/Ibsen's mouthpiece? Do Ibsen's values, ideas, and truths present themselves literally or ironically?

Connections

These learner portfolio activities reference many possible topics, from gender interactions to the concepts of truth and power, and the idea of complementary characters.

Stating the argument – the introductory paragraph

As the first paragraph of your essay, the introduction has several purposes:

- to catch the reader's interest

- to provide essential background about the literary work (author, title)

- to prepare your reader for the thesis (last sentence or sentences of the paragraph) so that it does not seem arbitrarily tacked on by making an attempt to link the thesis to the sentence that precedes it by building on a key word or idea.

The introductory paragraph has three distinct purposes.

Activity 10

In this activity, examine the introductory paragraph below and determine:

1) What is the nature of the argument described in this introductory paragraph?
2) Is the argument stated specifically? Paraphrase the argument.
3) Does the argument have more than one assertion? What are the assertion(s)?
4) What can you anticipate about this essay in terms of the order of presentation? Can you determine the subject of some body paragraphs?

Ibsen's *A Doll's House* presents an engaging view of late 19th-century family life in Norway through the marriage of Nora and Torvald Helmer. On its surface, the play works as a cautionary tale about the dangers of deceit. In the opening scene, Nora lies to her husband about consuming macaroons, a seemingly playful and benign behaviour, but this behaviour sets up what is to follow: a deeper revelation of lies, deceit, and corruption ending in the destruction of the marriage itself. The playful bantering between Nora and Torvald lays the foundation of the play's initial premise that Nora's power is equated with her ability to seduce and manipulate. Flirtation is her game and she plays it masterfully. She pretends to be a weak, silly woman, unable to manage her money, eager at the prospect of her husband, Torvald's, promotion and accompanying raise. What Torvald doesn't know is that Nora has managed money quite well, budgeting her household allowance and doing sewing work on the side to earn extra money to pay off a loan that she secured years ago without Torvald's knowledge. Ironically, the revelation of Nora's secret serves as a catalyst to the revelation of other characters' secrets — Dr Rank, Kristine Linde, Nils Krogstad, and Torvald each has a secret revealed through the course of the play, but only Nora's secret strips away the pretense of social norms and replaces them with a stark depiction of personal freedom.

Developing the argument – the body paragraphs

Body paragraphs support the argument, systematically and logically. Each body paragraph develops a part of the argument. The ordering of these body paragraphs is by no means arbitrary. The ordering of body paragraphs is a purposeful arrangement, essential to the logical development of the thesis. Each body paragraph will build upon the previous one, adding a new assertion and the textual evidence to convince and persuade the reader that the position taken in the thesis is valid and deserves consideration as an interpretation of the text.

Keep in mind that transitions within and between paragraphs allow your reader to follow your argument closely, seeing it carefully develop over the course of the essay.

> The ordering of body paragraphs is a purposeful arrangement essential to the logical development of the thesis.

Connections

Turn any of your ideas from activities 6–10 into a five-minute speech. Pretend you have to give the speech to your classmates. How would you begin your speech? What is your main point? What key information will you include? How much detail do you need to give your listener? What evidence will be most convincing or compelling for your audience? This is an exercise in narrowing, specifying, and ordering your brainstorming. Sometimes talking out ideas makes it easier to render them to paper.

Developing the argument – the concluding paragraph

The concluding paragraph should not simply restate the ideas present in the introductory paragraph. Instead, the purpose of the conclusion is to bring closure to the assertion you offered in your thesis statement and subsequently argued throughout the body of the essay. This closure can take several forms – from an evaluation of how well the thesis reflects on the text as a whole to an assertion as to how acceptance of the argument will lead to a deeper, perhaps more complex, understanding of the characters and the themes that emerge from their interactions. Another possibility is that you can assert how acceptance of your thesis will lead to clarification or an increased understanding of other aspects of the text that may have seemed incidental or insignificant.

Your conclusion can take several forms.

Understanding the HL essay criteria

Take a look at the two sections below. Both will help you better understand how your essay will be assessed.

Description of the HL assessment criteria

Criterion A: Knowledge, understanding, and interpretation

This criterion assesses your knowledge, understanding, and interpretation of your chosen text through the specific textual references.

Your references should:

- show that you not only know, but also understand the text that you read

- support your topic of analysis (thesis) in a purposeful rather than arbitrary way

- allow your ideas to be convincingly argued.

Criterion B: Analysis and evaluation

This criterion assesses your ability to offer an insightful and convincing analysis and evaluation of the textual features and/or authorial choices.

Your analysis and evaluation should:

- offer more than a description of some aspect of the text – a description frequently retells or describes the text and does not assert a claim or an inference that could be argued

- demonstrate an appropriate analysis of a topic that offers insight to the text

- evaluate the textual features and/or the broader authorial choices in relation to the topic.

Criterion C: Focus, organisation, and development

This criterion assesses your ability to develop a line of inquiry/thesis in an organised and cohesive manner, and your ability to integrate supporting examples into the sentences and paragraphs of your essay.

Your focus, organisation, and development should:

- demonstrate that the line of inquiry/thesis is developed as a cohesive argument

- demonstrate an organisational structure that is purposeful rather than random

- ensure that the essay reads logically with clear transitions within and between paragraphs

- ensure that supporting examples are well integrated into the body of the essay.

Criterion D: Language

This criterion assesses your use of language – your grammar, accuracy of vocabulary, sentence structure, and style.

Your use of language should:

- demonstrate language that is clear and carefully chosen

- indicate accuracy in grammar, vocabulary, and sentence construction

- show that register and style are effective and appropriate to the task.

Please note that a charted form of the HL essay assessment criteria is provided on page 291. You can download a copy of the form for your own use in your learner portfolio.

External assessment criteria – higher level (HL) essay (2021 onwards)

Criteria	0	1	2	3	4	5
Criterion A: Knowledge, understanding, and interpretation	The work does not reach a standard described by the descriptors.	There is little knowledge and understanding of the work or text shown through the essay chosen. References to the work or text are infrequent or are rarely appropriate in relation to the chosen topic.	There is some knowledge and understanding of the work or text shown through the essay in relation to the topic chosen. References to the work or text are at times appropriate in relation to the chosen topic.	There is satisfactory knowledge and understanding of the work or text shown through the essay and an interpretation of its implications in relation to the topic chosen. References to the work or text are generally relevant and mostly support the candidate's ideas in relation to the chosen topic.	There is good knowledge and understanding of the work or text shown through the essay and a sustained interpretation of its implications in relation to the topic chosen. References to the work or text are relevant and support the candidate's ideas in relation to the chosen topic.	There is excellent knowledge and understanding of the work or text shown through the essay and a persuasive interpretation of their implications in relation to the chosen topic. References to the work or text are well chosen and effectively support the candidate's ideas in relation to the chosen topic.
Criterion B: Analysis and evaluation	The work does not reach a standard described by the descriptors.	The essay is descriptive and demonstrates little relevant analysis of textual features and/or the broader choices in relation to the chosen topic.	The essay demonstrates some appropriate analysis of textual features and/or the broader authorial choices in relation to the chosen topic, but is reliant on description.	The essay demonstrates a generally appropriate analysis and evaluation of textual features and/or the broader authorial choices in relation to the chosen topic.	The essay demonstrates an appropriate and at times insightful analysis and evaluation of textual features and/or the broader authorial choices in relation to the chosen topic.	The essay demonstrates a consistently insightful and convincing analysis and evaluation of textual features and/or the broader authorial choices in relation to the chosen topic.
Criterion C: Focus, organisation, and development	The work does not reach a standard described by the descriptors.	Little organisation is present. No discernible line of inquiry is apparent in the essay. Supporting examples are not integrated into the structure of the sentences and paragraphs.	Some organisation is apparent. There is little development of a line of inquiry. Supporting examples are rarely integrated into the structure of the sentences and paragraphs.	The essay is adequately organised in a generally cohesive manner. There is some development of the line of inquiry. Supporting examples are sometimes integrated into the structure of the sentences and paragraphs.	The essay is well organised and mostly cohesive. The line of inquiry is adequately developed. Supporting examples are mostly well integrated into the structure of the sentences and paragraphs.	The essay is effectively organised and cohesive. The line of inquiry is well developed. Supporting examples are well integrated into the structure of the sentences and paragraphs.
Criterion D: Language	The work does not reach a standard described by the descriptors.	Language is rarely clear and appropriate; there are many errors in grammar, vocabulary, and sentence construction; there is little sense of register and style.	Language is sometimes clear and carefully chosen; grammar, vocabulary, and sentence construction are fairly accurate, although errors and inconsistencies are apparent; the register and style are to some extent appropriate to the task.	Language is clear and carefully chosen with an adequate degree of accuracy in grammar, vocabulary, and sentence construction despite some lapses; register and style are mostly appropriate to the task.	Language is clear and carefully chosen, with a good degree of accuracy in grammar, vocabulary, and sentence construction; register and style are consistently appropriate to the task.	Language is very clear, effective, carefully chosen, and precise, with a high degree of accuracy in grammar, vocabulary, and sentence construction; register and style are effective and appropriate to the task.

Evaluating the HL essay

Activity 11 Applying the rubric using the assertion/support/analysis model

With a partner, using the colour-coded annotations below and the detailed HL essay criteria on pages 289 and 290, determine the areas of strength and areas of weakness for the following essay. The areas of strength and weakness correspond to the four assessment criteria for this task:

- Criterion A: Knowledge, understanding, and interpretation
- Criterion B: Analysis and evaluation
- Criterion C: Focus, organisation, and development
- Criterion D: Language.

Annotation codes:

- assertions marked in yellow
- textual support marked in turquoise
- analysis marked in pink
- faulty integration of citations/quotation incorporation/parenthetical notes marked in bright green
- focus, organisation, development/clear transitions within and between paragraphs marked in grey
- errors in grammar, punctuation, vocabulary, and syntax highlighted in red
- vague generalisations, clichés, redundancies, and awkward or unclear word choice marked in red.

The sun as a symbol of truth in Albert Camus' *The Outsider*

In this essay it will be argued that the sun functions as a symbol of truth in Camus' *The Outsider*. The type of truth that is represented through this symbol is one of meaninglessness. Whilst Meursault, the protagonist, responds to it in an unthinking existential manner, society, emblematised by the justice system and the conventions of mourning, filters it and thus tries to prevent the truth from being known. The essay will examine this idea by discussing the use of the symbol in different passages of *The Outsider* with reference to the use of the style of the narrative and how this develops the characterisation of the protagonist.

... The style of the novel and the way that it evolves tells the reader much about the significance of the sun. Indeed, as the narrative of the first part unfolds and the sun reaches its zenith in a type of ongoing day, the sentences become more and more expressive. This progression is slow and it needs to be charted carefully.

At first bald statements such as 'it was very hot' (Camus 9) and 'it was a very bright room' (12) mirror the famous opening line of the novel 'Mother died today' (9) and the dispassionate description of the morgue and its inhabitants. This factual style suggests, like the undeniable heat of the sun, that the death of Meursault's mother is a hard fact with little meaning attached to it. Meursault expresses little emotional reaction to the death and seems to accept it in the same matter-of-fact manner of the style in which all of this is being told. The sun makes him sleepy and is described as 'beautiful' (13): Meursault is lulled by its presence but adds little comment to its potency and merely reminds the reader that it is there.

The next day, during the burial procession, the sun's intensity increases and so too does the expressivity of the narrative: the sun 'was beginning to weigh down heavily on the earth […] with the whole landscape flooded in sunshine and shimmering in the heat' (20). At the same time Meursault's narration becomes more and more impressionistic and poetic: he speaks of the 'heat-haze' (21), blood pounding in his temples(22) and gives the reader a series of fragmented images: 'the blood-red earth tumbling onto mother's coffin, the white flesh of the roots mixed in with it, more people, voices, the village' (22). All the while the sun has become so hot that it bursts open the tarmac of the road. Meursault has become so tired that he 'cannot see or think straight anymore' hence the style of the narration has become something of a stream of consciousness.

Therefore the sun represents the uncomfortable and inexorable fact of the mother's death in the first few chapters of the novel. This fact becomes increasingly oppressive as the sun's power radiates more and more heat, causing the narrative to enter into a slightly blurred internal monologue. In this way the sun also serves as a type of barometer for Meursault's act of narrating as it mirrors the change in his mental state.

… The truth of death is echoed by the truth of sensuality as the next major description of the sun comes with the time Meursault spends with Marie the next day by the sea. The poetic description of the 'whole sky' in Meursault's eyes shimmering in 'blue and gold' (24) correlates with the simple activities he engages in with Marie, swimming, lying on her stomach and laughing childishly. There is a simplicity in their interaction that represents a pure and unequivocal truth, that of the elements and the body. It is in this regard that we can look at the work as existentialist as the sheer uncommented existence of Meursault and Marie takes precedence over all else: the death of the mother; the protocol of mourning and the ethics of their relationship are swept under the carpet and instead of this there is a simple physical attraction.

… The climax of the sun's meaningless truth comes with the killing of the Arab on the beach at the end of the first part. The description of the sun is very powerful and mesmerising: 'The sea swept ashore a great breath of fire. The sky seemed to be splitting from end to end and raining down sheets of flame' (60). The sun is described as a 'dazzling spear', a 'flashing sword' and a 'red-hot iron', all connoting violence. Indeed, the use of the weaponry imagery furthers the idea that the sun is entering into Meursault, penetrating him and burning its way to his core (he describes it as 'gnawing' at him). At this high point of tension the style of the novel is at its most expressive and poetic: the reader is no longer within the tightly controlled and minimalistic voice of Meursault but deep in the throes of a type of vox dei that has taken control and swept up all in its fiery path. The truth of the sun is at its purest.

… This is the turning point in the novel as Meursault is knocking on the door of unhappiness and deciding his fate that will end with his execution. The sun at this point, at its most commanding, represents the utter meaninglessness of the act that Meursault perpetrates as he is now pushing himself into an act that later he will not be able to explain or justify, it is simply, as he states later in the trial, because of 'the sun' (99).

The second part of the novel dedicated to the trial is quite different in the way that the style builds up and as it concerns the sun as a symbol of the truth. Although the idea remains intact, the sun is less present and the theme of truth is played out in the shade of the court room. The style is, accordingly, fairly minimalistic and straightforward.

... Subtle hints tell the reader that the truth is not allowed to shine in the court; the prosecutor and journalists, representing a lie to portray Meursault as a type of monster, all have 'straw fans' (86) as if to protect them from the heat of the truth. The sun is less present in this part of the narrative, it is filtered by a 'net curtain' (66) in the lawyer's office and blinds (81) in the latter part of the trial. At the same time the style of the narrative is less expressive and more matter-of-fact, merely pointing to the ruthless indictment of Meursault by the prosecution and the way that the witnesses are manipulated.

... Interestingly, Meursault remarks that when it begins to get hot events seem to take their toll. He says: 'I knew that as soon as it began to get hot something was going to happen to me' (80). This indicates that the sun somehow creates action or galvanises characters into action, and in this there is a truth albeit an existential one, based simply on things happening and the idea that in the unfolding of events there is a truthfulness that cannot be denied. However, the action that is set in place is one of absurdity as it will be the sentencing of Meursault for the wrong reasons (chiefly the way he behaved at his mother's funeral).

... The emotional intensity of the narrative style increases once more as we approach the end of the novel and Meursault has the conversation about faith with the priest. It is here that he shows real frustration and decisive expression for the first time in the novel. At a crucial point in their conversation, contrasting either man's vision of truth, the priest asks what Meursault sees in the walls of the prison when he stares into them day after day. He claims that 'deep in my [his] heart I know that even the most wretched among you have looked at them [the stones of the wall] and seen a divine face emerging from the darkness.' Meursault replies 'maybe, a long time ago, I had looked for a face in them. But that face was the colour of the sun and burning with desire (page 118).

In conclusion, this essay has shown how the symbol of the sun in *The Outsider* is a complex one that evolves as the narrative develops. It represents the indifferent and ultimately meaningless truth of the world. This idea is suggested by the positive corollary between the intensity of the sun and the way that events take place — the hotter and brighter the sun, the balder and stronger the absurd and meaningless events take that place. In the courtroom, a place of deceit and charades, the sun is filtered and shaded. Camus' novel presents the reader with an omnipotent natural truth that can only be shaded by humans as they try to twist its truth into meaning. Ultimately, the sun exists in spite of human will and Meursault's acceptance of it makes him an existential hero.

Word count: 1499

Camus, Albert. *The Outsider*, (trans. Joseph Laredo) England, Penguin Classics, 1982.

General evaluation comments:

Assertions/arguable observations: *The student makes many valid and interesting assertions/claims that support the overall interpretation.*

Textual support/evidence: *Some good evidence is provided to support assertions, but not all assertions are backed up with textual support/evidence.*

Analysis/argument: *The focus of this somewhat sophisticated interpretation is not always clear. The thesis statement includes symbol, style, and characterisation which are not always clearly connected, resulting in a fragmented structure of the essay/ argument.*

Organisation/focus, development/transitions: *While the line of inquiry is well developed, the essay would benefit from a more precise organisation. Some paragraphs are one or two sentences long, while others are more developed. Transitions within and between paragraphs are not always apparent, which creates a lack of overall coherency.*

Incorporation of textual evidence/parenthetical citations: *Some parenthetical citations are incorporated well. Others are not pared down to a manageable size to incorporate into sentences. Punctuation is not always correct and some stylistic inconsistencies exist.*

Grammar, vocabulary, punctuation, syntax: *While the argument is a sophisticated one, sometimes the language obscures rather than clarifies meaning. Some sentences are unclear as a result of awkward or grammatically incorrect construction.*

Vague generalisations, clichés, redundancies, awkward or unclear word choice: *The more sophisticated the argument, the simpler the language must be to articulate it. This essay often lacks clarity of expression. Many vague generalisations and unclear word choices work against clearly understanding what the direction of the argument is or effectively persuading the reader to see the argument as valid.*

Because this essay is written out of class, the expectation is that there will be a minimum number of stylistic errors. Clarity and precision should be the rule and goal of the HL essay writer.

Activity 12 Examining the process of essay from inception to evaluation

Sample essays A and B below were both developed through using the learner portfolio activities that you have examined in this chapter.

1) Using the sample colour-marked essay above as a guide, highlight the assertions, support, and analysis in each of the sample essays below. You can download and print copies of the sample essay from your eBook.
2) Then compare their strengths and weaknesses using the criterion-based evaluation checklist below.
3) After you have done this task individually, share your responses with a small group and record your findings in your learner portfolio.
4) Write a brief reflection regarding the process and requirements of the HL essay.

Criterion-based evaluation checklist

Criterion A: Knowledge, understanding, and interpretation
- Which essay shows a clearer understanding of the work?
- Which essay makes better use of knowledge and understanding of the work to draw conclusions in relation to the chosen topic?
- Which essay's ideas are better supported by references to the work or text in relation to the chosen topic?

Criterion B: Analysis and evaluation
- Which essay offers a more persuasive interpretation of the text?
- Which essay better analyses and evaluates how the choices in language, technique, style, and broader authorial choices shape meaning in relation to the chosen topic?

Criterion C: Focus, organisation, and development
- Which essay is more effectively focused, organised, and developed?
- Which essay provides well-integrated supporting examples?

Criterion D: Language
- Which essay has more clear, varied, and accurate language?
- Which essay has fewer grammatical errors?
- Which essay is more appropriate in terms of choices of register and style (i.e. which essay shows more appropriate use of elements such as vocabulary, tone, sentence structure, and terminology for the HL essay)?

Sample essay A

The characters in *A Doll's House* differ in their beliefs about values, ideals, and truths and what role truth should play in their families. Nora Helmer cares for her family and makes many sacrifices for them. When Torvald is sick, she forges her father's signature to get money for their trip to Italy. Nora realises her actions are illegal, but she is willing to do whatever it takes to save her husband's life. Torvald, however, runs when it is his turn to sacrifice for his family. Torvald views family as an accessory. He doesn't actually love his wife and refuses to sacrifice anything for her. When Torvald finds out about Nora's forgery, instead of taking the blame upon himself, he scolds her for ruining his reputation. Torvald views Nora as a child and plays with her as one. After Krogstad shares her secret, Torvald explains to Nora how 'play time is over' (81) and now it is the time for lessons. Torvald and Nora have completely different views on family structure.

Nora comes to believe that she is most importantly 'an individual' (82). Torvald, on the other hand, believes Nora is primarily 'a wife and mother' (82). Kristine Linde shares the same traditional view of family that Torvald does. When her mother passes away, she cares for her brothers as a mother would. She marries a man she doesn't love because it benefits her brothers. She believes her duty as a woman is to her family, not herself. Kristine Linde sacrifices her own relationship with Nils Krogstad for what she believes is a better life for her family. She turns down Krogstad's invitation to marry and accepts the practical, though loveless, marriage offer because it will ensure that her brothers will be provided for. Although Krogstad is judged as morally deficient because of his business dealings, he does value family.

Torvald believes Krogstad 'poison[ed] his own children' (33) by his illegal financial dealings and Krogstad seems to agree. His very action of trying to reclaim his job at Torvald's bank implies that by doing so he could reclaim his good moral standing in the community as well. We see this attitude of valuing family when Krogstad speaks with Kristine Linde about the two of them renewing their old relationship. If Kristine will accept him once again, Krogstad doesn't mind sacrificing his plans to work at Torvald's bank. He would give up the fight if Kristine wants him to. He values his relationship with her more than he values his anger and competition with Torvald.

As the only character who questions the structure of the family, Nora Helmer is also consequently challenging the structure of the society at large. Late 19th century Norway is essentially patriarchal — it's a man's world. Nora feels that their society is corrupt and part of that corruption is that women are not valued as individuals in and of themselves. Society values women for what they can add to a man's life — companionship, children, and care. Nora questions 'who is right, society or [herself]?' (76) Torvald has an elitist view and believes that Nora is incapable of understanding the laws and ethics of Norwegian society. Society is right and anyone who questions it is delusional. One of his worst fears is that someone might discover Nora's behaviour, and then he, as her husband, would be judged poorly 'in the eyes of the world' (76). She is like a child that lacks understanding of issues larger than herself. Nora, on the other hand, does what she feels is right and believes that she doesn't need society's consent or permission to make financial decisions for her family. The laws that Torvald defends are 'very bad laws' (29) because they don't consider motive. Nora acted to secure a loan from Krogstad so that her family could travel to Italy, a warmer climate, for her husband's health. She believed that his life depended on this trip. But even after Torvald learns the truth of Nora's IOU with Krogstad and her motivation for doing so, he describes her actions as 'criminal' (76).

Ironically, even Krogstad, who Torvald regards as a criminal who got away with a crime (forgery), believes that Nora's lack of awareness of the seriousness of her crime is the result of her lack of knowledge of the laws and the value system that the laws were built upon. He tries to put Nora in her place by reminding her of the power that the law gives him over her. Nora's flippant disregard of the law is based on her belief that forgery was not such a bad thing to do considering the circumstances. Torvald's health was utmost in her mind and she would and could do anything to save his life. Even Kristine's decision to deny her own happiness to save her brothers' lives, which was regarded as 'magnanimous and self-sacrificing' (67), exposes the society's patriarchal expectations of women. In both cases, Nora and Kristine are limited in the roles that they are allowed to play within society. Limitation rather than openness governs their lives.

Kristine Linde also sees Nora's actions as criminal. She is traditional in respect to the laws that govern society including the one that would demand that Nora have her husband's consent prior to securing a loan from Krogstad. Kristine believes that 'it was rash' (74) to not secure the loan on her own, but also to not tell Torvald the truth about the loan — the truth that she forged her own father's signature to secure the loan. At first Kristine believes that Dr Rank was the man behind the money because she witnesses Nora's flirtatious behaviour around him. Dr Rank dotes on Nora and thinks that she has little understanding or knowledge of what society actually is; her childlike innocence in 'worldly matters' appeals to him and her physical beauty attracts him to her. This flirtation seems innocent enough, or so Nora thinks, until Dr Rank reveals his feelings for her. Nora is content to flirt innocently, but when she realises the extent of Dr Rank's feelings for her, she is alarmed and disgusted that he would think she reciprocated his feelings. Their relationship is now corrupted by Dr Rank's romantic view of her.

At the end of the play, Ibsen makes a clear statement about the nature of family structure in 19th-century Norway. When Nora walks out of Torvald's house, his doll's house, she relinquishes her doll status. For emphasis, she slams the door on the societal values of marriage that Torvald epitomises. For her, the risk beyond that doorway is less frightening than the life she currently leads. She claims herself. No longer a doll, who can be dressed up, cuddled, and played with, she asserts herself as an equal partner in life, deserving of learning what life has to offer her. She demands to know the truth of the world that has been locked away from her, symbolised by the lock on Torvald's office door. She demands entry.

Sample essay B

Each of the main characters in *A Doll's House* has a different understanding of the limitations and excesses of power because they fail to understand the fluid nature of power in all relationships. Nora, on whose decisions the play rests, is clever but doesn't always think through situations. She is attractive and is aware of how men respond to her beauty. She flirts, but seems to do so manipulatively to gain an edge in situations where men have a powerful advantage over her. When Krogstad tells her that her forgery is illegal, Nora brushes him off because she thinks that her good intentions supersede legality. She is insistent that 'the law must say somewhere' (29) that her forgery was acceptable. For her, the law exists outside the walls of her home. Her law is based on doing what is best for her family and herself because Nora is defined by family. Nora also loves living a comfortable life and sees that Torvalds' is the boss, both literally at the bank and at home. He treats her like a father would a child, chiding her for ruining her teeth with sweets, but she tolerates his authority over her, believing that his love for her is patently unconditional. When Torvald learns that Nora has stepped outside of the home and acted, without him, to make a decision, we see that the very nature of his power has been challenged. For Nora, power is fluid and dynamic, flowing beneath the surface of relationships. For Torvald power is a static force; hard to win, it must never be relinquished at any cost. Nora becomes Ibsen's mouthpiece in this play; she reveals the danger of traditional power dynamic in marriage where males have all of the power to act and women's power is to be acted upon.

Contrasting Torvald, Nils Krogstad feels as though he has lost the upper hand/power during most of the play. He understands that he made a bad decision when he forged a document years before, but now he thinks that he is losing opportunities unfairly. Krogstad had 'all paths barred' to him even though the case 'never reached the courts' (25), and so he feels he has been continually punished for an indiscretion and not a crime. He defines his power as coming from outside his family dynamic. A widower, Krogstad must play the role of mother and father to his children. Krogstad's powerlessness comes on two fronts, personal and professional. It seems that throughout the play, Krogstad is trying to reclaim some kind of professional redemption through securing a job with Torvald's bank even though he victimises Torvald's wife to achieve it. We see that it's important for him to at least have the chance to try and redeem himself on some front even though he may destroy someone else's marriage in the process.

Kristine Linde's power comes from her desire to take care of people; selflessness is one of her most prominent traits. When Nora comments that Mrs Linde must be relieved now that she no longer has dependents, Kristine replies that she is not relieved; instead, she feels as though there's 'nobody to live for anymore' (77). Honesty is also important to Mrs Linde; she can look past Krogstad's poor decisions to the honesty inside him. She also makes a decision that is key to the outcome of the play. She believes that 'everything must come out' with regard to Nora's secret loan transaction and the forgery of her father's name to secure it, and so she insists that Krogstad tell the truth. Ironically, once Kristine and Nils decide to restore their relationship, Nils no longer seeks to get even with Torvald through blackmailing Nora. He no longer needs the approval of the outside world. He has found his power through his redemption in his relationship with Kristine and so returns Nora's IOU.

While Kristine Linde is drawn to truth, Nora's husband, Torvald, is drawn to social appearances and his reputation, and he draws power in knowing that he is respected for his steadfast moral reputation. He appreciates Nora's physical beauty and enjoys showing her off at parties. He knows that other men consider him a lucky man to have such a beautiful, seductive woman as his wife. Nora even comments to Kristine that Torvald won't be 'quite so in love' with her 'when [she's] no longer so pretty' as she is now (15). In this way we see that Nora clearly understands that Torvald's values are superficial. Once again, at the play's end, we see this same attitude. Torvald says that he wishes he could risk 'body and soul' for Nora's sake (74) but less than a page later, after he finds out Nora's dirty secret, he doesn't think twice about 'sacrificing his honour' for her (75). In fact, he cares so much about his image, and the power that resides in it, that he wants Nora to remain in the house and pretend that nothing has happened even though he will not allow her to see their children or behave as his wife. They will instead live as brother and sister.

Dr Rank, who seems to be Torvald's closest friend as well as an admirer of Nora, understands that Torvald's inflated image of himself is based on a superficial belief system. Even with the severity of his illness, Dr Rank considers Torvald incapable of dealing with the harshness of his future incapacity and quickly approaching death. He tells Nora that he doesn't want Torvald to visit him when he is ill because he knows that his sickness will upset Torvald because he doesn't like to look at ugly things. Sickness is weakness and power does not like to look upon weakness. This willingness, or lack thereof, to give of oneself to ensure the happiness of someone else is one of the main ways in which Torvald and Dr Rank balance each other and provide an interesting contrast. A second contrast surfaces in their relationship with Nora.

Dr Rank and Nora have frequent conversations and appear to be good friends. When Dr Rank meets Kristine Linde, he recognises her name as one he's 'often heard mentioned in [that] house' (18). Torvald, on the other hand, shows no recognition of her name. We later learn from Nora that she doesn't talk to Torvald about school friends because he becomes jealous. This jealousy serves as an indication that Torvald sees Nora as his own perfect doll, while Rank views her as a woman that he can converse with on a variety of subjects, including his own imminent death and his fears about it. Nora seems to enjoy this friendship, and even though she flirts with Rank on occasion, she sees this behaviour as innocent and harmless because she does not have the slightest intention of venturing beyond surface flirtation. She does not see that power as an essential dynamic in their relationship. However, when Rank begins to declare his feelings for her, she cuts him off, explaining that there are 'those you love' and 'those you'd almost rather be with' (50) as a kind of defence of her verbal intimacy with him. Rank has stepped over the line of propriety and asserts an uncomfortable power over Nora.

In a way, Ibsen creates complementary characters through Torvald and Dr Rank. Together with Nora, they function as Ibsen's mouthpiece about the dangers implicit in power, its excesses and limitations. Nora can successfully maneuver her relationships with men — Torvald, Krogstad, and Dr Rank, manipulating each with her beauty and innocence until each asks her to accept their static definition of power. In this definition of power, Nora is helpless and victimised. She has to play by their rules, the rules of a patriarchal system that remind her at every turn that she is powerless in her position as wife and mother. This truth is realised at the play's end just before Nora walks out and slams the door. She tells Torvald that they have never before had a serious discussion like the one they are now having which is to say that they have never shared the power of their marriage as equal partners. Perhaps this play is a cautionary tale for 19th-century Norway marriages. Flirtation and sexual innuendo will not sustain a successful and happy marriage nor will rigid control — they are toys within a doll house, part of a game that no one wins.

Insights into the HL essay

1. The HL essay requires you to have a broad literary perspective.

2. The learner portfolio can provide you with helpful starting points for determining a text and a topic.

3. The learner portfolio can provide you with insights into establishing a line of inquiry.

4. Brainstorming activities play an important role in helping you determine and narrow a line of inquiry into an arguable thesis.

5. The HL essay requires you to provide a clearly stated arguable thesis about a single text which you have studied in the programme that you have not already used and which you do not plan to use in another assessment.

6. The format of the HL essay includes an introductory paragraph, body paragraphs, and a concluding paragraph.

7. The HL essay will be evaluated on four criteria that are supported by the assertion/support/analysis model.

Extended essay

General overview of the extended essay

The extended essay (EE) is at the heart of the IB core, along with CAS and TOK. The EE is a required component for all students seeking the IB Diploma and ties together several aspects of the IB framework including the **approaches to learning**, the **learner profile**, reflection, and **international-mindedness**. The EE provides an opportunity for you to develop a passion in a discipline that interests you through a serious piece of academic writing. This process will prepare you for university level studies that involve inquiry; allow you to engage with a topic that is meaningful to you; and inspire you to reflect on your academic and personal growth.

The extended essay is at the heart of the IB core.

The extended essay and the IB core

The IB core encourages the interconnectedness of learning. Through CAS you can deepen your knowledge in your subject areas by extending what you learn in class to service learning projects. TOK encourages you to think critically and transfer that critical thinking to all of your areas of knowledge. The EE gives you the opportunity to take research to a new level by exploring a topic through a specific disciplinary or interdisciplinary lens. The core supports the subject disciplines by enabling you to connect and extend your learning both inside and outside the classroom.

The connection between the extended essay and approaches to learning

It is important to remember that the approaches to learning that you have been applying to your English A: literature curriculum apply to all aspects of IB, including the extended essay. Working on your EE will enable you to hone your skills in research, communication, thinking, and self-management, and even social situations, as you work one on one with a supervisor.

The approaches to learning apply to all aspects of the IB, including the extended essay.

Key features of the extended essay

What is the extended essay?

The extended essay is a formal piece of academic research writing of no more than 4000 words accompanied by a required reflection form of no more than 500 words.

What is the extended essay worth?

- The EE in combination with the TOK assessments is worth up to 3 IB Diploma points.

- The point scale is 0–34 and the essay is scored from A–E. A score of E is a fail.

- A passing grade on the EE is mandatory in order to be eligible for the IB Diploma.

How is the extended essay scored?

The EE is scored on the following criteria:

Criterion	Description	Points
A	**Focus and method** topic, research question, methodology	6
B	**Knowledge and understanding** context, subject-specific terminology and concepts	6
C	**Critical thinking** research, analysis, discussion, and evaluation	12
D	**Presentation** structure, layout	4
E	**Engagement** process, research focus	6
Total		34

What do I write about?

- The great stories and discoveries (including self-discoveries) that have marked different cultures through time have all been the product of some form of research, be it formal or informal.

- Many of you will become specialists in a field, and the EE could be the first serious piece of study you undertake in that direction.

- But the EE is not about getting ready for future employment; it is about tapping into a passion you have for learning.

- The IB provides a long and varied list of approved EE subjects, along with subject-specific guidance for writing on your chosen subject.

- If you have a keen interest in a certain subject, writing an EE in this area will help you develop your knowledge and passion in more depth.

Connections

The connection between CAS and EE

Just as CAS encourages you to undertake new challenges, develop skills, and increase your awareness of your own strengths and growth through active learning outcomes, writing an EE reinforces these same skills through an academic lens.

How long does it take to write an extended essay?

The whole process takes approximately 40 hours and you will complete it over the course of your two-year IB diploma programme. Your school will set a timeline that includes initial steps, internal deadlines, and a final completion date.

Who can assist me with the process?

- You will receive support from a supervisor at your school who will spend approximately 3–5 hours with you as you go through the process.

- Supervisors act as guides. They can help you develop your topic and research question, and guide you through the research and writing process. They cannot construct your research question for you, do research on your behalf, or edit your draft.

- Your school librarian is another valuable resource who can help you navigate the research process.

What are mandatory and check-in reflection sessions?

- You will meet with your supervisor for three mandatory reflection sessions – one as you begin your EE journey, one in the midst of your research and writing, and one after you have completed your project.

- In addition to the mandatory reflection sessions, informal check-in sessions are also encouraged as are other communications such as emails or hallway chats.

- The third and final mandatory reflection session is the viva voce, which is the concluding interview with your supervising teacher. The reflection sessions will help you complete your required Reflections on Planning and Progress Form (RPPF) which will be turned in with your EE.

What is the RPPF?

- You will fill out your Reflections on Planning and Progress Form (RPPF) on three separate occasions, directly after each formal reflection meeting with your supervisor. The total word count on your form cannot exceed 500 words.

- The RPPF aligns with Criterion E: Engagement. This means that 6 of the 34 points for the assessment (17%) are devoted to how you reflect on your research and writing experience.

- You will not receive high marks for this criterion if you simply record what you did. Rather, you should aim for meaningful reflections on the effect the EE process had on your personal and academic development.

What is the format of the extended essay?

Your EE should include the following:

- title page (includes title, subject for which the essay is registered, research question, and word count)

- table of contents

- introduction

- body (research, analysis, discussion, evaluation)

- conclusion

- references and bibliography

- appendices (not required, only as needed).

Writing an extended essay in Group 1: studies in language and literature

As you study various works across **time and space** in English A: literature, you will develop:

- skills that enable you to interpret, analyse, and evaluate literary works

- an appreciation of authorial aesthetic (**creative**) choices and how such choices affect meaning in different contexts

- an understanding of relationships between texts and a variety of **perspectives**, cultural contexts, and local and **global issues**

- an appreciation of how various texts contribute to diverse responses and open up multiple meanings.

Studying literature not only provides an appreciation of the subject, but it also enables us to better understand the world around us and our place in it. Writing an EE in a Group 1 subject can further develop this appreciation as you strengthen your academic research and writing skills.

Info box

You cannot write your EE on any text that you are studying in your IB Language A course. However, it is permissible for you to base your EE on different texts by the same author.

Extended essays in Group 1: studies in language and literature fall into one of three categories. The first two categories are geared towards a literature essay, whereas the third category focuses on studies in language. This chapter will provide an overview of all three options.

Options for studies in language and literature extended essays	
Category 1	Studies of one or more literary works originally written in the language in which the essay is presented.
Category 2	Studies of one or more literary works originally written in the language of the essay (English) compared with one or more literary works originally written in another language (translation).
Category 3	Studies in language based on one or more texts originally produced in the language in which the essay is presented. Texts can be compared with a translated text originally written in another language.

General requirements for the extended essay (with subject-specific notes on studies in language and literature extended essays)

As you begin your EE journey, it is important to keep the following topics in mind.

Rationale

- Explain **why** your topic is worthy of investigation. This is important. Beyond the requirements, beyond the score, why have you selected this topic?

- If you are comparing two works, what is the significance of the comparison?

- What might be the point of tracing an image or motif through a novel or series of poems (Category 1 or Category 2) or analysing the significance of a world leader's rhetoric in two different contexts (Category 3)?

It is important to explain why your extended essay topic is worthy of investigation.

- If you can't make sense of a bigger picture, or find a reason for your argument to exist that answers the 'So what?' question, then it will be difficult for your examiner do so as well.

Literature review

- All EEs, regardless of subject, must include a literature review. This means that you need to research and consider what has **already** been written about your topic.

- Unlike the HL essay, which includes a broad literary focus, mainly on a primary text, writing an EE in Group 1 requires you to situate your analysis of your chosen texts in the wider context of the discipline. This could include background

A literature review asks you to consult critical secondary sources.

information about an author, time period, literary genre, or particular techniques.

- Literature does not exist in a vacuum, so it is important to provide a context from which to launch your essay, but this does not mean you should write several pages of unnecessary information that detracts from your argument.

- Always ask yourself: 'Is the contextual information I'm providing helping me to orient my reader to better understand my topic and research question?' 'Am I questioning/developing the views of critics or simply repeating them?' 'Do I end paragraphs with my own thoughts and evaluation rather than those borrowed from others?'

- It is important to remember that the purpose of undertaking a literature review is to contextualise your work to further enhance your own analysis. There is a difference between using secondary sources to develop your ideas at a higher level and allowing the voice of critics to eclipse your own. Extended essays that simply borrow from other sources will not score high marks, particularly under Criterion C: Critical thinking.

Primary vs secondary sources

All EEs will include both primary and secondary sources.

- A primary source includes the novels, poems, plays, or essays by authors whose work is the focus of your research.

- Secondary sources are scholarly works about the primary author's work and biography; the genre you are focusing on (i.e. gothic, dystopian, Greek tragedy); or literary techniques.

- Secondary sources can include books, academic journal articles, edited essays, and reviews.

A word on appendices

- Appendices are not required for EEs and examiners are not required to read them.

- However, if you are writing an essay in studies in language and literature, especially on small works of literature that you analyse in detail, such as poems or speeches, it is very helpful for the examiners to have them as a reference when they are scoring your essay. In this case, you should include the short works in an appendix.

- By the same token, if you are analysing a specific text, such as an advertisement or a panel of a graphic novel, and the analysis is integral to your argument, you should embed the graphic into the body of your essay rather than including it in the appendix. Since examiners are not required to read appendices, you may lose points by excluding essential information from the body of your essay.

Research question

- Formulating a **clear research question** is an important step in writing an effective EE.

- Your research question must be written in the form of a question.

- It must also be specific, sharply focused, and capable of being explored within the 4000-word limit.

- If your research question is too broad, you will have difficulty shaping your argument and addressing your topic within the word limit. If your focus is too narrow or obvious, then you limit your ability to construct a developed analytical argument.

- Consider the difference in the following two Category 1 research questions:
  1. An exploration of setting in Zora Neale Hurston's novel, *Their Eyes Were Watching God*.
  2. How does setting affect the development of Janie's character in Zora Neale Hurston's novel *Their Eyes Were Watching God*?

  Notice how the first question is not phrased as a question, is overly broad, and does not lend itself to the development of a cohesive argument. The second question is sharply focused and connects two different literary aspects – setting and characterisation – to a specific arguable idea.

- Later in this chapter you will have the opportunity to work with studies in language and literature research questions through a hands-on activity.

▲ Formulating a clear research question is an important step in writing an effective extended essay.

Self-management

- As an independent project, the EE requires much planning and discipline on your part. Although your school may set specific deadlines for meeting with your supervisor and completing parts of the essay in stages, the successful completion of this assignment will be up to you.

- This means that you need to build time into your schedule to complete research and reading before written portions are due.

- Your supervisor (and perhaps your school librarian) will be helpful resources, but you should make appointments for meetings (especially your mandatory formal reflective meetings) well in advance.

- Like you, supervisors are busy with their own commitments and will appreciate your proactive approach. Consider sending a short thank you note to your supervisor for taking the time to work with you. Such initiative not only shows your appreciation, but is also an important social skill that will serve you well after your project is completed.

◀ Build time for your extended essay into your schedule.

Academic integrity

- If you are found guilty of academic misconduct, you run the risk of not receiving your IB Diploma.

- The EE is perhaps the most daunting assignment in terms of academic rigour and required documentation.

- Make sure that you fully understand how to cite your works properly. Any information that did not originate in your own mind and is not common knowledge must be cited.

- This cited information could be in the form of direct quotes, summary notes, and/or paraphrases of quoted material.

- Any information that appears in your bibliography must be cross-referenced in the body of your essay.

- Your work will be checked in terms of IB's academic integrity policy.

- Proper documentation takes time. If you are unsure of how to document a source, make sure that you have resources to consult (perhaps your supervisor, your school librarian, or specific citation guides) so that you are sure that your essay meets IB's academic integrity standards.

Double-dipping

You may not base your studies in language and literature EE on any works you are studying in your Language A course, even if you aren't planning on using these works for an assessment. For example, if Ian McEwan's novel *Atonement* is one of the works studied in your Language A: literature course, you may not use that novel for your EE, even if you pair it with another text. You can, however, use other works by McEwan or perhaps explore the literary genre of postmodernism through another author.

The translation rule

- All studies in language and literature EEs must be written in the language of the Language A course. If you are a student of English A: literature, this means that you must write your studies in language and literature EE in English.

- While it is permissible to write about a translated work in this subject area, if you do this you **MUST** pair the translated work with another work originally written in the language of the course. (This pairing is required for Category 2 essays and permissible for Category 3 essays.)

If you write about a translated work, you must pair it with another work originally written in the language of the course.

- If you do **not** include a primary work that is originally written in the language of the essay (i.e. English for English A courses), your essay will be deemed inappropriate for the subject and you will lose 13 points across criteria A, B, and C due to penalty caps.

Additional subject-specific guidance for studies in language and literature extended essays

As mentioned earlier, Category 1 and 2 extended essays include a literary focus while Category 3 extended essays focus on language.

A closer look at Category 1 and 2 requirements and methodology

- Category 1 and 2 EEs always consider how text(s) work as literature, dealing with aspects such as the effects of the devices they use and the way they are written.

- You can choose literary works from any source including the *Prescribed reading list*. Your chosen texts should be of sufficient literary merit.

- Your topic can centre on a global issue arising from a work of literature, but the major focus of your essay should be literary, not social. You must not treat the literary work(s) simply as documentary evidence in a discussion of a particular issue.

For Category 1 and 2 EEs, you will:

- study a topic in depth through a literary lens, engaging in independent literary criticism

- contextualise and develop your arguments with critical comment (to contextualise means to use background sources as a foundation for your argument)

- develop the ability to put forward your views persuasively and in a well-structured manner, using a register appropriate to the study of literature.

In terms of *methodology*, primary methods involve analysing the author's collection of novels, poems, stories, plays, or personal essays. Secondary methods include contextualising your argument with books, journal articles, essays, or reviews about the author's work. The author's biography, literary genre, and techniques are also considered to be part of a qualitative secondary course of research. These secondary sources that are separate from the primary text provide insights into the primary text.

Connections

Secondary sources should support your methodology by helping to develop your argument and analysis within a specific context. Their presence should not pad the essay or include information that is irrelevant to your argument.

In a sense, your HL essay and your individual oral have already started preparing you for writing a solid Category 1 or Category 2 EE.

The connection between Category 1 and 2 extended essays and the HL essay

The HL essay requires you to follow your own line of inquiry on a topic of your choosing and refine your ideas into a focused, analytical argument. IB requires a broad literary perspective for the HL essay, which means that your line of inquiry covers the full texts, rather than extracts, and is derived from broad literary **course concepts** such as 'How do literary texts offer insights and challenges?' or 'How do diverse literary texts share points of similarity?' (These **conceptual questions** are also good starting points for the EE.)

While gothic elements can be explored in both literary EEs and HL essays, the scope of each assessment requires different methodologies.

Of course, the EE requires you to complete a full literature review and include secondary sources. For example, an HL essay may explore the gothic elements in a text such as Oscar Wilde's *The Picture of Dorian Gray*, limiting the argument to how gothic elements are presented in the text itself and how they are expressed through characters or setting.

Writing an EE with a gothic focus would require a different methodology that includes a literature review and a more contextual scope. For example, if you were interested in gothic elements in both Jane Austen's *Northanger Abbey* and Mary Shelley's *Frankenstein*, your literature review in this field would reveal the significance and effects of the gothic genre in a context. After reading some background information along with the primary texts, you might make connections between how the gothic elements in Shelley's text create a physical 'monster' while the mock gothic elements in Austen's text construct an imagined 'monster'. Further secondary reading could help you develop your argument as you answer your research question: 'What role do gothic elements play in producing real and imagined monsters in Mary Shelley's *Frankenstein* and Jane Austen's *Northanger Abbey*?'

The connection between Category 1 and 2 extended essays and the individual oral

While the individual oral requires you to discuss a global issue within a text through a literary lens, you also have the option to focus on a global issue in a literature EE. Global issues cross disciplines, but in literature-based assessments such as the individual oral or a literature EE, you need to focus on the authorial choices and how those choices express the global issue. Should you decide to write your EE on a global issue such as gender inequality, the use and abuse of power, or the effects of technological growth on individuals and societies, then your analysis, interpretation, and evaluation should be grounded in literary aspects of the text such as settings, characterisation, style, symbols, motifs, and narrative strategies. Of course, you will not cover all of these aspects, as your research question and argument should be sharply focused, but your lens should always be literary.

If your selected text for your EE is Alan Moore and Dave Gibbons' graphic novel, *Watchmen,* and your topic (global issue) focuses on how technological advances eclipse social responsibility, your literature review may begin with the context of the Cold War politics of the 1980s in which the novel is set. You might also explore the genre of literary realism and the evolution of the literary superhero. This background reading will help you develop a context for your topic and assist you as you answer your research question: 'To what extent do technological advances in *Watchmen* redefine the role of the hero?'

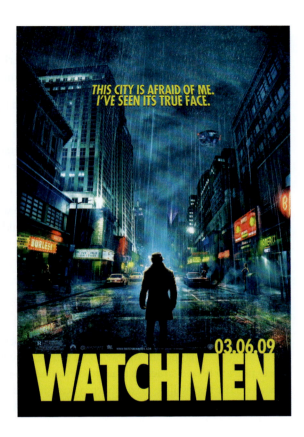

The graphic novel, *Watchmen,* redefines the role and perception of superheroes.

A closer look at Category 3 requirements and methodology

Students who select the Category 3 option for their EEs are often enrolled in the English A: language and literature course, which includes fewer works of literature and an additional focus on rhetoric, language, and non-print media. For Category 3 EEs, the focus is on language and how text works in context. You need to give critical attention to the text(s) being considered. The approach should aim to be balanced, coherently argued, and illustrated by relevant supporting examples. You are encouraged to adopt an analytical, critical position and show awareness of potentially conflicting viewpoints on the texts and their meaning in a wider social context.

For Category 3 extended essays the focus is on language and how text works in context.

For Category 3 EEs, you will:

- demonstrate skills of textual analysis by considering how language, **culture**, and/or context influence the ways in which meaning is constructed in texts

- examine critically the different relationships and interactions that exist between texts, audiences, and purposes

- develop the ability to put forward your views persuasively and in a well-structured manner using a register and terminology appropriate to the subject.

In terms of methodology, you should consider how language develops in specific cultural contexts, how it impacts the world, and the ways in which language shapes individual or group **identity**. Alternatively, you could consider the way language is used in the media, and how the production and reception of texts is influenced by the medium in which they are written.

Connections

Regardless of methodology, keep in mind that a focus on language is required for the Category 3 EE option. You won't be tracing a symbol or theme through a text, or exploring how characters react to certain settings or global issues. Rather, your focus on the text will be razor sharp; you will need to investigate the inner workings of language, and explore the effects of language on a wider scale in terms of how it relates to culture or media production and reception. Essays that attempt to interpret text(s) without considering the original audience and context are unlikely to offer a full discussion.

Category 3 EEs include the widest range of oral, written, and visual materials present in society:

- single and multiple images with or without written texts

- literary written texts and text extracts

- media texts, advertising campaigns, films, radio and television programmes, and scripts

- electronic texts that share aspects of a number of media texts, e.g. video-sharing websites, web pages, SMS messages, blogs, wikis, and tweets

- oral texts, e.g. readings, speeches, broadcasts, and transcripts of recorded conversation.

As with Category 1 and 2 EEs, your work with the HL essay and the individual oral can assist you in developing your topic and shaping your research questions for a Category 3 EE, though these components are a bit more suited to the Category 1 and 2 options. Reading through the samples below should help you decide which category is best geared towards your interests and skill set.

The significance of the research question

Activity 1 Identifying effective research questions

The table below includes all three EE category options; each with two sets of sample research questions.

1) For this activity you will identify each research question below as **Broad (B)**, **Effective (E)**, **Narrow (N)**, or **Unsystematic (U)**. (NOTE: 'Unsystematic' means that the research question doesn't fit the studies in the language and literature category, or breaks a rule such as the translation rule.)

2) Justify each choice in the column on the right. For each pairing, there will be one effective choice and one that is either too narrow, too broad, or unsystematic. You will find the answers and a downloadable version of this table in your eBook.

3) Once you have completed the activity, discuss your selections and justifications with a partner.

Extended essay: studies in language and literature research question analysis

Studies in language and literature, Category 1, 2, or 3	Sample research question	Broad (B) Effective (E) Narrow (N) Unsystematic (U)	Justify your rationale for questions that you identified as effective
Category 1	To what extent do the settings in Arundhati Roy's *The God of Small Things* portray entrapment?		
	What is the significance of apples in Robert Frost's poem *After Apple-Picking?*		
Category 1	How does the opening paragraph of *Heart of Darkness* show Joseph Conrad's effective use of imagery?		
	In what ways and for what purposes does Shakespeare present female ambition in *Macbeth* and *Antony and Cleopatra?*		
Category 2	How do walls in the dystopian texts *We* by Yevgeny Zamyatin and *Divergent* by Veronica Roth function as symbols of oppression and freedom?		
	Why are today's teens so interested in dystopian novels on a global scale?		
Category 2	To what effect do Wislawa Szymborska and Sylvia Plath use myth to convey their aesthetic visions?		
	To what extent does Isabel Allende's use of magical realism empower her characters to break barriers against oppression?		

Category 3	How do Apple's® changes to the apple symbol in specific advertising campaigns in the 1970s, 1990s, and 2000s reveal the evolution of both its relationship with its audience and its product?		
	How has Twitter® affected communication?		
Category 3	How and to what effect do Ghandi's rhetorical strategies change in the two letters he wrote to Hitler in 1939 and 1940 respectively?		
	What does the font on the September 1981 issue of *Vogue* reveal about the magazine industry?		

Extended essay assessment criteria

Activity 2 Unpacking the extended essay assessment criteria

1) Read through the EE assessment criteria below to familiarise yourself with the scoring process.
2) Look closely at criteria A–E in the table below.
   - What do you need to do in order to achieve high marks for each criterion?
   - Make a list of terms that are specific to this assessment.
   - How will your knowledge of these terms help you better understand the requirements of the assessment?
   - Discuss your responses with a partner or small group and record your findings in your learner portfolio.

Extended essay assessment criteria
Criterion A: Focus and method
This criterion focuses on the topic, the research question, and the methodology. It assesses the explanation of the focus of the research (which includes the topic and the research question), how the research will be undertaken, and how the focus is maintained throughout the essay.

Level	Descriptors
0	**The work does not reach a standard outlined by the descriptors.**
1–2	**The topic is communicated unclearly and incompletely.** • Identification and explanation of the topic is limited; the purpose and focus of the research is unclear, or does not lend itself to a systematic investigation in the subject for which it is registered.

	The research question is stated but not clearly expressed or is too broad. • The research question is too broad in scope to be treated effectively within the word limit and requirements of the task, or does not lend itself to a systematic investigation in the subject for which it is registered. • The intent of the research question is understood but has not been clearly expressed and/or the discussion of the essay is not focused on the research question. **Methodology of the research is limited.** • The source(s) and/or method(s) to be used are limited in range given the topic and research question. • There is limited evidence that their selection was informed.
3–4	**The topic is communicated.** • Identification and explanation of the research topic is communicated; the purpose and focus of the research is adequately clear, but only partially appropriate. **The research question is clearly stated but only partially focused.** • The research question is clear, but the discussion in the essay is only partially focused and connected to the research question. **Methodology of the research is mostly complete.** • Source(s) and/or method(s) to be used are generally relevant and appropriate given the topic and research question. There is some evidence that their selection(s) was informed. **If the topic or research question is deemed inappropriate for the subject in which the essay is registered, no more than 4 marks can be awarded for this criterion.**
5–6	**The topic is communicated accurately and effectively.** • Identification and explanation of the research topic is effectively communicated; the purpose and focus of the research is clear and appropriate. **The research question is clearly stated and focused.** • The research question is clear and addresses an issue of research that is appropriately connected to the discussion in the essay. **Methodology of the research is complete.** • An appropriate range of relevant source(s) and/or method(s) has been selected in relation to the topic and research question. • There is evidence of effective and informed selection of sources and/or methods.

Criterion B: Knowledge and understanding

This criterion assesses the extent to which the research relates to the subject area/discipline used to explore the research question, or in the case of the World Studies extended essay, the issue addressed and the two disciplinary perspectives applied. Additionally, it assesses the way in which this knowledge and understanding is demonstrated through the use of appropriate terminology and concepts.

Level	Descriptors
0	**The work does not reach a standard outlined by the descriptors.**
1–2	**Knowledge and understanding is limited.** • The application of source material has limited relevance and is only partially appropriate to the research question. • Knowledge of the topic/discipline(s)/issue is anecdotal, unstructured, and mostly descriptive with sources not effectively being used. **Use of terminology and concepts is unclear and limited.** • Subject-specific terminology and/or concepts are either missing or inaccurate, demonstrating limited knowledge and understanding.
3–4	**Knowledge and understanding is good.** • The application of source material is mostly relevant and appropriate to the research question. • Knowledge of the topic/discipline(s)/issue is clear; there is an understanding of the sources used but their application is only partially effective. **Use of terminology and concepts is adequate.** • The use of subject-specific terminology and concepts is mostly accurate, demonstrating an appropriate level of knowledge and understanding. **If the topic or research question is deemed inappropriate for the subject in which the essay is registered, no more than 4 marks can be awarded for this criterion.**
5–6	**Knowledge and understanding is excellent.** • The application of source materials is clearly relevant and appropriate to the research question. • Knowledge of the topic/discipline(s)/issue is clear and coherent, and sources are used effectively and with understanding. **Use of terminology and concepts is good.** • The use of subject-specific terminology and concepts is accurate and consistent, demonstrating effective knowledge and understanding.

Criterion C: Critical thinking

This criterion assesses the extent to which critical-thinking skills have been used to analyse and evaluate the research undertaken.

Level	Descriptors
0	**The work does not reach a standard outlined by the descriptors.**
1–3	**The research is limited.** • The research presented is limited and its application to support the argument is not clearly relevant to the research question. **Analysis is limited.** • There is limited analysis. • Where there are conclusions to individual points of analysis, these are limited and not consistent with the evidence.

	Discussion/evaluation is limited. • An argument is outlined **but** this is limited, incomplete, descriptive, or narrative in nature. • The construction of an argument is unclear and/or incoherent in structure, hindering understanding. • Where there is a final conclusion, it is limited and not consistent with the arguments/evidence presented. • There is an attempt to evaluate the research, but this is superficial. **If the topic or research question is deemed inappropriate for the subject in which the essay is registered, no more than 3 marks can be awarded for this criterion.**
4–6	**The research is adequate.** • Some research presented is appropriate and its application to support the argument is partially relevant to the research question. **Analysis is adequate.** • There is analysis **but** this is only partially relevant to the research question; the inclusion of irrelevant research detracts from the quality of the argument. • Any conclusions to individual points of analysis are only partially supported by the evidence. **Discussion/evaluation is adequate.** • An argument explains the research **but** the reasoning contains inconsistencies. • The argument may lack clarity and coherence, but this does not significantly hinder understanding. • Where there is a final or summative conclusion, this is only partially consistent with the arguments/evidence presented. • The research has been evaluated but not critically.
7–9	**The research is good.** • The majority of the research is appropriate and its application to support the argument is clearly relevant to the research question. **Analysis is good.** • The research is analysed in a way that is clearly relevant to the research question; the inclusion of less relevant research rarely detracts from the quality of the overall analysis. • Conclusions to individual points of analysis are supported by the evidence, but there are some minor inconsistencies. **Discussion/evaluation is good.** • An effective reasoned argument is developed from the research, with a conclusion supported by the evidence presented. • This reasoned argument is clearly structured and coherent, and supported by a final or summative conclusion; minor inconsistencies may hinder the strength of the overall argument. • The research has been evaluated, and this is partially critical.

10–12	**The research is excellent.** • The research is appropriate to the research question, and its application to support the argument is consistently relevant. **Analysis is excellent.** • The research is analysed effectively and is clearly focused on the research question; the inclusion of less relevant research does not significantly detract from the quality of the overall analysis. • Conclusions to individual points of analysis are effectively supported by the evidence. **Discussion/evaluation is excellent.** • An effective and focused reasoned argument is developed from the research with a conclusion reflective of the evidence presented. • This reasoned argument is well structured and coherent; any minor inconsistencies do not hinder the strength of the overall argument or the final or summative conclusion. • The research has been critically evaluated.

Criterion D: Presentation

This criterion assesses the extent to which the presentation follows the standard format expected for academic writing, and the extent to which this aids effective communication.

Level	Descriptors
0	**The work does not reach a standard outlined by the descriptors.**
1–2	**Presentation is acceptable.** • The structure of the essay is generally appropriate in terms of the expected conventions for the topic, argument, and subject in which the essay is registered. • Some layout considerations may be missing or applied incorrectly. • Weaknesses in the structure and/or layout do not significantly impact the reading, understanding, or evaluation of the extended essay.
3–4	**Presentation is good.** • The structure of the essay clearly is appropriate in terms of the expected conventions for the topic, the argument, and subject in which the essay is registered. • Layout considerations are present and applied correctly. • The structure and layout support the reading, understanding, and evaluation of the extended essay.

Criterion E: Engagement

This criterion assesses the student's engagement with their research focus and the research process. It will be applied by the examiner at the end of the assessment of the essay, and is based solely on the candidate's reflections as detailed on the Reflections on Planning and Progress Form (RRPF), with the supervisory comments and extended essay itself as context. Only the first 500 words are assessable.

Level	Descriptors
0	**The work does not reach a standard outlined by the descriptors, an RPPF has not been submitted, or the RPPF has been submitted in a language other than that of the essay.**
1–2	**Engagement is limited.** • Reflections on decision making and planning are mostly descriptive. • These reflections communicate a limited degree of personal engagement with the research focus and/or research process.
3–4	**Engagement is good.** • Reflections on decision making and planning are analytical and include reference to conceptual understanding and skill development. • These reflections communicate a moderate degree of personal engagement with the research focus and process of research, demonstrating some intellectual initiative.
5–6	**Engagement is excellent.** • Reflections on decision making and planning are evaluative and include reference to the student's capacity to consider actions and ideas in response to challenges experienced in the research process. • These reflections communicate a high degree of intellectual and personal engagement with the research focus and process of research, demonstrating authenticity, intellectual initiative and/or creative approach in the student voice.

Extended essay for studies in language and literature checklist

- The checklist below is designed specifically for students who are writing their EEs in the subject of studies in language and literature.

- If you fall into the category, make sure that you read through the checklist carefully throughout the research and writing process.

- In the beginning of the process the checklist will serve as a primer to make sure that you are in line with the requirements of a studies in language and literature EE.

- At the end of the process, it will serve as a final checklist to make sure that you make improvements as you move from draft to the final product.

- Good luck on your EE journey. Once you have completed this project you will have gained skills that will work towards your success at university and beyond.

Criterion	EE checklist for students: studies in language and literature
A: Focus and method	**This criterion focuses on the topic, the research question, and the methodology. It assesses the explanation of the focus of the research (this includes the topic and the research question), how the research will be undertaken, and how the focus is maintained throughout the essay.** ☐ Have you chosen texts that are capable of sustaining a detailed in-depth analysis of language/literature? ☐ Is the research question stated as a question? ☐ Is the research question sharply focused and stated clearly in the introduction of the essay? ☐ Is this focus sustained throughout the essay? ☐ Does the introduction state briefly why you have chosen your research question, what it has to offer, and how it relates to existing knowledge on the topic? ☐ Is your essay set up to move logically from beginning to end? ☐ For all essays: have you included a literature review (secondary sources)? ☐ Have you ensured that the secondary sources support your methodology rather than adding unnecessary padding to your essay? ☐ Have you properly cited all background information that is not common knowledge? ☐ For all Cat. 2 essays and selected Cat. 1/Cat. 3 essays: have you included a brief rationale for the pairing of texts chosen? ☐ For Cat. 3 essays: do you use secondary sources to put your analysis in a framework that shows how language, culture, and context shape meaning?
B: Knowledge and understanding	**This criterion assesses the extent to which the research relates to the subject area/discipline used to explore the research question; or in the case of the World Studies extended essay, the issue addressed and the two disciplinary perspectives applied; and additionally, the way in which this knowledge and understanding is demonstrated through the use of appropriate terminology and concepts.** ☐ Does your essay clearly and precisely communicate your knowledge of your topic including your primary and secondary sources? ☐ Has this knowledge been established in a wider framework for discussion? ☐ Do you use subject-specific terminology appropriately and key concepts to demonstrate your knowledge and understanding of the topic? ☐ Does this demonstration of knowledge continuously tie back to the research question? ☐ Does each sentence read clearly and crisply? Have you rethought and rewritten any sentences you can't explain?

C: Critical thinking	**This criterion assesses the extent to which critical thinking skills have been used to analyse and evaluate the research undertaken.** ☐ Does your analysis focus on the research question and support a personal interpretation? ☐ Have you developed your own argument rather than adopting one from other critics? ☐ Have you carefully analysed and evaluated secondary sources? ☐ Have you developed your argument with specific and appropriate examples? ☐ Does each example prove what you say it does? Do you explain each example fully? ☐ Do your paragraphs follow each other in a coherent logical order? ☐ Does the end of the essay draw a conclusion that synthesises the argument and leaves the examiner with something to think about regarding your position on the topic?
D: Formal presentation	**This criterion assesses the extent to which the presentation follows the standard format expected for academic writing and the extent to which this aids effective communication.** ☐ Does this essay follow the accepted formal format? ☐ Is the essay double-spaced with a readable 12 point font? ☐ Is the essay in the appropriate word range? (NOTE: Examiners won't read beyond 4000 words.) ☐ Does the essay include page numbers, title page, and table of contents? ☐ Is all material that is not original carefully acknowledged with a proper citation? ☐ Are all works identified internally cross-referenced in your Works Cited/References section? ☐ Is the Works Cited/References section formatted correctly? ☐ Have you carefully selected what information, if any, should go into the appendix? This may be copies of poems or candidate speeches, which may be helpful for the examiner. Charts and tables that contribute to the understanding of the argument should be integrated into the essay. NOTE: Examiners are not required to read footnotes or appendices, so any information that is essential to your argument should be embedded within the body of the essay.
E: Engagement	**This criterion assesses your engagement with your research focus and the research process. It will be applied by the examiner at the end of the assessment of the essay, after considering your Reflections on Planning and Progress form.** ☐ Have you completed each part of the RPPF accurately? ☐ Does the RPPF reflect your own voice? ☐ Have you demonstrated how you have engaged with the research topic and process? ☐ Have you demonstrated how you arrived at your topic as well as the methods and approach you used? ☐ Do you reveal your rationale for decisions made throughout the planning process? ☐ Have you demonstrated critical and reflective thinking that goes beyond describing the EE process? ☐ Does your EE stay within the prescribed 500 word limit? (Examiners will not read past 500 words.)

Insights into the extended essay

1. The extended essay is a formal piece of academic writing that is a required component for all students seeking the IB Diploma.

2. As you complete your extended essay, you will develop research, thinking, self-management, and communication skills.

3. The process of researching and writing the EE takes approximately 40 hours and you will complete it over the course of your two-year IB Diploma programme.

4. You will receive support from a supervisor at your school who will spend approximately 3–5 hours with you. The three mandatory reflection sessions where you meet with your supervisor will assist you with your research and writing process and provide details for you to complete your required Reflection on Planning and Progress Form.

5. All Language A courses fall under the extended essay subject of studies in language and literature. This subject includes three extending essay options: Category 1, Category 2, and Category 3.

6. You may not write your extended essay on any work that you have studied on your Language A syllabus. Additionally, extended essays in studies in language and literature must include at least one work that is written in the language of the essay.

7. There is a connection between the extended essay and the HL essay and the individual oral. Preparing for these internal and external assessments can help you prepare to write an extended essay in studies in language and literature.

8. All extended essays require a literature review and the use of primary and secondary sources.

9. Formulating a clear research question is an important step in writing an effective extended essay.

10. It is important to adhere to the IB's standards of academic integrity during all parts of the extended essay process.

11. As an independent project, the extended essay requires planning, self-discipline, and time-management skills.

12. The extended essay is scored with the following assessment criteria: A) focus and method; B) knowledge and understanding; C) critical thinking; D) presentation; and E) engagement.

13. Participating in the process of researching and writing your extended essay prepares you for university level studies, allows you to engage with a topic that is meaningful to you, and inspires you to reflect on your academic and personal growth.

Glossary

Alliteration The repetition of the beginning consonant sound in a series of two or more words in a line of poetry.

Allusion An indirect suggestion.

Antagonist The character who gets in the way of the protagonist of a play, poem or novel and tries to foul his or her plans.

Assonance The repetition of vowel sounds within a line or series of lines in a poem.

Autobiography An account of a life written by that person.

Biography An account of someone's life written by someone else.

Blocking A dramatic term to reference the movement of characters on stage, including entries and exits.

Caesura A stop in a line of poetry, often but not always indicated by punctuation such as full stops and semi-colons, or by a natural break in breathing.

Characterisation The creation and convincing representation of fictitious characters.

Climax A powerful ending to a play, poem, or novel.

Comparison To show/describe/demonstrate how something is similar.

Connotation When something connotes something else it suggests or infers it, rather than states it emphatically.

Consonance The repetition of a consonant sound within a line of poetry.

Context The set of circumstances or facts (background) that surround a particular event, situation, work of fiction, etc.

Contrast To show/describe/demonstrate how something differs from something else.

Denotation Showing or naming something directly.

Dénouement The final resolution or conclusion of a dramatic or narrative plot.

Dialogue Conversation between two or more persons in a novel or play.

Diction The specific vocabulary used by a writer or speaker to express his or her point of view.

Didactic Intended or inclined to teach, preach, or instruct.

Dramatic irony When the audience knows something about a character that the character himself or herself does not know.

Dystopian In fiction, the term references fearful imaginary worlds, usually set in the future.

Enjambment The continuation of a line of poetry into the next verse, a run-on line as opposed to an end-stopped line.

Epistolary novel A novel written in the form of letters.

Flashback A device that is used to go back in time to present material that will emphasise the present action of a text.

Foreshadowing Presenting material in such a way as to prepare readers for later events in a text.

Foil A character who underscores the distinctive characteristics of another character.

Genre A class, category, or type of artistic endeavour having a particular form, content, technique, etc.

Hyperbole Exaggeration for rhetorical effect.

Image A word (or words) appealing to at least one of our senses, and thereby generating a response in the reader.

In medias res Meaning 'in the middle of things' – a term used for the strategy of opening a story in the middle of the action without exposition.

Irony When things turn out differently, or are different, to what was expected or what was said.

Juxtaposition When two things are set alongside one another so as to create a strong contrast.

Linear approach Also known as a line-by-line or chronological analysis, one that follows the text in order.

Metaphor Saying that something is something else to express emotion or ideas (e.g. 'He is a God!').

Metre The rhythmic arrangement of stressed and unstressed syllables in verse, usually according to the number and kind of feet in a line of poetry.

Momentum In drama, the forward movement of the plot.

Monologue A form of dramatic entertainment, comedic solo, or the like by a single speaker. It is different to a soliloquy in that the character can address the audience directly.

Objective Not influenced by personal feelings, interpretations or prejudice; based on facts; unbiased: an objective opinion.

Onomatopoeia A device in which the word sounds like what it describes.

Persona The narrator of or a character in a literary work, sometimes identified with the author.

Personification The representation of a thing or abstraction in the form of a person.

Plagiarism When you take someone else's text or ideas and try to present them as your own.

Plot The events that enfold to constitute a story.

Point of view The vantage point from which a story is told, the perspective of a story.

Protagonist The leading character, hero, or heroine of a drama or other literary work, who drives the plot forward.

Register The style of language that is used in certain social contexts, such as formal or informal register.

Rhetoric The art of using speech effectively to persuade, influence, or please.

Rhyme scheme The pattern of rhyme established by a poem, based on the sound at the end of each line.

Rhythm In poetry, the rhythm of a phrase is created by its use of stressed and unstressed syllables.

Setting The location, time, place, and atmosphere (including historical time, clock time, and weather) which occur within a text.

Simile Comparing something to something else using the words 'like' or 'as'.

Soliloquy An utterance or discourse by a person who is talking to himself or herself, or is disregardful of or oblivious to any hearers present (often used as a device in drama to disclose a character's innermost thoughts).

Stanza A verse in a poem.

Structure The physical arrangement of a literary scene (including chapter breaks, white space/interstices, and the physical/visual form or shape of the text).

Subjective Placing excessive emphasis on one's own moods, attitudes and opinions, or showing personal bias.

Symbol Something that represents something else.

Syntax The way that words and phrases are arranged to form phrases, clauses, and sentences.

Tableau A pausing of action where actors freeze or hold in position and then resume action as before.

Thematic approach When you extract the themes, stylistic choices, messages, ideas, and developments of the text, and use them to discuss the work using your own organized structure.

Theme A subject, idea, or common element in a work of literature, which expresses an understanding of some aspect of human nature. Themes can be explicit or implicit.

Tone The writer's attitude toward his or her subject matter, such as anger, indifference, or irony.

Tragicomedy A dramatic or other literary composition combining elements of both tragedy and comedy.

Voice In fiction, the voice of the narrator as determined by perspective or angle of vision.

Index